A LOVELY GIRL

A LOVELY GIRL

The Tragedy of Olga Duncan and
the Trail of One of California's
Most Notorious Killers

DEBORAH HOLT LARKIN

PEGASUS CRIME

NEW YORK LONDON

A LOVELY GIRL

Pegasus Crime is an imprint of
Pegasus Books, Ltd.
148 West 37th Street, 13th Floor
New York, NY 10018

Copyright © 2022 by Deborah Holt Larkin

First Pegasus Books cloth edition October 2022

Interior design by Maria Fernandez

Library of Congress Cataloging-in-Publication Data is available.

ISBN: 978-1-63936-244-8

10 9 8 7 6 5 4 3 2 1

Printed in the United States of America
Distributed by Simon & Schuster
www.pegasusbooks.com

For my father, Bob Holt,
my inspiration to write this book.

And to the memory of a lovely girl, Olga Kupczyk Duncan,
my motivation for telling this story.

Note to Readers

This is the true story of a notorious 1958 murder case in my hometown that had an immense impact on our community, my family, and me. The book is based on extensive research and many sources. Details of the investigation and trial scenes have been drawn from over five thousand pages of trial transcripts, as well as newspaper articles and an unpublished account written by the young district attorney who prosecuted the case.

My father was the lead reporter who covered the case for the local newspaper. His personal files and recollections inspired this book. The commentary on the crime and the trial expressed by my father reflects our many discussions over thirty years about what he referred to as "the remarkable Duncan case." A few of the family chapters are based on his newspaper columns.

Some incidents have been recreated for dramatic purposes, and where necessary, I've made grammatical changes to witness testimony for the sake of clarity, as well as edits for the sake of brevity. But I have altered no facts.

I changed the names of several characters in the true crime chapters, but their actions and words are all based on the facts of the case. Detective Jim

Hansen is a composite character representing the many detectives on the Santa Barbara police force—too many to include in the book—who worked tirelessly to investigate Olga Duncan's disappearance. Again, the facts of the police work are unchanged. Bennie Jo Colton, the only female journalist assigned to cover the trial, is a fictitious name but based on a real person.

My school classmates are also composite characters, their names fictitious. These composite and fictitious characters are noted with an asterisk (*) the first time their names appear in the story. But I used the real names of my close childhood friends, the Alameda Avenue girls—Marilyn Waples, Judi Smith, and Linda Honer.

I apologize for any minor errors I may have made in my descriptions of 1958 Ventura—the layout of the town, the courthouse, the old *Star-Free Press* newspaper offices. It is impossible to see the past precisely as it was because we all look at long-ago events with knowledge of what we now know and understand. My memory is good, but obviously I cannot perfectly remember whole conversations that took place over sixty years ago. However, the dialogue in the book fully represents my recollections.

A Special Note about the Law

Police requirements and court proceedings have changed since 1958. The Olga Duncan murder occurred eight years prior to the enactment of the Miranda warning, in which the US Supreme Court ruled that individuals in police custody must be advised of their right to remain silent, their right to have an attorney present during questioning, and their right to have an attorney appointed for them if they cannot afford one. In 1958, an attorney was appointed without cost to the accused only after they had been charged with a crime in court.

PART ONE

THE DISAPPEARANCE

May 11, 1958–December 21, 1958

CHAPTER ONE

SHATTERED SECURITY

Ventura, California, 1958

The year Olga Duncan disappeared was the year my mother hired the convict babysitter. Mother worked as a psychiatric social worker at the state mental hospital in Camarillo, California. Over the years she had employed a string of babysitters to help watch my sister, Betsey, and me, as well as do the laundry, make the beds, and clean newsprint smudges from the doors. The year Olga disappeared, I was ten and Betsey six.

Mother was a little lax about checking the references of the sitters she employed, preferring to rely on her "intuition." She claimed that she could "read people" after so many years spent working at the mental institution. But the truth came out about our new babysitter when her parole officer called a few weeks into the job to check up on Jolene*.

At first it didn't bother me that Jolene had driven the getaway car in a liquor store heist. She was nineteen, a big, jolly girl with dark brown hair and twinkling eyes who always said cool stuff like, "You're the ginchiest." She painted our toenails with hot-pink polish, and she took us on our first city bus ride. But my father, a reporter and columnist for the *Ventura County Star-Free Press*, put his foot down.

"Hell's bells, woman," he said to my mother. "We can't leave the children with a criminal."

But before Mother found another sitter, Jolene's boyfriend got released from prison, and she ran off with him to Los Angeles to get married.

"She's in the wind," Daddy said. "Good riddance."

"Jolene eloped," Mother said. "Isn't that nice, girls?"

Maybe. But as that year progressed, I found myself gripped more and more by a dogged vigilance against danger. Every day I read newspaper headlines about children dying in school bus accidents, escaped convicts in high-speed shoot-outs, killer teenagers on a weeklong murder rampage in Nebraska. *Eleven innocent victims! Who's next?* Even before Olga Duncan vanished from her apartment, I had a lot on my mind.

Then, a month after Jolene disappeared with her criminal boyfriend, my cat Cinderella went missing.

"Don't worry, she'll come home when she gets hungry," Daddy assured me.

But a few days later, he came into the kitchen, where we were eating our oatmeal, and said, "Well, I'll be goddamned. That cat's dead in the backyard by the geraniums."

"But you said . . . YOU SAID . . ."

"These things happen, dear," Mother said. "At least you still have Pinky Lee."

Shortly after we buried Cinderella in the backyard, lost to "some cat disease," as my father said, my family held our annual neighborhood Fourth of July celebration. Daddy set off illegal fireworks in our driveway, and I found out that the Russians wanted to kill us.

It happened after all the firecrackers had exploded and the last sparkler had fizzled out. Daddy helped Mother pass out bowls of homemade ice cream that they'd hand-cranked in our old wooden ice cream maker. A group of the fathers hovered nearby, waiting for scoops and talking about the space race.

"You know, Sputnik isn't our biggest problem," one of the neighbors said. "That same rocket that launched the satellite could send a nuclear warhead anywhere in the world."

Another man nodded gravely. "Serious threat to US national security, all right. We could be looking at a nuclear attack."

Daddy laughed. "That nincompoop Khrushchev claims that the Sputnik launch proves the Russians can hit a fly on the wall from any distance. That's ridiculous. A hydrogen bomb weighs too much for that Russian rocket to carry it all the way to the United States."

The neighbor took a puff on his cigarette. "I don't know about that, Bob," he said in a mournful tone. "Those Ruskies want to annihilate us."

It had been exciting the year before when the Russians launched Sputnik. The neighborhood kids had all bounced on their toes in our driveway after sunset one night and passed around a pair of binoculars, oohing and aahing as we watched the little satellite scoot across the sky.

But now . . . *Annihilate us?*

I took some ice cream for myself and spooned in a mouthful while staring hard into the dark sky, remembering how we'd seen the twinkling Sputnik pass over our little neighborhood.

Sputnik's batteries had died a few months later, and Grandma said, "It's a miracle that thing didn't kill someone when it fell out of the sky."

Later in the week, I asked Daddy, "What about the Russians? And the fluoride stuff Grandma says the commies want to put in our water to poison us?"

Daddy peered at me over his newspaper. "Fluoride prevents tooth decay. It'll make your teeth stronger." He used his tongue to push his two false front teeth toward me and clicked them back into place. He'd lost the originals playing baseball as a boy. "Don't pay any attention to what your grandmother says." He folded his newspaper, stood, and turned to walk out of the kitchen.

"Do you think Jolene's boyfriend still has his gun?" I called after him.

The year Olga Duncan disappeared, my family was living just outside Ventura, a small California coastal town south of Santa Barbara. Main Street was only three blocks from the ocean. The small beach town had been transformed in the 1950s when developers bought up surrounding farmland and built tracts of houses for World War II vets and their baby boomer families.

We lived in Montalvo, an agricultural community a few miles inland from the coast. The subdivision of modest stucco bungalows, with long concrete front porches and big yards, had been built in the middle of an old walnut grove. Most of the houses still had a walnut tree or two growing in the yard and plenty of children to climb the branches. A dozen little girls between the ages of six and twelve lived within half a block of my home on Alameda Avenue. Daddy called us the Alameda Girls.

Montalvo was as safe a neighborhood as you could find in 1958. Still, it began to worry me that real danger lurked even in my own little community. Jolene had run off with an ex-con who carried a gun. Mr. Khrushchev had a nuclear bomb and plans to annihilate us. And my cat Cinderella had died under suspicious circumstances. But my parents remained clueless. Except for a fixation on automobile accidents and an unnatural fear of the house catching fire, they had stumbled through the 1950s in a fog of blind optimism.

Daddy couldn't get over the fact that we owned so many modern appliances—a Bendix combination automatic washing machine and clothes dryer, a self-defrosting refrigerator, a car with power steering and power brakes. After growing up on a cattle ranch in Montana with an outhouse and an icebox, he was giddy over our good fortune. "Progress, girls, progress," he crowed as he rubbed his hands together. Daddy was a big believer in progress.

I wanted to scream, "Open your eyes, for crying out loud! There's plenty to be worried about." We couldn't even count on God to protect us. My family wasn't saved, according to a devout Christian girl who lived up the street, because we didn't attend church like most of the other families in the neighborhood. And Grandma said Daddy was an atheist. I knew we needed to be careful, but we never even locked the front door. We'd lost the key.

On the evening of November 17, 1958, a foggy belt of cold coastal air settled over our neighborhood. The unseen ocean made its presence felt with a whiff of rotting seaweed tingeing the cooling coastal breeze. Olga Duncan would vanish later that night thirty miles to the north, signaling the end of our quiet 1950s life and shattering the sense of security for people in Santa Barbara and Ventura for years to come. But on that night, my family danced the polka.

Polka Go-Round was Mother's favorite Monday night show, and sometimes, if Daddy was in a good mood, we could get him to dance with us and the dancers on TV. Carolyn was my favorite singer on the show. She yodeled. And Lou played the accordion while he led the band. The polka was the only dance Daddy said he could do. But really, he just hopped and skipped to the music. Sometimes he got a little carried away.

"Slow down, Bob, before you hurt yourself," Mother cried that night, as Daddy galloped around our little living room with my sister and me on his arms. When Lou fired up the "Beer Barrel Polka" on his accordion, Mother danced too, and we all got going so fast, laughing and twirling, that Daddy stepped on Pinky Lee's tail, knocked over a lamp, and spilled a vase of roses on the floor.

"That's enough, Bob," Mother said. "It looks like a nuclear bomb went off in here." She shut off the TV after Carolyn yodeled good night to the viewers and told my sister and me to get ready for bed.

"But I want to watch *The Patti Page Show*," Betsey cried. "'How Much Is That Doggie' is my favorite."

A little while later, I stood on the bottom rung of the bunk bed ladder, watching Daddy as he struggled to close the three-inch gap between the windowsill and the sash.

"Could you please check the closet?" I asked.

He rolled his eyes. "There's no monster in the closet, honey."

I scrunched up my mouth and stared at him.

"Fine." He gave up on the window, walked over, and opened the closet door.

"Look behind the clothes."

Daddy made a big deal of moving the hangers this way and that. "Happy?"

I shrugged as he closed the closet door. "There's no such thing as monsters. It's all in your imagination, you know that, right?"

I nodded uncertainly and took another step up the ladder. "Do you think the Russians might be able to hit a fly on our wall with a nuclear bomb?"

Daddy laughed. "I can't even hit a fly on our wall with a fly swatter half the time."

"Yeah, but that doesn't mean that the Russians can't . . . Miss Peterson says we have to study harder or the Russians are going to take us over."

He made a shooing gesture toward the top bunk. "Come on, come on. Climb up. Jeez, Sputnik isn't a military threat. Khrushchev's using it as propaganda to scare us."

"Propa . . ?"

"Lies. You don't need to worry about this, honey."

"Uh-huh. That's what you said when Cinderella got lost."

"Well, maybe I misjudged the gravity of the Cinderella situation, but the Russians didn't kill her. Old age did. That is just nature. So don't worry about the Russians. Understand?"

"Okay, but that doesn't mean . . ."

Daddy put up his stop-sign hand. "No more. Get in bed." He headed for the door. "Where the hell is your sister?"

I finished climbing the ladder, lay down on the bed, and put my palms together to begin reciting the prayer that Grandma had taught me. I prayed every night and went to Sunday school with my friends. I was trying to save myself from God's wrath.

Pinky Lee curled up beside me. We both closed our eyes as I silently mouthed the words: "Now I lay me down to sleep. I pray the Lord my soul to keep. If I should die before I wake . . ." *Die? Does Grandma know something she isn't telling me?* I closed my eyes tighter. "I pray the Lord my soul to take." And finished off with my own last line: "Please, God, not tonight. I don't want to be buried under the ground like Cinderella. If you let me live, I'll be good."

The continuous hum of cars traveling from Los Angeles to Santa Barbara on Highway 101 at the end of our block drifted through the partially open window. The high whine of truck tires came from far away and faded in the distance. Pinky Lee purred in my ear, tickling my face with his whiskers. Smiling, I turned over and tried not to think about the Russians.

At that same time, just up the coast in Santa Barbara, a pregnant young nurse drank coffee and ate hot buns with two friends from work. She showed them the gown she was embroidering for her unborn baby and said good night, unaware that it would be her last.

CHAPTER TWO

GOODBYE

Santa Barbara, California,
November 17, 1958

The city of Santa Barbara, sandwiched between the Santa Ynez Mountains and the Pacific Ocean, ninety-five miles north of Los Angeles, is sometimes known as the American Riviera because of its beautiful coastline and almost perfect weather. But on that night, as a car moved slowly through the dark empty streets, it was cold by local standards. Forty degrees, with a slight whiff of rotting seaweed in the air.

The car's engine sputtered as it turned right from State Street onto a deserted street lined with Spanish-style buildings and slender-stemmed palm trees. The car stopped on the next block, idling under a streetlight across from the Santa Barbara courthouse. The clock tower, its huge Roman numerals shrouded in darkness, loomed overhead.

The driver pulled out a heavy object wrapped in an oil-stained rag from under the seat, examined it, handed it to his passenger, and strained to get a look at the clock on the courthouse tower. Ten past eleven.

After pumping the gas pedal until the engine ran smoothly again, the driver put the car in gear and pulled away from the curb. The engine sputtered momentarily as the car drove past low-slung, red-tiled buildings and headed through the shadowy darkness toward Garden Street.

Three blocks away, thirty-year-old nurse Olga Duncan called out a last goodbye as her friends from the hospital clambered down the open stairway, still laughing at Doreen's dead-on imitation of their insufferable head nurse. Doreen turned back toward her friend when she reached the courtyard below. "Now, girls," she continued in a high-pitched, haughty tone, "hasten, hasten. We mustn't keep Doctor waiting!"

Sylvia clapped her hands twice under her chin. "Go along to bed, my dear. We daren't be tardy for surgery in the morning."

Both young women dissolved into laughter before calling out a new round of goodbyes.

Olga giggled and covered her mouth. Glancing around at the dark windows of the neighboring apartments, she put a finger to her lips. "Shhhhh." Then she shook her head as she pointed toward the door of Mrs. Barnett, the manager of The Garden Street apartments, who always referred to Olga as 'that sweet lovely girl.'

Sylvia blew a kiss to her friend as the young nurses waved one last time, turned, and stepped onto the sidewalk.

Olga, a petite, quiet girl with large hazel eyes, brushed a few strands of auburn hair from her face and pulled her robe tight against the cool night. An electric stillness filled the air as she smoothed the quilted pink-and-white robe across her very pregnant belly. More laughter drifted up from the sidewalk as her friends waited for their cab. A car pulled up, doors slammed, and the sound of the taxi faded into the distance.

Olga slipped inside the sliding glass door of her apartment but didn't close it all the way. Instead, she leaned her hand on the glass and pressed her face through the partial opening to inhale the salt-scented air. She turned her face to the palm trees towering over the white stucco two-story building. A small sliver of a moon shone between the long fan-like fronds whispering as they swayed in the light breeze blowing off the Pacific Ocean.

A wistful smile turned up the corners of Olga's lips when the lonesome wail of the train whistle cut through the quiet night. She felt a pang of homesickness for the family she'd left behind in Canada, especially her railroad engineer papa. As the train chugged through town, she patted her pregnant belly. *Just six more weeks and your grandma will be on that train.* Olga moved her fingers to the side of her tummy when she felt the baby kick. *That's right. Grandma is coming here to help us.*

Olga felt a sharp pain from the neuritis in her hand. "Only the baby pressing on some nerves," the doctor had said. She massaged her tingling fingers as her thoughts shifted to her sometimes-husband, Frank. The handsome attorney didn't live at their apartment full time anymore. He just visited occasionally.

"Frank's a big baby." Doreen had exploded at her one afternoon at the hospital. "Enough is enough."

Olga sighed. Maybe. She had talked to that lawyer Sylvia had insisted on, but still . . . The baby kicked again. A hard kick this time, right under her ribs.

The train noise dissolved into the night, and an eerie silence descended again on the apartment building.

"Maybe your daddy will come see us tomorrow," she whispered to her unborn child. Olga smiled faintly as she remembered the silly grin on Frank's face when he'd tentatively put his fingers on her stomach to feel their baby move.

"Everything will be fine, honey. You'll see," Frank had said as he held her close.

The sound of a rough-running car engine creeping along the road below ended Olga's reverie. Headlights swept past the deserted courtyard as she shut the sliding glass door, pulled the drapes closed, and locked the latch. The sputtering engine abruptly died in the street.

CHAPTER THREE

MONSTER OF THE DEEP

Ventura, California, November 19, 1958

Looking back to my faraway childhood, I see it all so clearly. More than sixty years after Olga Duncan's disappearance, I still remember staring at the small headline on that fall afternoon.

MISSING NURSE SOUGHT BY POLICE, FRIENDS

I ran my finger along the tiny print. *Missing?* Lifting the newspaper from the kitchen table to get a better look at the blurry picture next to the story didn't help. I yanked open the junk drawer and rummaged through all the stuff. My magnifying glass was the only thing left from the Junior Detective Kit I'd gotten by sending in cereal box tops. Everything else—handcuffs, badge, miniature flashlight, and paper mustache disguise—had disappeared.

The scratched plastic magnifier made the picture of the smiling young woman wearing a white nurse's cap bigger but not much clearer.

Olga Duncan, 30, of 114 [sic] Garden Street, Apt. 11, was the object of a police search today. She has been missing from her home since 11:00 P.M. Monday, friends told police.

Mrs. Duncan is the wife of Santa Barbara attorney Frank
Duncan and was home alone Monday night after she said goodbye
to two friends who visited her at her apartment. She has not been
seen since. She is employed as a surgical nurse at Cottage Hospital.
However, she did not go to work yesterday and did not notify the
hospital of her whereabouts. Friends said she is expecting a baby.
Anyone with information is asked to call the Santa Barbara Police
Department.

Betsey banged the screen door open, causing me to jump and drop the magnifier.

Gosh. Home alone at night, and now she's gone. Vanished!

"Daddy, Daddy, come see the big fish at the Smiths' house!" Betsey ran into the living room and poked our father, who was napping on the couch. Sometimes on a slow news day, he came home after the paper went to press to "rest his eyes" before going out again to cover evening meetings.

"I already saw the fish. Big deal." He turned his back. "Can't you see that I'm busy?"

Betsey widened her eyes. "It's forty-eight feet long."

Daddy pushed himself up on one elbow and looked over his shoulder. "No, it is not. It's a forty-eight-pound sea bass. It's only five feet long. I have my sources."

"Well, it's a sea monster . . . of the deep, Mr. Smith says . . . and it's in the back of their station wagon, and it's so heavy that the whole back of the car is sagging. Everybody in the neighborhood is down there."

I walked through the archway that divided the dining and living room areas to join my sister at the couch. "I saw it, and it's dripping fish blood all over the place."

"He caught it by an island and flew it home in a helicopter," Betsey said. "Everybody says so."

"For God's sake." Daddy sat up. "You little chatterboxes won't let me sleep, will you?"

"I hardly said anything, Daddy. I've been very quiet reading this news-paper." I held up the copy of the *Santa Barbara News Press* that I'd found on the dining room table. "Didn't you say this paper is a rag and no one in their right mind should ever read it?"

He took the newspaper out of my hands. "You shouldn't read it."

"But you were. I saw you."

He set the newspaper next to him on the couch and sighed deeply. "Yes, I was reading it. It's my job to check up on those guys at the *News Press* to see if there's anything going on up in Santa Barbara that I may need to follow up on."

I lowered myself to my knees and put my face close to the folded paper. "What about this? 'Missing Nurse Sought by Police, Friends.' And look at the picture, Daddy." I held out my magnifying glass, but he didn't take it. "She looks nice."

"You don't need to worry about that." He pushed himself off the couch.

"But she disappeared in the middle of the night."

Betsey gazed at him. "Why don't we ever go fishing like Mr. Smith, Daddy?"

He waved her off. "Fishing is way overrated. I'm thinking of starting a magazine for us non-hunter, non-fisherman types. Might call it *The Great Indoorsman*."

We followed him into the kitchen, my sister's blonde curls bouncing as she hopped along on one foot. "And how come Mr. Smith always gets to fly everywhere?" she wanted to know.

Daddy opened the refrigerator door. "Because he's an officer in the Air Force Reserve, and he does something or other out at Oxnard Air Force Base once a week." He stuck his head in the refrigerator. "Something important for our national defense like going fishing."

"Myron flew a bomber on D-Day." My friends and I always called each other's parents by their first names. It was a very friendly neighborhood. I wasn't exactly sure what D-Day was, but I knew it was a big deal.

"What did you do in the war, Daddy?" Betsey persisted. "Were you an officer too?"

He ducked out of the refrigerator holding a slab of cheese and a jar of mustard. "I was a private first class," he said in a dignified voice. "PFC is a very important job. They just don't fly much. Too risky."

"Daddy was a typist," I told my sister.

"Fast typists were hard to come by in the war," he said. "They needed me stateside to type a lot of important messages."

I tugged on his shirt. "But what about this missing nurse?" I'd carried the newspaper with me. "What happened to her?"

Betsey pulled on his pants from the other side. "Did you see the fish eyeball? It's in a jar of salt water. Tommy Smith is taking it to school for sharing tomorrow."

Tommy had chased me home with the jar. I shivered and looked at the picture of the nurse to get the image of the floating eyeball out of my head.

"Wish I had an eyeball to share," Betsey pouted.

Daddy's head ping-ponged between our faces. Finally, he said, "Don't look at the eyeball. It'll give you nightmares. Don't think about it." He pointed toward the back of the house. "You're supposed to be in your room picking up those Rig-A-Jig things," he said to my sister.

Betsey hopped out of the kitchen on both feet.

Daddy tried to snatch the newspaper out of my hands, but I was too fast for him and whipped it behind my back.

"That isn't anything for you to worry about," he said. "It's nothing."

"Then why did you bring it home and fold it open to the story about the missing nurse?"

Daddy sat down on one of the kitchen chairs. "All right, I guess it can't hurt, but don't mention this conversation to your mother."

I rolled my eyes. That went without saying.

"I've got a source that tells me maybe this is more than just a domestic problem. This young woman could be in trouble."

"You mean somebody hurt her?"

He winced. "Not sure. Just have to see what the police come up with."

I brought the newspaper out from behind my back and looked at the picture of Olga Duncan. "It says she's expecting a baby." I stared intently into Daddy's face. "The police are going to solve it, find her, right?"

Daddy put his hand on my arm and guided me back to the bedroom. "Help your sister."

Betsey sat cross-legged on the floor, scooping the toys into a pile. She looked up at our father. "When are you going to start that magazine?"

"I got no time for a magazine. I've still got to write my column for tomorrow's paper. If you little girls would quit waking me up with a lot of nonsense about some poor fish Myron Smith dragged out of the ocean, I might get rested up enough to write it."

"You could write about Myron's fish," I said.

"Right. 'Big Fish Doings Afoot in the Neighborhood' or maybe 'Angling for the Couch' . . ." he muttered as he headed back to the living room.

I listened as his voice trailed off down the hallway. "Do you think somebody else could disappear like that nurse?" I called after him.

"I said *don't* worry about it."

But I couldn't stop thinking about Olga Duncan.

CHAPTER FOUR

THE SUSPENSION

Santa Barbara, California,
November 20, 1958

The Santa Barbara Police Department was headquartered in the basement of City Hall, a white two-story, Mission Revival–style building with a red-tiled roof standing on the northeast corner of the historic De La Guerra Plaza, in the heart of downtown Santa Barbara. Swaying palm trees lined the plaza.

Detective Jim Hansen* sat behind a gray metal desk outside his lieutenant's closed door in the airless, musty-smelling basement police station. Hansen's big shoulders hunched over his typewriter, his index fingers poised above the keys. He couldn't catch all the angry words from the other room—hell of a racket—but he'd heard enough to know that things weren't going well for his partner.

Lieutenant Peck's voice rose. "No evidence . . . just another one of your hunches, and we don't have the overtime budget for hunches."

"Good street sources said they were casing the place." Charlie Thompson bellowed back.

Hansen stared at the robbery incident report in his typewriter. A couple of other detectives also sat at their desks, moving papers around while their heads stayed tilted toward the commotion.

". . . couple of small-time guys . . . up to something big at Pep Boys auto parts . . . routine stakeout."

When Hansen heard pounding on the desk inside the small, thin-walled office, he gave up the pretext of working and swiveled his chair so he faced the door.

"You got your head up your ass. . . . You don't know shit."

"Insubordination!" the lieutenant screamed.

The door banged open. Thompson, red-faced beneath his trademark fedora, took a step out of the office.

"You're suspended." The lieutenant spat the words across his desk.

"What? Because I followed a tip?" Thompson shouted.

"Because you don't know how to follow orders. How many times—"

Thompson turned and headed for the exit. Everyone in the sweltering detective bay watched.

"What are you lookin' at?" he sneered as he passed a couple of patrolmen coming out of the coffee room.

Lieutenant Peck got up from his desk and moved to the doorway of his office. He stood, hands on hips, slowly shaking his head.

Thompson was almost out the door of the detective bay when he glanced over his shoulder and saw the lieutenant watching him. "You son of a bitch," he called to his boss.

"Two weeks!" Peck shouted. "No pay!" He was breathing hard. He shifted his gaze to Hansen. "You," he said and pointed. Hansen half stood. "You get back to the watch commander about that missing nurse yet?" Without waiting for a response, the lieutenant kicked his office door shut so hard it shook the room.

Hansen sat down, put both hands on his forehead for a moment, and then sorted through a pile of messages stacked on his desk. Finally, he found the one that had come from the watch commander earlier that day: *Young nurse reported missing two days ago. Pregnant. Hasn't turned up yet. Maybe more than a runaway wife.*

Hansen tapped the message with his index finger as he scanned the room. The other detectives all had their heads down. He stared for a moment at the empty doorway where his partner had made his grand exit. *Two weeks' suspension. Fucking Thompson. Can't he ever do things the easy way?*

Hansen got up and headed to the division that handled missing persons. Sergeant Vickers, the watch commander, was out, but patrol officer Peter O'Brian*, who'd taken the missing person report on Olga Duncan, was sitting at Vickers's desk with his chest puffed out.

Hansen stood next to the desk. "What about this so-called missing nurse?"

O'Brian swiveled his sergeant's chair to reach a folder. "It's been over forty-eight hours. We issued an all-points bulletin this afternoon. Sent it out on the teletype to all California law enforcement agencies."

Hansen perched his rear end on the desk. "What you got?"

"We called her family in Canada. Father's very upset, understandably. They haven't had a letter from their daughter in more than a week, and there were absolutely no plans for her to visit them in Manitoba."

Hansen grunted. "Yeah, well, women sometimes . . ."

O'Brian licked his thumb and flipped the page. "She got a job as a nurse over at Cottage Hospital about a year ago." He looked up. "Nursing shortage, you know."

Hansen circled his index finger impatiently.

"She's married to an attorney here in town by the name of Frank Duncan. Friends say she's seven months pregnant, but Duncan hasn't been living with her for a while. He's the one who called us with the report, but the friends are the ones who discovered she was missing."

Hansen took the folder and started reading for himself. "The friends? Not the husband?"

"It's all in the file. Husband says his wife's just sore at him. Probably took off to teach him a lesson." O'Brian raised his eyebrows. "But check with the landlady. She thinks there's no way this woman would run off and worry everyone."

Hansen read the interview of the husband, Frank Duncan, while standing in front of his desk in the detective bay. He sat down and dialed the black rotary telephone to call Duncan's office but had to leave a message when the receptionist told him the attorney was in court.

Hansen read through the interviews with the two nurse friends who'd last seen Olga. "So unlike her to go off without telling anyone. And she left her purse in the apartment."

The detective leaned an elbow on the desk and ran his fingers through his thick hair. *Must have gone out in an awful big hurry if she forgot her purse.* He underlined the name and address of Olga's landlady, Dorothy Barnett, then stretched his arms over his head, arched his back, and rolled his shoulders. He couldn't sit for too long, not since the war. His back ached.

Jim Hansen had been a Santa Barbara policeman for thirteen years, a detective for the last five. He'd joined the force right after he got out of the navy in 1946. He'd been on Battleship Row during the Japanese attack on Pearl Harbor and survived five torpedoes that sank his ship. Nothing so far in his job as a policeman had come close to the horror he'd experienced during World War II. He liked both the routine and the variety of police work, as long as he didn't have to spend too much time sitting at a desk.

He checked the notes on the interview with Olga Duncan's obstetrician. The report said she had visited him the day she disappeared. Pregnancy progressing normally. Gestation calculated at thirty-one weeks. Complained of a little neuritis in her hand. Otherwise a very healthy young woman. To the question about her emotional state, the doctor had replied, "Very weepy. Possibly a little depressed."

The detective stood and rotated his neck. *Runaway wife . . . or something else?* He took his coat off the back of the chair. In Santa Barbara, people don't just disappear.

Hansen parked on the residential street in front of The Garden Street apartments. A pair of seagulls soared above palm trees, very white against the blue sky, crying their high-pitched call. He entered through a courtyard of the small two-story apartment building lined with bright orange bird-of-paradise blooms and red bougainvillea climbing trellises along the wall.

Someone peered between the Venetian blinds of the window of ground-floor apartment 3 as Hansen read the small sign on the door. MANAGER. He flashed his police badge at the window.

Mrs. Barnett opened the door before he even had a chance to knock. The detective introduced himself and explained the purpose of his visit. "I know it's late, but . . ."

She waved his words away. "I'll do anything I can to help find Olga."

Mrs. Barnett sat on a faded brocade settee in her cramped living room/office and crossed her swollen ankles. A desk piled high with paperwork was crowded up against the wall beneath the window. She adjusted her rhinestone-decorated eyeglasses as she peered at the detective.

Hansen eased himself onto a small upholstered stool.

"You almost missed me." Mrs. Barnett fluffed one side of her puffy bluish hair at the handsome detective. "Just got back from getting my perm and rinse."

Hansen smiled politely. "I'd like you to tell me what you can about Olga Duncan. Where do you think she might go? Friends, relatives?" He put his notebook on his knee and patted his pockets until he found a pencil.

"I'm afraid I don't really know her friends." Mrs. Barnett twisted her fingers. "I want to help, but I have no idea where she might go."

"How about the last time you saw her?"

"Monday afternoon, the day she disappeared. I was in the courtyard watering my bird-of-paradise plants when she got home from work. She said, 'The garden looks lovely, Mrs. Barnett' when she passed. Olga is always so thoughtful that way. Appreciates things."

"You didn't talk to her again?"

"No, I watched TV all evening. I like to see *Polka Go-Round* on Monday nights and *The Patti Page Show*." She smoothed the hem of her skirt over her plump knees. "Two of Olga's nurse friends were there for a visit that night. I heard Olga say goodbye to them around eleven or so."

"Uh-huh . . . Do you think that she might have been depressed, maybe harmed herself . . . taken her own life?"

Mrs. Barnett slapped her hand on her chest. "Absolutely not. She might have been unhappy about some things, but she would never do anything to hurt her baby. She's a very even-tempered young woman."

Hansen tapped his pencil on his notebook. "Any men around? She likely to run off?"

"Never! Olga is a lovely girl, and very quiet, like a little mouse. Sweet. I wish all my tenants were like Olga."

"And you didn't hear anything unusual?"

"Like I said, it must have been a little after eleven o'clock when Olga's friends left. I couldn't help but hear them. They made so much noise talking and laughing as they came down the stairs. I was trying to get to sleep."

Hansen shifted his weight on the stool. "Just tell me anything else you can think of about that night."

"I made my rounds outside at seven thirty. I go out every night to check my roof lights. I'm like an old hen with a bunch of chickens. I want to know my tenants are safe. It's so dark up here at night, you know, and we have those two flights of steep stairs." Mrs. Barnett pulled her cardigan sweater close around her shoulders. "It was chilly and very quiet the night Olga disappeared, very still."

"And you were the one who found Olga's door open the next morning?"

Mrs. Barnett nodded. "I heard this strange thumping sound and went outside to check. Olga's sliding glass door was open with the drapes blowing through the opening. Very strange . . . drapes just flapping in the breeze. No sign of Olga. I thought she'd gone off to work and forgotten to close the door." Mrs. Barnett shrugged. "But while I was still standing outside her door, her nurse friends, the girls from the night before, came to check on her because she hadn't shown up to assist in surgery that morning. Never called. So unlike Olga."

"And you went inside the apartment?"

"Well, of course," the old woman stammered, "to check on her . . . We were worried. What if she was having an emergency with the baby, and . . ."

Hansen put up his hand. "Perfectly understandable. What did you find inside?"

"The lights in the living room were on. Some new baby clothes all neatly folded on the sofa. One of the girls checked the bedroom and looked in the closet. She said she didn't see the pink robe that Olga was wearing the night before." Mrs. Barnett put her hand to her mouth. "Olga's purse was still on her dresser."

"Strange," Hansen said as he continued to write in his notebook.

"There were a few dirty plates and cups from the hot buns and coffee still on the kitchen counter, but otherwise, nothing seemed out of order."

Hansen stopped writing. "So, did Olga have any problems you can think of? You mentioned that she was a little unhappy."

"Well . . . have you talked to the nurses yet?"

"The other policeman interviewed them, but I have them on my list of people I want to see myself. I'll get to everybody, of course . . . unless Mrs. Duncan turns up. Women have a way of doing that. Turning up, you know."

"I certainly hope you're taking this seriously, young man," the landlady huffed. "Olga wouldn't go away and worry everyone."

Hansen rubbed at a twinge in his back. "You said she was unhappy. Anything in particular?"

"Her husband, for one thing. He doesn't live here full time anymore." She ruffled her curls again. "I guess you could say that there were family problems."

"Like what?"

"I have no idea what was wrong between the two of them. I don't stick my nose into my tenants' business." The woman shifted forward in her chair. "But there was a bit of a bother with the mother-in-law."

"Like what?"

"I probably shouldn't say anything. I don't want to cause anybody any trouble."

"If you know something that will help us find her, anything . . ." Hansen said. "Let the police decide what's important."

The landlady lowered her voice. "Well, she was here one day, you see, kicked up a terrible fuss. Tricked me into letting her into the apartment."

"Who?"

"The other Mrs. Duncan. The mother-in-law." Mrs. Barnett looked away. "She claimed that Olga was unfit. Said she was a foreigner."

"When was this?"

"August, I think. She wanted me to kick Olga out of the apartment. Said her son wasn't going to be responsible for Olga's debts . . . some other crazy things."

Hansen turned to a new page in his notebook. "Like what?"

"I didn't really take her seriously." Mrs. Barnett hesitated. "I just thought she was a very interfering, buttinski type of woman, trying to run her son's life. My sister has a mother-in-law like that. You know the type. Sticks her nose into everything."

"Okay, Mrs. Barnett, you've been a big help." The detective paused for a moment before continuing. "Anything unusual that night?"

"Not really. Well, there was no light on in Dr. and Mrs. Williamson's apartment, so I figured they'd gone to a movie. Those two young people like to go out to a show, and I often hear them come home quite late."

"So that wasn't unusual?"

"No." Mrs. Barnett shook her head. "But a little after Olga's friends left, when I was trying to sleep after I'd finished reading a chapter in my Bible, I heard footsteps on the stairs outside my window, I thought to myself, 'There they are, the Williamsons coming home from the movie.'"

Hansen narrowed his brows. "I don't see how this . . ."

"Well, that's what I'm trying to tell you. When I saw Mrs. Williamson yesterday, we talked about Olga, and I told her, 'I didn't hear a thing that night except you and your dear husband coming home from the movie,' and she said, 'We didn't go out to a show that night. We didn't go out at all.'" Mrs. Barnett put a hand to her throat. "Then I realized that it was other footsteps."

"And those stairs lead to Olga's apartment?"

Mrs. Barnett nodded. "Her sliding glass door is at the top of the stairs."

CHAPTER FIVE

SNEEZES, SAUCES, AND SOURCES

Ventura, California, November 20, 1958

While Detective Hansen was questioning people who knew Olga Duncan, I sat at our gray Formica kitchen table carefully scanning the afternoon issue of the *Ventura County Star-Free Press*. Pinky Lee purred in my lap. There had been no stories since Olga had been reported missing. Every time I nagged my father for information about the investigation, he said, "How the hell do I know?"

I gave Pinky a nudge, put down the newspaper, and wandered out to the living room to stand at the screen door. Daddy was pacing the front lawn. He glanced at his watch and peered down the street.

Uh-oh. Mother's late again. "Do you think there might have been a head-on crash on the bridge?" I called out. Whenever Mother was late getting home from work, my father's mind jumped to catastrophic conclusions. So did mine.

Mother made the thirty-mile round-trip daily commute on Highway 101 to her social worker job at the state hospital in Camarillo. Daddy especially worried about fatal traffic accidents on the two-lane Santa Clara Bridge, which spanned the riverbed between Oxnard and Ventura. Considering all my parents' talk about trucks losing their brakes, cars going out of control because of tire blowouts or, worst of all, crossing that deadly bridge, it seemed a miracle to me that Mother was still alive.

She drove up five minutes later. "Sorry," she said. "My plate blew up at lunch." She stood beside me in the kitchen, still wearing her coat.

"Oh," I said.

Daddy wrinkled his brow.

"Hot chili beans, cold plate," she explained as she opened the refrigerator door. "Oh, gosh, I forgot to take the pork chops out of the freezer this morning." She opened a cupboard. "I could do some macaroni and cheese."

"Forget about it," Daddy said. "We'll all go down to the Wagon Wheel."

We drove to the end of the street and turned south at the signal onto Highway 101. Just as the light changed to green, Mother put her hand up in the air and made a muffled shrieking sound.

"Uh-oh," I said.

"Ah, ah, ah . . ." Mother sneezed a shuddering, convulsive "*Ker-choo!*"

Betsey leaned sideways and flattened herself against the window. Two or three more sneezes immediately followed. Daddy reflexively jerked the steering wheel, and we swerved partway into the next lane. A guy in a pickup truck laid on the horn.

"Jesus Christ! Quit doing that. You almost made me lose control of the car." Daddy shot her a sideways look. "Can't you give some kind of a warning?"

"I was gathering myself," my mother said in a dignified voice. She opened her purse, pulled out a Kleenex, and dabbed at her nose.

A short time later, Daddy found a space in the parking lot underneath the giant neon sign where large red letters blinked WAGON WHEEL RES-TAURANT AND MOTEL with an animated stagecoach driver cracking a whip over galloping horses. We walked across the gravel lot toward the low-slung ranch-style building. A weather vane perched on top of a cupola on the wood-shingled roof.

Betsey chattered away. "I want a double stack of pancakes."

"Uh, we'll have to see, dear," Mother said.

We entered through the heavy wooden double doors and stood in the small reception area just off the bar to wait for a table. A hostess wearing a flowing black dress and heavy silver-and-turquoise jewelry gathered up rawhide-covered menus for the couple ahead of us.

Daddy hated to wait. If he wasn't humming, he was sputtering. He impatiently blew air through his lips, making loud motorboat noises while he rubbed his face.

"It's an unconscious habit," Mother had told me a million times. "Relieves tension, I think. Might be a condition."

Betsey yammered on about pancakes in her booming little voice. I moved a few feet away, keeping my distance from my family.

I felt very grown up, waiting by myself, gazing up at the cow brands of local ranches burned into the wood beams of the building. It was dark and a little noisy, with clinking glasses and loud bursts of laughter coming from the bar. And in spite of the enormous bull horns hanging over the archway and the cowboy paraphernalia on the walls, to my small-town, ten-year-old mind, the place oozed sophistication. It was a steak house. Very classy.

A rumpled man sitting just inside the bar with his tie loose and his jacket lying across the next stool leaned out by the archway toward the reception area. "Hey, Bob," he called. "Got a minute?" He motioned Daddy into the bar with one hand while moving his jacket to make room for him to sit down.

Daddy mumbled to my mother, "Just be a second."

He climbed up on one of the cowhide-covered stools, waving off a bartender already sliding a little napkin in front of him. He put his elbow on the bar and leaned in to listen to the rumpled man.

I strained my ears to hear what they were saying until Mother called my name. Looking up, I saw the hostess leading the way into the dining room.

She seated us at a table near the red-leather-upholstered booths in the back. A flickering candle inside a small replica kerosene lamp sat at the center of the table. A basket of crackers, pats of butter on a little plate, sugar cubes, and a bowl of pitted olives surrounded the candle. I immediately got started on the sugar cubes.

"Don't eat those," Mother said. "You'll spoil your dinner."

Then she noticed Betsey putting olives on the ends of her fingers. I popped more sugar cubes in my mouth when Mother wasn't looking.

"Who was that man?" Betsey demanded in a loud voice when Daddy arrived at the table. She held up her hands with the olives for my father to see and used her teeth to pull one into her mouth. Diners at the next table turned to frown at the cute little curly-haired blonde girl sucking olives off her fingers.

"Shh," Mother hissed.

"Do something about her, Lois," Daddy said as he sat down.

"Wuth tha a sauce?" I said. "Wi infomation abou the nuse?"

Daddy glared at me. "What do you have in your mouth?"

"Nuh-ing."

I'd quit eating sugar cubes and Betsey had finished off the olives by the time a waitress dressed as a cowgirl wearing a MYRTLE nametag came to take our orders. She took a pencil from behind her ear.

"I'll have a cheeseburger with onion rings," I told her. "And a Shirley Temple."

Mother conferred with an unhappy Betsey. "You said," my sister whined. "You said I could have pancakes." Her lower lip quivered.

"I don't suppose . . ." Mother stammered, "we could get . . ."

"Sorry." Myrtle chewed gum. She pointed toward the rawhide-covered menu with a bright red lacquered fingernail. "See there, no breakfast after ten A.M."

Betsey glared at the table, arms folded across her chest, her feet kicking her chair.

Mother ordered some chicken for herself, then said, "She'll have a hamburger, plain, nothing on it."

"And french fries," my sister hissed. "No mayonnaise or anything or I'll throw up."

"Got a finicky one there," the waitress said as she wrote down Betsey's order. She turned toward my father. "And for you, sir?"

"I'll have a T-bone," Daddy said from behind the menu. "No sauces."

"I beg your pardon?"

Daddy lowered his menu. "I don't want any sauce on my steak, barbecue or otherwise."

"He won't eat it with sauce," I piped up. Mother put her hand on my arm.

"Or he'll throw up," my sister added.

Mother grabbed Betsey's arm, too, and forced a little laugh.

"None of that French stuff," my father elaborated.

After the waitress left, Betsey and I started spreading butter on saltine crackers while our parents talked. Mother quizzed Daddy about his conversation with the rumpled man at the bar.

"He told me about a Peeping Tom out on Telegraph Road."

"Well, I wouldn't think that's exactly big news," Mother said.

"It might be a little more than that. . . . Very strange. . . . Happened two nights after that nurse disappeared in Santa Barbara."

I choked on a cracker. *Olga?* I put my hand over my mouth to stifle a throat-clearing cough that would remind them that I was listening.

"A sixteen-year-old girl—that was her neighbor who talked to me—was babysitting out on the Campbell ranch and saw a man peering in the window."

"Well, you know teenage girls . . ." Mother waved her hand.

"She called the sheriff's office but didn't know the address of the ranch house. The sergeant who took the call told her to stay on the line—she was pretty shook up and crying—while he sent deputies to try and find the house."

Mother glanced our way. "Girls, put down those crackers."

"They're all gone," Betsey pouted. "Debby ate the last one."

I stopped chewing.

Mother returned her attention to my father, who had picked up a knife and some butter in one hand and was lifting the napkin covering the cracker basket with the other. "Bob," Mother snapped. "They're all gone. The girls ate them."

He gave us the stink-eye and lowered his voice. "This is where it starts to get really strange. Apparently, the guy came right into the house *twice* while the girl was on the phone with the sheriff."

Mother covered her mouth. I scooted forward on my seat.

"Each time the man came in, he approached the girl, and each time, she screamed. Then he'd run out of the house and go back to the window and continue to stare at her. Finally, the police called the girl's mother and got an approximate location for the house. When the sheriff's cars came up the drive, they saw a man wearing a long dark coat and white gloves flee into the ranch groves."

"Yee gads," Mother said, "that poor girl. She must have been terrified."

I shivered. *She could have disappeared.*

"Uh-huh. The neighbor said the girl was on the phone with the sheriff for almost twenty minutes while this guy was staring in the window or running in and out of the house."

I picked up a sugar cube and handed it to Betsey to keep her quiet while I kept my eyes focused on Daddy.

"According to this neighbor, the sheriff's investigator told the family today that the intruder fits the description of a man named John Lewis, age thirty-one." Daddy paused. "He escaped from Camarillo State Hospital four days ago."

My mouth fell open.

"*Nooo*," Mother said in a low breathy voice. "Not one of our patients."

"Yes, one of your patients. And I don't care what you say, they're not all harmless. They ought to have a fence around that place."

"It's a hospital, not a prison. Besides, the ones who walk off usually come back on their own. Sometimes they even call us to get a ride."

"Well, I don't think this guy's given anybody a ringy-dingy. The neighbor told me all this because he thinks there might be a connection to this nurse's disappearance. Told the Ventura police his theory but doesn't think they took him seriously. He wants me to write a story to get everyone's attention."

"And will you?" Mother asked. "Write a story?"

Daddy shrugged. "I'll check into it. I got a source at the Santa Barbara Police Department. I'll give Charlie a call." Daddy lowered his voice. "But this is where you can help."

"Me?" Mother said.

"It would be helpful if you could see what you can find out about this John Lewis."

"I will do no such thing." Mother's voice was loud and indignant.

Nearby diners turned to look at us again, but I was too engrossed in this startling development to care. I couldn't contain myself any longer. "A real clue, Daddy. He could be the one who took Olga."

My parents turned their heads toward me simultaneously.

"Now don't get ahead of yourself, Debby," Daddy said. "Nothing to connect the cases."

"Yet." My eyes widened. "But there's a mental patient on the loose. You know what you say about Mother's patients, Daddy. . . ."

He stuck his hand out to try to shut me up.

"You know, they're all nutcases, a bunch of psycho lunatics. That's what you always say, Daddy. . . . This could be the big break."

Mother put her hand over her mouth. Her shoulders heaved. "Ah, ah, ah, *ah* . . ."

Daddy shoved his chair away from the table, making a loud scraping sound, and stretched his hands out toward both my sister and me as if trying to shield us. "Don't!"

Mother exploded over the table with a burst of air that seemed to come from the depths of her entire being. "*Ahhhhhhhhh-chooooooooooooo . . . !*"

A woman at the next table said, "Well, I never," in a shrill voice.

"I want more crackers," Betsey said.

CHAPTER SIX

THE HUSBAND

Santa Barbara, California, November 20, 1958

After finishing the interview with Mrs. Barnett, Hansen folded his long frame into his car and sat for a moment in front of the apartment building, rubbing his left shoulder and stretching his back. Everything hurt by late in the day. *Fucking war.* He checked his watch . . . 6:00. *Shit. I told Beverly I'd pick her up at six thirty.* He sighed. *Yeah, well, I'll see her when I see her. She knows that.*

The detective checked his list of addresses and made a U-turn across Garden Street. *Frank Duncan ought to be home by now.*

Minutes later, he pulled his car to the curb at the corner of State Street and West Valerio and scanned the numbers until he found number seven. Hansen stared at the boxy two-story stucco building, wondering about Frank Duncan. *Footsteps at 11:15? Could be the husband.*

Hansen checked the mailboxes, then climbed the stairs and knocked on the door of apartment 4. Someone turned off the canned laughter of a television show as he waited. The door opened.

Frank Duncan, still wearing his lawyer suit, looked the picture of a successful young attorney, except for the dark circles under his red-rimmed eyes.

"Detective Jim Hansen." He flipped open his police identification. "Hope I'm not interrupting your dinner. I'd like to talk to you about your wife."

Frank searched his face. "Has there been any word?"

"Sorry. Just need to ask you a few questions."

Frank's shoulders slumped. He motioned the detective through the door.

Hansen glanced around the living room. New furniture, very modern. "I was in the neighborhood. Hoped I'd catch you in."

"Have a seat, Detective," Frank said. "I'd offer you a cup of coffee, but there isn't any. I just got home, and Mother's not here."

Hansen noticed that the attorney spoke with the slightest lisp. "Too bad. I'd like to talk to her."

"I'm not sure when she'll be home. She left a note that she's having dinner with her friend Mrs. Short."

"Maybe later." Hansen sat on the couch. "I want to go over some things you told Officer O'Brian when your wife was reported missing."

Frank sat in a low-slung chair facing Hansen. He raked his fingers through his dark wavy hair. "Anything. Anything to help you find her and clear up this mess. I've been going out of my mind. She's pregnant, you know."

The detective put his notebook on his thigh and clicked his ballpoint pen open. "Where were you the night your wife disappeared?"

"Here, right here with my mother. We were watching TV."

"How about at eleven that night?"

"I was asleep, of course. I had court in the morning, Detective. You don't think . . ." Frank shook his head. "You don't think I had anything to do with this, do you?"

Hansen watched the young attorney carefully. "You have no idea where your wife might have gone? She never said anything about going away?"

"Nothing, but . . ." Frank pursed his thin lips.

"But what, Mr. Duncan?"

"A few weeks ago, she threatened to make trouble for me if I didn't move back in with her. It should be in your report. I told Officer O'Brian the day she disappeared."

Hansen cast a suspicious eye on the man. "How would she make trouble for you?"

"I don't know. 'Unpleasant publicity' is all she said. She was upset about the way I was handling things . . . so maybe that's what she's doing now. Making trouble."

"Why was she so unhappy?"

"Because I'm staying here with Mother instead of living with her. I swear, one more week and I'd have been there with her." He held up a finger for emphasis. "One more week. This is just temporary, until Mother can . . . adjust."

"Adjust to your marriage?"

Frank ran his fingers through his hair again. "Believe me, it's a long story."

"I got plenty of time."

Frank hesitated. "My mother's terrified of being alone, and she's afraid of losing me."

Hansen lifted a brow.

"And I'm afraid she might try to harm herself." Frank stared at his feet. "She's tried it before."

"But you're not afraid your wife might harm *her*self?"

Frank jerked back. "Olga is a strong woman. I love her very much, and she knows it."

Hansen tipped his head to the side. "So you think your wife might be hiding out somewhere?"

"I don't know what else to think."

"Can you think of anybody she might stay with?"

"Olga's from Canada. She moved here when she finished nurses' training a year ago. The only friends I know about are a married couple down in LA that she knew from Vancouver and the people she works with. And all of them say they haven't seen or heard from her and have no idea where she might be."

Hansen glanced at his notes. "You told Officer O'Brian that some of your wife's luggage is missing from her apartment."

"Right." Frank nodded vigorously. "She keeps an imitation alligator-skin hatbox and a matching train-box on a shelf in her closet. Both gone."

"I understand your mother was unhappy with your wife."

Frank's mouth turned into a thin, straight line. "That's coming from Mrs. Barnett, that batty landlady over at Olga's apartment building, isn't it? Absolutely untrue. Mother is mad at *me*. I'm the one she's unhappy with."

"I'd like to talk to your mother," Hansen said. "See if Olga said anything to her."

"I don't think she can be any help. She barely knew Olga. She only met her once."

"Your mother only met your wife once?"

Frank looked away. "Mother's . . . very emotional . . . about the marriage."

After he left Frank Duncan, Hansen stopped by the police station. He was in no hurry to hear his girlfriend, Beverly, bitch at him for standing her up. He pushed aside the piles of paperwork covering his desk. *Damn Charlie and his big mouth. Gone for two weeks.* Hansen tossed his coat onto his partner's empty desk and sat down at his own. He grabbed his message slips from the nail on the paperweight. Two from Beverly. He threw those in the wastebasket.

He swiveled in his chair while he read the third message. It was for Charlie, but someone had added it to his pile. The message was from Bob Holt, a newspaper reporter from Ventura. Hansen knew that Charlie and Holt exchanged information sometimes. Off the record.

According to the message, Holt wanted to know if the police were investigating an escaped mental patient from Camarillo State Hospital in connection with Olga Duncan's disappearance. Hansen turned the paper over and continued to read. A man had harassed a girl in Ventura the night after Olga disappeared. Still on the loose.

Hansen paper-clipped the slip to the top of the case file, slung his jacket over his shoulder, and headed for the door.

CHAPTER SEVEN

THE INSTALLMENT PLAN

Santa Barbara, California, November 21, 1958

I t had rained a little during the night. The sky hung dense with cloud cover; the roads still glistened with moisture. Gus Baldonado's narrow shoulders hunched over the steering wheel as he weaved the battered Ford in and out of Friday morning traffic toward the Blue Onion restaurant. His baby-faced pal, Luis Moya, rode shotgun while Esperanza Esquivel, owner of the Tropical Café and Bar, sat slumped in a corner of the back seat.

Gus gunned the engine while he waited for other cars to clear the intersection and shouted "Boo!" out the window at a pretty girl stepping off the curb at the crosswalk. When she scrambled back onto the sidewalk, Gus made kissing noises. He leered a wide grin full of perfect teeth and laughed uproariously.

"Keep your mind on business, Romeo," Luis said as he gave the young woman a quick once-over of his own.

Gus threw the car into gear and roared through the intersection.

Luis faced backward in his seat to focus his steady black eyes on Mrs. Esquivel. "The lady should have the money for us by now."

Mrs. Esquivel stared out the window at the stores and restaurants lining State Street. Air smelling of ocean brine drifted through the wing window and mixed with the stink of stale cigarette smoke. She moved a lank strand of black hair away from her thin face. "I don't wanna do this. *You* talk to her."

Luis shook his head. "She wanted to talk to you. Besides, it's better this way. I don't want anybody seeing me or Gus with her."

As the big Ford rumbled through the next intersection, it barely missed clipping another car. Gus flipped the other driver the finger.

"You be careful with my car," Mrs. Esquivel said. "I don't like to let nobody drive it but me. Not even my brother."

"Hey, we help you out, cleaning all the time down at the Tropical."

Mrs. Esquivel continued to stare out the window. "And you drink up my beer."

"Yeah, well, you got us into *this*." Luis slapped the top of his seat, and Mrs. Esquivel jumped. "And if this lady tells you she doesn't have any money, don't take no for an answer. Tell her she better pay . . . or she'll be sorry. Two thousand dollars cash today."

Gus slowed the old Ford and turned left on Valerio into the parking lot of the Blue Onion Drive-In Restaurant. He put the car in neutral again, kept one foot on the brake, and pumped the gas pedal to keep the engine alive.

Luis shooed Mrs. Esquivel out the door and shouted after her, "Remember what I said. Cash only!"

Gus glanced sideways at his partner. "Do you think we have time to go down to the Frosty Freeze?"

Mrs. Esquivel spotted Elizabeth Duncan the moment she walked into the restaurant. The well-dressed matron and her old-lady friend, Mrs. Short, were sitting in a booth by the street-side window. Mrs. Esquivel shuffled their way.

Mrs. Short saw her coming, picked up her coffee cup, scooted out of the booth, and moved to one of the swivel stools across the room.

Mrs. Esquivel slid into the vacated spot. "The boys tell me you wanna talk to me."

Mrs. Duncan put down her coffee and smiled sweetly. She had thin lips and deep-set eyes behind cat's-eye glasses. "I'm sorry I haven't been able to get to the bank. . . . There's a lot going on right now."

"Yeah, well, I don't wanna hear your problems," Mrs. Esquivel wheezed. "I don' feel so good myself, and I got too much work all the time. Every morning, every night at the Tropical. Remember? I got to do everything now because Marciano's in jail, and your son . . ." More hacking.

Mrs. Duncan looked over to where Mrs. Short sat flipping through the music selections at the countertop jukebox. She took a quick look in the other direction. No one in earshot. She reached into her purse. "I do have something for you, though." She pushed a long white rectangular piece of paper over to Mrs. Esquivel's side of the table.

"What's this?"

Mrs. Duncan beamed. "A check."

Mrs. Esquivel tried to push the paper back, but Mrs. Duncan covered it with her hand to hold it in place. "It's all I've got right now, two hundred dollars."

"Two hundred dollars? Luis say no check. He want two thousand today. Cash only."

"I can't," Mrs. Duncan snapped, then softened her tone. "I'm so sorry. . . . You know me, Mrs. Esquivel. Remember? I was in the courtroom all the time during your husband's trial when Frank was defending him. You know I'm good for it."

"Talk to the boys."

Mrs. Duncan pulled the check back. "Fine," she said in a huffy tone.

"I'll tell 'em to meet you at the Woolworths a few blocks down." Mrs. Esquivel parted her cracked lips, showing small yellow teeth. "But Luis won' take no check. He want cash payment now, or too bad for you."

Mrs. Duncan touched a silver button on her cashmere sweater. "Frank doesn't give me money like that. I don't even have a bank account, haven't had one in years . . . overdrafts. And Frank, well, and the bank, for that matter, get very . . ." She flitted her fingers around.

Mrs. Esquivel slid out of the booth. "Tell your stories to Luis at Woolworths. He's the one you gotta worry about."

"Emma," Mrs. Duncan called across the room as soon as Mrs. Esquivel was gone.

Mrs. Short, holding a nickel over the coin slot in the jukebox, looked up from the plastic-coated list of song titles.

Mrs. Duncan motioned at her. Mrs. Short put the nickel back in her purse and followed her friend out of the restaurant.

"We got to get going to Woolworths," Mrs. Duncan said.

"Oh, good. I need some powder and a bottle of Jergens."

"Not shopping, you ninny," Mrs. Duncan snapped. "I need to take care of this business with the boys."

A bus groaned to a stop. The doors opened as compressed air hissed from its brakes. Mrs. Duncan stepped through the doorway. "You get the tickets, Emma. I don't have any change."

The bus lurched forward while Mrs. Short stumbled down the aisle, trying to close her purse. She was thrown one way, then the other, and finally plopped into the seat next to Mrs. Duncan. "I think this is the fourth time this week I've had to pay for the fares. I really don't . . ."

Mrs. Duncan waved the check at her. "Everybody wants my money," she pouted.

"I thought that was Frank's money that you were supposed to use to pay off his new typewriter, and I been wondering . . . What are you going to tell him?"

At Woolworths, Luis and Gus waited in the record department off a side aisle within sight of the front door. Gus leaned on the counter and nonchalantly flipped through a stack of records while Luis held a Frank Sinatra album in one hand. He whistled "Come Fly with Me" under his breath as he admired the bright blue cover picture of a jaunty Sinatra with a fedora perched on his head.

Mrs. Duncan yanked open the front door and strode inside like she owned the place, head held high with a wide smile for the salesgirl stocking a nearby display.

Mrs. Short shuffled in behind. "I'll be in cosmetics," she whispered.

Luis and Gus moved away from a couple of nearby shoppers. Mrs. Duncan's face brightened as she sailed down the aisle toward the men. She acknowledged each of them with a polite nod and held out the check. "It's good."

Luis stood rigid, arms folded across his chest. "Cash only. Esperanza told you."

Mrs. Duncan extended the check until it touched Luis's hand. "Two hundred dollars. It's all I have right now. Take it or leave it." Her lips froze in a closed-mouth smile.

Luis grabbed her wrist and squeezed. "You know what we said at the Tropical. You gotta pay up now . . . or else." He stared at her with dark, piercing eyes.

She twisted and yanked her wrist free. "I can get more money when I sell some of the stock certificates I've got up in Frisco. Just a few more days and I'll be able to get up there." She smoothed the sleeve of her jacket over her wrist. "I have a considerable portfolio. You boys do understand about stock certificates, I assume." She tilted her head a little. "It takes time to liquidate assets, you know."

Gus, slouching against the counter, shrugged and raised his eyebrows at his partner.

Luis shook his head, but his posture relaxed a little. "How much will you get?"

"All of it. Six thousand dollars by next week."

Luis looked at the ceiling and sucked in a breath. "I need that money. I got a vacation coming. Got permission from my parole officer to go to Texas to see my folks."

Mrs. Duncan held out the check again.

Luis hesitated, then snatched it out of her fingers. "Two hundred dollars? We'll call this an installment. Next week we want all of it."

Neither of them said anything while two shoppers passed. Then Luis handed her back the check. "You go across the street to that bank and get this cashed, then meet me at Silverwoods department store."

CHAPTER EIGHT

INJUSTICE

Ventura, California, November 21, 1958

I was upset when I got home from school Friday afternoon because my teacher had cut me off when I tried to tell the class about Olga's disappearance during sharing time. *Everybody should be on the lookout for Olga!* I couldn't stop thinking about her. Did a mad fiend drag her out of her apartment? It would have been dark outside. She must have been so scared.

I chewed my thumbnail. The house was quiet. Mrs. Alfred, our new babysitter, was in the kitchen reading one of her paperback novels. Daddy called the books trashy. Recently widowed and with no criminal record, she had replaced Jolene, the convict babysitter, earlier in the year. I tossed my books on the kitchen table.

My parakeet, Tweety, chirped from his cage, hanging over the washing machine in the kitchen. He jumped to one side of his perch and cocked his head.

"Sorry, Tweety," I said, climbing up on the counter to reach for the box of Honey Smacks. "I can't let you out. I'm not sure where Pinky Lee is right now." The little bird cocked his head in the other direction. "It wouldn't be safe for you."

Tweety wanted out of his cage so he could land on my finger. Sometimes he took off for a little fly around the house, but he always came back to me. Nowadays, though, he didn't get out much. Not since Pinky Lee had killed his brother, Chirpy.

The image was still vivid in my head. We'd come home late on a Sunday night in August after spending the day with my grandparents ninety miles away in Arcadia. I was the first one in the house because my parents were trying to get my sister out of the car without waking her up.

The moment I turned on the kitchen light, I screamed at the empty, overturned birdcage on the floor. Pinky was sitting on one of the chairs swishing his tail and washing his face. Daddy found Chirpy in the corner by the cat dishes, lifeless and partially plucked.

At first it seemed Tweety must be dead, too. I sat at the table, sobbing as my mother got a broom and a paper bag out of the closet after putting Betsey in bed. "Pinky is a bad cat," I wailed. "Cinderella wouldn't kill anyone."

"Honey, he's just being a cat. We should have known better than to leave him alone in the house with the birds for so long," Mother said.

Daddy threw Pinky Lee out the back door. "He's a natural-born killer."

I hiccupped and continued to cry.

"Yeah, we should have known better," Daddy said, "especially since that cat spends half his days staring up at the cage, licking his chops." He used the toe of his shoe to push Chirpy's body away from the wall.

I squealed, "Don't . . . hurt him any more."

"He's dead as a doornail, sweetheart. Can't feel a thing." Daddy flicked his hand at Mother. "You clean up the crime scene here, Lois. I'll go look for the second victim."

Mother surveyed the mess of green feathers. "I don't see any blue feathers. . . . Maybe Tweety got away."

"Now, don't get her hopes up."

I inhaled a deep shaky breath, getting ready to let out another howl, but stopped with my mouth wide open. I'd heard the flutter of wings high up in the drapes next to the table. "Tweety, Tweety!" I shouted. "You're alive."

That had been three months earlier, but even now, sometimes when I walked through the kitchen, I couldn't get the green feathers out of my mind.

I shook my head to forget about Chirpy's lifeless little body and poured the sugary cereal into a bowl, mixed two heaping spoonfuls of chocolate Nestle's Quik into a glass of milk, and carried both into the living room to sit in the Adirondack chair and contemplate the injustices of the world. Pinky Lee came out from under a table and jumped into my lap. He purred.

"You're not really a bad cat," I said. "You just made a bad mistake."

After I finished the last of my cereal, I plopped down on the living room floor. A warm breeze blew through the screen door as I spread my paper dolls on the floor. I preferred paper dolls because of the extensive wardrobe provided for each doll and the easy maneuvering to act out whatever drama I dreamed up for them.

The familiar thump on the lawn signaled the arrival of the afternoon edition of the newspaper. I left the dolls to go outside and walked barefoot across the lawn that my father mowed, fertilized, and cursed into a lush green landscape. I wiggled my toes in the small tufts of volunteer dichondra as I picked up the paper.

Our neighbor Gene had spent "a fortune," according to Daddy, to plant specially ordered dichondra grass seed, only to see the seeds blown by winds or dropped by birds into our yard, where it flourished in small spots. And it was spreading. Daddy commiserated with the neighbor over the fact that his lawn wasn't doing so well. But in private he was gleeful, rubbing his hands together, hoping that in time the dichondra clovers would take over our whole yard. He hummed "I'm Looking Over a Four Leaf Clover" whenever he surveyed the lawn.

I brought the newspaper inside and spread it out on the floor, sweeping the dolls aside. Pinky hopped down from the chair and tried to curl up on the paper. I pushed him away.

First, I turned to the B section to read the local stories, Dear Abby and, since today was Friday, my father's weekly column.

Daddy's smiling photo with the heading Bob Holt Reporting was on the first page of the B section. I traced my finger under the words as I read his column with ever-growing horror.

Rat Traps

I realize now that buying those traps was a mistake. We were in Korb's Trading Post for some other commodity, pencils as I recall. My oldest daughter, Debby, said she needed some.

Just why mousetraps should occupy the bin next to pencils, I can't imagine. Anyway, my youngest daughter, Betsey, spotted them.

"You should buy me a mousetrap, Daddy," Betsey said. "Remember the things I wanted for Christmas that I didn't get?"

I leaned in for a closer inspection, and right away I got a shock. "Good god, this thing is big enough to trap a rat or even a small bear."

"I need a rat trap," Betsey insisted. "I hardly got anything for Christmas."

By dint of a little fast talking, I was able to steer her over to some smaller traps. A little old mousetrap seemed like an easy way to satisfy some rather extensive obligation in the gift line, but I was wary. I telephoned my wife from the front counter of the store.

"Betsey wants some mousetraps. Three for twenty-five cents. How about it?"

"Well," she said, "go ahead and let her have them. Maybe we can use them after she's finished playing with them." Her whole attitude indicated this was a matter of little importance. "Can't hurt," she said before hanging up.

Those were fateful words.

A half an hour after we got home, I had forgotten all about the traps, Betsey approached me on tiptoe. "All set," she said cheerily.

"What?" I said.

"The rat traps."

"Where are they?" I asked as I shifted my eyes around the room without moving my head.

"I can't tell," Betsey whispered. "How will I catch anything if the traps aren't hidden?"

Then it hit me. The house was booby trapped. I hardly dared take a step in either direction. So much as a thrust-out finger might be an invitation to an ominous click.

Gathering my courage, I sidled toward the kitchen, determined to stay in the middle of the rooms and avoid dark corners. My mouth was suddenly dry. I needed a drink of milk.

Arriving at the refrigerator, I discovered that the pound of my favorite cheese was missing.

"Bait," was Betsey's cryptic explanation.

After considerable discussion, she was persuaded to bring the traps out of hiding and relocate them in plain sight. This in the interest of giving every family member a sporting chance.

The first casualty was almost the cat. He sniffed inquiringly, but when daughter Debby squealed, he withdrew his nose before touching the trigger. A fly crawled across the trap, and the whole family sat breathless, but he didn't prove heavy enough to trigger it.

"Could a person trip the trap and not get their finger caught?" Debby wondered.

"Sure, if the person's reflexes were fast enough," I said.

"How about yours, Daddy?" she asked.

My standing in the family seemed to be in the balance. I felt trapped to trip the trap.

My first try was successful, much to my astonishment. The trap flew halfway across the room, and when I looked down, my finger was still there. The children clapped wildly. Heady with success, I tried again. . . .

My theory now is that they have to make these modern traps so strong because modern mice, having gorged themselves and grown *supernaturally strong on today's rodent poisons, are a tough breed to bring down.*

Anyway, the swelling is going down now, and my finger is blue only on one side.

I slapped my forehead. *Oh no. I hope Eddie's* mother doesn't read that to his whole family like she did when Daddy wrote about accidently spraying Mother's hair spray on his face instead of shaving cream.* Eddie had told Jimmy the story at recess, and Jimmy had laughed and pointed his finger at me. Jimmy, the cutest boy in the class.

I let out a long hissing sigh and leafed through the rest of the second section without finding anything else of interest, and then reached for the front page to check for crimes, horrible accidents, and devastating natural disasters.

Just below an article with Daddy's byline, about a fifteen-year-old girl in Nebraska getting life in prison for her part in eleven murders, I caught sight of Olga Duncan's picture. She had a nice smile and pretty eyes. *Why would anyone want to hurt her?* The caption said to notify police if you saw her. I clamped my lips tight as I read the story below the photo.

Olga Duncan Photo Sent Out in Hunt

Santa Barbara city police are sending out copies of a photograph of Olga Duncan to other police departments on this coast today in the continuing search for the young woman.

She has been missing for five days. No one has reported seeing her since two women friends left her apartment about 11:00 on November 17th.

All-points bulletins were sent to police departments in California and neighboring states. However, police said that they can find no evidence that she left Santa Barbara. All her identification was left in her apartment. She has notified no one of her whereabouts, including her husband, attorney Frank Duncan, from whom she recently separated.

ALL-POINTS BULLETIN. Wowy zowy! I immediately tore out the picture so that I could be on the lookout for Olga. This was better than the MOST WANTED posters in the post office where my mother bought stamps. I never remembered the faces, but with Olga's picture in my pocket, I would have a chance. Maybe I could help solve this mystery, just like Nancy Drew, and save Olga.

CHAPTER NINE

THE DUNCANS AND THE DETECTIVES

Santa Barbara, California, November 21-22, 1958

D etective Hansen didn't need to look at the clock on the wall across the detective bay to know he was late. He dropped into his rolling chair and tossed his notebook on top of his desk.

"Shit." He'd just wasted the whole afternoon down in Ventura on a wild goose chase over some escaped mental patient Peeping Tom. Turned out, the night Olga went missing, the guy had been in Oxnard skulking through backyards and tapping on windows. Now Hansen had to type up his notes on the morning's interviews with Olga Duncan's hospital colleagues.

He typed quickly then organized and squared up the papers. He put aside the folder labeled "Frank Duncan" to review later and glanced at the unread messages stuck on the spike paperweight next to the telephone. He looked away. He'd promised Beverly he'd pick her up at six to take her to dinner.

"See you tomorrow," he called toward the lieutenant's open office door as he stood up. The message slips caught his eye again. Hansen hesitated.

He had a bad feeling about Olga Duncan. He'd known a lot of women, and he couldn't think of one who would voluntarily leave town without her purse. The detective snatched the messages off the spike and read them standing up. The first one was nothing, but the second got his attention. It was from Sergeant Meyers, who worked in vice and sometimes traffic. He wanted Hansen to call him at home. Underneath the number was scribbled "Duncan Blackmail."

Blackmail?

Hansen reached for the phone.

The next day, Hansen watched as the desk duty officer pointed Frank Duncan in his direction. Two P.M. Right on time, but . . .

Hansen half stood and stuck his hand out. "Thought you were bringing in your mother," he said as he motioned to one of the empty chairs on the other side of his desk.

Frank remained standing. "She's in the car. We expected to talk to Sergeant Meyers. I know him from court."

Hansen picked up the lisp again and thought about something Meyers had told him: "The girls down at the courthouse call him the Wicked Wascal Wabbit." Hansen kept his expression neutral. "I understand, but I'm handling your wife's disappearance, so . . ."

"I told Meyers that this business is totally unrelated to that. The blackmail started a week before Olga disappeared. Mrs. Esquivel down at the Tropical Café threatened her."

Hansen turned his hands out in a *what are you going to do?* gesture. "Well, Meyers isn't in today, and this isn't his beat anyway. The detective unit handles extortion cases."

Frank sighed. "Just don't confuse my mother. We need to concentrate on this extortion threat." Frank looked away. "Don't get me wrong. Mother's worried about Olga. We both are. But Mother's a little nervous about being here. She doesn't think she'll be able to identify the men who threatened her. Says she was too scared when it happened."

Hansen tilted the chair forward again. "Why don't you bring her in so we can get started?"

Elizabeth Duncan wore a green-and-white print dress, belted at the waist, with a white Peter Pan collar. Her wavy brown hair, streaked with gray, was meticulously styled and swept off her face. She was haranguing Frank as they came through the front door. "No. I said no."

Frank was silent, his face expressionless. He rested his hand on his mother's back and guided her forward.

When the pair reached the desk, Hansen stood. Frank made the introductions before he and his mother took seats facing the detective. Mrs. Duncan clutched a black patent leather purse in her lap. Hansen noticed that mother and son had identical thin lips set in straight lines across their faces.

"Tell me about your trouble with Mrs. Esquivel, Mrs. Duncan."

She looked at her son.

"You need to tell him yourself, Mother."

"You know they're probably going to kill us both if they find out we've talked to the police."

"I need to hear it from you, Mrs. Duncan," Hansen said.

She took a long-suffering breath. "Esperanza Esquivel's got two Mexicans going to kill me and Frankie if I don't give back the five hundred dollars she paid Frankie to defend her husband."

"This is Marciano Esquivel's wife?"

"Right." Mrs. Duncan looked surprised. "You know him?"

"Everybody in the squad room knows the Esquivels. I've made four or five arrests in that bar of theirs myself."

Mrs. Duncan slid her purse off her lap and handed it to Frank. Her face brightened as she scooted her chair closer to the desk. "Well, good. You know, then. You know the kind of people I'm dealing with here . . . dangerous. Frankie made Mr. Esquivel a deal with the judge, but now they don't like it. They're threatening us."

Hansen nodded. So far, this was the same story Meyers had told him on the phone the previous day. "What happened, exactly?"

"Well, I was down on Mason Street to look at some apartments and had lunch at the Pancake House. That's on Cabrillo down there by the beach."

"Yeah, I know where the Pancake House is, Mrs. Duncan. What about the Esquivels?"

"I'm getting to that. I'm trying to tell you about it."

Frank made a *take it easy* gesture to the detective and said, "I know you're nervous, Mother. Just tell Detective Hansen what happened."

"I'm more than nervous," she snapped. "I'm scared to death of these people, and you should be too."

"Back to the Esquivels," Hansen said.

"After lunch we saw the apartment, but I wasn't satisfied. So we looked at a few more."

"We? Someone with you?"

"Emma. My friend Emma Short."

"She's a witness, then."

"Mmm, yes and no. She was too far away when they threatened me. She couldn't hear what they were saying."

Hansen made a note in a tablet.

"We were going up State Street, waiting for the bus. It was getting along about three thirty or four, and the buses only come every hour. So we just kept walking. When we got in front of the Tropical Café, I was looking inside through the bamboo curtain they got in the front window. Just curious, you know. I never knew where the bar was located until we just happened to walk by that day. I'd heard of the place, what with Frankie defending the owners and all, and I saw Mr. and Mrs. Esquivel in court a couple of times." Mrs. Duncan folded her arms across her chest. "Bum rap."

Detective Hansen raised an eyebrow.

"Well, I go to court sometimes. I like to watch Frankie operate." She patted her son on the knee and gave him a radiant smile. "Brilliant!" She turned back to Hansen. "When we got to the door of the café,

Mrs. Esquivel and a Mexican guy stepped out in front of us. The man grabbed my wrist and pulled me into the café. I had black-and-blue marks for days." She held up her arm.

"When did this happen?" Hansen leaned a little closer to get a better look at the wrist. There was nothing to see.

"About ten days ago, I think."

"November 13th," Frank said. "She pawned her rings to make a payment that day. She's got the pawn ticket in here." He was still holding the purse. He opened it and started rummaging around.

Hansen watched Mrs. Duncan. "But you didn't tell your son about any of this until yesterday?"

"He has a lot on his mind right now with Olga missing and all."

"You say this all happened on November 13th?" Hansen wrote more in his tablet.

Mrs. Duncan looked at her son, who was still poking around in her purse. "Give me that. I'll find it myself." She snatched her purse out of his hands, reached in, and pulled out a slip of paper. "Here it is." She gave Frank a *can't you do anything right?* look and waved the pawn ticket in front of the policeman.

Hansen took the ticket and glanced at it before he set it on the desk. "So what happened at the café?"

"They threatened me, that's what happened. Blackmailed me." Mrs. Duncan's voice began to quiver, and she pulled a crumpled handkerchief out of her purse. "Mrs. Esquivel said she wasn't paying no lawyer five hundred dollars to get her husband sent to jail. Said they could have done that for free." She put the handkerchief over her mouth.

Frank shook his head. "It wasn't quite like that. Marciano Esquivel could have been sent to state prison for a couple of years. I got his sentence cut to a year. The case was worth fifteen hundred dollars. Five hundred was a bargain."

"Well, his wife didn't think so," Mrs. Duncan said. "Didn't agree with the way you'd handled the case at all."

Hansen shifted in his chair. "Where was this friend of yours, Mrs. Short, when all this was going on?"

"The other man, the tall one, walked her across the room to a little table over in the corner, out of the way. That guy never said anything. Just stood there. The shorter one did all the talking, the threatening. He took me over to the bar and sat me down on one of the stools."

"And what did you say?"

"I was frightened. It's hard to remember. I know I said I didn't have the money."

"So why did they come to you? Why didn't they go directly to your son?"

Frank interrupted. "Because they knew I'd give them nothing, Detective, that's why. I'd have had the idiots arrested for extortion. They just thought they could scare Mother into paying."

Mrs. Duncan nodded. "Told me not to tell Frank."

"So you agreed to pawn your rings to make a payment?"

"Right. I was terrified. The tall man followed me up the two blocks to Pacific Loan Company where I got $175 for my rings."

Hansen took notes. "What happened when you got back to the café?"

"I gave them all the money, and the short guy said, 'You'll hear from us later. We want the full five hundred dollars.'"

"She made another payment yesterday," Frank added.

Mrs. Duncan dabbed her eyes with the hanky. "He said that they knew where Frankie parked his car, and they would get him."

"How was the next payment arranged?" Hansen asked.

"Telephone. The short guy called me. Told me to meet Mrs. Esquivel down at the Blue Onion yesterday. I did that, and then Mrs. Esquivel said to go to Woolworths with cash."

Frank cut in. "But Mother didn't have the rest of the money. So she paid them with a two-hundred-dollar check I'd given her to pay for my typewriter."

"One hundred and fifty dollars," Mrs. Duncan said. "I kept fifty dollars for myself." When Frank turned his head toward her, she shrugged. "I needed some money."

"So here we are," Frank said. "When I got home yesterday, I asked mother for the receipt for payment on the typewriter. She didn't have it or the check. I hit the roof."

"I finally had to tell him," Mrs. Duncan said, "because by then they wanted even more money, another two thousand dollars . . . maybe six thousand . . . and I knew that I could never come up with that much."

"The whole thing's ridiculous," Frank said. "I still think I ought to go down to the Tropical and just settle this myself."

"Let us take care of it, Mr. Duncan." Detective Hansen stood up. "We'll start with the mug shots."

Mrs. Duncan stiffened. "Oh, I don't think I'll be able to identify them. It was dark in that café. And I was so scared."

"You've seen these guys twice, once in the bar and then again at Woolworths. I'll pull photos of people we know who hang out over at the Tropical. I think if you see one of the guys, you'll know him."

Frank reached for her elbow. "Come on, Mother, we have to give this a try."

They went into the office that held the large binders full of pictures of known criminals. Detective Hansen consulted with another officer, and the two took about ten minutes sorting through the binders. Finally, five pictures were laid on the table in front of Mrs. Duncan.

She shook her head. "Not here."

"You sure, Mother? You hardly looked. Try again."

She slapped her hand on the table. "I told you they aren't here! I'm not blind, you know."

Hansen cleared his throat. "I'm going to talk to the patrolman that works the Tropical beat. See if he has any ideas about the guys we're looking for, and then I'll get you some more photos to check."

"Good," Frank said.

Hansen turned to Mrs. Duncan. "When do you think they'll contact you again?"

"I don't know. Mrs. Esquivel is supposed call me to set up another meeting."

"We could put a recording device on your phone. Record the next call."

Mrs. Duncan shot her son a look. "Frank, I don't think I—"

Hansen talked over her. "We'll try to get it hooked up in the next couple of days."

"Great," Frank said.

"And, Mrs. Duncan, don't pay these people any more money," Hansen continued. "Don't meet them again. Notify me if they call you."

Mrs. Duncan said nothing.

The detective gathered up the mug shot photos and put them aside. "Since you're here, I'd also like to talk to you about your daughter-in-law."

Mrs. Duncan shot Frank another look. "But why? This hasn't got anything to do with Olga. I already talked to the patrolman about her."

Hansen folded his arms on the table and leaned forward. "Seems like if these people are threatening to kill you and your son, you might worry about what they'd do to Olga, too."

Thirty minutes after the Duncans left, Hansen finished typing up his notes from the interview and called Charlie Thompson. He wanted to bounce this crazy story off his suspended partner. Plus, he needed a drink.

Charlie didn't pick up until the fourth ring. "Hello," he barked.

Hansen tucked the receiver between his shoulder and his ear. "Thought you might like a little break from the drudgery of all the free time you have on your hands."

Thompson snorted. "Eleanor's keeping me pretty busy. I got a list."

"Think you could get away for a while? Meet me down at the Presidio for a beer? I'm just finishing up at the station."

Thompson sucked air through his teeth. "I dunno. Eleanor's not happy. No pay for two weeks."

"Maybe I can help you solve that problem," Hansen said. "We got a new case while you've been gone. Missing nurse."

"I read about that. Why are you at the station on a Saturday?"

"Why do you think? I'm working for two," Hansen said. "You can buy me a beer for all the extra work I've been doing because of your little temper tantrum."

"I'll get there if I can." Thompson hung up.

Charlie Thompson parked his beat-up Nash Rambler across the street from the police station, in front of the Presidio Bar. Inside, five or six men sat on stools or leaned on the old scarred mahogany bar with its pitted brass railing.

Hansen was sitting at the far end of the bar, reading the *Daily Racing Form* and sipping a beer. He glanced at Thompson as he approached, then put out his cigarette. "You look all tuckered out, buddy. Thought you were taking it easy."

"Just got back from visiting family in Chicago." Thompson slid onto the stool next to his partner. "Had an interview with the Chicago sheriff's department. I heard they were looking for good cops."

"That leaves you out." Hansen smirked.

"Ha-ha. Didn't work out anyway." Thompson set his fedora on the bar. "A couple of the deputies talked to me while I was waiting to go in for the interview. They bragged about how much money you can make in payoffs. That's not for me."

"Right. Every crime is personal with you."

Thompson grinned and pointed to his partner's flowered shirt. "See you changed into your pretty-boy aloha shirt."

"Hey, this shirt looks good, and when I wear it, I make it look even better." Hansen grabbed some of the material and shook like a hula girl. "It's a classic. Got it in Waikiki during the war. It's my 'victory' shirt." He wiggled his eyebrows. "The ladies love it."

Thompson wiped his hand over his bald head. "Yeah, yeah. You and the ladies. Spare me."

"So how's suspension agreeing with you? Having a nice little vacation?"

"Unpaid."

The bartender brought Charlie a beer without being asked. Charlie nodded thanks and took a sip.

"Uh-huh," Hansen said. "Seems like *I'm* paying for it."

"Sorry about all the extra work." Thompson made a sour face and drank more beer. "But the lieutenant's an asshole, all about regulations. Doesn't understand the street. I had a lead. I was doing my job."

"Uh-huh. Like calling him a son of a bitch on your way out the door?"

"What can I say? I'm passionate about my work." Thompson smiled into his beer. "Saw your old pickup out front. What happened to your baby?"

Hansen raised his voice. "Well, shit, I'm not parking a pristine '32 Ford Coupe in the middle of State Street on a Saturday night for some drunk to sideswipe."

"You ever going to drive that car?"

"I drive it . . . sometimes. It's not an everyday car."

Thompson coughed to suppress a smile. "So tell me about this missing nurse case you mentioned on the phone."

"Whatta you care?" Hansen lit another cigarette. "I'll have the case solved by the time you get back on duty."

"You're the one who wanted to pick my brain." Thompson eyed the box of Camels on the bar next to his partner's beer for a moment and reached over and took one.

"I thought you quit. Again."

Thompson shrugged.

Hansen flicked his lighter and said, "The nurse, Olga Duncan, just disappeared. She's pregnant and married to that defense attorney, Frank Duncan."

"Duncan? I know him. Tenacious little bastard. He was the attorney for some asshole I arrested last year on assault charges. Duncan got him off on a bullshit technicality." Thompson guzzled his beer.

"Sounds about right. And even though his wife is seven months pregnant, he left her and moved back home to live with his mother."

Thompson bunched his eyebrows. "So what happened with the wife?"

"One night about a week ago, she had a couple of her nurse friends from the hospital over to her apartment for refreshments and girl talk. The friends left about eleven, and nobody's seen Olga since."

"The neighbors didn't hear anything unusual that night?"

"Nothing. She just vanished." Hansen flicked his fingers into the air. "Poof."

"You think maybe the husband? No-alimony, no-child-support kinda divorce?"

"I don't know what to think. I've interviewed him twice. One minute he seems genuinely worried and upset, then he starts spouting off that his wife is pulling this disappearing act to make him look bad."

"Yeah, well, you know those scumbag defense attorneys. I've seen some Academy Award–worthy performances in court."

"Duncan says he was home at his mother's apartment watching TV at the time his wife disappeared, but Lieutenant Peck's not buying it. He thinks Duncan's involved. We're working on it, but so far no evidence."

"So you ain't got shit."

"There is one thing, though, about the mother-in-law. Olga's landlady says she came to the apartment a couple of months ago and made accusations about Olga not being a fit wife for her son. Wanted the landlady to evict her." Hansen took another drag off his cigarette. "We don't have much else to go on."

"What does this have to do with getting me off suspension?"

"I'll bet Lieutenant Peck would reinstate you on Monday if you'd apologize to him. We're shorthanded . . . and this case—Pretty Nurse Vanishes in the Night—is starting to get some notice in the press."

Charlie made a face. "So what's next?"

"Weirdest thing happened today. Frank brought his mother into the station to report that she's being extorted—she calls it blackmail—by the wife of one of his former clients." Hansen summarized the convoluted story.

"That's crazy."

"This case is getting more complicated every day."

"Well, I guess I could talk to the lieutenant. . . ." Thompson screwed up his face to show that he was thinking. "Eleanor's mad at me, as usual. We need the money."

Hansen slapped his partner on the back. "Great! Peck may not like you any better than you like him, but he's smart enough to know he needs you. He's getting some pressure from above to solve this thing."

"Yeah, well, it's my job. I don't want any other women disappearing." Thompson looked at his watch. "Jeez, I gotta get out of here." He raised his hand to the bartender as he stubbed out his cigarette in the ashtray.

"I'll get the beers," Hansen said. "You call the lieutenant."

Charlie slid off his stool. "You must really be desperate if you're offering to pick up the tab."

Hansen spread his arms, palms up. "I pay . . . sometimes. You get the next round."

Thompson pulled a couple of bills out of his wallet and set them on the bar. "Here, go crazy. I gotta get home. I told Eleanor I was going out to check in with an informant. I promised to make it quick."

"And that, my friend, is why I'm still single. No woman's ever going to keep me on a leash."

Thompson put his wallet back in his pocket and looked toward Hansen to say goodbye, but his partner already had his eye on the fuzzy pink sweater sitting a few stools down the bar, looking bored. She was sitting with a DA investigator, who was deep in conversation with one of the off-duty cops.

The girl lifted her drink toward Hansen and smiled.

CHAPTER TEN

THE WAGES OF SIN

Ventura, California, November 23, 1958

As I got myself ready for church Sunday morning, Betsey stirred on the bottom bunk. She looked so angelic. Ha! Mother didn't understand how my little sister tormented me, always taking my things without asking.

Betsey rolled over without opening her eyes.

And I'm the one in trouble? Why should I have to go to bed early and miss *Dragnet* because of Betsey ruining my doll's dress? *I don't care what Mother says; I wish Betsey had been the one to disappear instead of Olga.* I covered my mouth. *Oops. That's not very Christian of me.*

As I stepped through the bedroom door, wearing my poodle skirt and new pink sandals, I noticed the rumpled bed in my parents' room across the hallway. Daddy was always an early riser, and Mother had already left to work her monthly Sunday shift as the on-call social worker at the hospital. A coworker had picked her up.

At the end of the day, Daddy would drive us to the hospital to get Mother so we could all go out for Sunday dinner. Mother said that if she had to work on a Sunday, she wasn't going to cook, too. I liked the dinner out, but I hated going to the creepy hospital. If we got there early and the weather was nice, we waited on the big lawn outside her office building where blank-faced, glassy-eyed patients visited with their family members. Daddy said that all the patients had to take a lot of medicine so that they wouldn't cause trouble.

Off in the distance I could sometimes hear the wails and moaning of patients on what Mother referred to as the "locked wards." When I told her I was scared, she said to me, "You don't need to be afraid. They won't hurt you." She looked sad when she added, "They're sick, very, very sick people, and nobody really knows how to help them."

I walked to the kitchen and peered out the back door. My father was rummaging around in the garage. I hesitated for a moment then turned away.

No use bothering Daddy. He didn't believe in organized religion, only a higher being. A few Bible stories at bedtime and discussions about the Golden Rule were the extent of my parent-sponsored religious training.

That morning I'd arranged to walk to the Christian Life Revival Church with my friend Marilyn. Reverend Ralston* was the new pastor, and he said that everyone was welcome, even if your parents didn't go. I'd attended Sunday school at that church on and off since enrolling myself in their Vacation Bible School over the summer. I'd won a golden-tasseled bookmark with a picture of Jesus on the front for memorizing the names of all the books of the New Testament. Marilyn attended regularly. Her mother sometimes.

The church was just around the corner from our house. Marilyn and I traipsed over the front lawns of our neighbors' houses toward the corner. She carried a small white Bible I greatly admired.

When we got to the front yard of the house at the top of the street, I heard a knock on the picture window. Wendy* waved and then disappeared. The screen door banged. Wendy was a year ahead of me in school. I didn't like her because she said that my family wasn't saved. And once, when Daddy drove all the Alameda girls to the beach, she told me that her father said Daddy was a weirdo because he hummed all the time.

"Wait for me," Wendy called from the front porch. She caught up with us at the corner. "My mother said I get to walk with you today." She took Marilyn's arm.

The two girls chatted about a cute new boy at school as we continued toward church.

I'd been staring at my shoes as we walked. "Like my new sandals?" I wiggled my pink-painted toenails.

Wendy took in a sharp gulp of air. "You can't wear toenail polish to church. It's sinful."

"Really?" Marilyn said.

Wendy nodded. "God wants girls to be modest, not painted up." She squinted at me. "You'd know that if your family was Christian and read the Bible."

"We're Christian." I mumbled.

Wendy shook her head. "Your father curses and he smokes a pipe."

"No, he doesn't smoke anymore," I countered. "He had to quit the pipe because he kept setting himself on fire."

"When he put it in his coat pocket," Marilyn added helpfully.

Wendy raised her voice. "Well, Christian girls can't wear nail polish. Everybody knows that."

We stood on the curb at Victoria Avenue, waiting to cross the street. A big rig whizzed by and blew our skirts. Victoria was the only busy street in the neighborhood, a thoroughfare to the east part of town. Big-truck drivers used the road to bypass the weigh station on Highway 101. I wasn't supposed to cross Victoria on my own.

"You better hope you don't get hit by a truck and die," Wendy said, "because you won't be going to heaven with your toenails painted pink."

The Christian Life Revival Church was a plain stucco building with a peaked roof and a white metal cross on top. Sunday school met in a small, cold room off a hallway that ran alongside the main sanctuary. Most of the dozen or so children in the class sat cross-legged on the linoleum-tiled floor. I sat on my feet to hide the shame of my painted toenails. We waited for Mr. Dillon*, the Sunday school teacher, to get started.

Mr. Dillon had a pointy chin and wore a wrinkled black suit. He slapped his Bible to get our attention and scanned our faces as we quieted. He began to pace. "The wages of sin is death, boys and girls. I get no pleasure in speaking about this." His voice rose. He slapped his Bible after each word: "SIN, DEATH, HELL, and the LAKE OF FIRE."

I felt my toes cramping. I smoothed my skirt and gazed at Mr. Dillon with a solemn and hopefully virtuous expression as he continued with the lesson.

"I do not take pleasure, but it is my duty to warn you"—his voice rose— "of the divine wrath of God which awaits every one of you who defies His word." Mr. Dillon bowed his head. "Let us pray, boys and girls."

I lowered my head, shut my eyes tight, and silently apologized to God for wearing toenail polish to church.

Mr. Dillon reached for a strip of narrow white felt and smoothed it down the middle of the felt board. On one side of the strip, he put up a felt angel with golden hair hovering above a white cloud. On the other side he added a devilish-looking creature with horns and a red cape.

Mr. Dillon cleared his throat and pointed at the devil. "Murderers, whoremongers, sorcerers, idolaters, and all liars will be cast alive into a lake of fire burning with brimstone, and they shall be tormented day and night forever and ever."

I felt light-headed. *Fibbers too?*

He talked on and on about the end of the world . . . more wailing and gnashing of teeth. He finished with, "Remember, boys and girls, the wages of sin is death."

We prayed for God's mercy, and then he told Wendy and Marilyn to pass out crayons and coloring sheets with a mimeographed outline of a floating angel above the eternal lake of fire.

There was a fifteen-minute break before the church service started. Many people, adults and children both, stepped outside onto a covered cement area to stretch their legs and chat. Nobody smoked.

Mrs. Harris*, one of the helpers for my girl scout troop, caught my eye. She beamed at me as she zigzagged through the crowd in my direction. "Ha-ha." She shook her finger at me. "Debby, your father is such a card," she said loudly. "I get a real kick out of his columns."

I wished I could say "Shh."

"I can't believe it," she hooted. "Mousetraps for a six-year-old?"

Other children from my Sunday school class gawked. Wendy whispered something in Marilyn's ear.

"He must make that stuff up, right? Nobody buys mousetraps for little girls." Mrs. Harris giggled as she headed toward the coffee table.

I moved away. I was leaning against the rough stucco wall of the church, wondering about the meaning of *whoremongers* and *idolaters*, when I saw him: my father.

Oh no. I pushed myself off the wall and prayed for God's mercy as I watched him fast-step across the parking lot. I mumbled, "Got to go," as I passed Marilyn and ran to head him off.

"Daddy, what are you doing here?" He was dressed in his dirty, grass-stained yard clothes.

"What are *you* doing here? You didn't tell me you were leaving."

"I thought you knew." I shook off the image of the eternal lake of fire.

"Right," he said. "Let's go home."

"But I need to stay for church so I can go to the altar call."

"Altar call? What's that?"

"That's when the minister calls all the sinners up to the altar so they can be forgiven."

He laughed. "You don't need to do that, honey."

"I do. . . . Bad people are punished with God's wrath. . . . The wages of sin is death. . . . That was the lesson today."

"What sin?" He squinted in the sunlight. "Because of what you said to your sister about wishing that she'd been the one to disappear?"

I stared at my feet. "The polish," I said. I held up a foot.

"Jesus Christ. Who told you that?"

"Shhhhh. The people will hear."

I looked over my shoulder. Mr. Dillon was watching us from the covered area.

"Okay, we can go." I grabbed his hand and pulled him away from the church.

We stood on the curb waiting to cross Victoria Avenue as trucks thundered past. Wind whipped dirt and road trash around our feet. I took a step backward.

"You don't believe that 'hellfire and brimstone' stuff, do you?" Daddy asked.

I shrugged.

"This church has got things wrong, I think." He scratched his head. "My aunt told me about atonement for our sins."

"Atonement?"

"The need to do something to make things right. You don't need a church to do that."

"You mean like apologize?"

"That would be a start. Groveling at some altar won't help."

"But it's Betsey's fault. She took my doll's dress and ruined it, and then she hit me!"

"That's not right, either, sweetie, but she hit you after you said you hated her and you wished she'd disappeared instead of the nurse." He put his hand on my shoulder. "Blaming someone else doesn't help you learn from a mistake."

"The altar would be easier."

Daddy raised his brows.

I stared solemnly into his eyes. "I know what, I think I'm going to start a club." My face brightened. "*The Helpful Club.* We could help people. . . . They have children living at Mother's hospital, in the children's ward. That would be atonement, right?"

Daddy chuckled. "That would be . . . something."

There was a break in the traffic. He took my hand as we stepped off the curb.

"But Betsey can't be in the club," I said.

That night Daddy sat at his typewriter working on a story. The swelling on the finger he'd caught in the mousetrap was gone; most of the purple had turned to yellow.

"What's going on about Olga?" I watched his fingers punch the typewriter keys. "There wasn't anything in the paper today."

"I'm busy," he snapped as he continued to type.

"I've been wondering about her."

He blew out an exasperated puff of air. "The Santa Barbara police aren't saying much, and my usual source up there has been . . . uh . . . given a little time off."

I peered over his shoulder to try to see what he was writing.

"Goddammit. I'm trying to get my column finished."

I picked up some of the pages that he'd already typed and read a few lines about how he and my mother handled disagreements.

> *My wife starts reasonable but tends to end up unreasonable. I, on the other hand, start unreasonable and tend to move in the direction of sweet reason, perhaps because there is nowhere to go but up.*

"Can't you see that I'm working?" Daddy took the pages out of my hands and set them firmly back on his desk.

"But I've got something really important to ask you about, Daddy."

He rolled his eyes to the heavens as he continued to type.

> *But sooner or later, my temper gets out of hand despite all my resolutions to keep smiling. I'm afraid that my great failing as a conciliator is my regrettable tendency to become part of the problem.*

"I need your help, Daddy," I said as I perched on the arm of his ratty old nap couch. "Mother says the next time we go to Grandma's, we're going to leave Tweety with one of the patients that used to be in her therapy group at the hospital. She's afraid to leave Pinky Lee outside for so long because the Hallowells' Doberman might get loose again and hurt him. But if he stays inside with Tweety . . . well . . ." I shuddered.

Daddy looked up from his typing. "What? Leave the bird at the hospital?"

"No. She says that this lady, Beth*, is out of the hospital. She's on medicine so she's not crazy anymore. She's got job at the Coca-Cola plant, and she lives in a hotel downtown."

"Hmmm," Daddy said.

"Mother thinks it would be good for Beth to take care of a bird. Have some responsibility now that she's getting better. Thera . . . pootic."

"Uh-huh. Sounds okay." He looked at his notes, then back to the page in the typewriter. "Oh, shit. Your mother's not going to stand for that," he muttered as he rolled the paper back a line and banged the X key across the words. He turned to me. "Damn it. I'm trying to write here."

"But what about Tweety? He's nervous. He doesn't want to go stay in an old hotel with a crazy woman. It wouldn't be thera . . . pootic for him."

"*Former* crazy woman." Daddy put his fingers to his forehead and rubbed. "God, I think I'm getting one of my headaches."

"Why can't we just take Tweety with us to Grandma's?"

"Take that bird to your grandmother's house? That's not going to be thera . . . pootic for any of us. You know what she's like."

"A Republican?"

"Among other things."

"But Daddy, Tweety . . ."

He held up his hand. "Enough. I'm not getting in the middle of this. Talk to your mother."

"But she won't listen to reason. She's unreasonable." I pointed to the typed pages on his desk. "You say that all the time."

Daddy made a weird toothy smile, flexed his index finger, and examined the remaining yellow-purple bruise. "Listen to your mother. I'm sure the bird will be fine."

CHAPTER ELEVEN

PHONE TAP

Santa Barbara, California, November 26, 1958

M rs. Duncan opened the door a few inches with the chain still on. Her thin lips turned into a cat's smile.

"Afternoon." Hansen held out his badge. Thompson tipped his snappy fedora.

"Oh dear." Mrs. Duncan's face turned sorrowful. "Mrs. Short and I were just leaving."

"We need to hook this recorder up to your phone, remember?" Hansen indicated the small leather case and black box with cords wrapped around it that he carried under his arm.

Mrs. Duncan hesitated, then removed the chain.

Thompson took off his hat as he stepped across the threshold. Hansen followed.

"I don't think you've met my partner, Detective Charlie Thompson." Hansen tilted his head in Thompson's direction.

"Glad to meet you." Thompson extended his hand to Mrs. Duncan.

Mrs. Duncan clasped the detective's hand in both of hers. "I'm afraid this really isn't a good time. We were just going to the market."

Mrs. Short nodded vigorously. "She's cooking a big dinner for Thanksgiving tomorrow."

"Only take a minute," Hansen said.

Mrs. Duncan's mouth tightened. "You can come back when Frank's here. He understands about these things." She nodded toward the recorder in Thompson's hands.

"I know how anxious you must be to catch these criminals," Hansen said. "We can hook it up while you're out. Where's your telephone?"

Meanwhile, Thompson's gaze stopped at the elderly woman standing near Mrs. Duncan. "Mrs. Short, is it?"

Mrs. Duncan stepped in front of her friend. "I'm afraid I won't be able to work that thing. I'm not good with gadgets. They rattle me."

"That's right," Mrs. Short said. "She's no good with gadgets. Get on her nerves something terrible. And when she gets rattled, well . . ."

"Thank you, Emma," Mrs. Duncan said. "These men don't want to hear about my nerves." She turned toward the detectives, her mouth frozen in a brittle smile.

"We'll explain everything," Hansen said. "Simple as pie."

After a tense pause, Mrs. Duncan said, "The telephone's in the kitchen. I'll show you."

All four huddled around the wall-mounted phone next to a polished chrome-and-red Formica table pushed up against the wall. Mrs. Short pulled out one of the matching chairs and sat down. The others remained standing. Hansen set the equipment on the table and got to work hooking it up.

"That looks complicated. How am I supposed to operate that contraption?" Mrs. Duncan picked up the transformer box.

Thompson took the box out of her hands. "Let Detective Hansen do his job here. We can wait in the other room and come back when it's all installed, and he'll give you the instructions."

Mrs. Duncan turned to her friend. "Why don't you go to the store, Emma. I'll stay here with the detectives."

"But I—"

"Do you think you could stay for a few minutes, Mrs. Short?" Thompson asked. "I have a couple of questions about the incident at the Tropical Café."

Mrs. Duncan frowned and shook her head. "Emma doesn't know a thing. She sat clear across the room."

Mrs. Short nodded vigorously. "She's right. I know nothing."

"But you were there, right? In the café when the threats were made? That's what Mrs. Duncan said in her statement."

Mrs. Short worried her fingers. "Oh, well, yes . . . but I only know what Betty's said. What she told me."

"You'd be surprised how much people can remember once they get going," Thompson said as he guided Mrs. Short out of the kitchen. Mrs. Duncan followed.

The two women sat on the couch. The detective sat across from them in the chair. Thompson directed his questions to Mrs. Short. "Do you remember what the men at the Tropical Café looked like?"

"Not really. One tall, one short. Mexicans."

"What did they say?"

"I don't know. Those boys made me sit at a table in the back." She brightened. "Mrs. Esquivel brought me a cup of coffee."

"What about when you went with Mrs. Duncan to Woolworths to make the payment?"

"No, no, I never spoke with them."

"Anything you remember?"

"I was in Cosmetics."

"Isn't it obvious, Detective?" Mrs. Duncan cut in. "She doesn't know anything about the blackmailers. She just goes places with me."

The front door opened, and Frank Duncan stepped in. He stopped short. "Oh, you're already here." He looked from the detective to his mother. "I thought you were going to wait until I got home."

"He's talking to Emma."

Frank set his briefcase on the table by the front door. "You're Thompson, right? I remember you testifying against one of my clients. I thought I read in the paper you got suspended."

"Short vacation." He winked at Mrs. Short. "I came back early."

Mrs. Short giggled.

Detective Hansen stuck his head into the room. "Done, Mrs. Duncan. Come on in here, and I'll show you how to work it."

Mrs. Duncan and Frank sat at the table while Hansen explained. Thompson stood next to the table. Mrs. Short inched her way to a position right behind Mrs. Duncan's chair.

"This is the microphone that picks up the conversation." Hansen pointed at the little suction cup device he'd attached to the phone receiver. He ran his fingers along the cord that connected it to the recorder and opened the lid to show a spool of tape. He also pointed out the small transformer box. "This cord has to be plugged in at all times or nothing works. Got it? When a call comes in, all you have to do is hit this Record button."

Mrs. Duncan pushed her chair away from the table. "I don't know if I want all my conversations recorded. Sounds like McCarthyism to me."

"Mother, they're investigating a crime, not looking for communists."

"This isn't bugging your phone," Hansen said. "You don't have to record every conversation. Just push the Record button when you know the blackmailer is on the line."

"And call us afterward," Thompson said. "Don't go by yourself to meet them. Don't pay any more money. Understand?"

"I don't know if I can remember all those operating instructions."

"Look, Mrs. Duncan," Thompson said. "If we don't have your full cooperation, we're going to have to close this case. We can't conduct this investigation without your help."

"Mother, it's simple. When they call, just push the Record button." Frank turned to the detectives. "Thank you. I'll go over it again with her. I can take it from here."

He made a move to leave the kitchen, but Hansen stayed put.

"Before we go, we have some more mug shots to show your mother and Mrs. Short."

Frank nodded and reached to a shelf above the table to get a pair of tortoiseshell cat's-eye glasses. He handed them to his mother. Mrs. Duncan put the glasses on and blinked a couple of times while she chewed on her lip.

Mrs. Short moved closer to the table and used a crumpled handkerchief from the bodice of her dress to wipe her own glasses clean.

Hansen set a stack of small photos on the table and, one by one, spread them out in front of the two women.

"Look at each one carefully, Mother," Frank said.

Mrs. Short had her glasses back on. She leaned in close over Mrs. Duncan. "I'm looking carefully, too."

Mrs. Duncan swiveled her head around. "You already said that you don't remember what they looked like, Emma."

Mrs. Short pulled back. "Well, so did you."

"That's right, Detective, we just don't remember what they looked like. We were both so shook up that we were in shock."

Hansen said nothing, just used the side of one hand to sweep the pictures off table into his other hand.

"Why don't you leave the mug shots for a few days?" Frank said. "Maybe Mother will get her memory back."

"Fine," the detective said. "Call us if you think you can identify anyone. All these guys have records. It won't be hard to pull them in for a lineup."

"Oh, a lineup, Betty," Mrs. Short said. "Just like on TV."

Mrs. Duncan gave her friend a sideways, slit-eyed glance. "Do you want to get us killed? If we go to a lineup, they'll know we talked to the police."

"Just one more thing." Hansen pulled his notebook out of his pocket. "These men, the ones blackmailing you, did they ever say anything about Olga? Threats? Ransom?"

"Olga? Why would they mention Olga?" Mrs. Duncan said.

Frank shook his head. "Detective, it's a waste of time trying to connect the blackmail with Olga. I told you, I believe she's gone back to Canada. She's trying to make trouble for me."

The two detectives exchanged looks, then Hansen leveled his gaze first at Mrs. Duncan and then at Frank. "All the same, we're combining the two cases. Lieutenant Peck's decision. Thompson and I have been assigned full time to investigate your wife's disappearance and this extortion business." He closed his notebook. "So call if something comes up on either one."

"But this is about me and Frankie." Mrs. Duncan choked up. "Some men are threatening to kill us . . . and all you . . ."

"Mother." Frank put his hand on her shoulder. "It's going to be all right."

CHAPTER TWELVE

MINK, TURKEY, AND
J. EDGAR HOOVER

Ventura, California, November 27, 1958

Ten days after Olga vanished, our house was busy with Thanksgiving preparations. Mother and Betsey worked on dinner in the kitchen while my father tried to "neaten up" the living room. I sat out on the front porch in an aluminum armchair, alternately reading and acting as lookout.

"They're here!" I shouted. "Grandma and Grandpa."

Pinky Lee jumped out of my lap when we heard the crunch of walnuts under the tires of the big Chrysler Imperial rolling slowly up the driveway.

My father, in his new slacks and bow tie, stuck his head out the door. "Oh, God."

"Don't mention the election to my mother, Bob," Mother called out.

Daddy hummed "Happy Days Are Here Again" as he bounded down the steps. "Sure made good time . . ."

I wrapped my book in my sweater, pushed it under the chair, and followed Daddy down the steps. Grandma swung her short legs out of the big black car and kicked some walnut husks out of the way with the toe of her patent leather pump. She wore her mink stole even on this sunny

California autumn day. I waved at Grandpa, hugged my grandmother, and then stepped out of the way as she began to unload an assortment of boxes and packages from the back seat.

I fingered the chrome eagle hood ornament on the front of the car as she handed my father a pie tin covered in wax paper. "Now don't drop that, Robert."

Daddy smiled sweetly. "How about that governor's race, Mrs. Baker?" he said and let his hands drop a few inches before righting the tin.

Grandma let out a little "eek" and reached out to steady the pie before she realized he was just fooling with her. She snatched her hand away and smoothed the mink fur. "The election was a tragedy for this state, and I hold you responsible."

"*Meee?* I'm just one vote." He laughed. "That idiot William Knowland lost by a landslide. The Republicans were out of their minds to run him. How is that my fault?"

She wagged her finger. "The Commie press. That's what I'm talking about. You've been infiltrated. All the stories made him look bad."

Daddy took the paper grocery bag she held out to him and winked at me when Grandma picked up another box. "Now, Mrs. Baker, be reasonable. Knowland made himself look like a fool. Didn't need any help from me."

I stepped up and took a couple of small packages out of Grandma's hands and tried to think of something to make things better. "I thought Mr. Knowland looked good riding that elephant." I'd seen the front-page picture of the candidate riding an elephant, the Republican Party symbol, around an arena at a big campaign event.

Daddy laughed. "That buffoon looked like a circus clown."

Grandma turned her back on him. "Thank you, Debby," she said. "Do you know what the Democratic Party symbol is, dear?"

I shook my head.

Grandma smiled sweetly. "It's a donkey."

Grandpa, a short, stout man with thick silver-white hair, came around to the passenger side of the car.

"How's Lonesome and Ranger?" I asked.

He smiled and nodded.

"How's Lonesome?" I repeated in a much louder voice. "And Ranger?"

Grandma shouted, "Turn on your hearing aid, Arthur. Debby wants to know about the cat and dog." She huffed at him and turned to me. "They're fine. . . . Well, Ranger killed a chicken last week."

We managed to get all the bags and packages to the porch, where Mother and Betsey waited. My sister had on a clean dress, but her hair, dusted with flour, still wasn't combed.

Mother wiped her hands on a dishrag. "What's all this?" she asked, peering into one of the bags.

"Oh, Lois, I knew you'd need a few things for the dinner. I know how hard it is with you having to work at that institution." She gave Daddy a snide look. "No time to do justice to a real Thanksgiving meal."

Mother closed the bag. "I have everything under control, thank you."

"I got to bake a cake for today because I flushed the toilet every time for two whole weeks," Betsey crowed.

Grandma looked sideways at my sister. "Uh . . . uh . . ."

"She thinks the toilet is going to suck her into the septic tank every time she flushes," I scoffed, "so she—"

Daddy interrupted. "Mrs. Baker and I were just discussing the election, talking about what a beating the Republicans took."

"Eating?" my grandfather said. "Pelicans? Do we have time for a quick run to the beach for the girls to feed the birds?"

"He said Republicans, not pelicans!" Grandma shouted and waved the words away. "Arthur, turn up your hearing aid."

"Maybe he just wants to give his ears a rest." Betsey reached up and stroked the fur stole as we all walked up the steps. "How did they kill all those little minks to get their fur?"

Mother pulled her hand away. "That's enough."

"But, Mother, Daddy said that a lot of minks had to die so Grandma could get their skins."

Dinner was almost ready at a little after five, but by then Betsey was nowhere to be found. "She went up the street" was all the information I could provide. Daddy went outside yelling her name.

I slipped through the screen door to get the book I'd hidden under the chair on the porch and wandered back to my bedroom to wait.

"What's that you're reading?" Grandma was suddenly standing in the door of the bedroom.

I pushed the book under my pillow on the top bunk and slid down the ladder. "Is everything ready?" I said in a cheery voice.

She looked at me suspiciously and held out her hand. "Let's see the book."

I turned, climbed to the top bunk, pulled the book from under the pillow, and slid down the ladder again. I handed it to her, then stood, head bowed, and waited.

She exploded the second she saw the title: *Cell 2455, Death Row.* "What's the meaning of this?"

I tried to explain. "It's about a man on death row, Grandma, see?" I pointed to the red letters toward the bottom of the cover. *A Condemned Man's Own Story.*

Grandma turned the book to look at the spine. "Caryl Chessman? Where did you get this? Did your parents buy this for you?"

I shook my head. "It's Daddy's."

"And he's letting you read this garbage?"

"Not exactly," I said, scanning the room for a possible escape, but Grandma stood between me and the doorway. "It was in the bookcase." I frequently thumbed through my father's detective paperbacks and true crime books looking for anything interesting. I never asked permission, but it never seemed necessary since neither of my parents paid much attention to what I read. "You don't understand," I said. "I'm just trying to learn about bad people and crazy people . . . the mentally ill."

The front door banged open, and I heard Daddy yell, "I found her up at the Gottliebs, sitting down to join their Thanksgiving feast."

"The Gottliebs are having potato latkes," came Betsey's voice. "Why can't we ever have latkes?"

I used the distraction to duck under Grandma's arm and run to our small, cramped dining room. The redwood picnic table that Daddy had painted white was covered with a lace tablecloth and piled high with food. I slid onto the bench next to my grandfather.

Daddy stood over the turkey, holding his electric carving knife. He bent down to plug in the cord and blew through his lips, sounding like a backfiring motorcycle. "Who wants a drumstick?" He held the knife in the air, blade vibrating. Cackling his wicked villain laugh, "Heh, heh, heh," he bore down on the turkey.

Grandma sat next to Betsey. She set my book, cover down, between them on the bench. Mother brought plates filled with mashed potatoes, stuffing, green beans, and cranberry sauce from the kitchen and set them on a side table next to where my father was mutilating the bird. Tiny morsels of half-brown skin and meat sprayed the table.

"I don't know why you can't use a regular carving knife, Robert," Grandma said. "Look at it. It's just ripping the meat."

Mother held the plates as Daddy piled on the turkey.

Mother hurried back and forth to the kitchen two or three times before she finally brought the gravy in and sat down. Daddy mumbled a few words for Grandma's sake and said, "Amen."

After a few moments of quiet chewing, Grandma said, "Thankfully, the turkey's not too dry."

Mother brightened. "Why don't each of us say what we're thankful for this year?" She started and said that she was thankful for her lovely family.

Betsey went next. "I'm thankful for my mousetraps, and that I've been flushing the toilet so I could bake a cake this morning for our dessert."

Grandma stopped her fork midway to her mouth. "Mousetraps?"

Daddy looked at me pointedly. "Your turn, Debby."

I furrowed my brow and glanced at him sideways. "I'm thankful that Betsey didn't disappear like Olga."

"Very nice, dear," Mother said. "You're next, Bob."

"Who's Olga?" Grandma asked.

All eyes turned to my father. Mother shook her head ever so slightly and mouthed the word *no*.

Daddy cleared his throat. "I'm thankful . . ." He rocked back and forth in his chair a couple of times and began again. "I'm thankful for all of us, and especially for our children, that sanity has returned to this state and that three weeks ago the Democrats won the governorship and took control of the legislature for the first time in seventy-five years. We will have responsible liberalism in our state. Finally, progress, not retreat!"

Mother put her elbows on the table and rested her forehead on her hands. She looked like she was praying.

Grandma glared at Daddy. She picked up the book from the bench and held it up so everyone could see. "Is this what you call responsible?"

Daddy squinted at the book. His vision wasn't the best, even when he wore his glasses.

Mother looked up and put her hand to her throat. "What's that?"

"It's your daughter's reading material. 'Responsible liberalism,' I suppose your husband would call it."

"Nancy Drew?" Mother said in a faltering voice. But everyone could see that the picture of the convict on the dust cover wasn't a blonde-haired girl detective. The words *Cell 2455, Death Row* in big block letters seemed to pulsate off the cover.

"Debby?" I heard my father say in a bewildered tone.

"I found it in your bookcase. . . . I thought you said you wanted me to read the classics you've got in there."

"The classics aren't on the top shelf," he said through gritted teeth.

"But I want to learn about the mentally ill, like Mother's patients."

"That man's not mentally ill," Daddy said. "He's a—"

"You don't need to know anything about that bad business," Grandma said.

"I do. Mother's going to have one of her patients take care of Tweety next time we visit you."

Daddy threw down his fork. "Jesus, Debby, Caryl Chessman's a psychopath. He's not psychotic."

"What's the difference? You called him crazy."

Daddy rubbed his temples like he was getting one of his headaches.

Mother reached across the table and took the book from Grandma. She turned it cover-side down and put it on the floor.

"You never said *not* to read those books." My eyes welled. My voice quivered. I turned to my grandmother. "You know, people really do disappear sometimes, and I thought it might help with the investigation to find Olga."

"Investigation?" Grandma said.

Mother shaded her eyes with her hand. "Oh, God."

"You know, to learn about bad men like this Caryl Chessman who hurt women, and then try to figure out, you know, what might have happened to Olga. . . ." My voice trailed off. "So I don't vanish too." I burst into tears.

"Who's Olga?"

Mother patted my arm. "Some nurse up in Santa Barbara who disappeared. . . . Sort of a local mystery."

Betsey reached toward the breadbasket at the center of the table. "Debby likes murder," she said to Grandma. "She's going to be a detective when she grows up. Maybe a policewoman. Could someone pass the rolls?" No one moved. "Pleeeeease!"

Grandma turned toward Mother. "Your daughter likes murder? Am I to understand that my granddaughter is fascinated by killers?"

Daddy worked his temples again.

"No, wait a minute. Olga's not murdered," I said. "They're going to find her. . . ."

Betsey got up on her knees and grabbed her own roll. "I'm going to be a veterinarian when I grow up, Grandma. I don't like killing. I'm going to save all the little minks."

"Don't reach. It's not polite." Grandma swatted at her hand.

I used my sleeve to wipe away tears. "I don't like murders. I'm afraid of them. That's why I need to learn."

"That's enough, Debby." Daddy held out his hand to stop Grandma from speaking. "This Caryl Chessman is a very bad man. He's not mentally ill. He knew exactly what he was doing."

"And . . ." Mother put out an imploring hand toward Daddy.

He sighed deeply. "I shouldn't have left the book out where the children could find it." He folded his arms and looked at the ceiling.

Grandma smirked. "Thank you, Robert. I appreciate that you can admit when you've made a serious error of judgment, and I hope—"

Daddy picked up his knife and tapped it vigorously on his water glass. "Now let's finish this lovely meal."

"We have so much to be thankful for," Mother murmured.

Grandma held her water glass up toward my father. "We can be thankful that at least there's still a Republican in the White House. Thank God for General Eisenhower."

Daddy made a mean-smile face at her.

Mother removed the plates and set my sister's lopsided cake in the middle of the table while Grandma and Daddy carried on toasting with their water glasses.

Grandma took another drink of water.

"And let's not forget to give thanks," Daddy said, picking up his own glass again and grinning at Grandma, "for the fluoride in this water." He gestured toward the new water cooler in the kitchen. "No tooth decay for this family."

Grandma started choking. She struggled to keep the water in her mouth while she coughed. Water gurgled out of her nose.

"Help her!" my mother cried out. "Do something, Bob!"

Daddy was partway out of his chair when Betsey jumped up and walloped Grandma on the back. Water flew from Grandma's mouth and sprayed across my sister's cake.

As Grandma gulped for air, Betsey started wailing. She tried to wipe the water off the listing, soggy cake with her napkin but instead smeared the chocolate frosting across the lace tablecloth.

"Grandma!" she cried. "You shouldn't spit on the cake. It's not polite!"

CHAPTER THIRTEEN

I CAN TELL WHEN MOTHER'S LYING

Santa Barbara, California,
December 1, 1958

Five days after installing the recording device on Mrs. Duncan's phone, Thompson and Hansen were running out of leads on both the extortion case and the nurse's disappearance. Mrs. Duncan claimed that the blackmailers hadn't made any more calls.

The detectives drove up to the corner of State and Canon Perdido and stopped in front of the Howard-Canfield Building, a flat-roofed two-story stucco structure that could best be described as "plain." Its only recommendation was that it was downtown and close to the courthouse.

"Frank's office is on the second floor," Hansen said.

The men got out of their unmarked sedan and slammed the doors. A cool breeze smelling of ocean pervaded the bright December morning.

Thompson gazed up at a second-story window while he waited for Hansen to join him on the sidewalk. "The lieutenant still has Frank Duncan at the top of his list of suspects. What do you think?"

Hansen shrugged. "No evidence. And I'm not picking up anything that suggests he's covering up a murder."

"Maybe Olga told him she'd had enough of his mama's boy routine and wanted a divorce," Thompson said, "and Frank didn't want to cough up the alimony."

Hansen opened the door of the office building and held it for his partner. "But why would he drag us into this whole extortion investigation if he's involved in his wife's disappearance? Doesn't make sense."

"What kind of man walks out on his wife when she's seven months pregnant and still claims he loves her?" Thompson said. "Something's off there."

"Then there's his mother. Talk about a controlling woman." Hansen shuddered. "When O'Brian talked to Olga's nurse friends, they said that Mrs. Duncan had been harassing Olga, making threats, trying to get her to leave Frank."

Thompson grunted and started up the staircase.

Frank Duncan's wooden desk almost filled his small, cramped office. The desk was covered with papers jumbled together with a stack of big leather-bound books. Law books, according to the gold-embossed letters on the spines. A small window overlooked State Street.

Frank motioned to the two chairs in front of his desk. "Any news on my wife?"

Hansen shook his head. "We have a few more questions."

Thompson studied the framed diplomas hanging over Frank's desk, one from the University of California at Santa Barbara and the other from Hastings Law School in San Francisco.

"When did you last see Olga?" Hansen asked.

"Haven't we been over all this already?"

"We need to make sure we haven't missed anything."

"November 7th. My birthday," Frank said in a flat tone.

"That would be ten days before she disappeared?"

Frank rocked his chair back on two legs. "Sounds right."

"Any particular reason you didn't see her after that? Your wife is over seven months pregnant. You didn't feel the need to check on her for ten days?"

Frank frowned at one of the piles of papers. Hansen waited, but Frank just sat there shaking his head. Thompson and Hansen exchanged glances.

"Doesn't seem like your marriage is working out very well," Thompson said. "Kind of convenient that she disappeared."

Frank let the chair bang back to an upright position. "I love my wife. For God's sake, she's carrying my child."

"But you weren't living with her in the apartment," Hansen said.

Frank took a deep breath and blew it out. "No, not at that time."

"At what time *were* you living with your wife, Mr. Duncan?"

"Look, we have a little bit different living arrangement for the time being, okay? But it's all going to be fine when the baby arrives. I told Olga, 'You'll see. Mother will come around after the baby's born.'"

"You'll all be one big happy family. Is that the way you see it?" Thompson scoffed.

Frank's gaze wandered to the window beside his desk. "They just never hit it off, my mother and Olga. Mother didn't think Olga was good enough for me." He turned back to face the officers and gave them a sad smile. "Guess that happens with a lot of mothers and sons."

"Wouldn't know," Hansen said.

Thompson cleared his throat. "We got people telling us that your mother was harassing your wife. Calling her at work, threatening her. Showed up at her apartment unannounced."

Frank picked up his pen and fiddled with it. "Oh, she bothered Olga a little, I'll admit that. Mother can be very intense, very possessive about me. Hysterical, even, sometimes. But she never threatened to harm my wife. Never."

"Olga didn't tell you that she was afraid of your mother?"

"Absolutely not."

Hansen leaned forward. "It ever occur to you that your mother might have something to do with your wife's disappearance?"

"Never."

"We've been talking to Olga's friends at the hospital," Thompson said, "and I interviewed her landlady again yesterday. Mrs. Barnett had a little more to say this time. She claims your mother said 'nobody is going to take my son away from me' and that your mother made threats against Olga when she visited her apartment building in August."

Frank put up both hands. "Whoa, whoa, whoa. That landlady's crazy. I never heard mother threaten to harm Olga. Never."

"Where were you the night Olga disappeared?" Hansen said. "On November 17th?"

Frank threw his pen on the desk. "I already told you. Home watching TV."

"And your mother?"

"Same. We were watching Patti Page, I think, then the news. We went to bed about eleven o'clock."

"Our lieutenant thinks there's a connection between your wife's disappearance and this blackmail story," Hansen said. "You worried about that?"

Frank ran his fingers across the page of an open law book beside his desk and slammed it closed. He met the detective's eyes. "I'm worried about everything. The whole situation. Olga's gone and her purse is still at the apartment, but I think she took her suitcase . . . and now this extortion." Frank swept his arm over the jumble of paperwork and books in front of him. "I can't get any work done. I can't keep my mind on anything, and now I think I'm about to get fired. Boss doesn't like the newspaper publicity about it all."

"Have you talked to your mother about what might have happened to Olga?" Hansen said.

"Of course I have. Practically cross-examined her."

"What'd she say?"

"No. She said no, she didn't have anything to do with it, and she thinks Olga ran off to scare me and force me to move into the apartment with her when she comes back."

"Do you believe that?"

Frank didn't respond.

"Do you believe your mother, Mr. Duncan?" Thompson repeated.

Frank turned to face him and said, "I can tell when Mother's lying, and I'm sure she's not lying about this. Olga's just mad. That's all." He pulled his black-rimmed glasses off his face and squeezed the bridge of his nose. "And I can hardly blame her," he muttered.

He waited a few seconds and opened his desk drawer. "Almost forgot." He held out the stack of mug shots the detectives had left when they hooked up the phone recorder. "I think Mother recognizes a couple of these men." He took two pictures out of the pile and turned them around so the officers could see. "These guys."

Hansen reached for the pictures and squinted at the faces. "Once we pick them up, we're going to need your mother to come down to the station to see if she can identify them in a lineup."

"Shouldn't be too hard to find them," Thompson added." Everybody in that pile of mug shots hangs out over at the Tropical."

Hansen handed the mug shots to his partner.

Thompson glanced at the two photos and did a double take. "Well, well, what do you know?" He laughed harshly, like he didn't think it was funny, and slipped the pictures into his jacket pocket. "One of my Pep Boys."

Thompson pulled the pictures from his pocket the second he slammed the passenger-side door. "Well, I'll be damned."

Hansen started the car. "You recognized those guys?"

"This guy"—Thompson held up a small photograph for his partner—"is Luis Moya. He's one of the guys that I heard was going to burglarize the Pep Boys auto parts store. I set up that stakeout because I was sure about my information, even though that SOB Peck told me not to do it." Thompson laughed again. "Waste of resources, he said."

"And that's when you got—"

"Suspended." Thompson pointed to the picture again. "This shithead cost me a week's pay."

"Uh-huh," Hansen said. "Him and your big mouth."

Thompson rolled down his window a few inches, letting in warm air tinged with the scent of sage. The ocean breeze had died, and a hot wind blew in from the east.

CHAPTER FOURTEEN

THE BIRTHDAY BLAZE

Ventura, California, December 3, 1958

W here are my fire clothes?" my father shouted. "What the hell have you done with my FIRE CLOTHES?" I could hear him rooting around in the hall closet outside my bedroom door. "There's a fire, goddammit."

I didn't jump out of bed to run for safety. Needing his fire clothes, as Daddy referred to the pile of smoke-smelling, soot-covered rags on the garage floor, didn't mean the house was burning. It meant that there was a wildfire somewhere within the circulation boundaries of the *Ventura County Star-Free Press*, and he'd been assigned to cover the story.

I'd woken that morning to the sound of dry leaves skittering across the driveway outside my window, driven by the hot Santa Ana winds that swept into Ventura County that first week of December in 1958. It was my birthday.

I knew Daddy had found his clothes when I heard him humming a few minutes later. He liked covering fires, and the unseasonably hot weather combined with wind that tore through the mountains and squeezed through the canyons was fire weather.

"Um-mum um-mum um um-um . . ." When the east wind blew, Daddy switched into high-gear humming.

Sometimes it was hard to recognize the songs he hummed, although he had two favorites: "Rudolph the Red-Nosed Reindeer" and the church hymn "In the Garden." The hymn was probably left over from his days growing up in Montana with his devout aunt and uncle. But I guessed he was humming Rudolph that day, it being December.

Much to my embarrassment, Daddy frequently hummed in public. I'd asked him once why he did it, and he said that he hummed so he wouldn't talk to himself. "Other people get nervous when you're always mumbling under your breath," he told me.

I got out of bed and went to the kitchen. Pinky Lee was sitting on the floor staring up at Tweety's cage. I shooed him away.

"Happy birthday." Mother reached out and gave me a pat on the shoulder as I passed.

Daddy arrived in the kitchen dressed in his sooty clothes. He smelled like the incinerator and started humming "Happy Birthday" when he saw me.

"Stop humming," I said. "Don't do that, Daddy." So he started singing "Happy Birthday" instead, loud and off-key. I tried not to smile. "Wendy's father says you're an oddball."

"That Bible thumper?" Daddy said. "He's the oddball."

"Their whole family is saved," I said.

Daddy gave me a pitying look before he turned and noticed that Pinky Lee was back under the bird's cage. "Goddammit, Lois. Do something about that cat!"

Mother glanced at Pinky. "He's not doing anything."

"Look at him. He's thinking. . . . You can see the wheels turning in his savage little brain." Daddy kicked the air near Pinky. "Get out of here, dammit." He clapped his hands at the cat. I opened the back door, and Pinky ran out.

"Don't worry, Daddy. He won't try anything unless he's alone in the house, and remember, Mother has it all set for Beth to take care of him when we go to Grandma's next week."

"Hmmm, right. Beth, the ex-mental-patient bird babysitter."

I shifted my eyes to my mother. "You said that Beth is well enough, now, right? She's got a job and everything."

"Of course," Mother said. "At the Coca-Cola plant."

I watched Daddy as he measured instant coffee into a cup and added boiling water.

"I don't know how competent you have to be to stand in front of a conveyer belt watching Coke bottles glide by." He blew on his coffee. "It might drive somebody over the—"

"Bob," Mother said. "You're not helping."

"I mean . . . that job is probably very soothing, you might even say mind-numbing."

I nodded uncertainly at Daddy. "You know I'll turn eleven at two thirty this afternoon?"

"Eleven, is it?" he said.

"Uh-huh. How old are you, Daddy?"

"Thirty-nine," he mumbled into his coffee cup.

"Wow! That's old. No wonder you need glasses."

"He's forty." Mother laughed. "And a half."

Daddy fake smiled at her. "I'm young at heart."

"Practically a child," Mother agreed.

"I gotta go," Daddy said. "I'm late for the fire."

"Eat something," Mother said. "The fire's not going anywhere. In this weather it will only get bigger."

Daddy walked to the sink and gazed out the window. "No smoke on this side of the mountains," he said, "yet." The wind whistled down the driveway.

"Will the barefoot Jesus men be fighting the fire?" I asked.

Daddy was now rummaging through cereal boxes in the cupboard next to the sink. The box tops were all missing, mailed in along with dimes and quarters for various premium offers. Some of the boxes were missing, too, because the cereal came with instructions on how to use the containers to construct a log cabin or a make-believe TV set.

"Krishna Venta and his followers?" he asked as he threw aside two de-boxed wax paper bags. "Probably. The fire's near their compound in Box Canyon. Goddammit. I'm tired of playing cereal grab-bag. Who screwed up all these boxes?"

"It's Betsey," I said. She was still in bed. "I only look for the prizes."

He cocked his head at me.

"I might have used a few box tops to send away for another Junior Detective Kit. I need a new one."

Mother changed the subject. "Have you been telling her about that Krishna Venta criminal?"

"Daddy didn't tell me," I said. "I read about him in the newspaper."

"Same thing," she said. "Mr. Venta thinks he's the reincarnation of Christ."

"Actually, no," my father corrected her as he poured cereal into a bowl. "His business card says he's the 'Fundador.'"

"Fun?" Mother finished up the lunch preparations and turned to look at her husband. "Fun? Those poor deluded souls."

"He and his followers have their annual meeting at the bar at the Elks Lodge. I went last year and asked him about his arrest record up in San Francisco. He said that those arrests were in another life."

"What kind of messiah sips cocktails at the Elks bar?" Mother asked.

"He does good. Krishna and his followers clear firebreaks, dig trenches, those sorts of things. They don't get too close to the flames," Daddy said. "They're just trying to be helpful neighbors, I think."

"Like me, Daddy; I started the Helpful Club, you know. Did Mother tell you yet? My friends and I are going to have a lemonade stand to raise money to buy a doll for Cathy. She's a little girl that lives on the children's ward at Mother's hospital. It's so sad. She doesn't have her own doll."

Daddy patted my head. "Very nice, dear."

He finished his cereal and said goodbye.

"You'll be back for my party on Saturday?" I said hopefully. He was sometimes gone all night when he covered big fires.

"Of course. That's three days away."

Before I got to school, the black cloud above the coastal mountains to the south had doubled and tripled in size. Smoke billowed thousands of feet into the air then spread across the sky. Wailing sirens sounded from the highway as I walked with my friends to school. I stared at the smoke. *An eternal lake of fire. . . . I hope Daddy's okay.*

Miss Peterson tried to keep the hot air out of the classroom by shutting all the windows and pulling the heavy drapes we usually used to darken the room to watch *You Are There* films. By ten o'clock the heat was so oppressive that she opened everything up again. By noon, the thermometer on the science table read eighty-nine degrees.

Hot, dry wind swirled dead leaves through the open door and left a film of grit on our desktops. Our voices were shrill, our laughter too loud. We bounced on the edges of our chairs while Miss Peterson kept telling us to settle down. Eddie*, the big hulking boy who sat at the desk in front of me, picked his nose and ate the booger.

When it was my turn to tell the class about my current event, Miss Peterson stopped me before I even got out of my chair.

"This isn't about that missing nurse again, is it?" She eyed me suspiciously as she wiped sweat from her plump face.

"No," I said. "It's about the school fire in Chicago. Ninety-two dead children and three nuns." I held up my newspaper clipping so she could see the picture of the charred, smoking building.

Miss Peterson glanced at the clock and rubbed the back of her neck like she was trying to get a kink out. "Sorry, dear, it's almost time for lunch," she said. "Put your books away, class, and Angela, please pass out the milk tickets."

Angela held up her hand as she scurried across the room to get the tickets. "I have an important announcement."

"Make it fast," Miss Peterson said.

"Starting this week, my church, the Baptist church, is sending a special bus to take children to Sunday school. We do lots of fun things at my church, and our pastor says all of you are welcome. I have a list of all the stops and times." She waved a paper at us.

Wow, a special bus to Angela's church. Wonder if Baptists allow nail polish.

CHAPTER FIFTEEN

FINAL PAYMENT

Santa Barbara, California,
December 3, 1958

Detective Hansen spent his day off in his garage drinking beer and tinkering with the engine of his prized '32 Ford Roadster. He listened to fire department calls, on his shortwave radio, about the inferno roaring through the Malibu Hills. Beverly had called twice about going to a movie at the Arlington down on State Street. *The Sound of Music. God. Maybe if it was something with John Wayne.*

Hansen picked up his chamois and rubbed at an invisible smudge on the Roadster's gleaming red fender. Original paint. It had taken him two years to restore the engine, but he rarely drove the car. He bragged that it had never seen rain. Once in a while he might take it on a little spin along Cabrillo Boulevard when the weather got nice. Take the top down, maybe, but Hansen had a fear of leaving his flawlessly maintained classic in a parking lot or on the street. Too risky. Might get door dings.

The detective took another sip of beer and adjusted the dial on the shortwave radio, trying to get better reception on the fire calls. *Sounds bad.* He left the garage and stood at the top of the driveway of his hillside cottage to watch the smoke to the south. The hot wind was picking up. He lit a cigarette as he watched the sky over the distant ocean turn vibrant orange and luminous pink. Contrails of gray smoke from the fire floated north across a huge scarlet sun as it slipped below the horizon.

He ignored the ringing of the phone in the house. Probably Beverly again. *That woman is getting to be a nag.*

After a dinner of a Spam-and-Velveeta-cheese sandwich with cold green beans right out of the can, Hansen settled himself in his old La-Z-Boy with another beer to watch *The Real McCoys*. The phone rang again.

"Goddammit. I'm not going to some crap musical." He didn't move from the chair. The theme song was just starting. Someone on the TV rang a dinner bell and introduced the McCoy clan.

The phone stopped ringing for a few seconds and then started up again.

"Son of a . . ." Hansen pulled the lever on his La-Z-Boy and shot from reclined to upright with a jarring thud, spilling some of his beer in the process. "Shit!" He got to the kitchen in three long strides and grabbed the receiver off the wall.

"Yeah, Beverly, now what?"

"I'm worried about my son. He hasn't come home yet."

Hansen pulled the receiver from his ear, squinted at it, and put it to his head again. "Who is this?"

"It's Betty. Betty Duncan. Frankie isn't home yet, and I'm worried. Very worried."

"How'd you get this number?"

"What's that matter?" Mrs. Duncan said in a peevish tone. "It's an emergency."

Hansen glanced at the clock on the stove. "It's only seven. He's probably working overtime."

"I've called his office, and there isn't any answer. There's something wrong. He always calls me if he's going to be late."

"Let's give it a little more time." Hansen reached for a bottle of Jim Beam on the kitchen counter. "Call back if he isn't there in a couple of hours."

"He's not safe. It's those Mexicans. They probably found out we talked to you and—"

Hansen hung up and poured himself a shot.

Mrs. Duncan slammed her phone into the cradle on the kitchen wall and stared at the reels of the recorder. They had not moved.

"Frank's going to be here any minute," Mrs. Short said. "He'll see you got that thing unplugged."

Mrs. Duncan pushed the plug back into the wall.

"Maybe he's over at Olga's apartment again," Mrs. Short said, "waiting like he does. I can just picture him sitting there in the dark, hoping against hope that she'll walk through the door and—"

"That's ridiculous. Quit being so melodramatic, Emma." Mrs. Duncan pushed away from the counter. "He doesn't care about her!"

"Right." Mrs. Short tried to smile. "Anyhoo . . . Olga still might come back, right? No one knows for sure."

Mrs. Duncan looked away.

Both women turned toward the sound of the front door opening.

"Don't worry," Mrs. Short whispered. "I won't mention the envelope you had me take to the Blue Onion."

Moments later Frank Duncan appeared in the kitchen doorway, holding his briefcase in one hand, his suit jacket slung over his shoulder. His tie was loose. He walked to the stove and lifted the lid of a pot. It was empty. "No dinner?"

Mrs. Duncan twisted her hands together. "I've been worried sick, Frank. Where were you? I thought Mrs. Esquivel's boys had you for sure."

Frank plopped his briefcase on the table next to the recorder and threw his jacket over a chair. "I went to Olga's. It's quiet there. I go sit in the apartment to try to figure this out, and wait."

"Wait? Wait for what?"

"For my wife. Olga knows that I sometimes go over to the apartment after work."

Mrs. Duncan put her arms around him. "You know how terrified I am to be alone."

Frank gently pushed her away. "I'm fine, Mother, and so are you. We're letting the police handle this, remember?" He looked at the recorder.

Mrs. Short cleared her throat and started to get up. "I think I'll be going. Way past my—"

"No, stay, Emma," Mrs. Duncan said. "You can eat here. But I've been so upset I haven't even started the stew."

"Stay for dinner? Well, that would be nice."

Mrs. Duncan patted her friend on the shoulder. "Be a pet, dear. Just get this all started"—she motioned to the vegetables—"while I go out into the living room to talk to Frank. There's meat in the icebox."

Frank got an apple out of the fruit bowl and followed his mother through the doorway. Mrs. Short had opened the refrigerator door and stuck her head inside when she heard Frank shout, "What? When did they call?"

Mrs. Short removed her head from the refrigerator. She couldn't hear her friend's reply to Frank's question, but she knew the answer was, "Around three o'clock." She was there when the boys had called and told Betty to put two thousand dollars in an envelope and address it to "Dorothy." That was the code name the boys had made up. Mrs. Short had taken an envelope and dropped it off at the register at the Blue Onion, as instructed. But all her friend had had to give them was ten dollars from her grocery money.

"Why didn't you call me right away?" Frank shouted.

"I've been trying to get ahold of you . . ." The rest of Mrs. Duncan's words were too low for Mrs. Short to hear.

"Two thousand dollars?" Frank screamed. "This is ridiculous. Why didn't you call the police?"

"I did . . . sort of . . . I called Detective Hansen at home."

The voices came closer. Mrs. Short grabbed a package of meat and backed away from the refrigerator. She moved down the counter toward the colander of vegetables as Frank stormed into the kitchen.

"What about the recorder? Did you get them on tape?"

Mrs. Duncan followed on Frank's heels. "It doesn't work. I told you."

Frank's face grew red; his nostrils flared. He pressed the Play button, and the tape began to turn. "This isn't rocket science. Just press the button when the call comes in."

"It's that contraption hooked up on the phone. The suction cup keeps falling off."

The phone rang.

Mrs. Duncan reached for the receiver. Her son's arm cut in front of her.

"Wait, Frank, let me . . ."

Frank picked up the receiver on the second ring. He pushed the Record button at the same time.

"Oh, hello, Detective Hansen." Frank pushed Stop. "Yes, I'm home. I got here just a few minutes ago. Sorry about my mother bothering . . ." He watched his mother while he listened to the detective.

"Yeah, I know. . . . We've got a new development, though. The black-mailers called this afternoon." Frank paused and listened. "No, no recording. Sorry about that. Seems the recorder malfunctioned." He narrowed his eyes at his mother. "I'm not sure. I was just hearing about this when you called. . . . Right." Frank held out the phone to his mother. "Detective Hansen wants to talk to you."

Mrs. Duncan shook her head.

Frank stretched the coiled phone cord to its full length. "Talk."

She put the phone to her ear. "They want more money. Two thousand dollars this time. I told him we didn't have it." She paused and listened. "I tried. . . . It won't work. . . . I don't know." She stomped her foot. "I'm not a mind reader! He didn't say when he'll call back. Told me to get the money, or else. That's why I'm so terrified, why I was so afraid when Frankie was late." Another pause. "I was going to tell you. You just didn't want to listen." Her voice was rising. "My nerves can't take all this. You're just as bad as those Mexicans, trying to—"

Frank grabbed the phone out of his mother's hands. "It's me, Detective. I'll talk to her. She's working herself into hysterics here. You're not going to get any more information tonight." He watched his mother tug her hanky out of her pocket and turned his back on her. "Okay, good. When do you want us down there?" Pause. "I understand. We'll be there." He hung up. "They located one of the guys you identified in the mug shots. Hansen's setting up a lineup for tomorrow evening." He switched his eyes to Mrs. Short. "Both of you. They want you both down there at five o'clock to identify the blackmailer."

"Oh, Frank," his mother said, "I don't think I can do it. He'll know. They'll come after us. We aren't safe with—"

"And I got fired today," Frank said. "Too much bad publicity. Boss doesn't like what he's reading in the newspapers." Frank threw his apple core into the trashcan under the sink. "This blackmail business has to be resolved, Mother, and we have to find Olga. We can't live like this. Who's going to hire me in this town now?"

Mrs. Short looked away. "I think . . . I'm busy tomorrow."

CHAPTER SIXTEEN

IT'S NO PICNIC

Ventura, California, December 6, 1958

The Santa Ana winds of the previous week had died, and the Malibu fire was out. Daddy had stayed near the fire lines for two days, with winds gusting to seventy miles per hour. When he got home Friday morning, he wrote a story about the twenty thousand acres that had burned.

> *Silence, desolation hang above the fire-blackened hills and canyons.*
> *Forty homes burned to the ground. Two fire trucks lost in a flare-up.*
> *The firemen had to run for their lives.*

But by Saturday the weather had cooled to a pleasant sixty-eight degrees, just in time for my birthday picnic. By midmorning we were close to being ready to leave for Steckel Park. I wore my new pink-and-purple pedal pushers. "No, I will not get them dirty," I had told Mother a hundred times.

I'd invited five girls from the neighborhood, including Wendy, the girl who said that wearing toenail polish was sinful and that Daddy was a weirdo. Mother said I had to invite her because she lived on our street. But

Wendy couldn't come, thank the Lord, because she had to go to Bakersfield for a Bible study family retreat.

So instead I invited Angela, my best friend from my fifth grade class. But Angela presented a problem, being that she was such a devout Baptist. She'd visited our home once before, when my father was trying to unclog the kitchen sink, and left crying and reported to her mother that he had been taking the Lord's name in vain.

Her mother had called before the party to ask about it.

"He must have been having a bad day," my mother said.

"I read his columns in the newspaper," Angela's mother said. "Such a fine family man. I just knew Angela must have misunderstood."

"Yes," Mother said, "a misunderstanding." She probably had her fingers crossed. "I'll speak to him."

We all climbed into our new orange-and-white nine-passenger Plymouth station wagon. Daddy had gotten a really good deal on it because nobody else wanted an orange car.

I sat on the rear-facing bench seat with my friends Marilyn, Linda, and Judi. Angela had to sit in the middle seat facing forward because she got carsick. Most of the party supplies were in the middle seat with her and the other Alameda girls. Betsey sat between my parents in the front seat.

I don't remember if there were seat belts, but I'm sure that no one used them if there were. Daddy believed that your best chance of surviving a car crash was to be flung free of the vehicle. He thought the car was likely to explode upon impact.

We cruised north along the 101, the sun bright, no clouds. Facing backward, my friends and I made faces at the people in the cars behind us.

"Slow down, Bob, you're driving too fast." Mother grabbed the dashboard.

"Hold your horses, Lois, I'm just passing this blue bastard." Daddy liked to add the color of the bad driver's car when he cussed them out.

The four-lane highway, divided by a dirt median, ran through lima bean fields and orange groves. Forest Lawn Cemetery was on the left, the grass bright green against the farm fields. The cemetery was so close I could see flowers marking some of the graves.

There were lots of big double-trailer trucks on the road. Marilyn, Judi, Linda, and I kept raising our arms to the long-haul truckers we passed, motioning up and down as a signal to the driver to honk the truck's air horn. A couple of big rigs passed with no response. Then a gasoline tanker pulled up behind our car. Linda made the sign. Judi plugged her ears.

The truck got closer and came within a few feet of our back bumper. I watched the driver's face. He wore a demented grin. Marilyn signaled again.

"Oh, no," I said under my breath. The trucker blasted his horn. It was deafening.

The blare unnerved Daddy and sent Mother into what Daddy called "a conniption fit." She waved her arms around and pointed at the other lane. "Bob, Bob, pull over." She turned her head to check for cars on the right and shouted, "All clear! Get out of his way, Bob. He wants to pass."

I looked past the truck and fixed my gaze on the dots of color in the cemetery grass fading in the distance, trying not to think about all the dead people lying in the ground next to the highway. *How did they all die?* I wondered every time we drove by this graveyard. *Multicar pileups?* I crossed my fingers and prayed.

"What's that son of a bitch truck think he's doing?" Daddy yelled. He stepped on the gas, throwing the four of us in the back against the tailgate window.

"Bob, the girls . . . Angela's mother!"

The horn blasted again. The truck inched closer. I held my stomach.

"That jackass is trying to kill us!" Daddy screamed.

Finally, he pulled into the slow lane to let the big rig pass. "Bastard! Going like a bat out of hell." He raised his fist to the window. "Someone get his license plate. Jesus Christ! He's a menace on the road."

Angela began to cry.

"Not Jesus." I got up on my knees to pat her shoulder. "Not Jesus, Angela. He's not the menace."

The truck flew past, rattling our car in its wake.

Steckel Park was situated in a secluded spot along a small creek sheltered by oaks and sycamores. The parking lot was mostly deserted, even with the warm weather. When the car stopped, the doors flew open. I pushed the button to roll down the automatic window in the back. We didn't bother to unlatch the tailgate. Instead, the four of us climbed out the window. I was the last one out.

"Stop." Mother put out her hand to block my path. "I need you to carry some of these bags."

Angela stood next to the car waiting for me, her pretty face stained with tears. She wasn't used to all that carrying on. She wiped her eyes and looked at Mother. "Can I help?" Angela was always very helpful, not selfish like me. Probably because her family went to church every Sunday and lived a good Christian life.

"Thank you, dear," Mother said.

I stepped in front of Angela and grabbed a brown paper sack out of Mother's hands. It had a bag of marshmallows on top. I wanted to run to join the others. I could hear their voices. But I waited for Angela to get loaded down. She took two sacks of food and carried some towels over her shoulder. We walked slowly down the path.

I'm lucky to be Angela's friend. All the girls wanted to sit by her at school. And her family was very normal and . . . peaceful. It was heavenly to spend the afternoon at her house. So quiet that you felt like you should tiptoe across the room when you got up to go to the kitchen to get another cookie that Angela's mother had baked herself. The cookies were always warm. The chocolate chips melted on your fingers.

When Angela's father got home from work, he hardly said a word, just hugged and kissed them both and said, "How's my girls?" and told them, "I love you," before he disappeared into the back of the house.

Gosh. He said "I love you" right out loud.

They prayed before every meal and had a big picture of Jesus on the mantel in the living room watching over them. "We're blessed by God," her mother said.

Angela and I stopped at the restrooms on the way to the picnic tables because Angela had to go. I opened the bag of marshmallows and ate some while I waited. When she came out of the restroom, she gave me a sorrowful look and said, "Your father's going to hell."

The bag I was holding started to rip. "No!" I said, trying to catch the marshmallows before they hit the ground.

"I'm sorry," she said.

"I'm coming to Sunday school at your church tomorrow," I said.

Steckel Park was a magical place to me. The stream rushed and tumbled under the oaks as we walked along the path. The winter sun slipped through barren branches of sycamores, sparkling on the yellow leaves scattered along the bank and the golden rocks lying beneath the crystalline water in the stream.

Angela and I caught up with the others where the wide creek was only a couple of inches deep. The soft sound of the water flowing across rocks mixed with the chatter of squawking blue jays and squealing girls.

We followed the others across large stones to get to a small island in the middle of the creek, but the rocks were slippery, and we ended up wading most of the way. Our tennis shoes were soaked. We continued to where the water pooled upstream of a large boulder near the bank of the island. The water was smooth and calm except where bugs rippled the surface. Invisible frogs chirped.

Some of my friends carried plastic cups for scooping tadpoles out of the water and a coffee can with holes poked in the lid to take them home.

"I see one!" Marilyn shouted.

Marilyn always said the tadpoles would turn into frogs when we got home. It had never happened. The tadpoles all died. I didn't want to catch them. Too slimy.

I walked across the island to the other bank, my shoes squishing in the mud, and climbed to the top of a big granite boulder under some cottonwood trees. I found metates, small hollows in the rocks' flat surfaces created by Indians grinding acorns into flour thousands of years before. *The Mupu Indians*, I thought. We'd studied them in third grade.

I called out to my friends. "There's metates up here," I said. "Let's get acorns and make acorn mush."

It was easier to climb up the rock than down. I turned on my stomach and slid, ripping my new pink and purple pedal pushers and skinning my knee. Soon the others arrived, and everyone joined the Indian village game, but my knee was bleeding.

"I gotta go back," I told my friends while they gathered acorns.

Judi offered to walk back to the picnic table with me. "I want to look at the food, anyway." Judi didn't like to eat at other people's houses. Sometimes at birthday parties she ran home when food was served.

"Don't worry. Mother doesn't make anybody eat anything they don't want. She's used to it. She says our family is impossible to cook for."

"I need a Band-Aid," I said when I found my mother at the picnic table. Judi, convinced by my argument, had gone back to the grinding rocks.

Mother's shoulders slumped. "You ruined your new pedal pushers."

I glanced at the rip. "But you can sew it, right?"

She searched around for a roll of paper towels and ripped one off for me. "Go wash your knee at that faucet over there." She barely looked up as she rummaged through a bag. "I'm going back to the car, Bob. Can't find the mustard."

I took a few steps toward the water spigot but stopped next to where Daddy was working on the fire. He'd whittled points on some thin sticks and propped them against the table to use for roasting the hot dogs and marshmallows. I climbed up on the picnic table next to the firepit and sat down to inspect my knee. The bleeding had stopped. "Do you believe in God, Daddy?"

He kept whittling. "Not the one Reverend Ralston talks about. I don't think God, if there is one, causes or prevents tragedies."

"Then what good is He?"

"A creator of all this?" Daddy swept his arm toward the trees and the creek. "A higher spirit to give us strength when life gets hard?" He shrugged. "But I don't think there's a God that punishes or rewards people based on their behavior."

I shook my head emphatically. "That's not what they say in church. Only God can save you."

He picked up a piece of wood from his scavenged pile of oak branches and threw it on the smoldering coals. "The world isn't ever going to be perfect."

I watched the fire smoke. "Do you think there's a hell, an eternal lake of fire?"

Daddy stirred the wood. "I don't think so."

"Well, what happens to bad people when they die, then?"

"Like thieves and murderers?"

"Yes, like that man in that book, Caryl Chessman, the one on death row."

He splashed gasoline onto the smoking coals and jumped back when it flared. He put down the can. "Your grandmother was right, Debby. You shouldn't have looked at that book."

I crisscrossed my legs and leaned my elbows on my knees. "He says he's innocent. He wrote in the book that the police got it all wrong. And it seems true to me. He admits that he's been bad most of his life but says that he's not the Red Light Bandit. The police are lying."

"I think he's the liar." Daddy raised his voice. "He's like a lot of criminals I've come across covering the courts. They're never guilty, or it's never their fault. Some of these men live a life where other people aren't people, they're just things." He folded his arms. "Chessman's made a mockery out of the law by twisting the facts. And what's troubling is that there's a whole bunch of do-gooders out there lining up behind him because of that book. They believe his crap, and they're trying to stop his execution. He's been on death row for over ten years. . . . He . . ." Daddy looked away. "Caryl Chessman did terrible things, Debby, and I don't want you reading about it."

"I just wondered . . ." I lowered my gaze to rub at a spot of mud on my wet tennis shoe. "What's rape?"

"Oh my God." He slapped his forehead. "The man hurt women. That's all you need to know."

"But . . ."

Daddy picked up a piece of wood and threw it hard into the fire. "That bastard ought to be executed tomorrow."

I nodded solemnly. "The wages of sin is death, right? Reverend Ralston says God throws bad people into the lake of fire."

"That's not what I meant. Let's leave Reverend Ralston out of this."

"Mother doesn't believe in the death penalty. She says it's barbaric. She thinks some people can change if you give them a chance."

"Your mother has her beliefs and I have mine. She's big on rehabilitation." He shook his head sadly. "Don't get me wrong, the death penalty shouldn't be taken lightly or used often. But . . ." He pointed an oak twig at me. "But some people won't change."

"Reverend Ralston says the wrath of God awaits everyone who defies His word." I leaned my chin in my hands. "The wages of sin is death."

Daddy mumbled, "Jesus," and stirred the coals again. He looked up from the fire and searched my face. "What's all this? Are you worried about something?"

"Why do all these bad things happen? How does someone just disappear?" I gazed at the shadowed mountain towering in the distance. Blue jays squabbled and scolded overhead, hidden in the oak canopies. "What could have happened to Olga Duncan?"

He waved smoke away from his face. "Christ! I don't know. The police are going to figure this out." He glanced over his shoulder. Mother was coming back.

I unfolded my legs and swung them over the tabletop to the bench. "So after they put Mr. Chessman in the gas chamber, he'll go to hell?"

Daddy sighed. "Oh God."

"What about people who use bad language? Take the Lord's name in vain?"

His lips twitched into a crooked smile. "Are you afraid God will 'smite' me? That I'll be condemned to eternal damnation for a few"—he paused—"strong words?"

"No! No! I wasn't talking about you." My birthday cake sat on the table next to me, covered with wax paper. I stuck my finger under the paper, scooped up a little chocolate icing, and licked my finger. "Besides, you're never going to die, anyway, so who cares about the bad words?"

I jumped off the table and ran toward the creek. I heard him laugh.

CHAPTER SEVENTEEN

LUIS MOYA

Santa Barbara, California,
December 6, 1958

The same day as my party, Luis Moya arrived at the Blue Onion restaurant twenty minutes early for his lunch shift as a fry cook. He didn't own a car but sauntered up the sidewalk to the parking lot entrance whistling "Come Fly with Me," stopping outside the kitchen door for a cigarette. He had a little time to kill before he had to go in.

Moya was known as a hard worker at the restaurant. In six months, he'd gone from dishwasher to cook to night manager. But he'd quit the manager job a few weeks earlier and was only filling in as a fry cook today because his ex-boss was short-handed.

"Just temporary," he'd told a girlfriend. "'Til my ship comes in. Plus, Haywood's a good guy. Took a chance on me last year when I got out of Soledad and needed a job."

A lot of guys working in the kitchen at the Blue Onion were in the same boat. Frank Haywood was willing to give a guy a chance. That was how Moya's buddy Gus Baldonado had hired on as a dishwasher.

Moya pulled a comb from his back pocket with his free hand and ran it through his shiny black hair. He was twenty years old, with soulful dark eyes and a fast smile. The girls loved him.

Mr. Haywood banged open the kitchen screen door and held out a small white card. "Some detective was here looking for you today."

Moya didn't say anything, just took the card and stared at it.

"You still on parole?"

"I'm clean, boss, honest. I meant it when I told you I came to Santa Barbara to get a fresh start."

"Yeah, well, guy wants to talk to you. Seemed pretty insistent. I wouldn't be surprised if the cops come here looking for you tonight."

"Probably just a mix-up," Moya said.

"Maybe you better go down to the station. Get things straightened out. I'll cover for you for an hour."

Moya sat opposite Hansen, his hands folded on the oak interview table, marred with scratches and intersecting circular watermarks. Moya's eyes, wide and alert, scanned the small, high-ceilinged room. His gaze lingered on the closed door and the small rectangular window above it, suspended from a chain. It hung open a crack.

"What's this all about?" He furrowed his brow. "How can I help you, Detective?"

Hansen put a tablet on the table and pulled a ballpoint pen from his inside jacket pocket. "We got a complaint. A woman says you're trying to blackmail her."

"What?" Moya laughed. "Blackmail? That's crazy."

"She identified your mug shot."

He shook his head. "You got the wrong guy."

Hansen leafed through a folder with Moya's mug shot clipped to the front. "It says here you got out of prison eleven months ago and that you're still on parole."

"I'm clean. My parole agent says I'm the best guy he's got. You check with him."

"What were you in prison for?"

"You got the file."

Hansen raised his voice. "I'm askin' you, hot shot, what were you in prison for?"

Moya mumbled, "Selling marijuana, but it wasn't my—"

"Spare me." Hansen kept flipping the file pages. "Seems you been in trouble most of your life. In and out of juvie in Texas for drugs, burglaries, bunch of other petty crimes. You got quite a few bad habits for such a fine, upstanding fellow."

Moya slouched in his chair. "I been unlucky. Picked the wrong friends, got caught up in a bunch of shit I didn't do. . . ." He wiped his mouth with the back of his hand. "That's why I came here to Santa Barbara, to change my luck, rehabilitate myself."

The detective gave him a long look. "Rehabilitate? Big word for a guy from a border town in Texas."

"You think I'm a stupid spic? Check with my boss at the restaurant. He'll tell ya. I'm a quick learner." Moya reached across the table and tapped his finger on the folder. "And I don't do blackmail."

"That's not what this lady says. Says you threatened to kill her and her son if she didn't pay you . . . you and your buddies Gus Baldonado and Esperanza Esquivel."

Moya pushed his chair away and stood up. "No way. I'm not blackmailing nobody."

"Sit down!" Hansen barked. "Tell me about Mrs. Esquivel."

Moya dropped back into the chair. "Esperanza? That lying bitch."

"You hang out at her bar, the Tropical Café, right?"

"I help out around the bar. Do odd jobs sometimes. She needs the help. Her husband's in jail."

"I heard her husband had a lousy lawyer."

"Don't know anything about his lawyer. Just know Marciano Esquivel's in jail now."

"So you think Esperanza's a liar? Interesting. She says the blackmail never happened too. That this other lady is making it all up."

"Well, yeah. That's the truth, but that other lady is making a big mistake. She picked out the wrong picture." He scanned the blank walls of the little room. "White people think all Mexicans look the same. Just my luck. Mistaken identity."

Hansen closed Moya's file. "You even want to know who this lady is? The one who ID'd you?"

"All right, I give. Who is she?"

"Elizabeth Duncan. Her son's name is Frank."

Moya furrowed his brow. "Never heard of them."

Both men turned as Thompson walked in.

"Am I under arrest?" Moya asked. "Because if not, I gotta get back to work." He started to stand up again.

Thompson raised a hand. "Sit down and shut up. You're not going anywhere. You're on parole, remember? We'll tell you when you can leave."

Moya lowered himself back into his chair. Thompson took a seat at the table.

Hansen turned to his partner. "Moya here says he doesn't know anything about any blackmail. Says he never heard of Mrs. Duncan or her son."

"How about Frank's wife, Olga? You ever meet her?" Thompson leaned toward Moya, got into his space. "I think you kidnapped her."

"Wait a minute." Moya held up his hands. "I don't know anybody named Olga." He looked back and forth between the two detectives. "Kidnapping? Thought we were talking about blackmail."

"Why don't you just tell us what happened to Olga," Thompson said in a steady tone.

"How would I know? I never killed anybody in my life." Moya smiled weakly. "Everybody knows I'm a lover, not a killer."

The room stayed silent for a few seconds.

"Nobody said you were a killer," Hansen said softly.

Moya sucked on his upper lip.

"I'll tell you what I can do for you," Thompson said. "If you want to clear this up, we'll put you in a lineup. Let this lady see you."

"Anything. If she can see me, I'm sure she'll change her mind."

"I'll go get things started." Hansen headed for the door but turned before he got there. "How about your buddy Gus Baldonado. Seen him lately?"

"Wouldn't know about Gus. I'm not in the habit of consorting with felons."

"Consorting?" Thompson hooted. "Well, la-de-da. That how they talk in Texas?"

Moya gave him a sulky look. "I happen to have an excellent vocabulary."

"Well, good. Does it include *incarcerated*? Because you might want to start thinking about the meaning of that word."

Luis looked from one detective to the other with steady black eyes. He didn't blink. "Put me in the lineup. I'm not worried. No way anybody's going to identify me."

The lights on the other side of the one-way glass came on, illuminating gray-smudged walls and yellowing linoleum with black lines painted at intervals across the stained floor. Five men, each holding a large card printed with a black numeral, walked single file through the door. Luis Moya held number four.

Hansen stood with the Duncans in the little room behind the mirrored glass. He barked orders into an intercom. "Stand on the marks on the floor. Hold your numbers up."

Mrs. Duncan adjusted her cat's-eye glasses. "Four of them look like prisoners out of county jail. Look, they got jail shoes on."

Frank moved to her side. "Don't worry about their feet, Mother. Look at their faces."

Mrs. Duncan didn't respond.

"Mother? You know you recognize him. I recognize him from the mug shot."

"Mr. Duncan, please," Hansen said. "You need to let her do this on her own."

"No, I don't see anybody I recognize," Mrs. Duncan said. "The man who threatened us is not there."

Frank made a loud hissing noise. "The man in the mug shot, Mother. Just point him out."

The detective watched Mrs. Duncan and her son. This was far from a normal police lineup procedure, but he didn't say anything to stop Frank's prompting.

"I can't be sure," Mrs. Duncan said. "He looks so young."

Frank threw down his hands. "That's the man that you already identified in the mug shot." Frank spun away from his mother.

"His hair looks different," Mrs. Duncan fretted. "I don't know . . . something's wrong about his hair."

Hansen wound down a back hallway and met Thompson, who was coming from the other direction with Moya in tow. A uniformed officer a few steps behind collected numbers and directed the other men from the lineup through a doorway into the custody of a jail guard.

"She didn't recognize me, did she?" Moya said to Hansen and grinned. "Told ya, you got the wrong guy."

Hansen looked over Moya's shoulder and called to the officer. "Take this guy to a room and wait with him until one of us gets there."

After Moya left with the officer, Hansen turned to Thompson. "That woman's playing us."

"Didn't identify him, huh?"

"Nope. Says his hair's wrong." Hansen walked along the hallway with his partner. "There's never going to be a prosecution on this extortion case."

"Agreed," Thompson said.

"But if we think this is connected to Olga somehow," Hansen continued, "maybe we should let it play out."

Thompson nodded. "That's the priority. You let Peck know what's going on. I'll get the Duncans. Let's see where Ma and Frankie can take us with this."

When Hansen walked into the interview room where Frank and Mrs. Duncan were waiting with Thompson, Frank was in his mother's face.

"You know you recognized that man, number four. A blind man could see it's the same guy you picked out of the mug shots."

Mrs. Duncan sipped coffee. "I couldn't be sure. I don't want to point the finger at an innocent man."

"Innocent?" Frank slapped his hand on the table. "Okay, you want to be sure? Let's get number four in here and get a good look at him, face to face."

"Face to face?"

Frank turned and addressed Hansen. "Could you please bring number four in here? My mother wants to get a better look."

"You all right with that, ma'am?" Hansen said. "You want me to bring him in here?"

Mrs. Duncan crossed her ankles. Thompson held his breath.

"Listen, Mother, you either tell the truth or I'm leaving home tonight. You understand? I'll move out."

"I can't believe you're being so mean about this, Frankie. That boy looked as innocent as a little lamb in there. And you, acting like one of those lying crooked DAs you hate so much. I thought we were always on the side of the defense. You always say that we fight for the underdog. And here I am, the victim, but I feel like I'm being prosecuted."

Frank stared, stone-faced. "Will you see him or not? It's up to you."

"Fine," Mrs. Duncan said. "I'll take another look if it'll make you happy."

"It will make me extremely happy."

Hansen stepped out of the interview room and met with Lieutenant Peck in the hallway. "Frank wants us to bring Moya in there," he said in a low voice. "So his mother can get a better look."

"Highly irregular." Peck shrugged. "But . . ."

Hansen turned up the corners of his mouth. "I'll get Mr. Moya."

When the door to the interview room opened, Moya strutted into the room, Hansen right behind him. Moya held out his hand to Mrs. Duncan and said, "Just want to get this mistake cleared up."

Mrs. Duncan shook his hand. They didn't make eye contact.

Moya also extended his hand to Frank, but Frank refused it. "Let's just get this over with."

Moya turned back to Mrs. Duncan. "These policemen are accusing me of terrible things. They say I'm blackmailing you, and they think I had something to do with your daughter-in-law's disappearance." Moya gazed intently into her face. "I wouldn't do anything like that."

Mrs. Duncan looked him up and down and said, "No, this isn't the man that I thought it was. I know I picked him out of the mug shots, but the man doing the blackmailing is much taller."

Moya broke into a broad grin. "I'm glad you corrected your mistake, ma'am."

Frank's facial muscles twitched.

Thompson asked Mrs. Duncan if she was sure.

"I'm sure. It's not him."

Hansen led Moya out of the room and arranged for the duty officer at the front desk to keep an eye on him.

When the detective got back into the interview room, Frank was interrogating his mother while Thompson leaned against the wall and watched.

"I know you're lying, Mother. Either you tell these detectives what they need to know or I'm moving out of our apartment tonight."

Mrs. Duncan's mouth tightened. "But that other man is still on the loose. He could kill us."

"The police will protect you." Frank looked at Hansen for confirmation, but the detective didn't respond. Frank turned back to his mother. "We can't let this blackmail business go. You'll never be rid of them, and I'm telling you, Mother: tell the truth, or I'm leaving tonight."

"Frankie, please. I feel sorry for him. Even though he did that to me, he looked like an innocent little boy in that lineup."

"So you *did* recognize him?" Thompson pushed himself away from the wall. "He's the one who's been blackmailing you?"

Mrs. Duncan hesitated, then nodded.

"Thank you." Frank threw up his hands. "Finally."

"But I'm not signing a complaint."

Frank slammed both of his hands on the table. "For heaven's sake!"

Mrs. Duncan stared at her son. "God knows jail is a terrible place. I'm not for putting people in jail. I can't help it. I'm just not."

A look passed between the detectives. Hansen turned to Mrs. Duncan. "I told you the first time you came in about these extortion charges that if you didn't cooperate with us, we'd have to drop the case."

Mrs. Duncan picked up her purse.

"We said that you had to tell us the whole truth. Had to record telephone calls from the blackmailers and tell us if they called you again. You haven't cooperated on any of these things, not completely, and now you don't even want to sign a complaint." Hansen put his hands in his pockets. "I think we're done here. Case closed."

Frank turned away. Mrs. Duncan got out of the chair, head held high, and walked toward the door. She glanced back at Frank as if she expected him to follow.

"You've wasted everyone's time, Mother. Go to the car. I want to talk to the detectives."

Mrs. Duncan stepped out and quietly closed the door behind her. In the corridor, Moya sat on a bench, his head down, his arms resting on his knees. As Mrs. Duncan passed him, he spoke in a low voice. "I think everything's going to be okay now."

Mrs. Duncan hesitated for an instant and nodded almost imperceptibly before continuing through the police station, up the stairs, and out the double doors into the fading sunlight.

Nurse Olga Duncan disappeared from her Santa Barbara apartment November 17, 1958.

ABOVE: Luis Moya and Augustine Baldonado with Ventura County deputy sheriff Ray Higgins. Baldonado confessed to Higgins that he and Moya kidnapped and murdered Olga. BELOW: Baldonado led authorities to Olga's shallow grave on Casitas Pass Road in Ventura County.

ABOVE: Luis Moya with deputy Ray Higgins on December 26th, the day of the grand jury hearing. Moya had confessed to Higgins on Christmas night, backing up the details in Baldonado's confession. BELOW: Mrs. Duncan seemed to be in a cheerful mood while being questioned by reporters the day after her daughter-in-law's body was discovered. She claimed that she knew nothing about Olga's death.

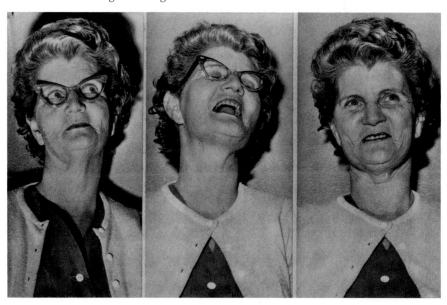

ABOVE: Elizabeth Duncan poses with her famed Los Angeles criminal defense attorney S. Ward Sullivan. Frank hired Sullivan to represent his mother as soon as Olga's body was discovered. BELOW: Moya, Baldonado, and Mrs. Duncan with deputy Higgins in the Ventura courtroom during their arraignment on charges of first degree murder.

ABOVE: Mrs. Duncan stands beside her attorney Ward Sullivan at her arraignment hearing. Ventura County District attorney Roy Gustafson sits at the table to her left. BELOW: Moya, Baldonado, and Elizabeth Duncan wait for an elevator on their way back to the jail. Mrs. Duncan covers her face while reporters snap photos.

RIGHT: Elizabeth Duncan kisses her son Frank goodbye after he visits her at the jail to discuss her upcoming trial. BELOW: Mrs. Duncan poses with attorney Sullivan and insists to reporters that she's innocent and the victim of lies.

ABOVE: Ventura County District attorney Roy Gustafson, the youngest district attorney ever elected in the county at age 32, had just begun his third term in office at the time of the trial. BELOW: Elizabeth and Frank Duncan pose for reporters before court begins.

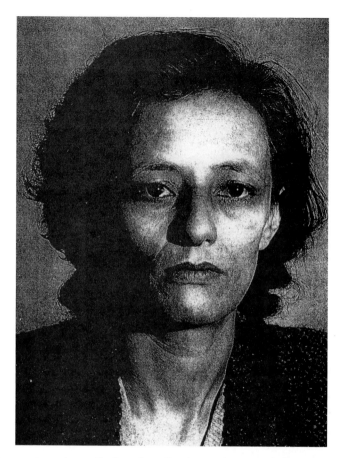

ABOVE: Prosecution witness Barbara Jean Reed, a carhop at the Blue Onion Drive-In restaurant in Santa Barbara, testified that Mrs. Duncan tried to hire her to kidnap and murder Olga. BELOW: Prosecution witness Luis Moya testified in excruciating detail about the brutal murder of Olga.

ABOVE: Eighty-four-year-old Emma Short was Elizabeth Duncan's constant companion and the chief prosecution witness against her friend. BELOW: During a court recess, Mrs. Short passes in front of the defense table. Mrs. Duncan screamed at her friend, calling her a bitch, a thief, and a liar. Reporter Bob Holt (in bow tie) is at the end of the line of men walking behind Mrs. Short.

ABOVE: Elizabeth Duncan testifies in her own defense. She claims that she is innocent and calls the prosecution witnesses liars. BELOW: Frank Duncan was his mother's only defense witness against the charge that she conspired to murder his wife and unborn child. At the end of the trial Frank testified, ". . . if I had a choice for a mother again, as much as I've been humiliated and hurt, I would still pick the same mother."

RIGHT: Elizabeth Duncan crosses her fingers for luck before the district attorney began his final arguments. BELOW: As his mother watches during final arguments, Frank closes his eyes while DA Gustafson relates the brutal details of his wife's murder.

ABOVE: Elizabeth Duncan is escorted to jail after the jury retired to deliberate her guilt or innocence on charges of arranging for the murder of her daughter-in-law. BELOW: After the penalty trail, Mrs. Duncan stares straight ahead at the jury (unseen) as the court clerk announces her sentence—death in the gas chamber.

Picture that appeared above my father's weekly column, Bob Holt Reporting. During his thirty-four-year career as a reporter for the *Ventura County Star Free-Press* he penned a weekly column on every subject imaginable. From the mundane to the lofty, he wrote about anything that interested him and everything interested him.

LEFT: My ten-year-old self at the time of Olga Duncan's disappearance. I couldn't stop wondering and worrying about what happened to Olga. BELOW: My sister, Betsey, and me all dressed up in dresses our grandmother made for us.

LEFT: Betsey, our father, and me. This photo is a "mug shot" taken by a deputy during an outing to the Ventura County Sheriff's office. BELOW: My mother Lois Holt holding me. She was the sane, calming voice in a hectic household.

ABOVE: The Elizabeth Duncan murder trial was the highlight of my father's career as a crime reporter, but he covered an eclectic array of stories, from crime to politics to local happenings. He always said that he loved the variety of people he got to meet and the subjects he got to write about while working for a small-town newspaper. BELOW: Interviewing a pilot at Oxnard Air Force Base.

CHAPTER EIGHTEEN

THE BIRD AND THE BOMB

Ventura, California, December 10, 1958

Mother had promised to come home early on Wednesday so we could take Tweety to her ex-patient's hotel room. She said it would be a good idea for Beth to practice taking care of Tweety for a few days before we left for Grandma's house.

When I got home from school that afternoon, Mrs. Alfred put down her cigarette and helped me take Tweety's cage from the hook over the washing machine in the kitchen.

I looked through the pages of the afternoon newspaper as I ate chips from a small bowl at the dining room table. Nothing about Olga's disappearance. It had been three weeks since she'd been reported missing, and there hadn't been any new stories for days.

"How can someone just vanish?" I said. "And why can't anyone find her?" Tweety chirped. "That's really scary."

When Mother got home, I carried Tweety's cage to the car, put it on the back seat along with a bag of birdseed, and climbed in next to it. Betsey followed and got into the front seat next to Mother.

"Why was Beth in the hospital, anyway?" Betsey asked. "Did she have her appendix out like me?"

"She was crazy," I said in a glum tone.

"Mentally ill," Mother corrected. "She has a psychiatric illness . . . delusions, paranoia . . . but she's much better now."

"Daddy says he hopes Tweety doesn't need a bird psychiatrist after all this is over," I said.

We drove down Victoria Avenue, waited for the stoplight to change to green, and turned right on Highway 101, heading north toward town. Mother drove along at a comfortable pace through the lima bean fields and orange groves, past the cemetery and the drive-in movie theater, until we reached the intersection of Five Points at the edge of town. I pointed at Merle's Drive-In as we waited at the stoplight. A huge tower sign rose from the roof with MERLE's spelled out on three sides. Four or five cars angled along the building with trays hanging from the driver's-side windows.

"Hey, I've got a good idea," I said. "Let's go to Merle's for dinner on the way home. Daddy could meet us there."

"I don't think so," Mother said. "That Krishna Venta's YKFL headquarters blew up last night. A bomb, your father said. He got a call in the middle of the night."

"The barefoot firefighting Jesus man? What happened to him?"

Mother sucked air between her teeth. "I really have no idea . . . big explosion . . . dynamite, I think Daddy said. But I'm pretty sure your father won't be home in time for dinner. He called me at work and said he could be out half the night."

We found a parking place in front of Mother's ex-patient's hotel on a side street off Main. I peered out the window at the old three-story clapboard building with peeling, dirty white paint, a gabled roof, dark turrets, and tall, narrow windows.

"This place looks haunted," Betsey said. "Let's go home."

One of the curtains on the second story moved. I caught a glimpse of a black-gloved hand pulling the curtain closed, and I put my arm protectively over Tweety's cage. "I don't think Tweety's going to like this place."

Mother opened my door. "Let's get this over with."

I didn't move.

"Come on, dear," Mother said encouragingly. "We want to hurry so we can get to Merle's before it gets too crowded. I can almost taste those onion rings."

I got out of the car. "I guess this will be better for him than staying in the house alone with Pinky Lee pacing under his cage, licking his chops."

Mother picked up the cage. I carried the bag of birdseed. We walked up the steps to the sagging porch. Mother opened the large, weatherworn, ornately carved door.

"Go on in," she said. "Beth will be waiting for us."

I followed Betsey into the hotel lobby. The room was small and dark and too warm. A faded brocade-upholstered sofa took up all the space on the far wall. A torn, yellowing shade covered the only window.

"Pee-ew," Betsey said. "This place stinks to high heaven."

"Shh," Mother said. "It's just an old building . . . a little musty."

Betsey held her breath, and her cheeks puffed out, her eyes wide. I put my hands on either side of her face and popped the air out of her cheeks.

"She hit me!" Betsey wailed.

"I didn't. I just touched your cheeks. I was helping you breathe. Daddy says you'll pass out if you keep holding your breath all the time."

"Both of you," Mother hissed. "Stop it. Beth should be down here any minute." She looked at her watch. "I told her to meet us in the lobby."

We "stopped it" at the sound of creaking footsteps coming from the narrow wooden staircase that led from the shadowy dimness of the upper floors. I held on to Mother's arm as the shuffling sound approached. Betsey took another breath and held it. She ducked behind Mother.

A thin, middle-aged woman with dull brown hair, wearing a shapeless gray dress, descended into the lobby. She wore black evening gloves that came all the way up to her elbows. "Hello, Mrs. Holt." She held out one of her gloved hands to Mother, who had to set the birdcage on the floor to shake it.

"This is Beth, girls. She's kind enough to take care of Tweety even though she's also working very hard over at the Coca-Cola plant." Mother beamed.

I squinted at the woman's expressionless face. White skin, pale lips, dark circles under her eyes.

"We can't thank you enough for helping us," Mother continued. "Right, girls?"

Betsey stared at the woman from behind Mother's skirt. She had her fingers in her mouth. Mother nudged the backs of my legs with her knee.

"Uh," I said. "Did you ever have a bird yourself?"

"No," Beth said in a toneless voice.

"Beth is very meticulous about following directions," Mother said. "She's one of the most conscientious clients I've ever worked with." She gave Beth another big smile.

"What's that smell?" Betsey said as she poked her head out from behind Mother.

Mother pushed Betsey back with one hand as she held out the cage to Beth with the other. Betsey took in another noisy breath and held it.

Beth hesitated before taking the cage with her black-gloved hand. She held her arm rigid, keeping Tweety as far away as possible.

"There's nothing much to do except fill the water bottle and add new birdseed to the feeder every day," Mother said in an enthusiastic tone. "Give Beth the birdseed, dear. We don't want to keep her."

I looked pleadingly into Mother's narrowed eyes. She shook her head.

I reluctantly held out the paper bag, but quickly pulled it back again. "And Tweety likes to talk. Don't forget to talk to him every day."

Beth frowned. "The bird talks?"

"No, he chirps when *you* talk," I said. "Just tell him he's a pretty boy . . . and cats are stupid . . . stuff like that."

Beth looked to Mother. "This bird won't say things to me, will he?"

"No, no, he can't say a word. He's only a parakeet, not a parrot. No talking," Mother emphasized. "Debby just pretends sometimes. . . ." She gave me a stern look.

"No talking, no voices." Beth took a step backward. "Just pretends sometimes," she repeated in her monotone voice.

Mother frowned and bit her lip. I held out the bag of birdseed again. Beth took it with the fingertips of her gloved hand.

I pressed my face to Tweety's cage. "Now, don't worry, we'll be back to get you on Sunday."

Mother placed her hands on my shoulders. "We need to get going."

I folded my fingers up and down to wave. "Goodbye, Tweety. I'll miss you."

Tweety croaked a little chirp.

"You girls go and wait for me in the car. I need to talk to Beth for a moment."

"It smells like a dead mouse in here. . . . That's what it is." Betsey wrinkled her nose. "Like when—"

Mother shooed us toward the door. "No, no, no . . . just a little musty."

We waited in the car for about five minutes, Betsey kicking the back of my seat every couple of seconds.

"You're probably going to end up at Camarillo yourself," I said. "I wouldn't be surprised."

When Mother got back, she slid into the front seat and put the key into the ignition. "Now, wasn't that nice, girls? This is going to work out fine for all concerned."

"What's wrong with that lady, anyway?" Betsey asked.

Mother winced. "I think there might be a little problem with her medication. She might be taking too much of her Thorazine. I'm going to talk to her doctor tomorrow."

"But how come she's wearing those black evening gloves?" I asked.

Mother turned to me. "Hygiene. Beth worries about germs."

My face fell. "You said she wasn't crazy anymore. That's why they let her out of the hospital."

"Mentally ill, dear. And she's doing much better."

CHAPTER NINETEEN

THE INVESTIGATION CONTINUES

Santa Barbara, California,
December 12, 1958

Two days later, Hansen was standing by the door between the detective bay and the front desk, angrily cramming folders into a metal filing cabinet and ruminating over the call he'd just received from Canada. Olga's father, the poor man, had wanted an update on the investigation. It was hard to understand him through the static on the line.

"She wouldn't go off without telling us," he said and then broke down. "My wife's in the hospital, sick with worry." His voice cut in and out during the long-distance call. "Have you? . . . mother-in-law? . . . She's been . . . Olga's afraid of . . ."

"I know, Mr. Kupczyk. We're looking into everyone and everything."

"Thank you. Thank you for helping us."

Hansen ended the conversation and looked up front when he heard his name called.

"Someone out here wants to see you." The duty-desk sergeant gestured toward a young woman in a white nurse's uniform sitting by the front door, fiddling with a business card. "Gina . . . something."

The detective took a few steps in her direction. "Detective Hansen," he said.

"I'm Gina Gallo*, Olga Duncan's friend. I was with a patient when Detective Thompson came by yesterday to ask more questions of everybody." She held up the card. "He left this at the hospital."

"Thompson's my partner. He's out right now, but we're working together on the investigation," Hansen said as he escorted the nurse back to his desk. He pulled a chair over for her. "Can I get you a cup of coffee?"

Miss Gallo shook her head, causing her shiny brunette ponytail to sway. "No thanks. I don't drink coffee."

Hansen moved his chipped mug aside. "Well, I probably drink too much . . . coffee." He smiled at her pretty face, then looked down and fumbled together some message slips that were scattered across his desk. When he tried to put the messages on the spiked paperweight, he knocked it off the desktop. "Son of a biscuit eater," he muttered. His face turned red as he leaned over to pick things up off the floor. "Excuse my English."

Gina bit her lip to hide a smile.

"So, you're one of Olga's friends?" he said as he struggled to get the little papers onto the spike.

Gina placed her delicate hands on the desk. "I decided to come down here and try to talk face-to-face so I can find out what's going on. I just hope you're not too busy to . . ."

"No, no, not too busy. Of course not," Hansen stammered as he reached for a folder in the metal basket at the corner of his desk. "I read through these initial statements of the nurses who reported Olga missing. Someone did a follow-up interview with everyone at the hospital the next day, right?"

"Not really an interview. An officer came by to see if Olga had showed up yet. It seemed like he'd already decided she took off on her own."

"That's all changed now. Our lieutenant's made this case the number one priority in our department." Hansen pulled a page out of the folder. "You don't think Olga's run off?"

"No." Gina's ponytail snapped back and forth. "She was being threatened and harassed almost daily by her mother-in-law. It started before she married Frank, and it never let up. When Olga changed her home phone number, the woman started calling the hospital."

"You witnessed this harassment firsthand?" Hansen pulled out a tablet to take notes.

"No. I never met the woman, but she called the hospital all the time, and Olga told me about the threats. Poor Olga was so upset that she broke down crying during surgery a few times. She would have to leave the operating room."

Hansen wrinkled his brow. "Frank know about this?"

"Yes, but he's an idiot when it comes to his mother. The last time I saw Olga, she told me she'd finally realized that Frank was still a little boy. 'He's never grown up,' she said. 'He still does whatever his mother tells him to do.'" Gina leaned in closer to Hansen. "You know, from the first, when Olga didn't show up for work that morning, I knew something was terribly wrong. She told me once that she went into nursing to help humanity. Olga was the most conscientious nurse I've ever known. She never missed a shift. After they found the sliding glass door of her apartment wide open, and her purse . . . well, I just knew Olga was dead." Gina's eyes welled. "How can something like this happen?"

I ask myself that question every day, honey. Hansen held her gaze for a moment. "You don't think she just got fed up and decided to leave her husband?"

"Olga loved Frank. She told me many times, 'Frank has so much feeling for his mother, I just know he'll have the same for our child.' She hoped that after the baby came, things would be better. I think she believed that Frank loved her, too . . . as much as he could."

Hansen scratched his scalp with his pencil. "And you're sure she'd talked to Frank about the harassment, the threats from his mother?"

"She told him about it over and over, but he's such a mama's boy."

Hansen scribbled a few notes. "Anything else you want to tell me?"

"Isn't that enough? Can't you just arrest Frank's mother and make her tell you what she did to Olga?"

Hansen smiled a little. "It ain't that easy. We need evidence."

The young nurse nodded uncertainly and sighed. "Well, is it okay if I check in with you once in a while to see if you have any news?"

"Sure, why don't you leave me your phone number in case I have any more questions?" Hansen ripped a piece of paper from his pad, and his hand knocked over the spiked paperweight again. He had to grab his coffee cup to keep it from tipping over.

Her face brightened. "Sure, call me. I want to help all I can."

Hansen smiled a crooked smile as he handed her the paper and a pencil.

An hour after Olga's friend left, Thompson got back. "More dead ends. The body that washed up in Carpinteria was a man, not a woman. I also talked to the switchboard operator at the hospital. Got more accusations about Mrs. Duncan making threats, but no real evidence." He took off his jacket and threw it across his desk. "Anything new here?"

"Busy, very busy." Hansen summarized his interview with Gina, without mentioning that he had her phone number in his shirt pocket. "She says Frank loves Olga."

"He's got a funny way of showing it." Thompson dropped into his chair. "Goddammit, Olga disappeared three weeks ago, and all we've got is his mother's alleged threats and her bullshit story about being blackmailed."

They sat in silence for a moment, then Hansen said, "Why don't we pay Mrs. Short a surprise visit? But this time we'll make sure she's on her own."

"Good idea." Thompson stood up. "And I'd like to be the one to take a crack at her."

As Thompson knocked softly on the door of number twelve, he glanced uneasily at the apartment just above, where Hansen had gone to talk to Mrs. Duncan and keep her busy. Thompson waited a few seconds, then knocked again, a little harder. No response. He put his mouth right next to the door and called out softly, "Mrs. Short?"

The door opened a few inches. The chain was on; Thompson couldn't see much inside the dark apartment. But he heard the old woman's timid voice clearly enough: "Yes?"

"Detective Thompson, Santa Barbara Police." He flashed his badge in the gap of the doorway. "Remember me? We talked earlier in the week when my partner and I installed the recording device on your friend's phone."

"What do you want? I'm not feeling very well." The old woman finally appeared in the doorway, wearing a ratty cardigan over a cotton housedress. She pulled the sweater close around her throat.

"I just need to ask you a few more questions about Olga Duncan."

"I don't know anything. I never met her. Sorry."

She tried to close the door, but Thompson held it open with one hand. He put his face close to the opening and peered down at the old woman. "This won't take long."

After a few seconds, she unlatched the chain and stepped back. Thompson walked into a musty-smelling room. The windows were closed and the shades drawn even though it was nearly eighty degrees outside, another unseasonably warm Santa Barbara winter day.

Mrs. Short stuck her head outside and looked around before closing the door and locking the deadbolt.

Thompson took off his hat. "Do you mind if I sit down?" He nodded toward a sagging upholstered chair.

Mrs. Short made a sweeping motion with her arm and took a seat on the sofa. "Betty warned me not to talk to you. She said you're just going to try to trick me." Her hands trembled as she fiddled with a string of glass beads around her turkey neck. "And Betty does things to people who cross her."

Thompson made himself remain very still. "What doesn't Betty want you to talk about? Olga?"

"Yes . . . Olga . . . the annulment . . . the Mexicans . . . everything."

Sweat trickled down the detective's spine. *Annulment? Mexicans?*

Mrs. Short hugged a small blue pillow. "If I talk to you, she'll find out what I said. Betty always knows what people are doing against her."

Thompson leaned forward. "Mrs. Short, you don't have to worry about Betty. She doesn't know I'm here, and my partner's upstairs with her right now, keeping her busy checking the phone recorder. Now, tell me about this annulment."

Mrs. Short covered her mouth and stifled a little bleat. A tear rolled down her cheek.

"A young woman is missing," Thompson said firmly, "and you may have been a witness to a crime. That's serious business, Mrs. Short. We have to check out everything, and you have to tell us the truth. What's this about an annulment?"

"I only went with them to Ventura to see the lawyer and go to the courtroom," she whimpered. "I didn't *do* anything."

"You're saying Frank got his marriage annulled in Ventura?"

"Not Frank. Betty. She did it. Frank didn't even know."

Thompson wrinkled his forehead. "Mrs. Duncan got her son's marriage annulled without his knowledge? How is that possible?"

"She hired a man."

The detective pulled a small notebook and pencil out of his breast pocket. "A lawyer?"

"No, a man from the Salvation Army . . . to do odd jobs. She called the Salvation Army to get someone. . . ." Mrs. Short fluttered her fingers. "Betty isn't allowed to go down there anymore. You know, problems, but she can still call. The odd-job man was supposed to wash the windows. That's what she told them on the phone."

Thompson stopped writing. "She called the Salvation Army to hire a man to wash her windows? I don't think I follow. How did this man annul Frank's marriage?"

"He pretended to be Frank. Betty pretended to be Olga, and we all went to a judge in Ventura last summer." She folded her hands in her lap. "But I didn't do anything. I just went along for the ride."

Thompson worked to process what he was hearing. "Mrs. Duncan paid this odd-job guy to impersonate Frank?"

"She promised him a hundred dollars, but when we got back from Ventura, she told him she didn't have the money. . . ." Mrs. Short's voice trailed off.

Thompson leaned back. "What about these Mexican men you just mentioned? How do they fit into this? Are they the same guys Mrs. Duncan's accusing of blackmail?"

"I really can't say." Mrs. Short dabbed at her eyes again. "I'm an old woman. I mind my own business, and I've never hurt anybody. Can't you just leave me alone now?"

Instead of leaving, the detective moved to the sofa next to Mrs. Short. "I can see that you're afraid."

The old woman sniveled. She nodded vigorously.

"I think we should finish this conversation down at the police station. Your choice, but make it fast. My partner's going to be finished talking to your friend in a little while."

Mrs. Short stood up. "All right, but I'll have to think of something to tell Betty when I come back . . . about where I've been."

"We can protect you. You tell us what happened to Olga, and you won't have to worry about Elizabeth Duncan. If you help us, we'll help you."

Mrs. Short darted around the coffee table and sprang for the front door with the agility of a woman half her age. She unbolted the lock and said, "Good, because the Mexicans are after us. She didn't pay them either."

Thompson escorted Mrs. Short through the side entrance of the Santa Barbara Police Department while Hansen parked the car.

"This won't take too long, will it?" Mrs. Short said when they reached the bottom of the stairs. She adjusted her glasses and looked around, blinking in the bright florescent lighting. "My programs start in an hour."

Thompson escorted Mrs. Short into an empty interview room. "Would you like something to drink? Coffee, water?"

"Glass of water, if you don't mind." She folded her wrinkled hands on the table. "Ice would be nice."

"I'll be right back."

Hansen and Lieutenant Peck were waiting outside the room. "Whatta we got?" the lieutenant barked the instant Thompson closed the door. "This old biddy know anything?"

Hansen answered for his partner. "We think she knows a lot. She's Mrs. Duncan's sidekick, so to speak. They're together practically twenty-four hours a day."

"But does she know where Olga is?"

"She's not saying, but she knows plenty," Thompson said. "Get this: she just told me Betty got her son's marriage annulled."

The lieutenant laughed. "*She* got his marriage annulled?"

"She says Mrs. Duncan hired some guy to play Frank and impersonated Olga herself at an annulment hearing in Ventura. Mrs. Short was there when it happened."

The lieutenant raised his eyebrows. He barked out another laugh. "That's crazy."

"She also mentioned something about Mrs. Duncan owing money to some guys."

"Might be the blackmailers, Moya and Baldonado," Hansen said.

"You sure she's dealing with a full deck?" the lieutenant said.

Thompson shrugged. "She's afraid of the Duncan woman. I only got her talking by saying that we'd protect her. I think she's ready to get it all off her chest. This could be the break we need. What can I give her?"

The lieutenant rocked back on his heels. "Promise her anything you want. Just get her to tell us what happened to Olga Duncan."

Thompson sat opposite Mrs. Short. "You need to tell me everything you know about what Elizabeth Duncan said or did regarding her daughter-in-law," he said in his kindest voice. "If you're truthful and you help us find this young woman, I'm going to help you."

Mrs. Short sat hunch-shouldered at the table. "I can't go back to my apartment after this. You don't know Betty."

"We'll put you up in a hotel. You'll have a guard." *Didn't the lieutenant say to promise her whatever it took?*

She perked up. "Hotel? How about the Miramar? You know the one with the blue roofs?"

"Hold your horses," Thompson said. "You need to tell us what you know before we start making reservations. Let's start with the annulment." He looked down at his notes. "You say she hired a man from the Salvation Army to impersonate Frank."

"Un-huh, Ralph." Mrs. Short smiled. "I have a boyfriend named Ralph."

Thompson looked up. "Your boyfriend is the man Mrs. Duncan hired to impersonate Frank?"

Mrs. Short fluffed her hair. "No, no, not *my* Ralph. It was another Ralph, from the Salvation Army."

"Okay. When did this annulment take place?"

"August, I think. Betty called an attorney in Ventura to do the paperwork."

"Just like that?" Thompson snapped his fingers.

"Yes, sir. She told the attorney's secretary on the phone that she wanted to go to court the same afternoon and have the annulment granted by the judge. Said she was in a hurry."

"She told the secretary what to do?"

"Oh yes, Betty's very well-versed on the subject. She knows all about annulments. She's done it herself many times."

"Really?" Thompson made a note. "What happened when you got to Ventura?"

"The lawyer had all the paperwork ready. He didn't ask for any identification. Just had Betty and Ralph swear under oath that they were Frank and Olga, and then they went to court that afternoon and told the judge that they wanted the annulment."

"Anything else?"

"Betty wrote the lawyer a check for $100, but it bounced." Mrs. Short reached for her pocketbook. "I'm tired. Can't we finish this tomorrow?"

Hansen entered the room carrying a glass of water. No ice. He set the glass in front of Mrs. Short and took a seat next to his partner.

"You're doing really well, Mrs. Short," Thompson said, "but let's go back a bit. When did Betty become upset about her son marrying Olga?"

"Why, before the beginning. Before they even got married, Betty was upset about it." Mrs. Short took a sip of water. "Frank promised Betty that he would never marry Olga. Then he went out and married her secretly. But Betty found out anyway. The same day."

"And how did Betty find out?" Hansen asked.

"She called the hospital where Olga works and asked to speak to her. She was going to warn her again not to marry Frank."

"Again? Betty had called Olga before?" Thompson said.

"All the time, but the person who answered that day said Olga wasn't there. Said she had the day off because she was getting married." Mrs. Short fiddled with the clasp on her purse and pulled out a crumpled tissue. "Boy, was Betty mad. She said, 'My son will never live with her . . . over my dead body. . . .'" The old woman put the tissue to her nose and blew out a long blast. "Or maybe she said, 'I'll kill her first.'"

Thompson stopped writing and looked at his partner. "I'll kill her first?"

"How do these guys you mentioned earlier fit into this?" Hansen asked Mrs. Short.

"When the annulment didn't do the trick, Betty hired two boys at the Tropical Café that Mrs. Esquivel introduced her to. They were supposed to take Olga to Mexico." Mrs. Short glanced back and forth between the detectives. "They were supposed to get rid of her . . . somehow . . . maybe kill her in Mexico, I think, and get rid of the body. Betty said she had pills and acid if they needed them." Mrs. Short twisted her fingers around the tissue. "I don't suppose one of you would have a cigarette?"

Thompson did not move. Hansen set his pencil on the table and lined it up next to the yellow pad. Muffled voices drifted in from the squad room outside the door.

Finally. Thompson looked at his watch and wrote *4:30 p.m.* on the pad. "You've been a big help, Mrs. Short. But this is going to take a little while longer. Detective Hansen's going to step outside for a moment and speak to our lieutenant."

He walked his partner to the door and spoke a few words before returning to the table and giving his head a quick shake to compose himself. He folded his fingers together and looked intently into the weary eyes of the old lady sitting across from him. "Mrs. Short, our lieutenant is going to call the district attorney's office. You need to tell them everything you've told me. Understand?"

Mrs. Short's eyes welled. "What about the hotel?"

CHAPTER TWENTY

DUM-DE-DUM-DUM

Ventura, California, December 12, 1958

While Detective Thompson was questioning Mrs. Short, Daddy was sitting at our dining room table eating a warmed-over dinner and telling mother about his return to the Krishna Venta bombing site. I listened quietly from the living room.

"You oughta see what's left of the Wisdom, Knowledge, Faith, and Love Fountain of the World headquarters. Jesus," Daddy boomed. "What a mess. I went back out there today. It's nothing but a big smoldering hole in the ground. A little like the burning brimstone Debby worries about after her visits to that idiot Reverend Ralston's church."

I glimpsed Mother standing next to the table with a plate of overcooked pork chops in her hand. "Want another chop?"

Daddy shook his head as he shoveled a spoonful of potatoes into his mouth. "You ought to see it."

"I don't want to get anywhere near that, that burning . . ." Mother searched for words.

Well, *I* would have liked to see it, but I didn't say anything. Didn't want my parents to know I was sitting on the living room floor at an angle where I could just see them.

"Bomb set a brush fire that burned more than two hundred acres around the compound," Daddy said as he struggled to cut a leathery piece of pork. "Poor Krishna. That firefighting barefoot messiah would have loved to fight that blaze. . . . That man appreciated a good fire."

"What happened to him?" Mother asked.

"Huge fireball. My god, it was an awful sight. I'm afraid the bomb blew the Fundador clear to kingdom come." Daddy looked heavenward. "Nothing left of him."

I pressed my lips together to stifle a gasp.

"Snuffed out seven followers, too," Daddy said. "The sheriff found an empty dynamite box in a pickup truck near the blast site, and there was a rambling monologue on a tape recorder in the truck. The man on the tape said he didn't like Krishna's leadership of the Fountain of the World. Plus, he claimed the master was sleeping with all the women, including the guy's wife."

I covered my mouth. *The wages of sin is death.*

"And they're sure Krishna's dead?" Mother said.

Daddy chuckled. "Well, maybe the messiah has risen, at least into the oak trees. There's a lot of debris from the explosion hanging in the branches."

"Bob, stop it. This isn't a joking matter."

As I listened to Mother scold Daddy about showing some respect for the dead, I picked up the book I'd been looking at before all the bomb talk. It was one of my father's Perry Mason paperbacks, *The Case of The Vagabond Virgin*. I thumbed through the pages again, looking for parts about the virgin that I wasn't supposed to read.

"God, I'm exhausted." Daddy yawned. "They'll have to use dental records to identify everyone . . . but get this. One of the cult members who wasn't in the building when it exploded told all the reporters that Olga Duncan had been living at the compound with Krishna. Claimed she might be one of the victims. He said he recognized her from her picture in the newspaper, and that Krishna was helping her find Wisdom, Knowledge, Faith, Love, et cetera."

"Sounds a little . . . implausible. . . ."

I rushed, wild-eyed, through the open archway into the dining room. "Olga was there?"

"I thought you were doing your homework," Mother said.

"Calm down, Debby." Daddy tossed his fork on the plate. "I talked to a detective about it, and he just laughed. He said the guy's crazy."

I pouted. "They could check a little bit more."

Daddy yawned again. "By the way, the crazy guy is one of your patients from the hospital, dear. Just got out of Camarillo a few weeks ago and—surprise, surprise—he ran from one nuthouse to another."

I furrowed my brow at Mother. "Hey, what about your other patient, you know . . . Beth? Did she call you yet? She's supposed to let us know how Tweety's doing before we leave for Grandma's."

Mother busied herself clearing the table. "Beth's hard to reach at the hotel. She doesn't have a phone in her room, and she's out all day working at the Coca-Cola plant."

"But did you call her?"

Mother wiped crumbs from the table onto a plate. "I'm sure Tweety's fine."

"Maybe we should go down to the hotel and check," I said. "Just to make sure."

"No time for that," Mother said. "We have to leave first thing in the morning."

"Hey, what do you know?" Daddy said in a jolly tone. "It's almost time for *Dragnet* to start."

Mother stacked the dishes she'd collected on the table and put her hands on her hips. "You shouldn't be encouraging her to watch that show. It's affecting her. All this talk about the police . . . and missing nurses . . ."

"But it's Daddy's and my favorite show. We like the facts, nothing but the facts. And I learn stuff from Sergeant Friday."

"This family . . ." Mother put her hands to her head. "We're scaring the children, Bob. Obsessing over danger. It's no wonder my mother says that the girls are being exposed to too much negativity."

"For Christ's sake, seeing *Dragnet* won't hurt her." Daddy tossed his napkin on the table. "Your mother's a mollycoddler."

Daddy flopped onto the couch and stretched his arms over his head. "I'm exhausted. Nothing like the aftermath of a big dynamite blast to knock the wind out of your sails." He loosened his tie, extended his legs, put a couple of the little blue pillows behind his head, and closed his eyes.

Dum—de-dum-dum. Dum—de-dum-dum-DUMMM.

"It's starting," I said without taking my eyes off the screen.

"Ladies and gentlemen, the story you are about to see is true. The names have been changed to protect the innocent."

I adjusted the volume and scooted back from the screen so as not to ruin my eyes.

"Daddy." I shook his arm. He rolled his head away. The smell of smoke clung to his clothes. Pinky Lee jumped up on his chest. Daddy swatted the cat away, but Pinky popped right back onto the couch and curled up against the cushion beside my father's head.

I turned my attention to the television.

"This is the city, Los Angeles, California," Sergeant Joe Friday said. "I work here. I'm a cop. I carry a badge."

Ooooh, this is going to be good.

I stretched out on my stomach, elbows on the floor, chin in my hands. My feet almost touched the Adirondack chair by the front door. The chair, like the rest of the redwood patio set in our house, including a double-chair settee and the picnic table in the dining room, had been painted white to make it look more "indoors." It didn't. It looked like it belonged on a red-wood deck someplace. Except it was white. Daddy was sleeping on the only real piece of furniture in the room, a turquoise Naugahyde couch embossed with a dark squiggly design.

The camera moved to a close-up on Sergeant Friday sitting at his desk in the police station. His partner rifled through some messages at the desk opposite Sergeant Friday's. "Anything doing with the jewelry store burglary?" he asked Joe.

I wondered if there was "anything doing" on the disappearance of Olga Duncan. I wished Joe Friday were on the case and wondered if Daddy knew anything new. I'd heard my parents talking in low voices in the kitchen before Daddy sat down to eat. Mother had shushed him when I walked through the room.

I focused on the TV. Joe wore a neatly pressed white shirt and a dark tie. Every shiny black hair on his head was in place. The phone rang. Joe answered. "Burglary, Friday." He listened and scribbled some notes. "All right, Father, we'll be right over." He hung up the phone and picked up his hat. "Father Rojas from the San Fernando Mission. The baby Jesus is missing."

Joe and his partner arrived at the old adobe church and interviewed the priest. "A life-sized statue of the baby Jesus was stolen right out of the manger," the priest said. "It disappeared sometime last night." He pointed to the nativity scene at the altar, where Mary looked lovingly at an empty spot on the straw bed.

I poked at my father. He lifted his head an inch and glanced at the screen. "It's that Christmas rerun," he mumbled as he turned over and went back to sleep.

A knock sounded on our front door, but I ignored it. Daddy turned over again, and Pinky's tail shot up. The cat turned his butt into my father's face and glared at the door with his squinty eyes.

On the TV, the priest talked about the Baby Jesus. "It means a lot to the people here. We put it out every year. For some of the children, it's the only Jesus they know."

Joe wrote it all down in his notebook. "When did you last see it?"

"At six o'clock mass last night."

Joe closed his notebook. "I promise you, Father, that we'll do everything we can to find the statue in time for mass on Christmas morning."

Joe Friday's wide mouth didn't smile or frown as he surveyed the church, but I could tell that he cared about the missing baby Jesus. He'd care about Olga's baby, too. Joe just had to act unemotional because he was a policeman.

The knock at our front door repeated, louder this time. Betsey ran out from the kitchen and threw open the door.

"Hi there, little girl," a man's voice boomed. "Your parents home?"

People didn't usually stop by after dinner, and I didn't recognize the voice. Betsey stood with her fingers in her mouth, looking up at whoever was on the porch.

"Your parents home?" the man repeated.

Uh-oh. Now I recognized the voice: Reverend Ralston from the Christian Life Revival Church. The "Wages of Sin Church," Daddy called it, since I'd told him about the Sunday school lesson. He said I wasn't supposed to go back there again.

The reverend was new to the little church, but he'd already made a reputation for himself in the community as an aggressive crusader out to find and convert new church members. The "Divine Wrath Evangelist," my father called him. I looked at Daddy stretched out on the couch, spittle drooling from the corner of his open mouth. I sighed. We were ripe for being saved.

Betsey nodded to the man on the porch, ignoring my arm waves and head shakes. I glanced back at the TV. Joe and his partner were walking out of the mission. "We have a man to find," Joe said. "Our only clue: he's been to church."

Betsey took a step backward, her fingers still in her mouth, as the reverend stepped into the living room. He was a youngish-looking man dressed in a white short-sleeved shirt with a dark tie. His blonde flat-top haircut was waxed and stiff, and he held a worn black Bible in one hand.

Dum—de-dum-dum rang out just as the program cut to a commercial.

Mother came to the door, wiping her fingers on a dish towel.

The preacher stuck out his hand. "Reverend Hank Ralston, Christian Life Revival Church. I'm doing some visits for our Family Ministry Program."

Mother hesitated before she took his hand. "This really isn't a good time."

Reverend Ralston shook her hand vigorously as he looked in my direction. "We are so pleased that Miss Deborah has joined our Sunday school the last few months. Such a nice young lady." He smiled and crinkled his eyes at me. "I want to invite the whole family to join us next Sunday."

"I don't think so, Mr. Ralston." Mother glanced at Daddy asleep on the couch.

I gazed at my bare feet and wiggled my toes. *Whew! The polish is all chipped away.*

The reverend bared his teeth in a big grin. "Little Deborah here came to our Vacation Bible School last summer, too. Smart girl." He winked at me. "Knows her books of the Bible. First one in the class to memorize all the books of the New Testament."

I glanced across the living room at the gold-tasseled bookmark with a picture of Jesus on the front sticking out of my latest Nancy Drew mystery.

Mother gave me a look.

"I didn't go there last Sunday," I stammered. "I went to the Baptist church. They have a bus for Sunday school to pick you up at the corner."

Reverend Ralston frowned momentarily and turned back to Mother. He pulled out a mimeographed sheet from inside his Bible. "Let me leave you a copy of our *Church Times*. It has the schedule of all our services on the back."

Mother took the paper, reluctantly, but used her other hand to pull the front door wide open. Cool night air breathed into the room.

Reverend Ralston didn't take the hint. Instead, he sat down on the edge of the Adirondack chair and pulled a little booklet from his shirt pocket. "I have the Four Spiritual Laws tract here," he said. "Would you mind, ma'am, if I shared this with you and your precious family?"

I heard the *Dragnet* theme music chime in again. *Dum—de-dum-dum.* The commercial had ended. I turned a little to keep one eye on the screen. Joe and his partner were checking out pawnshops for the statue.

Daddy started to snore. Really loud.

"No, I don't think so," Mother said.

The reverend kept an eye on Daddy and raised his voice. "Won't take but a minute to share. 'First law: God loves you and offers a wonderful plan for your life.'"

Mother shook her head. "Not now, Reverend. We're not interested in joining your church." She moved to one side to make room for him to walk out the door.

"'The second law of spirituality . . .'" the reverend intoned as he stood up.

Sergeant Friday interrupted. "You're half-wrong already, buster," he said as he grabbed a suspect by the arm to drag him down to the police station.

The reverend glanced at the TV and then at Daddy. "'Man is sinful and separated from God. Therefore, he cannot know and experience God's . . .'"

Daddy stirred. He blinked a couple of times, a mix of confusion and surprise on his face, and struggled to sit up. He gave Mother a groggy, accusing look.

"All we want are the facts," Sergeant Friday said.

The suspect said he didn't know anything about any baby Jesus.

Daddy's eyes rolled around, and his head tilted back against the couch. He was asleep again, which wasn't surprising. Daddy bragged about how he could sleep sitting up, like it was some kind of special gift he possessed.

"He's just leaving, Bob," Mother said.

But the reverend reached down and took my hand, pulling me to a standing position. He reached out for Betsey's hand, too. "Let us pray before I go."

Mother's gaze searched the room as if evaluating her options, and she stepped forward, teeth set. I think she just wanted the guy out of the house, and if that meant praying, so be it. But Reverend Ralston wasn't happy with just the three of us. He let go of my hand and grabbed Daddy by the elbow to stand him up.

"*Nooo!*" Mother cried.

But Daddy wobbled forward. Both my mother and I put our hands out to steady him. He seemed to be in a semi-conscious, eyes-half-closed, sleepwalking state.

We all held hands in the circle. "Our heavenly Father, God in heaven, we request your immense blessing on this wonderful family," Reverend Ralston said.

I kept my eyes open. Daddy's were shut. He looked peaceful, even reverent, standing there, swaying a little.

The reverend continued. "We are so happy to have young Deborah as part of our Sunday school, and we pray for the rest of the family to know and experience God's love. . . ."

And then it happened. The snore started as a guttural sound deep in Daddy's throat and blasted through his mouth and nose: *SNK-KKKRRRRTTTT.* His chin rose from its resting position on his chest. As his head moved upright, the snore got louder. The reverend was cut off mid-prayer by the horrible roar. By the time Daddy's head had tilted all the way back, the sound was so loud it seemed to shake the house. Rattle the windows. Drown out the TV. Scare the cat. It reverberated off the walls of the little living room and echoed in my ears. When Daddy's head snapped forward like a bobblehead doll, it woke him.

The reverend started praying again, but now really fast: ". . . and experienceGod'slove andaplanforyourlifeAmen."

Daddy blinked around the circle. His blurry gaze stopped on the reverend. Silence. No one moved.

"Uh . . . Reverend Ralston?" Daddy shook his head as if to clear the cobwebs. "Afraid you caught us at a bad time." He yawned. "We're in a bit of a state about my good friend, the master, Krishna Venta. Maybe you heard? Some devil blew up the messiah with twenty sticks of dynamite."

"Possible messiah," I muttered.

"Not much left, I'm afraid," Daddy said sadly. He lowered his head and stared at the floor.

Mother began to shake. For a moment I thought she was crying. She had her hand over her mouth, and she coughed a couple of times. Then the cough turned into a hysterical-sounding giggle before she threw her head back and roared with laughter.

The reverend held his Bible in front of his chest like he was trying to ward off evil spirits.

Daddy laughed too, a big belly laugh. Betsey cried in the confusion, and I was just plain mortified. I wasn't worried so much about us all going to hell, although I knew it was a strong possibility. I was more worried about my family being so out of step in our neighborhood. Wendy would hear all about this and tell everyone. Grandma was right. We were doomed. Liberal agnostics with patio furniture in the living room and a mother who worked at the state mental hospital, living amongst God-fearing, church-going families with stay-at-home mothers and smartly furnished homes. We were just plain weird.

The reverend left, but not before telling Mother that if she let her little girls watch programs like *Dragnet*, we would get nightmares "or worse."

When he was gone, I said, "Don't worry. I'm not going back to that church. I'm a Baptist now. I go on the bus."

My parents moved into the kitchen, still laughing like hyenas. Betsey picked up Pinky Lee and walked down the hall toward the bedroom. I sat on the empty couch to watch the last few minutes of *Dragnet*.

Joe and his partner were in the church, telling the priest that they were very sorry that they couldn't find the statue of the baby Jesus in time for Christmas mass, when the big double doors at the back of the church banged open. A small boy walked slowly up the aisle pulling a little wagon carrying the white porcelain statue of the baby Jesus.

The priest clapped his hands together. "Where did you find him, *hijo*?"

The boy bowed his head. "I didn't find him. I took him."

Sergeant Friday looked from the boy to the statue.

"I prayed to the baby for a red wagon many times." The boy's lips quivered into a tumultuous smile. "I promised if my prayers were answered that the baby Jesus would get the first ride. So when I got the wagon at the firemen's Christmas party last night . . ." The boy glanced sideways at the priest. "I picked him up after early mass this morning."

The camera zoomed in for a close-up. The boy's large, soulful dark eyes stared into Joe Friday's equally beautiful deep, dark eyes.

Organ music played in the background, building to a crescendo as the boy and the priest gently lifted the statue out of the wagon and into the empty manger of the nativity scene. One side of Joe Friday's mouth twitched. He was so happy.

"It's time for bed." Daddy stood in the doorway.

"Too bad we don't have a policeman like Joe Friday looking for Olga," I said.

He pointed down the hall. "To bed."

"What were you telling Mother tonight when you first got home? It sounded like a secret. Were you talking about Olga?"

Daddy sat down next to me on the couch. He ran his hand across the black squiggly pattern embossed in the turquoise Naugahyde.

"I don't think I'll be able to sleep until I find out," I said.

He huffed. "The Santa Barbara Police have some new information. Something about Olga's mother-in-law saying she was being blackmailed around the time of Olga's disappearance. It seems someone threatened to have her and her son, Frank, killed if Mrs. Duncan didn't give him money."

I grabbed my father's arm. "But they only threatened to kill Frank Duncan and his mother, right? Not Olga."

"But it's Olga who vanished. . . ." Daddy took off his glasses. He pinched his nose. "Now the police are looking for a couple of ex-convicts. . . . That's all I know."

"I can't believe this." I searched his face. "It's not just on TV?"

Daddy nodded. The phone rang.

"Bob, telephone," Mother called out from the kitchen. "And, Debby, you need to get to bed. We're leaving early tomorrow for Grandma's house."

I turned to the TV. *Dum—de-dum-dum* . . . I watched as the big metal hammer pounded out the numeral 714 on the screen. Badge 714, Joe Friday's number. *Clang. Clang. Clang.*

CHAPTER TWENTY-ONE

IT'S SO CRAZY IT MUST BE TRUE

Santa Barbara, California, December 12, 1958

After Lieutenant Peck called the DA to tell him about the new witness, the detectives drove Mrs. Short four blocks north to the district attorney's office at the courthouse. Hansen was at the wheel of the unmarked police car. Thompson rode shotgun with Mrs. Short in the back seat. It had been twenty-five days since Olga disappeared.

"Betty might be looking for me." Mrs. Short's frizzled gray head swiveled from side to side as she slumped in the seat. Purple-and-gray clouds blew from the ocean over the city. A shadow fell across her wrinkled face. "She'll be expecting me for our highballs soon."

Thompson made a big deal of looking in every direction. "You're safe with us." He tried to keep his breathing steady. *This old bat could be the key to solving the disappearance of Olga Duncan. Jesus.*

Hansen swung the car into the parking lot at the south end of the courthouse. The massive Spanish-style building took up an entire city block. The face of the four-story clock tower was already illuminated in the gloom of the winter twilight. Fiery orange shafts of light pierced the dark clouds in stark contrast to the plain white walls of the courthouse.

"Where did you say we're going?" Mrs. Short blinked at the enormous wooden door at the entrance to the building.

Thompson turned in his seat. "Like we told you back at the station, you're going to talk to the Santa Barbara district attorney."

Vern Lawton*, a thin bald-headed man, sat at a grand mahogany desk. No clutter. The district attorney didn't get up when the trio entered. He nodded at Thompson. "Sounds like you got something."

"This is Mrs. Short, our witness," Hansen said.

Mrs. Short stood dwarfed between the two detectives, squinting up at the framed diplomas on the wall above the DA's desk. "I don't know anything. You should talk to Betty."

"She's just a little nervous," Thompson said. "Thinks Mrs. Duncan is going to hurt her if she talks."

"Mrs. Short is Elizabeth Duncan's best friend. Constant companion," Hansen added.

"Confidante, so to speak," Thompson said.

The old woman sat down. She smoothed her skirt across her knees. "I like to keep myself to myself."

Lawton narrowed his eyes at her. "I like to put bad people in jail, so why don't you give me a little summary of what you know about your friend Betty and the disappearance of Olga Duncan."

Mrs. Short ducked her head. "I don't know . . . Betty just didn't want her son to have a wife. I tried to reason with her. I said, 'Let's just leave things alone. Maybe it'll all work out.' But she was so determined. . . ."

"Let's start," Lawton said, "with this annulment you told Detectives Thompson and Hansen about."

With constant prodding from Thompson, Mrs. Short repeated her story about going to Ventura to get the phony annulment.

"And you need to tell Mr. Lawton," Hansen coaxed, "about what Betty said the day she found out that Frank married Olga. And about the guys at the Tropical Café."

Mrs. Short hesitated.

Thompson muttered the word "hotel" to her under his breath.

"Well, the day she found out that Frank married Olga, she told me, 'My son will never live with her. I will kill her first. Destroy her.'"

"Kill her?" Lawton said. "Anyone else hear her say this?"

"No, not then. I was the only one there."

"Any other time?"

"Oh, lots of other times. She asked a lot of people to help her get rid of Olga."

All three men leaned closer.

"She asked people to kill Olga?" Lawton said.

"Get rid of her. Betty wanted to keep her son all for herself. Wanted him to only live with her. No wife."

"Those other people? You're talking about the men who met with Mrs. Duncan at the Tropical Café?"

"Yes, and she asked the owner of the Tropical, Mrs. Esquivel, to help her find those men. And then there were the others who didn't come through."

Lawton ran his hand over his bald head and pulled a tablet from a drawer. He reached for the gold fountain pen on a stand at the corner of his desk. "Who all did Mrs. Duncan talk to about getting rid of Olga?"

"Well, let me see." Mrs. Short furrowed her brow. "She tried to make a number of transactions."

"Transactions?"

"That's what Betty called them . . . getting other people to get rid of Olga. Like she asked Ralph, the man from the Salvation Army, to 'take care' of Olga."

The DA looked to Thompson for help.

"That's the guy she paid, the window washer, to impersonate Frank when they went to court down in Ventura," Thompson said.

"Right," the DA said, like it made perfect sense. "Go on, Mrs. Short."

"Ralph didn't want any part of it. Refused to help, except he sometimes moved Frank's car around to hide it, because Betty didn't want Olga in that car."

Mrs. Short went on to tell the men about a carhop at the Blue Onion who Mrs. Duncan had asked to help with the "Olga problem." "But she wasn't any use at all, so then Betty asked one of Frank's clients and his wife, but they turned her down, too. And a lady we met named Becky was supposed to try to find someone to do it when she went to Oxnard to visit her sister."

"Last names?"

Mrs. Short shook her head. "That's all I can remember. Can I go to the hotel now?"

Lawton leaned back. "And what about you, Mrs. Short? What did you think about your friend wanting to 'get rid' of her daughter-in-law?"

"Well, I disapproved of the whole thing. Of course."

"You ever tell anyone about all these plans? Olga? Frank? The police?"

"Well, not Frank. That man is not what you would call approachable." Mrs. Short looked at Hansen as if seeking confirmation. When he didn't react, she shifted her gaze to the window. "I don't know . . . Betty was just very determined. She wouldn't tolerate being contradicted."

Lawton turned to Hansen and Thompson with an incredulous look. "So this woman, Elizabeth Duncan, solicited people all over Santa Barbara looking for a killer, and you guys never heard a word about it?"

"Nothing," Thompson said, "until we talked to Mrs. Short today—and at first all she told us about was the annulment and the men at the Tropical."

The DA turned back to Mrs. Short. "Tell us about the men from the café."

Mrs. Short picked at something on her skirt. "Mrs. Esquivel, the owner, introduced Betty to two Mexicans, Luis and Baldo, I think. That's when everything was agreed. I wasn't privy to the discussions. I sat at another table."

"But what did Mrs. Duncan tell you?"

Mrs. Short continued staring at her lap. "She said that the boys were going to kidnap Olga and take her to Mexico for $6,000. Betty told them she could get some acid and pills if they needed it." Mrs. Short looked up. "And Luis was supposed to call when the job was done, and Betty would pay him. But she doesn't have any money."

Lawton leaned forward. "And did he call?"

Mrs. Short nodded. "'She's gone,' that's what he said. He told Betty that she won't have to worry about Olga causing any more problems."

The three men looked at each other.

"Now Mrs. Esquivel keeps calling," Mrs. Short continued, "trying to get Betty to pay the boys. We went down to Woolworths to give them two hundred dollars. She used Frank's typewriter money. That's why she told Frank she was being blackmailed; she had to come up with an excuse."

For a moment, the only sound in the room was Lawton's pen scratching across paper.

"I need to powder my nose," Mrs. Short said.

"What do you think?" the DA asked the detectives after a jail matron escorted Mrs. Short down the hall to the bathroom.

"Don't think she could make all that up," Hansen said. "It's so crazy it must be true."

"And she hasn't changed her story since we started talking with her this afternoon," Thompson said. "She just keeps adding more details."

The DA swiveled in his chair. "We don't have enough to arrest anyone on the disappearance yet. Mrs. Duncan, Moya, Baldonado . . . no solid evidence to file charges against any of them. All we got is Mrs. Short's wild, uncorroborated story." He laced his fingers together. "But we should be able to put something together on the phony annulment. Only one problem: the old lady says it all happened in Ventura, so we'll have to get their cooperation. And—" The DA wrinkled his nose. "Shhhhhit. That means Gustafson."

Thompson bunched his eyebrows. "Gustafson?"

"Roy Gustafson, the district attorney in Ventura County. Always on the lookout to make a name for himself. Pretty sure he's planning to run for governor someday. He'll be happy to jump all over this."

"I'll get started trying to find out about the annulment," Hansen said.

"And find some pictures of Olga and Frank, everybody involved. See if the judge and the attorney in Ventura can identify Mrs. Duncan. If we get solid IDs, I want her brought in for questioning immediately. Tomorrow if we can. Get the Ventura people to move fast, take her by surprise before she realizes Mrs. Short spilled her guts. Then we keep her in jail down there in Ventura while we work on finding out what happened to Olga up here."

"What do you want us to do with Mrs. Short in the meantime?" Thompson asked.

Lawton squared his notepad on the desk. "We need to get some kind of verification before we go out on a wild goose chase. There's a guy who works with the Los Angeles Police on polygraph tests. He's an expert. I'll call and get it set up for tomorrow. One of you drive Mrs. Short down to LA for the test and then call me with the results. I don't care what time. I want to know what we've got here."

"And get her a hotel room?" Hansen asked.

"Fine," the DA said, "but keep it cheap."

"I'll stay on Moya and Baldonado, work with Lieutenant Peck," Thompson said, "and interview Esperanza Esquivel again in the morning. When we talked to her the last time, she said she never talked to Mrs. Duncan."

Thompson looked out the window. "You think Olga could still be alive?"

"Not a snowball's chance in hell," Hansen said.

PART TWO

THE SEARCH
FOR THE BODY

December 13, 1958–December 26, 1959

CHAPTER TWENTY-TWO

OFF TO GRANDMA'S

Ventura, California, December 13, 1958

On Saturday morning, we were supposed to make an early start to Grandma and Grandpa's house, seventy-five miles south in Arcadia. The plan was to be on the road by six thirty A.M., arrive sometime around nine, and head home by three. Most important of all—*avoid the weekend traffic!*

At 7:15, our orange station wagon still sat in the driveway. I waited in the back seat, barefoot and yawning, watching Daddy as he paced the driveway, humming a gravelly, agitated, off-key tune. He glanced at his watch and muttered to himself, "Son of a bitch." Sometimes he stopped to ask me a question through my partially opened window. "You have your shoes, right?"

I dug around on the floor of the car to find my new ballet slippers. "These are real shoes," I said as I held them up for inspection, ready for an argument, but he'd already turned away.

"Hurry up!" he yelled toward the house.

Mother stuck her head out the back door and hissed, "Shh, Bob, the neighbors."

"For God's sake, the *traffic*!"

The muffled sound of a ringing telephone came through the open back door. Daddy never looked up. He was too preoccupied with his pacing and muttering to notice.

The ringing persisted.

"Daddy." I pointed at the house. "Phone's ringing."

He bounded up the back porch steps and through the open door.

I kicked my bare feet against the back of the driver's seat.

The ringing stopped. Daddy screamed, "Christ almighty, Lois! Can't you pick up the damn phone?"

Mother appeared at the back door, holding a big shopping bag overflowing with assorted clothes and cereal boxes in one hand and gripping my sister's hand with the other. Betsey was still wearing her pajamas.

"The phone? You said to hurry up and get ready. I can't do everything at once."

Daddy followed her onto the porch and slammed the door behind him. "That call could have been important."

Mother settled Betsey into the back seat next to me. "It was probably just a wrong number."

"At this time in the morning?"

Mother climbed into the front. Daddy stood with one hand holding the driver's-side door open. "You know, a lot is going on with the Duncan case right now. I keep hearing things. They might be close to making an arrest, and . . ."

Mother sat stone-faced, staring out the windshield.

". . . maybe I should stay here. You take the girls and go to your folks. You could stay the night if you like," Daddy said in a cheery tone. "Come back in the morning so that you won't have such a long drive after dark."

Mother turned slowly until she was gazing directly into Daddy's face, her mouth pinched, her eyes narrowed to slits.

Daddy looked away. "All right, all right. Let's get going. Don't want to hit the traffic."

Mother rolled her eyes to the heavens. "Calm down, Bob. It's Saturday morning, not Friday night."

"Yeah, well, that Conejo Grade can be a bitch any day of the week," he mumbled.

I opened my Nancy Drew, *The Clue in the Diary*, as Daddy backed out of the driveway. Betsey was already asleep.

Traffic wasn't bad. No problem as we drove up the grade. When we passed the little sign posted to notify drivers that they'd entered Los Angeles County, Daddy grabbed his throat and pretended to have a coughing fit. "The smog is killing me," he croaked. "Hold your breath, girls. He-he-he," he cackled his maniacal laugh.

He quit his coughing routine and looked at us in the rearview mirror. "You know what's happening right now, girls, at Cape Canaveral?"

Betsey stirred and looked out the window. "Smog?"

"No. Gordo is about to blast off! Today's the big day."

"The space monkey!" Betsey squealed.

Daddy met our eyes in the mirror and laughed gleefully. "Gordo's going to show those Russians a thing or two about the American space program."

"Will the Russians shoot the bomb into space, too?" I asked.

"Stop worrying about the bomb," Daddy said.

"Keep your eyes on the road, Bob. . . . That poor little monkey. It's just cruel."

"Gordo is going to be fine," Daddy said. "He's a trailblazer . . . He's making aeronautical history."

Betsey clapped her hands. "I love his little helmet. Can I get one of those for Pinky Lee?"

"Did you feed the cat, Bob?" Mother said.

After we arrived at our grandparents' home, I went down the rickety wooden stairs to the basement. I wondered if it would make a good bomb shelter, but then I got distracted rummaging through boxes of old clothes and costume jewelry. I liked to dress up, especially in Grandma's wide-brimmed hats decorated with feathers and ribbons. I went upstairs to show off my costume and twirled around in my ballet slippers.

Grandma tilted the hat to one side of my head and said, "You look very smart, dear."

Daddy was in a bad mood for the whole visit, but at least he was too pre-occupied about getting home "in good time" to start any political arguments with Grandma. He kept pestering Mother about what time she expected us to leave. "Something's happening with that Duncan case. I just know it." He eyed the wall telephone in Grandma's kitchen.

"Don't make any long-distance calls," Mother said.

We ate a big lunch around two. Grandma served ham with corn on the cob and salads and home-baked bread. There were also chocolate lace cookies and a coconut cake, both her specialties.

"Don't eat the corn from the cob, Bob," Mother said. "You know it makes your lip swell." She looked at Grandma. "New allergy."

Mother reached for his plate. "Let me cut the kernels off for you."

Daddy pulled the plate away. "I'm not a child," he said.

Grandma snorted a laugh.

"Eat up, girls," Daddy said. "We aren't stopping for dinner on the way home."

CHAPTER TWENTY-THREE

THE ARRESTS

Santa Barbara, California,
December 13, 1958

S ince Mrs. Short's interview the previous night, the Santa Barbara PD had been working almost nonstop on Olga Duncan's disappearance. On Saturday morning, while my family was on our way to Grandma's, Hansen was driving Mrs. Short along the same highway to Los Angeles for a polygraph test. At the same time, up the coast in Santa Barbara, Esperanza Esquivel, owner of the Tropical Café, was being led into an interrogation room at the police station.

Detective Thompson watched as the police matron helped Mrs. Esquivel into one of the straight-back wooden chairs. He grabbed a chair on the opposite side of the table and swiveled it around before straddling it to face the trembling woman.

He tossed his yellow tablet down on the table between them. "I'm going to give you one chance to answer my questions, and answer them truthfully. Understand?"

Mrs. Esquivel began coughing. Her whole body shook. She covered her mouth with one hand and wrapped her other arm across her chest. Finally, the coughing stopped, but her labored breathing continued. She wiped a spot of spittle from her chin.

"I said, do you understand? If you don't tell the truth, I'm going to have the matron here take you down to the jail. We'll charge you with conspiracy to commit murder."

Mrs. Esquivel coughed again and pulled a crumpled, pink-stained hand-kerchief from the bodice of her dress to dab more spittle from her mouth.

"And don't tell me you never met Mrs. Duncan. Mrs. Short told us everything."

The woman twisted the handkerchief in her fingers. "Mrs. Duncan and the other woman come to the café for coffee and talk," she finally said.

"Talk about what?"

Mrs. Esquivel's mouth quivered. "She say her son is married and the woman is no good. She want to know if I have friends to"—Mrs. Esquivel wheezed—"to help her get rid of this woman, get her out of the way."

Thompson stiffened. "And what did you tell her?"

"I think I say I might know some boys. Maybe."

"Mrs. Short said you told Mrs. Duncan to come back the next day—and when she did, you introduced her to two men to help her get rid of her daughter-in-law."

"I dunno what they talk about." Mrs. Esquivel ran a shaky finger under each eye to wipe away tears. "I'm busy in restaurant. I just introduce them. I dunno nothing else."

"Names?" Thompson picked up his pen. "Who were the men?"

Her lower lip trembled. "Luis and Gus. They clean up the café some-times, help me get ready to open."

Thompson tried to steady his own hand as he wrote. "Last names?"

"I'm not feeling so good. I been sick for a couple of months."

"Let's finish this interview. Then you can lie down." He turned to the matron, who was sitting in a chair by the door. "Get her some water."

"I gotta go back to the Tropical," Mrs. Esquivel said. "My husband's in jail. I gotta be there all the time."

"Last names," Thompson said again, his voice stern.

More coughing. "Luis Moya and Gus Baldonado. That's all I know."

Thompson wrote the names on his tablet and underlined them. "All? I don't think so. Mrs. Short says you're the go-between to help these men try to collect payments from Mrs. Duncan . . . for services rendered, so to speak."

Mrs. Esquivel put her head in her hands. "I dunno what happen. I just drive the boys to some places on State Street. Help them out so they help me at the café. With Marciano in jail, I got no one to help me."

"Weren't you arrested for the same crime as your husband, receiving stolen property?" Thompson asked.

"I was afraid they going to send me back to Mexico, but the lawyer got the charges dropped." Mrs. Esquivel looked up through wet, bloodshot eyes. "I get up at five thirty in the morning and go to the café to cook breakfast. I walk home at nine to rest a little and then be back down there again to open up for lunch. I stay until after two in the morning. Every day, I do this." She began to sob. "I got no time to notice what Luis and Gus are up to."

Thompson waited for her crying to subside, then spoke in a softer tone. "Look, Mrs. Esquivel. You help us, and we can help you. That's what Mrs. Short is doing. You want to go to jail? Because based on what we know so far, you're up to your eyeballs in this thing. You helped arrange for Olga Duncan to disappear, or maybe worse." He leaned forward. "I think you're part of a conspiracy to commit murder."

"Please. Please . . . I din't do nothing. I'm sorry I help that lady. . . . I din't know!"

"You can help yourself now. What did Mrs. Duncan say to these guys about doing a job for her?"

Mrs. Esquivel hugged her arms around her waist. "Maybe I hear her ask, 'Will $3,000 be all right? And . . . and something about pills and acid."

Pills and acid? The same crazy detail Mrs. Short mentioned. Thompson scribbled on the yellow tablet. "And was $3,000 enough?"

"No. Luis say $6,000."

"The night Olga Duncan disappeared. Did you see these men?"

Mrs. Esquivel nodded. "I remember the night. The next day my husband will find out about going to prison." She took a ragged breath. "I hear Gus and Luis come in. Gus stays in a room at my house sometimes if he don' have no place else to go."

"What time?"

"After two thirty. I was in bed. The noise wake me up." She cleared her throat and spat into the handkerchief. "I go to the kitchen to get a drink of water, and they are there. They got blood on their pants. They are washing off the blood."

Thompson's head jerked up. He enunciated his next words carefully. "Blood? What happened to the pants they were washing?"

"I dunno. I go back to bed. In the morning the boys are gone. I hear a few days later, the woman disappear, and it sticks in my mind." She coughed. "I dunno nothing more."

After sending Mrs. Esquivel to a cell with the matron, Thompson gulped coffee from a paper cup and glanced at the wall clock as he hustled through the squad room. *Almost ten thirty.* He felt electrified just thinking about everything Mrs. Esquivel had said. *Blood on their pants.*

When he got to his desk, he found a note from an officer named Bagley in the traffic division telling him they were holding a guy on a DUI and possible stolen car charge. Knows Baldonado. The words were underlined.

Thompson grabbed the phone. When Bagley picked up, he told Thompson, "I heard you and Hansen are looking for Gus Baldonado."

"That's right." Thompson lowered himself into his chair as he searched through a pile of papers with his other hand.

"Well, I'm holding a guy named Chico Rojo, and he says he loaned his car to his buddy Gus Baldonado last month. Rojo was very eager to tell me that when Gus returned the car, the back seat upholstery was ripped and burned. I looked inside. You can still see what looks like dried blood."

Thompson blew out a long whistle and popped out of his chair. "Where's the car?"

"Got it in impound. Beat-up 1948 gray Chevrolet. Looks like someone tore big pieces out of the back seat upholstery and burned the edges to get rid of something . . . and recently."

"You still got Rojo?"

"Hasn't made bail yet."

Thompson hung up the phone. "Jesus!"

Lieutenant Peck called out from his office: "Lawton just phoned and said the Ventura DA—what's his name, Gustafson—is sending people up to arrest Elizabeth Duncan on the fraudulent annulment charge later today. They confirmed all the information Mrs. Short gave us about the annulment."

Thompson crossed the few steps into the lieutenant's office and told his boss about the car with the bloody upholstery. "How do we handle this now?"

"Ventura sheriff's deputies and a DA guy will be here in a couple of hours." Peck glanced at the clock above his desk. "Probably sometime after lunch, and then you and I'll go with them to the Duncan woman's apartment to make the arrest. Lawton wants her brought to the Santa Barbara jail first so we can take another crack at her about her daughter-in-law's disappearance. Then, assuming Mrs. Duncan doesn't have a change of heart and spill her guts, she goes to Ventura and gets booked on the fraudulent annulment charge. In the meantime, I'll check out the car."

Peck leaned back in his chair. "I sent a couple of guys to talk to Baldonado's ex-wife in Oxnard. She just got out of the hospital after having twins. Gus was down to visit last week. Seems he's the father even though they're divorced. They have two other kids, and he hasn't paid child support in years. Gustafson thinks we can get the ex-wife to sign a complaint for failure to support and hold him in jail. Somebody from Ventura is going to call as soon as they pick him up."

"Shit," Thompson said. "That means Baldonado will be staying in Ventura. They got jurisdiction on this one, too." He tossed his paper cup into the wastebasket. "I'm going over to the Blue Onion and picking up Moya while we wait for the Ventura boys. I talked to his parole officer this morning, and we've got enough to hold him on a couple of probation violations—driving, hanging out with felons at the Tropical."

"Good. Don't want him to run when he hears we've got old lady Duncan in jail." The lieutenant pulled a pack of cigarettes out of his shirt pocket and tapped the package on his hand to slide one into his fingers. "At least we'll have Moya here in Santa Barbara to work on."

A little after one P.M., Peck, Thompson, two Ventura sheriff's deputies, a jail matron, and a Ventura DA investigator named Tom Osborne all marched up the open stairway to apartment 3 of the Valerio Street apartments. Lieutenant Peck knocked on the door. Thompson and the three men from Ventura stood back. No answer. After a moment, the lieutenant put his ear to the door and listened. He shrugged.

Osborne moved the lieutenant aside, made a fist, and pounded. "Police! Open up!"

The curtain in the window next to the door moved slightly. A pair of angry eyes framed in tortoiseshell cat-eye glasses glared at the group gathered outside the apartment.

"Police," Osborne yelled again.

"What do you want?" Mrs. Duncan called through the glass.

Peck moved over to the window. "We have a warrant for your arrest."

"Let me see it."

Peck held up the warrant. After a moment, Mrs. Duncan moved away from the window. The deadbolt turned and the door opened a crack.

"Let me see that warrant. I know the law." Mrs. Duncan snatched the paper out of Peck's hand. She pulled it through the opening.

"It's all in order," Osborne said. "You're being charged with fraud and forgery for—"

"I can read," Mrs. Duncan spat.

The officers pushed the door open, and Mrs. Duncan stepped outside. Charlie Thompson pried the warrant from her fingers.

Neighbors on both sides of the Duncan apartment peeked out their doors. A woman with her hair in curlers put her hand over her mouth.

"I need to call my son," Mrs. Duncan said in a loud voice. "He's a lawyer and he'll be representing me."

"You can call him when you get to the jail," Thompson said. "Turn around and put your hands behind your back."

As Thompson snapped the handcuffs on her wrists, Mrs. Duncan called out to the woman in curlers. "It's all a misunderstanding. Frank will get this whole mix-up straightened out." She turned her head to Thompson. "I know what happens to innocent people. They get their words twisted back on them in court. I'm not saying another word."

"You do that," Thompson said as he finished with the cuffs.

Mrs. Duncan looked down at her cotton housedress. "I need to change my clothes. I can't go out like this."

"You'll get a nice new dress when they book you into the jail," Thompson said. "Very stylish . . . if you like gray, that is."

Thompson took one elbow, and the matron took the other to guide her toward the stairs.

Mrs. Duncan tried to twist out of Thompson's hand. He held on tight. She screeched as they passed a neighbor. "These handcuffs are killing me! You're cutting off my circulation!"

The lieutenant and the two Ventura officers brought up the rear as the parade clomped down the stairs.

"Somebody call Frank!" Mrs. Duncan yelled up to her neighbors. "He'll get this all straightened out!"

CHAPTER TWENTY-FOUR

NO GOOD NEWS ON THE RADIO

Ventura, California, December 13, 1958

We left Grandma's at about four. All went well until we approached the Conejo Grade. Traffic was at a total standstill near the top of the pass before heading down the hill toward Ventura.

"What the hell?" Daddy said. He flipped on the radio, twisting the knob to find a news station with a traffic report.

"Oh no," Mother moaned. "A truck's probably lost its brakes again."

"You don't know that," Daddy said as he rubbed his mouth. His upper lip was red and a little swollen. "I'd rather speed through hell than be stuck on this godforsaken highway." He threw up his hands. "Damnation! Look at it. We'll be here all night."

"Calm down," Mother said.

Some cars had pulled off on the shoulder of the road. A few people milled around. Daddy rolled down his window. "Hey, what's going on up ahead?"

A man threw his cigarette to the ground and squashed it under his boot. "Another big rig lost its brakes. Hell of a mess."

Mother turned to us in the back seat and smiled serenely. "I hope no one died this time."

Daddy let his head drop. His forehead hit the top of the steering wheel. "Dammit," he yelled. He gingerly touched his lip with his fingertips and fiddled with the radio dial until he found a news station. He turned up the volume.

"The search for Gordo the monkey, fired into space this morning in the nose cone of a Jupiter rocket, has been called off."

Betsey and I leaned forward. "Oh, good," Betsey said happily. "Gordo. I like his little space helmet."

"Shh," I said. "Listen."

"Scientists say the monkey survived the fifteen-minute journey into space, but that the parachute failed to open at reentry, and the nose cone sank in the Atlantic, taking Gordo—"

Mother twisted the tuner dial to a music station.

"I want to hear about Gordo," Betsey said. "Where did the man say Gordo went?"

Daddy said, "Well, it sounds like Gordo didn't—"

"He went back to Florida," Mother cut in. "He's probably at Cape Canaveral eating bananas and playing with those monkeys who thought up his mission." She glared at Daddy, daring him to say more.

I furrowed my brow. "I think the man on the radio said Gordo sank—"

"He did not," Mother said. "The man said the *capsule* sank, not Gordo." She twisted in her seat to face Betsey. "Why don't we play I Spy? I'll start. . . . Let's see . . . I spy a Greyhound bus."

Betsey and I both stared at her.

"I really like Gordo's little space helmet." Betsey frowned. "He'll be safe as long as he had his helmet on, right?"

Traffic finally began to move. We sat quietly as our car inched along behind a huge gasoline tanker truck in the growing darkness. I could just make out the bold letters painted on the back of the truck: FLAMMABLE. NO SMOKING. I turned to scrutinize the shadowy profiles of other travelers in nearby cars, looking for the telltale glow of a burning cigarette. When I spied a floating red sparkle in a car in the next lane, I sank into my seat and closed my eyes and waited for the explosion. "Please God, please God, not tonight," I whispered.

"I knew we should have left earlier," Daddy fumed as we finally crested the grade and began the three-mile descent. "All because some imbecile truck driver can't take the time to get his brakes checked. Lunatic."

Lunatic? I stopped praying and opened my eyes wide. "What about Tweety? Are we still going to go over to Beth's hotel and pick him up?"

"Not tonight," Daddy said. "We won't be home for hours."

"But, Daddy, you promised we'd pick up Tweety tonight." I burst into tears.

"Look at this mess." Daddy jabbed his finger at the endless stream of red taillights snaking down the grade, police lights pulsating in the distance. "We'll be lucky if we ever get home."

"Don't say that. Please, Daddy, don't say we won't get home." I started to pray again.

Betsey burst into tears.

"Oh, Bob," Mother pleaded.

"Stop your crying and goddamn praying," he bellowed. "Both of you . . . before I push my ejection button and send you into space like that stupid monkey." His finger hovered near one of the push buttons on the dashboard.

Betsey cried harder.

"That's enough, Bob." Mother reached over the seat to pat my sister's knee. "There's no ejection button, dear. You know that." She turned back to my father. "Just stop your nonsense!"

Daddy sighed noisily.

I kicked the back of his seat. "We are *too* going to get home. Mother knows the way."

Daddy squinted at Mother. "I'm getting a headache. I don't suppose you thought to bring any aspirin."

"I don't suppose I did," she said. "I'm not the one who gets headaches."

"Right," he mumbled. "I'm a getter, in a family of givers."

Mother turned up the volume on the radio.

"Yakety Yak" blared from the speaker. Daddy turned the dial to the news again.

A newscaster said the name Duncan.

Daddy shushed us all even though no one had said anything. I sat forward. Daddy turned up the volume.

"Mrs. Elizabeth Duncan, mother-in-law of missing nurse Olga Duncan, was arrested this afternoon at her home in Santa Barbara on charges of forgery and fraud for obtaining a fraudulent annulment for her son and his missing wife. It is believed that Mrs. Duncan is also a key figure in the disappearance of the young woman. And now for the national news. . . ."

Daddy pounded on the steering wheel. "I never should have gone today! I knew something was going to break."

The radio announcer continued. "I'm sorry to report that Gordo the Space Monkey did not . . ."

Mother snapped off the radio.

"What's a key figure?" I asked. "Do they know what happened to Olga?"

Betsey leaned forward. "How about Gordo?"

CHAPTER TWENTY-FIVE

EX-BEST FRIENDS

Santa Barbara, California, December 13, 1958

O n Saturday evening after her arrest, Elizabeth Duncan was led into the Santa Barbara DA's office. She wore a loose-fitting, dingy gray jail uniform and an ugly scowl.

"Over there," Lawton said to the escorting officers, indicating the chair next to Thompson. "Cuff one of her hands to the chair and then wait outside."

The DA was anxious to take another crack at Elizabeth Duncan before she got whisked away to Ventura to face the phony-annulment charge. The local press had been hounding him for two days about why he hadn't charged Mrs. Duncan with something . . . anything. Lawton's repeated response to reporters' questions had been "Not enough evidence" or "I have nothing to say," while Olga's friends gave detailed interviews about Mrs. Duncan's campaign of threats and harassment to get her daughter-in-law to leave Frank. Frustrated by the silence coming from official sources, the Santa Barbara papers printed front page stories speculating about the lack of progress with the investigation.

Lawton asked the first question. "What happened to Olga, Mrs. Duncan? We have a couple of witnesses telling us you hired two men to kidnap her. 'Get rid of her' is the phrase we heard."

"The only thing I'm telling you is that I'm innocent and I'm a victim of blackmail." She rubbed the wrist of her cuffed hand. "Where's Frankie? He should be here by now. He's my lawyer. Talk to him." She turned away.

Someone knocked on the door. Hansen stuck his head inside. "Sorry we're late. Hit some traffic on the grade coming back from LA. Some trucker lost his brakes again. Ready for us?"

"Join the party," Lawton said.

The detective held the door open and guided Mrs. Short inside. "Everything's going to be fine," he whispered in her ear. "She's handcuffed, and I'm right here beside you."

Mrs. Short took a step backward. "I'll stand."

Mrs. Duncan stretched her free arm across the table. "For God's sake, Emma, what are you doing here?"

"They made me," Mrs. Short mumbled. She kept her eyes on the floor.

Mrs. Duncan looked wild-eyed at Hansen. "What did you do to her?"

Mrs. Short said, "Betty, I—"

"Don't say anything. Don't you say anything until you've talked to a lawyer. Haven't I always told you never to talk to the police without a lawyer present?"

Mrs. Short finally looked up. "Don't worry, Betty. No harm will come to you if you just tell the truth. We have to help them prosecute those boys from the Tropical. *They're* the ones who got rid of Olga."

Mrs. Duncan screamed, "Stop it, Emma!"

Mrs. Short dropped into the chair Hansen was holding for her. "I had to tell the truth. They made me take a lie detector test."

"Shut up. Shut up right now."

The DA raised his voice. "Let's talk about the meeting with Baldonado and Moya at the Tropical."

"I already told you about that meeting," Mrs. Duncan snapped. "That's when Mrs. Esquivel got those two thugs to threaten me if I didn't give her back the five hundred dollars she paid Frankie for defending her husband."

Mrs. Short shook her head. "I already told them how those boys were supposed to take Olga to Mexico and get rid of her."

Mrs. Duncan leaped out of her chair but was yanked back by the handcuff chain. "Those are lies! Filthy lies." She kept jerking at her handcuff. "She's a crazy old woman. Doesn't know what she's saying half the time."

"I passed the test, Betty." Mrs. Short eyed the handcuff on her ex-friend's wrist. "The machine detected that I was telling the truth."

"You didn't have to do that. It's a trick. They're trying to trick you."

Everyone turned to the sound of angry voices outside the office. The door flew open, and Frank Duncan burst into the room, a uniformed deputy right behind him. "Sorry, boss. I couldn't stop him."

DA Lawton waved the deputy off. "Nothing to worry about. We've been waiting for Mr. Duncan to arrive." He stood. "Glad you can join us, counselor. Pull up a chair. We were just about to get started."

Frank remained standing. "There's not going to be any interview."

"No problem." Lawton sat down. "We've been interviewing Mrs. Short here."

Mrs. Duncan opened her mouth.

Frank put up his hand. "Don't say anything, Mother."

"But—"

"Nothing. We'll talk later." Frank surveyed the room. "Since when are the Santa Barbara DA and the Santa Barbara Police Department interested in an alleged fraudulent annulment in Ventura County?"

"We just wanted to check on a few details about your wife's disappearance before your mother left for Ventura, that's all." Lawton produced a toothy grin.

"Emma's helping them," Mrs. Duncan said through clenched teeth. "She's telling lies."

"Mother. Enough."

Mrs. Short said, "I told them how Betty hired two boys to get rid of Olga."

Frank spun around to look at the old woman for the first time. "What did you say?"

"The boys were supposed to take her to Mexico." Mrs. Short shifted her gaze nervously between the DA and Frank Duncan. "No harm was supposed to come to her. They were just going to pack her bags and take her on a trip. Like a vacation. No harm was to come to her. I believe they said that." Mrs. Short patted her chest. "Ahmmm. I feel like I'm catching something."

Frank snapped his head toward his mother.

"It's a lie!" Mrs. Duncan yelled. "It's a filthy lie!"

Frank closed his eyes.

Lawton stood up and spoke sharply to Frank Duncan. "I'll have the guards take your mother to an interview room. You can talk to her before they transport her down to Ventura."

When he was alone with Detective Thompson, the DA reached into the desk drawer for a pack of Lucky Strikes. "You hear Mrs. Short changing her story at the end? A *vacation*? Jesus." He jabbed a cigarette into his mouth. "Think we learned anything new from that little drama?"

Thompson shrugged.

The DA lit his cigarette, took a long drag, and blew out the smoke. "Although I will say, I think it was quite enlightening for Frank Duncan."

CHAPTER TWENTY-SIX

GETTING INTO HEAVEN

Ventura, California, December 13-14, 1958

W
e didn't get home until after nine that night. My father went straight to his office and shut the door. I lingered in the hallway, listening as he talked on the phone.

"Secret witness?" he exclaimed, but then he lowered his voice. I opened the door a crack to hear better, but he saw me and yelled at me to go to bed.

I couldn't fall asleep. When I closed my eyes, I saw the overturned truck, windshield shattered, huge double tires rising into the air. It looked like a giant turtle flipped on its back. The image of the accident site moved by in slow motion. Flattened pieces of cars, bumpers, and fenders, some of them scorched, lay near the red glowing flares scattered along the roadway marking the trail of destruction.

I yawned and turned over. "Secret witness?" I mumbled as I drifted off to the clicking sound of Daddy's typewriter keys coming from across the hallway.

I awoke late on Sunday with barely enough time to dress for church. I put on my purple plaid wool skirt and yellow sweater set because they were still lying across the chair where I'd thrown them after school on Friday.

I called out, "I'm going."

Daddy poked his head through the kitchen doorway. "Where?"

"Sunday school at the Baptist church. I told you last night. Remember?"

He shrugged a shoulder.

"The lesson this week is called 'Getting into Heaven.' I don't want to miss it."

He nodded absently. "Right." He had a box of cornflakes in his hand and shook it near his ear to see if there was any cereal left.

"Mother said that you're taking me to pick up Tweety after I get home from church. I can hardly wait to see him."

Daddy looked toward the kitchen sink. "Yeah, well, I've got to put in the new garbage disposal today. Your mother wants it by Christmas dinner, so she'll have to take you to get Tweety."

I slipped out the front door, ran across the neighbors' lawns, and reached the corner out of breath. Black smoke belched from the tailpipe of the old green Baptist Sunday school bus as it slowed at the curb. After I boarded, the driver ground the gearshift into first, and with a shudder and another blast of smoke that wafted up to the back window, the bus rumbled down the road toward salvation.

When I got home, Daddy was in the kitchen staring at some tools he'd put on the floor near the sink.

"Where's Mother?" I asked.

He didn't look up. "She went down to the hotel to get the bird."

"I was supposed to go with her," I complained.

Daddy rolled a screwdriver around in his hands. "She'll be back soon."

I looked down at Daddy's tools and then at a cardboard box sitting on the kitchen floor. The word In-Sink-Erator was printed on the side of the carton in bold black letters. "Does Mother know what you're doing?"

"I'm surprising her."

I sat at the table, moved aside a bowl of soggy cornflakes swimming in a pool of milk, and picked up the morning newspaper. The headline read:

KEY WITNESS GIVES DA VALUABLE INFORMATION. According to the story, "A witness has made information available to investigators regarding the whereabouts of Olga Duncan, and the witness is being held at a secret location because she fears for her safety."

Secret! This must be the person I heard Daddy talking about on the phone last night.

The article also said that Olga's mother-in-law, Elizabeth Duncan, had been arrested for obtaining a fake annulment for her son and his missing wife.

Daddy was standing in front of the kitchen sink scratching his head. He frequently started his projects with a long period of head-scratching. He said it helped him become better acquainted with the problem.

"What's an annulment?" I asked.

He fingered some screws he'd taken out of the carton. "It means the court says the marriage was never valid."

"So what's that got to do with Olga disappearing?"

Before he could answer, Mother walked through the back door. Her hands were empty, her face pinched. She chewed on her lower lip as she glanced at me and then away.

"Where's Tweety?" I asked.

Her gaze bounced around the kitchen until she zeroed in on the In-Sink-Erator box.

"What do you think you're doing, Bob?"

"Surprise! I'm installing 'Jack,'" he said. He always tried to make a joke when he had his tools out. He'd started calling the disposal 'Jack the Ripper' after he first opened the box and cut his finger on a staple in the safety instruction manual. Then he lost interest and left it all sitting in the garage for a month.

Mother sank into one of the kitchen chairs.

I got up from the table, walked to the door, and stuck my head outside. "Is Tweety still in the car?"

"Ummm . . ." Mother said.

"Where is he?"

She put her hand over her mouth and shook her head. "I'm so sorry, dear. There seems to have been a, well, a mishap."

I raised my voice. "A mishap?"

Daddy groaned. "Oh, God, Lois. I knew something would go wrong."

I looked back and forth between my parents' faces. "You said he would be fine. 'Nothing to worry about,' you said."

Daddy gazed at the floor. "I don't think I want to hear this."

Mother reached out to touch my arm.

"What happened?" I wailed.

"Well . . ." Mother looked toward Daddy, but he was fiddling with the In-Sink-Erator box. "I think you should sit down, dear." She patted the chair next to hers.

I didn't move. "Where is he?"

She grimaced. "Bird heaven?"

"What?" I screamed. "He's dead? He can't be. You promised."

Mother looked toward the driveway. "Beth must have stopped taking her medication. . . . I don't know. . . . The hotel manager said she'd been complaining that Tweety was talking to her and that he could read her mind. . . . Last night, Beth went screaming down the stairs with her hands over her ears. She yelled something about Tweety being sent by the hospital to control her brain."

I slumped down in the chair to cry.

"So what happened to the bird?" Daddy said.

"The manager found him in his cage. He wasn't, you know . . ."

"Chirping?" Daddy said.

I covered my face. "No!" I wailed. "She killed Tweety! Anybody could see she was crazy. She wore those long black gloves." As I ran out of the kitchen, I screamed at Mother, "I hate you!"

I had mostly stopped crying, except for some intermittent hiccupping breaths, when I heard the bedroom door open. I lay crosswise on the top bunk, staring with unseeing eyes at the ceiling. Daddy stood on the first rung of the ladder and put his hand on my shoulder. I shrugged it away, scooted myself toward the wall, and put the pillow over my head.

"Your mother feels terrible about what happened," he said.

"It's her fault," I said in a muffled voice. "She made me leave Tweety in that stinky old hotel with a murderer."

"*Murder* is a little harsh," he mumbled. "Maybe diminished capacity, or bird slaughter?"

I sat up and used my hand to swipe at my tears. "Don't joke. This is your fault, too. You called Beth a lunatic. You knew it was a bad idea, but you said that you 'didn't have time to worry about some nutcase bird babysitter.'" I flung myself back onto the bed and sobbed.

Daddy patted my shoulder. "Shh, shh, I'm sorry. I know that this is very serious, but sometimes parents make mistakes."

"Mother didn't care about Tweety. All Mother cared about was Beth." I gulped for air in between words and sobs. "I should call those humane people that Mother's always giving money to and tell them about this."

"Your mother is very, very upset about what happened. She's in the other room crying, too."

I sat up again. "She is?" I sniveled. "Crying?"

"You need to apologize for saying that you hate her. You don't hate your mother."

I made a sad face.

Daddy pulled his crumpled gray-white handkerchief out of his pants pocket and handed it to me.

I blew my nose. The handkerchief smelled like pencil lead and newsprint.

"Mother didn't mean for any of this to happen."

I sniveled some more. "Can we bury Tweety in the backyard with Cinderella?"

Daddy stammered, "I'm afraid there's no, uh, *corpus delicti*."

"What?"

"The hotel manager disposed of Tweety."

I sat up again. "Disposed?"

"Don't worry about that, sweetheart. Tweety has gone away . . ." He sucked air through gritted teeth. "To a better place."

"Heaven?"

"I think so." Daddy bit his lip. "Tweety was a happy bird. I've seen paintings with little birds hovering around the angels in heaven."

I brightened. "Horses go to heaven. I heard Reverend Ralston say that chariots of fire, pulled by horses, carried someone to heaven." I blew my nose again. "But being happy doesn't get you into heaven, does it? There's all these rules you need to follow. Today, the Sunday school teacher told us that we have to believe Jesus died for our sins and rose from the grave to go to heaven."

"But I think happiness must be very important to God," Daddy said. "Happy people do the most good in the world. It's the unhappy ones who cause all the trouble."

Mother stuck her head into the bedroom as she knocked gently on the partway open door. Her nose was red. "I'm so sorry about Tweety, dear."

Daddy nudged my leg.

"Sorry," I said in a petulant tone. "I don't really *hate* you."

Daddy nudged my leg again. I slid down the ladder.

Mother hugged me. I put my head on her shoulder and cried quietly.

"Looks like you two don't need me anymore." Daddy said. "I've got some work to do."

"Not the garbage disposal, Bob. It can wait." Mother patted my back. "We've had enough trouble already today."

"I have to work on my—"

"Don't write about this in your column," Mother and I cried in unison.

"I never make light of family tragedies," he said, all huffy.

"You wrote about Chirpy. You said he was 'dead as a doornail.'"

Daddy gazed into the distance. "Fine, fine with me. I've got plenty of other things to do since they arrested Elizabeth Duncan." He started inching toward the door. "She's being arraigned on the fraudulent-annulment charges tomorrow morning. Good thing they got her before she tried to make a run for it."

I broke away from Mother's arms. "Why don't you tell the police to arrest Beth?"

My parents glanced at each other.

"Beth took off, and no one knows where she is." Daddy wiggled his eyebrows up and down. "Must have been something Tweety said that scared her away."

"Bob!"

CHAPTER TWENTY-SEVEN

PUT UP OR SHUT UP

Santa Barbara, California, December 15, 1958

Lieutenant Peck called Hansen at home early Monday morning. "I've got a blood-and-fingerprint expert from LAPD coming up this morning to process the car Baldonado supposedly borrowed. I need you to meet him at the impound yard."

Hansen pulled himself out of bed.

"If he finds anything, we'll call the press," Peck continued. "Let them take pictures, tell them it 'might' be connected to the disappearance of Olga Duncan. That ought to get them off our backs about progress in the investigation."

Hansen yawned. "They'll go crazy."

"It could help the case, you know. Get the public more involved. Maybe somebody will remember seeing the car around the time the nurse disappeared."

An hour later, while Hansen was watching the expert take samples from the rust bucket at the impound yard in Santa Barbara, his partner Charlie Thompson was thirty miles to the south, marching up the steep sidewalk leading to the Ventura County Courthouse. The white Beaux Arts–style building, with its hundred-foot Doric columns, Roman-arched windows, and copper dome and cupola, perched like a massive stone villa on a hillside above California Street.

Thompson paused at the top of the hill to catch his breath. He listened to the sounds of a train crossing the trestle near the shore and the ever-present cry of seagulls and then turned west, toward the sweeping view of the Pacific Ocean. He was there in case he had to testify at the phony-annulment arraignment hearing for Elizabeth Duncan.

Santa Barbara DA Vern Lawton had called him earlier that morning. "Gustafson wants to meet with you after Mrs. Duncan's hearing. Just make it short. Tell him the basics, but don't waste too much time down there. We need you here. We've *got* to find the body. Those hacks at the *News Press* . . . they're killing us, and those SOBs in the Ventura district attorney's office are a bunch of glory hounds." Lawton blasted a shaky breath into the phone. "We just *have* to find her body, that's all."

The detective passed the ten-foot-tall concrete statue of Father Junipero Serra that loomed over the walkway at the front of the building. The Roman Catholic priest had established missions throughout California, including Ventura's San Buenaventura Mission in 1782. Hansen continued up the wide steps to the courthouse door. He stopped at the top of the stairs and stood beside a giant white stone pillar at the courthouse entrance. He cupped his hand around a cigarette as he lit up. When he straightened again, he stared down California Street toward the ocean and the pier. Men with fishing poles dotted the pier railings near the bait shop's faded green canopy. Pelicans flew in a V formation along the water's edge, dipping down to skim across the whitecaps, gliding on the warm breeze that blew offshore from the east.

Thompson searched the vast landscape north toward Santa Barbara. *Where are you, Olga?* He took another drag on his cigarette. *Screw Vern Lawton. I'm telling these Ventura guys everything we know. Olga Duncan's been missing for a month. If Gustafson and his guys can figure out what happened to her, more power to 'em.*

A man wearing a bow tie and a rumpled sports jacket hurried up the wide concrete steps, humming a few bars of "It's Beginning to Look a Lot Like Christmas."

"Hey, Bob," Thompson said.

Bob Holt stopped humming in the middle of the "everywhere you go" stanza and sidled up to the detective. "You're here about this crazy annulment scheme?"

"Right. In case I have to testify."

Bob nodded. "Gustafson put out the word to the local press about the hearing last night. Likes to get his name in the paper. You got anything new up in Santa Barbara?"

Thompson glanced around. "I think we found the car. A guy we picked up on a traffic stop says he loaned it to Baldonado the day before Olga disappeared."

Bob pulled a little spiral notebook out of his breast pocket. "Guy's name?"

"Can't tell you that yet."

"How about the make and year?"

Thompson made a face. "Old rusted '48 Chevy sedan." He lowered his voice. "But get this: It looks like someone tried to get rid of bloodstains in the back seat. Burned the upholstery and ripped some of it out."

Bob raised his eyebrows as he scribbled something in his notebook. "Anything more on the mother-in-law's blackmail claim?"

"No comment, but . . ." Thompson lowered his voice to a whisper. "We can't thank her enough for reporting that little fantasy to us. You can tell your readers it might be the key to cracking this case."

"What about Frank? You think maybe Olga gave him an ultimatum? Threatened to divorce him?"

"No evidence. Her friends say she still loved the guy."

Bob nodded as he wrote a few more words. "I owe you one," he said as he slipped the notebook into his pocket.

"I appreciate you getting the facts right in your stories. Not clouding the issues with a bunch of bullshit. Plus, I just want to get these guys. We need all the help we can get. Maybe someone saw something that night and doesn't realize the importance yet."

"I'll put out the word."

Thompson reached for the heavy wooden door and held it open. "But anonymous sources, right?"

"Every time." Bob resumed humming his Christmas song as he stepped into the courthouse.

Thompson dropped his cigarette to the pavement and followed the reporter inside and up the elegant stairway to the second floor. The courtroom was at the top of the stairs, the sheriff's office at one end of the long marble-floored hallway, the district attorney's office at the other.

There were plenty of seats available in the dark mahogany-paneled courtroom. Thompson sat down in the first row of wooden chairs, just behind the prosecution table. Frank Duncan fidgeted in his chair across the aisle at the defense table as he rifled through a stack of papers. A lock of dark hair hung over his forehead.

Woodruff Deem, chief deputy district attorney, turned around. "You Thompson?"

The detective nodded.

"I'll only have to call you today if the judge needs convincing when it comes time to set bail." He was taking papers out of his briefcase while he talked. "Never know with Judge Heaton. Just sit tight. And don't leave when the hearing's done. I'll be taking you back to the boss's office. He's got a lot of questions."

Thompson sat back, stretched out his legs, and scanned the courtroom. The only spectators were a few regular court watchers and a half dozen or so members of the press. Bob Holt sat in a row by himself, behind a group of reporters from Santa Barbara and Oxnard. His jaw set, his eyes focused on the notebook on his knee, he wasn't humming anymore.

Mrs. Duncan was led into the courtroom wearing the gray jail uniform. Her usually immaculately styled hair drooped. The matron removed her handcuffs, and she started whispering furiously to Frank the second she sat down at the table.

The only thing Thompson picked up was Frank's repeated refrain after every barrage of words: "Let me handle this, Mother."

Judge Heaton entered the courtroom and called court to order. Mrs. Duncan was formally charged with four counts of fraud related to the phony annulment. She and Frank stood before the judge. Frank whispered in his mother's ear. She immediately stood straighter and quit glaring at the prosecutor.

The judge asked for her plea. Before Frank could answer, his mother shouted, "Not guilty."

The rest of the short hearing was taken up with arguments over bail. The assistant DA stood up. "The people request that bail be set at $100,000."

Frank popped out of his seat. "That's outrageous, Your Honor. My moth—I mean, my client has no criminal history and is a long-standing member of the community of Santa Barbara, where she has lived for over ten years until she was dragged down here and thrown in jail."

The judge motioned for Frank to sit down. "In a moment, counselor. Let the prosecution finish."

"As I was about to tell the court, Mrs. Duncan's daughter-in-law, Olga Duncan, has been missing for a month. The Santa Barbara authorities have witnesses who say Mrs. Duncan threatened to kill her daughter-in-law on numerous occasions."

Frank stood up. "I object, Your Honor. There's no evidence. He's just—"

"Sit down, Mr. Duncan," the judge said.

Deem continued. "The Santa Barbara Police have evidence that links this defendant to the disappearance of her son's wife. The investigation isn't complete, and we're extremely concerned that she might be a flight risk if she's released on bail."

Frank flew out of his chair again. "Pure speculation and totally unrelated to this case."

The judge banged his gavel. Frank sat down. The judge turned back to the prosecutor.

"I have a detective in the courtroom from the Santa Barbara Police Department." Deem glanced over his shoulder at Thompson. "He's ready to testify about the information I just referred to."

The judge eyed Thompson for a moment and looked over at Frank. "Proceed, counselor."

Frank addressed the court. "My client is not a flight risk. She has multiple ties to this community. She has no history of serious crimes."

The judge raised his eyebrows. "I thought you just said '*no* criminal history.'"

Deem opened a file folder on the table in front of him. "She was arrested for solicitation in San Francisco."

Mrs. Duncan stuck out her chin.

Reporters mumbled to each other in the press section.

"Misunderstanding," Frank said.

"And then there's the arrest on check forgery," Deem said in an even tone. "Convicted in 1938."

"These aren't the kind of things that should affect bail in this matter. These"—Frank seemed to be searching for a word—"situations . . . occurred a long time ago. My client has had an unblemished record for years. She is an upstanding citizen."

Judge Heaton picked up some papers from the bench and tapped them square. "Bail is set for $50,000."

Mrs. Duncan gasped. Frank's shoulders slumped. Deem turned to smile at Thompson.

"But I'm going to set another hearing for"—the judge thumbed through his calendar—"December 17th. That's the day after tomorrow. I'll hear arguments about a bail reduction at that time."

Bob cornered Frank on his way out of the courtroom. "You think the bail amount is unfair, Mr. Duncan?"

"For falsification of a legal document? Forgery of a signature? You've got to be kidding me. Fifty thousand dollars is ridiculous. Accused armed robbers get out for less than that."

Two more reporters stepped up. One said, "The DA just told the judge that there's a witness who says your mother threatened to kill your wife. Have you anything to say about that?"

"The Ventura DA's on a fishing expedition for his friends in Santa Barbara. It's time the authorities in Santa Barbara either put up or shut up. If they've got any proof or evidence, then let them bring it to court and file charges."

"What's your own theory on your wife's disappearance?" a reporter in the back called out.

"I've heard so many stories . . . blackmail, the extortion plot . . . I just don't know." Frank scanned the faces of the reporters and continued in a halting voice. "My mother would be insane to be involved in this . . . this insanity. I don't recall her ever being cruel in any sense."

He elbowed his way through the growing crowd of reporters. "If you'll excuse me, gentlemen. I need to go arrange bail for my mother."

Deem took Thompson down the hallway to the district attorney's office.

"I ought to warn you. The boss is *very* interested in this case. He thinks Olga Duncan was murdered, and murder is his specialty. Gustafson's got three death penalty convictions under his belt."

"Okay," Thompson said as they walked along the marble floor. "But Olga was kidnapped up in Santa Barbara. We believe her body isn't far from where she disappeared."

The deputy DA shrugged. "Gustafson thinks he can help solve the case. He wants to nail whoever took this girl. It's all personal with him."

Roy Gustafson was on the telephone when Deem and Thompson entered his office. Two men were sitting in straight-back chairs on either side of the DA's desk.

"I'm telling you, Phillips," Gustafson said into the phone, "you put up bail for that Duncan woman, you're going to lose all of it. She's going to skip. She'll be facing a murder charge in a week, and she's not going to be sticking around with the kind of evidence we've got."

Thompson smiled to himself as he waited in the doorway. *My kind of guy. Plays hardball.*

Gustafson drummed his fingers on his desk. "Right. Anybody who puts up money for the Duncans will lose their shirt. Spread the word, Saul."

The Ventura district attorney hung up, stood, and extended his hand toward Thompson. Gustafson was a tall, thin man with slightly stooped shoulders. Known in his office as a relentless taskmaster, he'd held the office of district attorney for eight years, having been the youngest district attorney ever elected in the county. At age forty, he'd just begun his third term. No one had run against him in the last election.

Gustafson introduced the men in the chairs. "My investigators, Clarence Henderson and Tommy Osborne. Nobody better in the state. Couldn't prosecute a case without them."

Both Thompson and Deem remained standing.

The DA rubbed his hands together. "Let's get started."

"We got bail set at $50,000," Deem said.

"I heard, but even if Frank comes up with some money, I don't think he's going to find a bondsman in Ventura to do business with."

"Boss just took care of that," the investigator named Osborne said.

Gustafson turned to Thompson. "Tell me what you've got on Ma Duncan."

Thompson recounted everything the SBPD had turned up so far: the supposed blackmail scheme, Mrs. Short's and Mrs. Esquivel's statements about Mrs. Duncan hiring Moya and Baldonado, Mrs. Esquivel seeing the men at her house the night Olga disappeared, washing blood off their clothes.

"Blood?" repeated Clarence Henderson, Gustafson's chief investigator.

"Blood all over their clothes." Thompson took some folded papers out of his breast pocket and held them toward the DA. "I brought some of the reports."

Osborne reached for the paperwork. "I'll take those, boss. Start making notes."

"I'll need to get those back before I leave," Thompson said.

Gustafson swiveled in his chair. "What's the latest on Moya and Baldonado?"

Henderson answered. "Moya's still in Santa Barbara on the probation hold, but we got Gus Baldonado down here. SBPD picked him up early this morning on a 'failure to support' charge, but since the ex-wife lives here in Ventura County, he's with us now. Got him in a cell next door."

Gustafson leaned back. "Anything else you want to tell us, Detective Thompson?"

"Mrs. Short thinks the men were supposed to take Olga to Mexico, but Mrs. Esquivel says they were back at her house covered with blood a few hours after Olga disappeared." Thompson tilted his head. "Can't get from Santa Barbara to Mexico and back in a couple of hours, and I don't think either woman is holding back. They just don't know what these guys did with her."

All of the men were silent a moment. Gustafson pushed his glasses onto his forehead. "Seems to me we aren't going to be able to find her body without the cooperation of the killers. We need the weak link." He pinched the bridge of his nose. "Which one do we think is most likely to break?"

Thompson was quick with his response. "Definitely not Mrs. Duncan. Every word that comes out of her mouth is a lie. You catch her on one thing, and she just comes up with a new lie to cover the first one."

"I wasn't thinking about her," Gustafson said. "She's got her son telling her to keep her mouth shut. What about Moya or Baldonado? Either of them have a lawyer yet?"

"Not Moya. He's still in the Santa Barbara jail."

"Neither one has the dough to hire a lawyer," Henderson said. "And there's no question in my mind who the weak link is. Baldonado is dumber than a box of rocks."

"Okay. We got a place to start." Gustafson pushed his glasses back onto his nose. "Henderson, you and Tommy get started right away on Baldonado before he gets his hands on any legal advice."*

---

* There was no requirement for a Miranda warning in 1958, and attorneys weren't appointed for defendants until they were formally charged with a crime.

CHAPTER TWENTY-EIGHT

OUR CIVIC RESPONSIBILITY

Ventura, California, December 17, 1958

S hut up. I'm getting it, you little bastards."

I propped myself up on one elbow and yawned, listening to the commotion coming from the kitchen. Daddy was feeding the cats breakfast. Not just Pinky Lee but also a scrawny black cat we called the Panther, who flitted from tree limb to tree limb in the backyard during the day, and a beat-up yellow tomcat known as Old Yowler. The two strays were in the early stages of worming their way into our family.

"Goddammit," my father yelled. "Now look what you made me do. I'm bleeding, you son of a bitch."

Sometimes when he used the can opener, Daddy nicked his finger on the ragged edges of the lid. A cat yowled and a cupboard door slammed shut. I sat up and swung my legs out of bed and stumbled into the kitchen, still rubbing my eyes. The yellow cat paced and glanced furtively in my direction while the other two circled Daddy's feet, bleating and pleading. Pinky Lee hissed at the intruders as he waited for the food.

Daddy lowered three small paper plates filled with cat food to the floor. "There, that ought to shut you up for a while." He threw the empty can in the trash container under the sink as the cats gobbled down the meal.

"What are you doing up early?" he asked me.

"I need to find a current event for school." I yawned.

My father settled himself at the kitchen table and picked up a newspaper.

"Are you going to the courthouse today for Mrs. Duncan's bail lowering hearing?"

The cats finished gulping down their feast and sauntered to the back door, high tails swishing, shrilly demanding to be let out.

Daddy nodded absently as he read. "Yeah, should be quite a circus." He glanced at the clock and folded the paper. He heaved himself out of the chair, dumped the rest of his coffee in the sink, and opened the back door for the cats. "Mrs. Alfred will be here soon. She'll make you some oatmeal. I've got to get going."

"Do you think the judge will let her out of jail?"

"Hard to say. Plus, Frank will still have to find a bail bondsman around here to post her bond." He put his hand on my shoulder. "Lois!" he called out. "Mrs. Alfred's going to have to make the oatmeal. I'm late!" He turned back to me and tapped the paper he'd folded on the table with his index finger. "And don't cut any holes in this. I may need it later."

I sat at the table in the empty kitchen eating dry Honey Smacks, sipping a glass of cold milk mixed with chocolate Nestlé's Quik and reading Daddy's paper. I held scissors in one hand as I searched for a story to take to school. Civic responsibility was the topic of the week.

An article caught my eye: Authorities in Santa Barbara were asking for the cooperation of all citizens to report any suspicious activity on the night of November 17th that might be connected to the disappearance of Olga Duncan. A man from Summerland had already come forward. He'd seen a car parked along Casitas Pass Road and two men climbing up to the road from an embankment in the early hours of the morning after Olga Duncan disappeared.

Wow! That's a good example of civic responsibility, someone trying to help the police find Olga.

I checked the other side of the page. Only an advertisement for a Christmas tree lot. We already had a tree, so I clipped out the article. *Even Miss Peterson will have to admit that this is an appropriate current event.*

At school, fifteen minutes before the dismissal bell sounded, Miss Peterson stood at the front of the classroom in a yellow gingham shirtwaist dress, collecting the SRA Reading Lab cards and answer sheets. She told my row to get their current event articles out of their desks. I smoothed the edges of my clipping, which included Olga's picture.

The teacher called on Angela first. "What do you have for us today about civic responsibility?"

"I have an article about a pageant at the Civic Center in Ojai."

Miss Peterson picked up her red pencil and began scanning the SRA answer sheets while she listened.

"There will be a 'Living Nativity' scene in Ojai tonight and tomorrow commemorating the birth of Christ," Angela read from her clipping. "It's sponsored by the Baptist Church and the Ojai Chamber of Commerce, with two showings each night, one at seven o'clock and another at eight thirty."

Miss Peterson frowned. "And how is that related to civic responsibility, dear?"

"My mother says that the Chamber of Commerce is a civic organization and, well, it's at the Civic Center."

"I see." Miss Peterson fiddled her pencil back and forth. "Maybe you can give us more information about that."

Angela bit her lip. She ran her index finger down the article. "'This year, the Chamber of Commerce has become involved with the pageant, and the public response has been greater than I ever dreamed,' said the Reverend Gene Vaught, director of the pageant. 'All of the wise men are portrayed by Chamber members.'"

Miss Peterson pursed her mouth. "Thank you, dear. Put your article in the assignment basket. Name and date, please." She scanned the row. "Next?"

I raised my hand and popped out of my seat. Miss Peterson nodded.

I read from the article. "The Santa Barbara Police and the district attorney released a statement yesterday asking for the cooperation of anyone knowing anything about the disappearance of Olga Duncan, the missing nurse." I glanced sideways at Miss Peterson. She was looking down at her desk, her red pencil poised midair over the papers.

I turned back to the class. "It's our civic responsibility to help the police whenever possible. We need to keep our eyes peeled for Olga." I held up the article and slowly moved Olga's picture from left to right so everyone could see. "A man already reported that he saw two men out on Casitas Pass Road late at night after Olga disappeared. Very suspicious."

Miss Peterson propped her chin on her hands. She sighed. "Thank you, Debby, that's enough. We need to clean up before the bell."

"Also," I said really fast, "they have Olga's mother-in-law in jail here in Ventura for something. I don't really know about that exactly . . . 'nulment or fraud, but anyway, a man from the DA's office said, 'There are indications that more serious charges may be filed against Mrs. Duncan in Santa Barbara.'" I heard the teacher's chair scrape on the linoleum. "One of the reporters asked, 'What indications?' And the assistant prosecutor said, 'When we have a suspected murder case, we don't give hints.'"

Somebody gasped. Probably Angela.

I waved my hand in a 'no-no' motion. "But Olga's not dead. That guy doesn't know what he's talking about. He's only the *assistant* DA. A helper." I saw a flash of yellow gingham.

Miss Peterson stood next to me with her hand out.

"I need to put my name on it," I mumbled.

The teacher tapped her foot as I pulled a pencil out of my desk, and I kept talking. "So we must all do our civic responsibility and help the police. We have to find Olga as soon as possible." I scribbled my name across the headline and handed her the article.

Angela put her hands over her ears. "My mother doesn't want me thinking about that nurse disappearing."

"That's enough," Miss Peterson said to me in a stern tone. "Get ready for the bell, class."

I sat down.

Eddie swiveled around in his chair and leaned over my desk. His breath smelled like peanut butter. "I'd like to find a body."

CHAPTER TWENTY-NINE

PITIFUL

Santa Barbara, California,
December 19, 1958

On Friday night, Investigator Clarence Henderson arrived at the Ventura DA office's Christmas party late and rumpled. He'd come directly from the jail after the latest round of questioning Baldonado. He scanned the crowded room at the Pierpont Inn for his boss.

Some of the partygoers were still in their chairs, joking and laughing over dessert at tables strewn with green garlands and white-tipped pinecones. Roy Gustafson watched from a table next to a tinsel-covered tree and discreetly lifted his palm toward Henderson. Both men headed for the bar.

Only one stool stood empty, at the far end, near a window that overlooked the coast road and the beach beyond. It was dark outside; headlights and taillights coming and going were visible along the roadway.

Gustafson told Henderson to sit. The smaller man hoisted himself up on the stool with his back to the window. The room was noisy. The voices of the usual Saturday night drinkers mixed with the sounds of Christmas music and laughter drifting in from the DA's office party.

"Has Frank bailed his mother out of jail yet?" Gustafson asked.

"Nope. She's still in her cell even though the judge lowered the bail to $5,000. None of the bondsmen will put up their money. You really spooked them, boss. Everybody's afraid she'll skip."

Gustafson smiled. "And how are things going with Baldonado?"

Henderson shook his head as the bartender put down the drinks. "We've been talking to him off and on for three days now. We get close. . . . He admits that Mrs. Duncan propositioned him and Moya to get rid of Olga, but he claims they refused." Henderson downed half of his drink. "I thought he was going to give it up a couple of times. Today he blurted out that he 'had a secret' . . . and said, 'Whatever comes out, comes out,' but says he can't say anything."

Gustafson raised his eyebrows. "'Whatever comes out, comes out?'"

"Yeah, but nothing more helpful comes out of his mouth. Osborne told him that we have witnesses who say he and Moya killed Olga Duncan, hoped that might loosen his tongue, but Baldonado clammed up." Henderson put his elbow on the bar. "But something did come up that might help."

Gustafson took an almost dainty sip from his drink while he kept his eyes on his investigator.

"There's a deputy at the sheriff's office name of Ray Higgins who worked a beat in Camarillo years ago. He arrested Baldonado a couple of times. Baldonado was just a boy but already in and out of trouble. Higgins says he got along with the kid."

The man sitting next to Henderson got up. Gustafson took his stool.

"Higgins made the connection when he heard one of the other inmates call Baldonado 'T'lene.' Everyone called him T'lene back then . . . short for Augustine."

"And Higgins thinks he can get Baldonado to talk?" Gustafson said.

Henderson nodded. "Higgins is good. He's had a lot of success getting tough criminals to talk."

Gustafson gave his investigator a suspicious look.

"No, nothing rough. Higgins just, I don't know . . . builds trust . . . and he's already got this connection with this prisoner. Remembers the whole

Baldonado family. There were eight kids, and he says they might as well have been raised by wolves for all the care they got. The house was a garbage pit. The kids ran wild all over town. Hungry, stealing food, out all night . . . pitiful." Henderson shook his head. "Higgins arrested the father three or four times for public drunkenness, disorderly conduct. Same thing with the mother. Neighbors called the police all the time. If the old man wasn't slapping the mother around, he was beating the kids."

Gustafson took another sip of his drink. "So Higgins thinks he can convince Baldonado that telling us where Olga is buried would be in his best interest?"

"Yeah."

Both men sat silently for a few moments, heads bowed. Henderson worked on his second drink; Gustafson turned his glass slowly around on the bar top.

"Right now, Baldonado's the only hope for finding Olga," Gustafson finally said. "And Olga can't be in Mexico if Moya and Baldonado were in Mrs. Esquivel's kitchen washing blood off their clothes at two thirty in the morning."

"Not a chance," Henderson agreed. "But Santa Barbara hasn't sent anyone down to talk to Baldonado in a couple of days. Guess they're focusing on Moya."

Gustafson threw his head back and finished his drink. "Get Higgins in there first thing tomorrow to take a crack at Baldonado. He's got no money for an attorney, and I need a confession before somebody gets a lawyer for him."

CHAPTER THIRTY

T'LENE

Santa Barbara, California,
December 20, 1958

The next morning, a guard brought Augustine Baldonado into the ten-by-ten interrogation room with dirty white walls and gray linoleum where DA Investigator Henderson and Ventura County deputy sheriff Ray Higgins waited.

Higgins was an excellent interrogator, but he'd failed the written civil service exam for promotion numerous times, and at the age of forty he still hadn't made detective. Nevertheless, he was a much-admired deputy, a soft-spoken, understanding, and patient man who took crime, especially murders, personally. His identification with the victim and the pain of the victim's family was a huge motivation for him, yet he always played the "good cop" at interrogations.

The guard pushed the prisoner into a chair, took the handcuff off one of his wrists, and reattached it to the metal arm of the chair. There were no windows in the room except for a small pane of glass in the door so the guard could keep an eye on the inmate.

Henderson began the interview by reminding Baldonado, "We got two witnesses say you and your buddy Luis Moya kidnapped and murdered Olga Duncan for her mother-in-law."

"How many times I got to tell you? I got nothing more to say." He looked everywhere but at the faces of his two interrogators. Finally, his gaze rested on the ceiling tiles. "Wonder how many little holes they got in one of those square things up there?"

"Don't think you can count that high," Henderson said.

Higgins exchanged a look with Henderson. "Oh, I don't know about that. I remember T'lene here when he was a smart little boy. Outfoxed me one time."

Baldonado tilted his head forward. A puzzled expression crossed his face.

"That's right, T'lene. Camarillo. Deputy Higgins. Ring a bell? Remember how Mr. Ellis called all the time to say you and your brother were stealing apples from the bin out front of his store?"

Baldonado twisted his mouth to keep from smiling.

"Yeah, you remember." Higgins chuckled, then turned to Henderson. "I never could get the goods on those boys, though. By the time I caught up with them, I couldn't find a thing. Those Baldonado boys always got away with it."

Henderson made a sour face.

"What'd you do with those apples, anyway?" Higgins asked. "Where'd you hide them?"

Baldonado bit his lip. "It's a secret." He burst out laughing. "We ate the evidence."

Higgins laughed a little, too. "Well, you really got me all right. Too bad I didn't have any corroborating witnesses back then. Might have been different."

None of the men spoke for a moment. Sounds from the jail—shouting voices, clanging metal doors—grew louder in the quiet of the little room.

Higgins stopped smiling. "But we got a witness now, T'lene. Mrs. Esquivel says you had blood on your clothes the night Olga Duncan disappeared."

Baldonado shifted his gaze from Higgins to Henderson. "You got nothin'."

"We got Mrs. Esquivel, and Mrs. Short, too," Higgins said. "They both say the same thing: you kidnapped Olga and got rid of her for Mrs. Duncan. Come on, T'lene, tell us what you did with Olga's body."

Baldonado hunched his shoulders. "Nothing. I told you. I didn't even know that woman. Why would I do something like that?"

"Money," Henderson said.

Baldonado laughed and then stopped abruptly. His gaze zigzagged around the closed-up little room. "You're crazy. Whatever comes out, comes out. That's all I got to say. I want to go back to my cell."

After the guard took Baldonado away, Henderson tossed his pencil onto the table. "Well, that was productive."

Higgins looked sideways toward the door that led back to the jail. "Wait until tomorrow."

CHAPTER THIRTY-ONE

MISTLETOE

Ventura, California,
December 19-20, 1958

Lying on my stomach across the bed, I opened my pink plastic treasure box to take out the "Merry Christmas Sweetheart" card Jimmy had slipped into my desk during our class Christmas party the day before.

When Miss Peterson had called for us to get ready for the bell, I'd opened my desk to get my math book out. Mother wanted me to practice long division over Christmas vacation. My hand stopped in midair when I spotted a long red envelope with my name, first and last, written in ornate cursive letters. I took the big oblong card out of the envelope. "Merry Christmas Sweetheart" was printed across the top—"Sweetheart" in red velveteen—and "Love Jim" underneath. I looked toward Jimmy. He was grinning at me and wiggling a candy cigarette between his lips. Eddie had passed the candy out to boys only during the class party.

My face burned. I ducked my head behind my raised desktop while I shoved the card back in the envelope and stuck it inside the pocket of my binder. "Boys are so . . . stupid," I muttered and peeked around the desktop.

A dark lock of hair fell across Jimmy's freckled forehead as he sucked on his candy cigarette. I watched while he pretended to blow smoke from the side of his mouth, and then he ate the cigarette.

At home that evening, I turned on my back in my bed, adjusted the pillow behind my head, and examined my prize again. This time I noticed that although the words *To* and *From Jimmy* were written on the front of the red envelope in ink, my name was in pencil. And there were eraser marks underneath it. I looked closely to see if another name had been erased but couldn't make out anything.

With my fingers, I traced the words *I love you big* above the kissing chipmunks. *Love* was underlined in ink, and he'd signed the card "Love Jim" *five times*.

"Hmmm," I said, putting the card back into my treasure box and picking up the mimeographed postcard from the Billy Clower Dance Studio and Clubhouse.

Dear Pre-Teen and *Christmas Dance* were printed in purple letters across the card. The words *Gentlemen will wear coats and ties. Ladies will wear semi-formal dresses* were in a box at the center.

My friends and I had started going to Billy Clower ballroom dancing lessons the summer before fifth grade, the first opportunity allowed, and tomorrow night was to be our first real dance after seven months of lessons. It was the biggest social event of our lives, ever.

Angela had told me that she was wearing a new red taffeta dress that she'd gotten at Masseys dress shop. "I get to wear my sister's double-layer petticoat," she'd added.

"But she's so tall. . . ."

Angela shrugged. "I can roll the elastic at the waist." She lowered her voice. "And I hear there's going to be mistletoe."

I put a hand over my mouth.

Angela nodded solemnly. "My neighbor Mary Sue said so."

I whispered, "Does your mother know?"

Angela shook her head briskly. "And don't tell her," she hissed. "She thinks the dancing's bad enough." Angela looked longingly across the classroom at Larry*—tall, blonde, his cheeks filled with punch. He swished the drink around in his mouth and held his cup to his lips, as if getting ready to spit it back in. Angela recoiled a little and turned back to me. "I heard Larry daring the boys at lunch, you know . . ." She pursed her lips primly. "Well, I hope he doesn't try any . . . funny business with me."

When I got home from school after the party, Mrs. Alfred was gone. My father's car was parked at the curb in front of our house.

Daddy sat at the table in the kitchen eating a cheese sandwich and drinking a glass of milk while reading the newspaper. I resisted the urge to check if Jimmy's card was still tucked in the pocket of my binder. My parents didn't approve of mushy stuff.

Daddy folded the paper, put it in the basket next to the phone table, and stood up. "I gotta do a little incinerator burning. There's a lot of crap piling up in the garage."

After he left the room, I got his newspaper out of the basket and stood at the table checking for stories about the investigation. The main story covered the ongoing police search for Olga and also how Mrs. Duncan had gotten her bail reduced but was still sitting in the Ventura jail because she couldn't find a bail bondsman to put up the money.

In another article, at the bottom of the page, Frank Duncan was quoted as saying, "I truly believe that Olga is still alive," and "I'm still very much in love with my wife."

I put the newspaper back in the basket and pulled Jimmy's card out of my binder. It was a big accordion card with multiple pages. I fingered the two chipmunks sitting in a heart-shaped chair on the front, and the *I Love You Big* words but slammed the card shut when I heard Daddy humming down the hallway.

"What you got there?" He was wearing his yard clothes: old wrinkled gray slacks covered in grass stains and a torn long-sleeved plaid shirt.

"Nothing." I stood with my hands behind my back.

He eyed me as he passed. "If you need to burn anything, I'll be incinerating in the backyard."

I shoved my card back inside the binder, left it on the table, and followed Daddy down the porch steps and into the "way back" yard behind the garage. He'd stopped next to a rusted fifty-five-gallon drum partially burned out on one side and half-full of ashes. He began tossing cardboard and newspapers into the incinerator.

I walked up beside him. "Do you think Frank Duncan loves Olga?" I took a few pieces of cardboard from the wheelbarrow and handed them to him. "Do you think he ever got Olga a special card that said she was his sweetheart?"

Daddy struck a match on the side of the incinerator barrel, then touched it to some of the cardboard. The flames spread and swooshed a foot into the air as the newspapers ignited. "Frank Duncan keeps telling anyone who will listen that his wife ran off to punish him." The fire crackled as it ignited the rest of the cardboard. He reached for the broken pool cue stick—his incinerator stirrer, he called it—and poked at some glowing ashes before he tossed what was left from the wheelbarrow onto the fire. "Frank seems to think this whole thing is just a big mess his wife created to hurt him. It's her fault? HUH? She's to blame."

"I guess she wasn't his real sweetheart." I bent down to pick up a scrap of cardboard from the ground and tossed it into the smoldering fire.

We stood watching the flames for a few moments.

"Can you pick us up from the Billy Clower dance tomorrow night?" I asked. "We need someone with a station wagon. Everybody's going. Judi's father's taking us."

"Yeah, yeah. All right. But no more Olga Duncan talk."

"Okay, and you just wait in the car when you get there. No looking in the glass doors and making faces at me."

He smiled. "Now, would I do that?"

Saturday night, my friends and I sat fidgeting in folding metal chairs along the wall of the dance studio while the boys bounced around on their seats on the other side of the big room. More than seventy-five fifth and sixth graders from all over Ventura were waiting for the dance to start. My stomach tingled.

I tugged the hem of my dress over a scab on my knee and scanned the room, wondering what it would be like to hold Jimmy's hand. Our fingers had touched a few times during square dancing at school. But that was over so fast, with the do-si-dos and the allemande lefts and all.

Angela whispered to me nervously, "Larry's late, but he's coming, and I know he'll ask me to dance. Do you see him?"

I craned my neck, but I was looking for Jimmy.

Some of the girls pointed and tittered at the mistletoe hanging above the doorway of the refreshment room. I searched the ceiling of the dance floor to make sure there wasn't more mistletoe there.

"Do you see Larry?" Angela asked again.

Billy Clower and his wife, Audrey, our ballroom dance teachers, waltzed onto the floor to announce the first dance. Billy was dressed in a tuxedo. Audrey, in a flowing red chiffon dress, her dark hair pulled elegantly on top of her head, glided across the dance floor with him. She wore three-inch silver lamé heels and never missed a step. Billy and Audrey had really good posture. I threw my shoulders back. Grandma said I slouched, that I needed to stand up straight or I was going to get curvature of the spine, which is very bad.

After a few best-behavior reminders, Billy announced, "Gentlemen, please ask the ladies to dance."

Two or three of the boys bolted across the room like bulls barreling out of a bucking chute, but most of them shuffled like livestock going to slaughter. I kept my eyes down, afraid of being asked to dance by someone other than Jimmy and even more scared of not being asked at all.

A tide of dark pant legs and scuffed shoes stuttered back and forth in front of me.

Billy repeated in a loud voice, "Gentlemen, please find your partner."

"May I have this dance?"

I looked up. Monty Fisher stood there, grim-faced in a red blazer and a dark, narrow tie. I had to be nice to him. His sister was blind. I got up silently and followed him to the middle of the dance floor, where we both stood straight, facing each other, and waited for the music. I looked over his shoulder for Jimmy and spotted him with a girl named Joanne. She was a foot taller than him; her lace-ruffled chest was right at his eye level. I didn't really know the girl. She went to another school, but I'd heard her bragging in the cloakroom about getting a new training bra. Angela said it was stuffed with toilet paper. Jimmy had a stupid grin on his face.

On Billy's signal, Audrey put the needle on the record. Violins played. Monty stepped forward and put his right arm around my waist, then stuck his left arm straight out to the side. I put one hand on his shoulder and extended my other hand to meet his. He held me at arm's length. We began to waltz, haltingly, in a circle.

"Did you watch *Alfred Hitchcock Presents* last week?" he asked as we bumped into another couple.

Violins played as a woman sang about fascination and love. I searched the room for Jimmy. He was dancing close with Joanne, his cheek inches from her toilet-paper-stuffed bosom.

"Did you see that new Hitchcock show?" Monty repeated. "Neato."

"On TV?"

We turned and glide-stumbled in the other direction.

"You know, that scary show. I was wondering if you saw that one where the guy was stuck in bed with a rattlesnake on his stomach."

"My mother turned it off. She doesn't like snakes."

"Really rattled her cage, huh?" Monty brayed a high-pitched laugh. "Eddie says it was a real snake, and . . ."

I didn't hear the rest of what he said. Something about the actor actually dying right there on TV, I think. When the music stopped, I bolted for the wall of chairs.

The rest of the first half of the dance was more of the same. Foxtrots, tangos, cha-chas, a few jitterbugs and bebops. A couple of times I saw, out of the corner of my eye, that Jimmy seemed to be headed in my direction. But he was such a slowpoke that someone else always asked me to dance first.

On ladies' turn to choose, Angela asked Larry to dance. But I had to go to the bathroom, and when I came out, all the boys were taken. The Everly Brothers record "Wake Up Little Susie" blasted from the speakers while everyone did the bebop. Larry kept twirling Angela all over the floor, bumping into people. After the music stopped, Angela was so dizzy she could hardly walk.

"The Purple People Eater" came next, and Arnold asked me to dance. He knew how to dance a little and was a nice partner, especially now that his ringworm had cleared up and he didn't have to wear that white cloth cap on his head anymore.

When the song ended, Billy announced that refreshments would be served. A stampede for the kitchen door started but quickly stalled when everyone remembered the mistletoe tacked up on the center of the door frame. The line split in half, boys on one side, girls on the other, and reformed along each side of the door. I gave Angela cuts.

Boys pushed each other under the mistletoe, and girls giggled and pointed. I kept as far to the right as possible as I squeezed through the doorway and checked above to make sure I was clear. But it didn't matter. Out of nowhere Jimmy appeared, propelled forward by the boys behind him. I barely had time to shut my eyes before I felt his lips brush my cheek. Laughter erupted all around. My face burned.

I ducked out of the way just as another boy ran forward and kissed the girl next to me. Girls squealed. Boys roared. I pushed my way through the crowd and headed for the cloakroom. Angela called my name as she turned to follow. Just as I squeezed through the kitchen doorway and onto the dance floor, another boy bumped into me. He lowered his head and lunged in my direction, lips puckered. I ducked my head, but he managed to plant a big wet kiss somewhere near my ear. It was Larry.

Angela squealed.

Hey, there isn't even any mistletoe here.

Billy stood near the refreshment line, shouting at everyone to act like ladies and gentlemen. He elbowed his way through the crowd with a small stepstool and yanked down the mistletoe with a disgusted grunt.

I ran to the cloakroom and stood with my back to the door, my face against a scratchy wool coat that smelled like Grandpa. My cheeks were on fire. Other girls were already inside, hiding and giggling. Angela came in a few seconds later with an entourage trailing her.

"You're going to get a bad reputation," she said stiffly. "You kissed two boys in one night." The wide-eyed girls behind her nodded in unison.

"They kissed *me*. I was just standing there."

Angela wrinkled her nose. "Doesn't matter. Same thing. It's still very bad for your reputation." She looked like she might cry.

I wanted to stay in the cloakroom, but Audrey came through, high heels clicking, saying that refreshment time was over. She shooed us back to the chairs at the edge of the dance floor. Jimmy danced by with that Joanne girl again to the strains of Ricky Nelson's "Poor Little Fool."

It was the worst night of my life. In spite of all the big talk on the Christmas card, Jimmy hadn't asked me to dance once. Near the end of the dance, I sat in a chair at the far corner with my elbows on my knees, face propped in my hands, waiting for the misery to be over. But then, as if things weren't bad enough, Eddie skidded to a stop in front of me, shirt-tail hanging out, a ring of cookie crumbs circling his mouth, and asked me to dance.

I pretended I couldn't hear him, but he shouted, "It's the last song. Billy says everyone has to dance." I followed him robotically onto the floor. As we waited, I saw my father standing in the back row of parents at one of the glass doors, craning his neck.

Billy ended every dance session with the same music, "Dream" by the Pied Pipers. I thought it must be his favorite song. The record sounded worn and scratchy, like he played it a lot at home.

The music started. Eddie took my hand in his sweaty palm and pulled me close. I pulled in the other direction. After a brief, wordless tug-of-war, we settled at about a foot and a half apart.

The woman crooned with xylophone notes in the background. Eddie moved stiff-legged and out of rhythm, doing the box step. He counted,

"One, two, slide together, four," under his breath while looking at his feet. The tip of his thinking tongue stuck out of the side of his mouth.

I spotted Jimmy dancing with a cute blonde girl. He said something and she laughed. I sighed deeply.

Eddie said, "I think I'm getting a BB gun for Christmas."

"Hmmm," I said.

He turned and shouted in Angela's direction. "Hey, it's snowing down south!"

Angela stood on the sidelines, sniffling and being comforted by a couple of girls. Her sister's petticoat drooped a few inches below the hemline of her dress.

I pushed us in another direction.

"I had to promise not to shoot any birds when I get my gun," Eddie said.

I pulled away, narrowing my eyes at him.

"And I'd like to find that nurse's body you shared about for your current event yesterday. Any ideas where she might be buried?" Eddie stumbled over my feet.

"Ouch," I cried as I jerked free and hopped, one foot in the air, toward the French doors.

Eddie grabbed my hand and swung me back to his shoulder.

"She's not dead," I said half-heartedly. "She probably ran away from her stupid husband."

Oh no. I glimpsed Daddy's face at the glass doors. He'd managed to move himself into the front row of waiting parents.

As a saxophone played the mournful refrain of the song, Daddy waved and pressed his nose to the glass, making a crazy face at me.

I giggled and then caught myself. He'd promised to wait in the car. I took my hand off Eddie's shoulder and pointed emphatically toward the parking area. Daddy shook his head and shrugged like he didn't understand, then flashed me a goofy grin.

I turned away. *Oh well.* I hummed along with the last lines of the song. *"Dream, dream, dream."*

CHAPTER THIRTY-TWO

THE SEARCH

Santa Barbara, California,
December 21, 1958

Higgins and Henderson had Baldonado returned to the interrogation room at nine on Sunday morning. Henderson didn't say much. Just listened and glowered at the prisoner.

"All right, T'lene," Higgins said. "Where's Olga?"

Baldonado chewed on a fingernail. "I got nothing to say."

Again, Higgins brought up the old days in Camarillo. Mentioned a couple of guys that both he and Baldonado had known. Reminded the prisoner of how he'd cut him some slack a few times, sent him home with a warning instead of to jail. He asked Gus about his wife, daughters, and newborn twins before returning to the subject of Olga Duncan.

"I got nothing to say," Baldonado mumbled, his finger still in his mouth.

"You keep saying that, but think about it," Higgins said. "When it comes out of someone else's mouth—Moya, say, or Mrs. Duncan—who's going to get the blame? Huh?" He pointed. "You, that's who. You need to tell us your side of the story, T'lene. Do the right thing. Tell us where Olga and her baby are."

"I can't." Baldonado took his finger out of his mouth. "If I tell you what happened, what Luis did, I'll end up in the gas chamber for sure."

Henderson went still. His brows lowered.

Higgins chose his next words carefully. "Do the right thing, T'lene. You're a family man. You got two little girls, two baby boys. How would you feel if they were missing, and for the rest of your life you didn't know how to find them or where to even start looking?"

Baldonado ran his fingers through his hair. He hung his head.

"At least give Olga's father and mother the comfort of taking their daughter home for a decent burial . . . and Olga's baby, too. We need to send them home to their family in Canada."

Henderson cut in. "You're nothing but a fucking baby killer, Baldonado, and you know what that means, right? What happens to baby killers in jail?" He pointed toward the cells. "When word gets out you murdered a baby, I'm the least of your problems."

Higgins moved his hand toward Henderson, his fingertips inches from the investigator's arm. "I can help you, T'lene, just like I did in the old days. Get you a special cell at the jail."

Baldonado tapped his foot on the dirty linoleum floor. The sound of pounding on a metal door and muffled cries came from somewhere deep in the building.

"Do the right thing, T'lene," Higgins said. "Be a man."

Baldonado's foot-tapping grew louder and stronger. He shook his head back and forth in the same rhythm. Suddenly, he jumped halfway out of the chair. "All right, I'll do it for my family."

Higgins nodded and took care not to even glance at Henderson. "Yes, T'lene, yes, for your own children. . . ."

Baldonado dropped back into the chair and closed his eyes. "We didn't know she was pregnant." Tears erupted and streamed down his cheeks. "That Duncan bitch never told us she was pregnant."

"I know this is eating you up inside," Higgins said in a soft voice. "I know you, T'lene. You didn't mean for this to happen. It couldn't have been your idea. It's just like when you were a kid, following the wrong crowd. . . ."

Baldonado sobbed softly. His body shook; his limbs twitched.

"There's only one thing to do now to make this right, to be the decent man I know you want to be," Higgins continued. "Get it off your chest. Tell us where Olga is."

Baldonado wiped his eyes. Higgins and Henderson both held their breath.

"I got two things I want you to promise me first," Baldonado said.

Henderson nodded. He clenched a fist under the table.

"I'll show you where she is, but I want to see a priest."

Henderson spoke quickly. "Okay. You tell us where she is, and I'll get you a priest."

Baldonado remained silent for a time. The investigators didn't move. Finally: "I don't think I can tell you the exact spot. She's way out there somewhere on Casitas Pass Road near where they're building the dam." He looked away. "I'll have to show you myself . . . if I can even find it again."

Henderson tore a sheet of paper out of his notebook and slid it across the table in front of Baldonado. He slapped a pencil down and said, "Draw a map."

Baldonado dried his face on his sleeve. He picked up a pencil and began to sketch. "She's on Casitas Pass next to some new pipe in a big ditch in a hole we dug with our hands. Somewhere between Santa Barbara and Ojai."

"That's where you killed her?" Henderson asked.

Baldonado nodded. "Luis is the one wanted to do it because he needed the money."

"I'll call Gustafson," Henderson said. "You get his statement in writing."

Baldonado wiped his nose with his hand. "Wait, you didn't promise the other thing yet."

Henderson stopped halfway out of his chair. "What's that?"

"Promise I don't have to watch you dig her up."

At noon, Baldonado signed the statement, admitting that Elizabeth Duncan had hired him and Luis Moya to get rid of her daughter-in-law. He included details of the meeting at the Tropical Café and how he and Moya had kidnapped, beaten, and strangled Olga Duncan and buried her off Casitas Pass Road at the bottom of a ravine in a hole they dug with their own hands. Baldonado mostly blamed Moya.

By one P.M., Higgins and Henderson stood on either side of their prisoner at the jail entrance and waited in the drizzle for the car. Higgins lit a cigarette.

"I hope this isn't some wild goose chase," Henderson said.

Higgins nodded.

When Tom Osborne, Gustafson's other investigator, pulled the squad car to the curb, the men led the cuffed Baldonado to the back door and put him inside. Higgins slid in next to the prisoner. Henderson sat up front with Osborne.

They drove up Main Street past the white-walled bell tower of the old San Buenaventura Mission, turned onto Ventura Avenue, and followed rural Highway 33 toward Ojai. For the first few miles, no one spoke. Only the dull, rhythmic thudding of the windshield wipers, along with the intermittent crackling voice coming from the police radio, broke the silence.

Henderson rotated the piece of yellow paper that Baldonado had used to draw a crude map, trying to figure out which way was up. He looked over his shoulder at the prisoner. "About how far out on Casitas Pass?"

Baldonado slouched in his seat, staring out the window. He shrugged.

"Hey," Osborne called over his shoulder. "He asked you a question, dumbshit. You know where we're going, or we just out for a Sunday drive?"

Higgins leaned closer to Baldonado. "We're here to bring Olga home. Remember, T'lene? For her family. For your kids."

Baldonado turned his head toward the front seat. "Like I already told you, I'll know it when I see it."

None of the men talked again until Osborne slowed the car as they approached Ojai, near the gravel parking area of a ramshackle liquor store at the side of the road. Baldonado stared at the partially lit blue-and-red neon sign for Pabst Blue Ribbon beer. Osborne turned left onto Highway 150, heading toward Santa Barbara.

Baldonado twisted his head to keep his eyes on the sign. "Anybody wanna stop for a beer? We might need a little something . . ."

Higgins pulled out a pack of Camels and offered one to the prisoner. Baldonado took a cigarette with both hands and stuck it between his lips. Higgins struck a match and lit it.

"What are we looking for?" Henderson asked.

"Not sure. It's been a month." Baldonado slouched lower in the seat and took a drag on the cigarette, two-fisted because of the cuffs. They passed a dirt road with a tilted dead-end sign. It looked as if someone might have backed into it.

Higgins snatched the cigarette out of Baldonado's mouth. "Think."

Baldonado gave Higgins a pouty look. "Watch for a sharp curve in the road. It'd be on the left . . . just after one of those little bridges that cross over a gully." He put up his hands toward the cigarette. Higgins handed it back. "She's down the embankment."

No buildings were visible as they climbed higher into the oak-covered hills. The terrain was covered with big boulders, chaparral, and grass, with steep drop-offs to the sandy washes below the mostly deserted two-lane highway. The windshield wipers squeaked.

Henderson scratched his head. "All looks pretty much the same to me."

Osborne turned off the wipers. "I think he's wasting our time. Just wants a nice little Sunday afternoon drive in the country." The investigator looked at the prisoner through the rearview mirror. "Did you beat her to death or strangle her? Which one?"

"This is Moya's fault. Always got to be the big shot."

"So Moya made you beat her with the gun?" Osborne sneered.

"Bitch didn't want to die," Baldonado mumbled.

"But she was dead when you dumped her in the hole?"

Baldonado took a long drag on his cigarette. "I'm pretty sure. . . ."

Osborne whipped his head around; the car swerved. "*Pretty* sure?"

Higgins gave Osborne a quick shake of his head before saying, "Concentrate on the road, T'lene. We gotta find her. You're smart telling your side of the story before Luis blames it all on you."

Baldonado dropped the last of his cigarette on the floor and crushed it with his shoe. "We're getting close, but I need another smoke. Helps me think."

Higgins lit a cigarette for himself and blew a lungful of smoke in Baldonado's direction. He was getting tired of Baldonado's attitude, tired of being the good cop.

Baldonado pressed his face close to the window. "Slow down," he said.

Osborne stepped on the brakes.

Baldonado shook his head. "Never mind. False alarm."

Osborne drove on through the pass and down the hill then made a U-turn. "Maybe he can recognize the landscape better if we're driving in the same direction they came from," he said.

Now driving east, the car slowed to a crawl. Twice they stopped, and Higgins helped Baldonado out of the car each time. Henderson held on to Baldonado's arm while he stared down into the ravine that ran below the roadway, where large new drainage pipes were laid for the new dam. Both times, Baldonado ended up shaking his head.

Henderson muttered again, "All looks the same to me."

They'd been searching up and down the pass for over an hour when they crossed another bridge as the road curved sharply to the right.

"Stop!" Baldonado shouted.

Osborne edged the car to the shoulder next to Ventura County's 6.9-mile marker. Baldonado sat on the edge of his seat. "This looks right. I think this is it."

Higgins, Henderson, and Osborne got out of the car. The drizzle had stopped. Osborne opened the back door. "Get out."

Baldonado didn't move. Osborne tugged on the prisoner's wrists just above the handcuffs. Baldonado resisted. "You said I didn't have to see her."

Higgins stepped up, the good cop again. "Get out of the car, T'lene. You have to show us where she is so we can take her home."

He pulled gently on Baldonado's wrists, and the prisoner climbed out of the car, head hanging. Henderson grabbed the cuffs and dragged him across the narrow dirt shoulder. The wind whistled through the hills.

Higgins followed. "Look, T'lene."

Baldonado raised his head and gazed into the bottom of the ravine, twenty feet below the road. The end of a large corrugated steel pipe stuck out of a sandy-bottomed drainage channel that came from under the highway.

He nodded. "This is it. Dig in front of that pipe." He turned away. "Can I get back in the car now?"

Henderson stared down at the drainage pipe then glanced at the curve in the road running over the little bridge. His eyes rested on the mile marker. "Shit. We're in Ventura County."

"This is the spot?" Osborne asked Baldonado. "You're sure?"

Baldonado nodded.

"She was still alive when you got here?"

Baldonado nodded again.

Higgins took off his jacket and laid it across the hood of the car. "I'll check down below. We got a shovel?"

"Crap," Osborne said. "Sorry, didn't think to bring one."

Higgins rolled up his sleeves. "Guess it doesn't matter. They didn't use one to bury her. I don't need one to find her. She can't be very deep."

"Can I wait in the car now?" Baldonado whined.

"Shut up," Henderson said.

"You promised that I didn't have to watch you dig her up."

"Fuck you." Osborne shoved him toward the car. "We oughta bury you next to her."

While Osborne threw Baldonado into the back seat of the car, Higgins surveyed the surrounding wildlands. He shivered, standing in his shirt-sleeves. The wind blew in damp air from the ocean ten miles to the west on this sunless gray Sunday afternoon.

Finally, he slid carefully down the embankment in his smooth-soled leather shoes, holding on to manzanita branches for support. At the bottom he walked ten feet to a flat, triangular area formed by the edge of the embankment and the sides of the ravine. He stopped where the pipe protruded from the slope and looked around the creek bed in the eerie quiet. He knelt in front of the pipe and gently scraped some of the loose, sandy dirt aside. Then he used both hands to dig deeper.

When his fingers touched something solid, he quickly withdrew his hands. A sickening-sweet odor assailed his nostrils. "Olga," he whispered. "We're going to get you home." A fly buzzed near his eyes. He batted it away and listened to the wind rustling in the bushes on the hillside above him for a moment before he dug down again with both hands.

Henderson called from above. "Got anything yet?"

Higgins didn't answer. He scraped off more sandy soil, carefully piling it along the sides of his small excavation. One more handful, and he saw it: pink cloth caked with dirt. He brushed more soil away from a patch of mud-stained, quilted fabric. The stench of death grew stronger.

Higgins stood up and brushed dirt off the knees of his pants. "Got her!" he shouted up to the road, and then, in a softer voice, "We've got you, sweetheart. We've got you."

CHAPTER THIRTY-THREE

HANDYMAN

Ventura, California, December 21, 1958

O n that momentous morning, I'd skipped church because the Sunday school teacher wanted us to share something about the way our families worshipped God at home. I couldn't think of anything that wouldn't be a lie.

When I got up, Daddy was in the kitchen with the In-Sink-Erator box again. "Only four days until Christmas," he said.

"Hold on," Mother said as she walked in with her arms full of laundry. "We need to get somebody who knows what they're doing." She dumped the laundry on top of the Bendix.

"Too late," he said. "If you want this by Christmas, time's running out." He picked up his hammer and began taking "dojiggers" out of the box. Daddy called all machinery parts "dojiggers" because he didn't know the right name for anything.

"Bob, stop it before you lose something important," Mother continued in a loud, firm voice. You could always tell when she wasn't fooling around.

He put down the dojigger and said, "If we get somebody, it'll cost a fortune. I'll just give it a try. See if I can't get this baby going. If it doesn't work, I'll call Pete." Pete owned a service station and fixed cars.

Mother moved between my father and the In-Sink-Erator box. "Pete doesn't have time for this. Anyway, I already talked to Donna Honer. She says Rich can help you."

"Rich? *Rich?* I don't want to bother him. That poor guy's got his hands full—five kids, works two jobs." Daddy threw down the hammer. His face turned red.

"Shh." Mother glanced over her shoulder toward the neighbors' house. "Donna says he can install this In-Sink-Erator with his eyes closed. Everybody in the neighborhood knows that Rich Honer is a genius with his hands."

"Genius?" Daddy sputtered.

I looked down at my father's smooth, ink-smudged fingers.

"Rich single-handedly built their bedroom and bathroom addition last year. He's a very handy man around the house."

"Big deal," Daddy muttered. "He's so busy he doesn't even have time to read the newspaper."

"I'm going up to the Honers'," Mother said.

"I read the newspaper, Daddy."

He gave me an unenthusiastic, thin-lipped smile. "Good. Good girl," he said, and picked up the screwdriver to inspect the tip. He scratched his head with it.

"I read about how 'sources' say the district attorney in Santa Barbara has a witness who says she saw two guys with blood on their clothes the night Olga disappeared. I'd sure like to know more about that."

"Uh-huh," Daddy said. He used the screwdriver to try to pry open the cardboard wrapping that encased more In-Sink-Erator dojiggers.

Mother returned through the kitchen door. "Donna is sending Rich over."

"Son of a bitch." Daddy kicked the box. "It doesn't take a genius to install a garbage disposal."

But it might help.

Rich arrived a few minutes later lugging a large metal box of tools. He was a tall, thin man with a nice smile. Always very calm. I heard one of my friends' mothers say that he was handsome.

"Wow, Mr. Honer," I said, "you've got a lot of tools."

Daddy gave me a narrow-eyed look.

Mother pulled out all the cleaning supplies and other odds and ends from under the sink. Rich lay on his back and scooted under the sink to take a look.

"Bob, you just stand over there by the toolbox and hand me the tools when I ask," Rich said, his voice muffled from being inside the cupboard.

Daddy rolled his eyes at me, but he moved next to the tools. Rich called for the adjustable spanner, and it took my father three tries to find the right tool. He was really starting to get put out—my father, not Rich.

"So what's going on with that Duncan case, Bob? You think the girl's dead, or do you believe the husband's story that she probably just took off 'cause she's mad at him?"

Daddy mumbled something unintelligible in an irritated tone and then raised his voice. "It's all in the newspaper, Rich, if you're interested." Mother gave him the stink eye, so he added, "That phony annulment Mrs. Duncan got for her son in August does seem suspicious." He squinted at Mother as if to say, "There, you satisfied?"

Rich removed the pipe from the sink drain and poured the remaining water in a small plastic bowl that he handed up to Daddy, who looked around absently for someplace to put the water. Finally, he just poured it back into the sink.

I heard a gasp and some gurgling. Rich inched his way out from under the sink, water streaming off his hair and face. No one said a word for what seemed like a very long time before Rich burst out laughing. I jumped out of my chair and handed him a dishtowel. We all laughed.

"I really don't need any more help, Bob," Rich said. "I can do the job myself, no problem."

Daddy apologized over and over and offered to pay Rich to install the disposal, but Rich said it wasn't necessary. He was just being neighborly.

So Daddy offered the only thing he could. "About the Duncan case, Rich, it looks like Olga's mother-in-law is heavily involved. The Santa

Barbara DA is getting ready to file murder charges against her and two men. They have evidence from a couple witnesses who know things about the crime, but it will be hard to prove the case without a body."

Rich came out from under the sink to get another tool. "So what do you think happened to her?"

"We're working on a story. The police have letters from Olga Duncan that she wrote to her parents in Canada saying she was afraid of her mother-in-law and wanted Frank to get his mother psychiatric help."

Rich whistled and disappeared back under the sink.

The phone rang in the dining area next to the kitchen. I jumped up to answer, just as Betsey flew into the room through the archway from the living room. We both charged the telephone table.

"My turn!" Betsey screamed.

I snatched up the receiver and said, "Holt residence," very official like, while pushing Betsey away.

"I never get to talk on the phone," she wailed.

Mother arrived and put an arm around Betsey. She looked at me and hissed, "You don't always have to be first."

I covered the mouthpiece with my hand. "It's for Daddy, someone from the paper." I widened my eyes. "Sounds important."

CHAPTER THIRTY-FOUR

THE BODY

Ventura County, California,
December 21, 1958

I t didn't take long for people to start showing up after Henderson radioed the report to headquarters. Within thirty minutes, the Ventura County sheriff arrived at the roadside turnout, brakes screeching and gravel spraying. He jumped out before the engine died. "Whaddya got?"

"Looks like we found her." Henderson pointed into the ravine. "Higgins is with her."

The sheriff towered over the DA's investigator. He spat tobacco juice on the road. "Olga Duncan?"

"Pretty sure. The body's right where Baldonado said to dig."

The sheriff spat another loogie of brown liquid next to the county road marker. "There's no doubt this is in Ventura County."

Henderson nodded. "Baldonado says they killed her here." He paused. "I'm not even sure they knew if she was dead when they buried her."

"Jesus," the sheriff said.

Both men turned toward the sound of more cars.

Two sheriff's deputies and a police photographer stepped out of an all-black squad car, red light flashing on top. A white Chevrolet station wagon with a Ventura County emblem and the word *Coroner* printed on the door pulled diagonally into the gravel turnout behind the police car.

The coroner inched down the slope, a deputy at each elbow. His assistant brought up the rear, carrying a black rubber body bag and two shovels. The sheriff followed. Sirens sounded in the distance as the men descended the steep embankment.

Higgins stood next to a boulder in the bottom of the ravine, smoking while he watched them come down.

The sheriff shook his hand. "Good job."

The coroner set his small case on the ground and opened it, put on gloves, and told the deputies to start digging. "Slowly," he said. "I want the body to stay the way we find it."

Higgins moved closer to the grave site.

Osborne joined him, his hand over his nose. "There must be thirty cars up there already. Gustafson's on his way."

When the shovels got down a little way into darker, wetter soil, the only sound to be heard was the scrape of sand on the metal shovelhead and dirt hitting the ground when the deputies tossed it aside. The wind had died. A little sunlight broke through the clouds. The putrid smell grew stronger.

Osborne bolted for the bushes. Retching noises followed. One of the sheriff's deputies gagged, too, threw down his shovel, and headed in Osborne's direction. The remaining deputy kept digging.

"Stop," the coroner said. He knelt and began using his hands to scrape around the body. Gradually its form emerged.

The sheriff stepped to the edge of the grave. He took out a plastic Vicks Vapo Inhaler and used it in each nostril. The police photographer moved in closer too, snapping pictures.

An ashen-faced Osborne stumbled out of the bushes and rejoined Higgins next to the grave. The detectives could see the curve of Olga's back, the swell of her belly. She'd been folded sideways into a fetal position, her pink robe pulled up over her head.

"This whole thing makes me sick," Higgins mumbled.

Osborne took out a handkerchief to wipe his brow and moved it over his mouth and nose.

The coroner gently moved the robe from Olga's head and touched her skull with a metal instrument. He lifted a limp strand of dirt-brown hair and examined her scalp. "Traumatic lacerations," he said to his assistant, who took notes on a clipboard. "Look, she's been beaten right down to the bone."

"Animals," Osborne muttered through the handkerchief.

Higgins moved to the other side of the grave and leaned against the drainage pipe. He stared at the corpse, curled, its hands pressed together and taped at the wrists, the arms bent at the elbows in front of the body. The pulled-up robe revealed a shorty pajama set. He barely made out a flower print on the muddy fabric. A speck of gold on one of her bloated black fingers caught Higgins's attention as it sparkled momentarily in the sunlight. *Wedding ring . . . the symbol of Frank Duncan's unbroken circle of eternal love.*

Lighting another cigarette, Higgins squinted toward the buzz of voices mixed with the sound of roaring engines and slamming doors coming from the roadway above. The excited words, "We've got a body," were repeated over and over for the benefit of the new arrivals. The roar of a bigger engine caught the deputy's attention. Higgins recognized the accompanying voice.

"Where is she?" Roy Gustafson shouted. "I don't want her moved until I see for myself what they did to her."

Rocks and loose dirt tumbled down the hill, followed by Gustafson and Deputy DA Deem. Their suit jackets flapped, and their polished shoes sank into the ground as they made their way to the grave.

The coroner stood back. Gustafson walked the perimeter of the hole. Everyone quieted while he checked the scene from every angle. He took notes then walked over to the foot of the slope and back again. He turned to Higgins. "Baldonado led you here?"

"It wasn't the first stop he had us make, but he kept saying the same thing . . . curve in the road at a bridge, down a steep embankment, next to a drainage pipe. He knew this was right the minute we stopped the car."

Gustafson nodded. "And he told you that they killed her here?"

"We got a signed confession."

The DA stood silent as he watched the coroner scrape more dirt away. The body looked mummified, the upturned knees and bowed back frozen in the curled position of a sleeping child. Gustafson fixed his eyes on what was left of her face. Her lips and nose were gone, the eye sockets caked with mud. "Those bastards," he mumbled.

He turned to the coroner. "I'm taking charge of the crime scene. She was murdered here." He raised his voice. "Santa Barbara's out of it now."

Higgins pushed away from the pipe and moved closer as the coroner probed Olga's remains. The deputy willed himself to keep his eyes on the upturned, unrecognizable face, the skull still partially covered with fragments of black, decomposing tissue.

"*Bitch didn't want to die.*" He stiffened as he remembered Baldonado's chilling words. Small, white, hook-shaped blobs covered parts of her throat. Higgins took in a quick involuntary breath when one of the blobs moved. Maggots.

He glanced up toward the road when he heard one of the deputies yell, "Hey, you fellows get back where I told you."

A row of faces, some of which he recognized, peered down from the roadside. Charlie Thompson, the Santa Barbara detective who'd cracked the case by getting Mrs. Short to spill her guts about her friend Betty, was there, along with that reporter from the *Ventura Star-Free Press*, the one who was always humming. He stood next to a guy pointing a camera at the grave site. A flashbulb popped.

One of the reporters from the Oxnard paper called down to him. "Hey, Higgins. You find Olga's body? You get the confession?"

Higgins flicked ashes from his cigarette onto the sand near the drainage pipe. He waved a dismissive hand toward the reporters.

An arm clothed in the khaki shirtsleeve of a deputy sheriff moved in front of reporters to back them away from the slope. "I told you guys to stay back; Sheriff will be up here as soon as he can to give you a briefing."

Two more flashbulbs popped. "We're not in the way," one man argued. "Just trying to do our jobs."

Bob Holt kept shaking his head as he mumbled, "What a god-awful business. Jesus Christ, that poor girl."

The coroner worked for an hour before he was ready to remove the corpse from the grave. "Get the bag," he said to his assistant as he pointed to the long black rubber bag folded on a rock a few feet away.

Gustafson squatted next to the grave. "Got any idea about cause of death?"

"I won't know for sure until after the autopsy, but . . ." The coroner pointed to small, jagged lacerations above the forehead. "One, two, three . . . nine wounds. She's been hit so hard that a few of these hair strands are buried deep inside the wounds in her skull." He shrugged. "But you never know until they get her opened up on the table."

A deputy manipulated Olga's arms to fit her body inside the bag. Higgins and Osborne helped, and the coroner's assistant slowly pulled the metal zipper past her swollen abdomen, her bound wrists, and her shattered head as he closed the black bag on Olga Duncan and her unborn child.

The coroner stood with the sheriff and his deputies at the foot of the slope, the zippered bag at their feet. "There's no way we're going to be able to carry her up this hill."

"You'll have to tie a rope around the end of the bag and drag her up," the sheriff said.

Gustafson spoke to the sheriff before he left. "I plan to convene the grand jury on Friday, indict all three."

The coroner, stooped over his black case, struggling to get it closed, frowned. "The day after Christmas? That's five days from now."

"Right," Gustafson said. "Tell Dr. Johnston I'll need the autopsy report in time."

A chill settled over the crowd, the unseen ocean making its presence felt in the late afternoon gloom. Bob and Charlie Thompson watched the deputies at the bottom of the hill struggle to tie the rope on the body bag.

"Ventura gave us a call . . . let us know they found her here," Charlie said.

"Terrible business," Bob muttered. "What kind of a . . ." He shook his head. "Would do this to an innocent, pregnant . . . ?" His voice trailed off.

"Devils," Charlie said.

"They're saying they murdered her down there." Bob gestured into the ravine. "If that's true, it looks like Santa Barbara is out of it."

Charlie worked his mouth around. "They got the son of a bitches. That's what matters."

"We wouldn't be standing here if Santa Barbara hadn't broken the case."

"Yeah, well, Olga got found. That's all I care about." He turned toward Bob. "And as far as Ventura prosecuting the case, fine with me. Gustafson's a better DA than what we got." Charlie turned to go.

"What are you going to do now?" Bob said, keeping his eyes on the men as they started to pull the black bag up the embankment.

"Help the Ventura guys any way I can." Charlie took a long last look at the black body bag at the bottom of the ravine. "All I care about is seeing those animals sucking gas in the chamber."

Gustafson returned to his office and worked almost nonstop through the rest of the weekend preparing for the grand jury hearing scheduled for the following Friday. During this time, he refused all calls from the press. When he arrived at his office on Monday morning, the DA was met by over twenty newsmen representing local and metropolitan newspapers, radio and television stations, and national wire services. They all insisted that Gustafson make some sort of statement. He finally relented and wrote out the following in longhand:

The brutal, calculated, revolting killing for hire of Olga Duncan is one of a number of horrible crimes which have recently been committed in California. I simply cannot understand how some of our leaders can seriously contend that the death penalty is not appropriate punishment for such a crime.

Many persons contend that the death penalty does not deter a murderer. Frankly, I am sick of this illogical argument. Of course, penalties do not completely deter crimes. But that is no reason to dispense with penalties.

Retaliation is a basic instinct of the human race. From biblical times, a life for a life has been recognized as just and fair. The alternative in California, a life sentence, which permits a prisoner to be paroled in seven years, simply is insufficient . . . What are you going to do, rehabilitate them?

The statement was widely printed in the afternoon papers and broadcast on TV and radio, along with details about the discovery of Olga's body and the story of Baldonado's confession. Mrs. Duncan's defense attorney later called the DA's words "inflammatory and prejudicial" against people not yet charged with a crime.

Gustafson later told colleagues that his intention had been to defend capital punishment in connection with Olga's murder in the wake of the newly elected governor's and attorney general's campaigns urging the abolition of the death penalty.

Gustafson pointed out that he hadn't named any suspect and insisted that he only wanted to imply that *whoever* did such a thing ought to be executed. Nevertheless, the DA's emotionally charged statement would plague him throughout the trial and for years to come.

CHAPTER THIRTY-FIVE

CHRISTMAS SHOPPING
AT THE JAIL

Ventura, California, December 23, 1958

O n Tuesday afternoon, two days after Olga's body was discovered, Marilyn invited me to go Christmas shopping. Going anywhere with Marilyn's mother, Florence, was always an adventure. She was "offbeat," according to my father. Another neighbor called her an "old battle ax," but that was because she'd cussed him out after Marilyn's dog bit his son on the leg. I'm not sure why Florence was doing the cussing, because it was her dog that did the biting, but that's just the way she was. You never wanted to get on her bad side.

She started complaining as soon as she backed their maroon Mercury out of the driveway. "I don't know about this drizzle and my hair," she muttered as she patted her tight blue curls with one hand and steered the car with the other. She had just had her hair washed, set, and blued the day before at the neighborhood beauty parlor.

I inspected Florence's head from the back seat. She had prematurely gray hair and said she had to take the yellow out with a blue rinse. She never discussed her hair without mentioning the "premature" part a couple of times. The beautician told her to sleep with her hair rolled in toilet paper to keep the "set" longer, but Florence said, "That's a load of crap."

Florence squinted at me in the rearview mirror. "What the hell happened to your hair, Debby?"

"I got a pixie cut at the beauty college for $1.25, but Linda had to trim my bangs. She said the girl didn't do it right." I smoothed my hair. "Linda knows. She's going to be a beautician when she grows up."

"Uh-huh. Well, somebody didn't do something right. You look like a little boy."

"For goodness' sakes, Mother," Marilyn said. "It's the latest style."

Marilyn and I started playing rock-paper-scissors in the back seat, and I was squirming around trying to get away from her rock, when Florence erupted. "Hey, you girls, quit fiddle-farting around back there. Do you hear me?"

You'd have to be deaf not to hear the woman. Florence never had to tell me anything twice. And I knew she appreciated that about me. I'd heard her tell my mother, "Debby's no trouble to have around. You hardly even know she's there." That was a pretty big compliment coming from Florence, because she had a lot of trouble with her nerves.

That's why Marilyn's stepfather, Gene, had to sleep in a patio room off the garage. He drank a lot. ("Who wouldn't?" my father said.) Florence couldn't tolerate any aggravation, and Gene just wouldn't stop getting on her nerves no matter how much she yelled at him to stop it.

We pulled into a diagonal parking place on Main Street and got out of the car.

Florence took a plastic shower cap from her purse and put it on her head. She looked up to the sky and adjusted the cap. "This drizzle's going to ruin my set."

I stared, my mouth open, at the blue curls poking out from under the green cap. Florence noticed. "I lost my rain hat," she snapped.

Marilyn looked at the sidewalk, out into the street, anywhere but at her mother. "Can we go to the dime store?"

"I have money," I chimed in and held up my purse. "For Christmas shopping. I need to buy my sister a present."

"We gotta go to the shoe store," Florence said to Marilyn. "Your feet are growing so fast I'm going to have to cut holes in the toes if I don't get you a new pair."

When we got to Rain's Shoe Company, I stopped to admire the display of girls' shoes in the front window while Marilyn and her mother went inside. Florence kept repeating, "You're getting something sturdy this time."

I stood perfectly still as I gazed at the most beautiful shoes I'd ever seen: royal-blue Mary Janes with two slightly diagonal pink straps across the top of each shoe. A leather bow was attached to the straps. Also pink. And they had one-inch heels. Wow!

A folded card with the price balanced on the toe of one of the shoes: $2.98. I opened the clasp of my purse to check my wallet. One, two, three dollars. I fingered the bills and glanced inside the store. Florence still had the shower cap on her head. She gestured at the salesman while Marilyn tried on a pair of saddle shoes. Florence caught my eye and motioned me inside.

I walked to the salesman and said in a bold voice, "I'd like to try on the blue shoes in the window. The ones with the pink bows."

The salesman looked to Florence.

She put a hand to her head, noticed that she was still wearing the shower cap, and snatched it off. "You don't need shoes, Debby."

"I do," I said. "I need them to wear to church 'cause I have to cover up my toes."

Florence snorted. "Since when does your family go to church?"

"I go to church sometimes. . . . I go to lots of churches," I said. "And Reverend Ralston visited our house to pray with my whole family."

"Ha," Florence hooted. "I'd like to have seen your father praying."

"Uh-huh . . ." I said. *Dum-de-dum-dum.*

"Well, your mother didn't say nothin' about getting any shoes." Florence told the salesman that they'd take the saddle shoes for Marilyn and turned back to me. "You talk this over with your mother, Debby."

On our way out of the store, I lingered at the window. Florence put the shower cap back on her head and said she needed to go to the Great Eastern department store to pick out some last-minute presents.

"Can we go to See's Candies while you shop?" Marilyn asked. "We won't get into anything."

"I thought you wanted to go to Woolworths."

"They give out free samples at See's," I said.

Florence checked her watch. "Okay. Half an hour. Then you meet me"—she pointed up the block—"over there on the corner at the Jack Rose shop. And don't be late. I gotta get home to fix Gene his food."

Marilyn and I went to the See's store, then walked a half block to the corner of Main and California Streets and waited for a break in the traffic. The streets were crowded with last-minute Christmas shoppers. Green plastic garlands, adorned with red and silver Christmas decorations and lights, were strung across the intersection. A man in a raggedy Santa suit stood next to a Salvation Army pot, ringing a bell. I gazed up California Street toward the courthouse on the hill, a block away. The drizzle had stopped. We stood on the corner chewing our molasses chips, that day's free samples from See's.

"You heard they found the missing nurse, right?" I asked Marilyn. "She was buried right up on Casitas Pass. You know, the road where my father made a wrong turn on our way to Steckel Park for my birthday?"

She shuddered. "Good thing he turned around. The killers might have still been up there. I heard my mother say that nurse was 'pistol-whipped.' I wonder what that means."

"It means they beat her with a gun."

"Oh." Marilyn hesitated. "My mother uses a fly swatter."

"The killers buried her in a hole."

Marilyn nodded. "I know that. My Ganny and Papa live out that way where they found the body. Papa says he knew she was there all the time."

"Really? Did he tell the police?"

"No. Says why should he do all the work when the police are the ones getting paid? He's tired of getting screwed when everyone steals his ideas for free . . . like when he invented air brakes."

"Uh-huh." I was afraid of Marilyn's papa. He liked to reach out and pinch her on the chest when she passed close to him. He called it giving her a "titty twister." Everyone in the family laughed, even though I could tell Marilyn didn't like it. I stayed way out of his way.

"They got one of the men who killed Olga Duncan up there." I pointed up California Street. "I know everything about Olga. My Daddy's going to be the lead reporter on the case from now on. The editor told him."

"Really?" Marilyn stared up the hill at the huge white-pillared building. "And the jail's up there?"

I nodded. Marilyn was a year and a half older than me, and two years ahead in school. She'd just started junior high. There wasn't much I knew that Marilyn didn't. Except criminal information.

I puffed up my chest. "We can see it if we walk up behind the courthouse. And if we're lucky," I added, "we'll see one of the killers."

Marilyn looked up and down the street. No sign of her mother. "Show me."

We climbed the steep sidewalk up California Street and crossed in front of the Father Serra statue. Fog was creeping in from the sea. When the walkway at the edge of the big marble building ended, we looked around. The area was deserted.

"Maybe we should go back." Marilyn stopped and checked her wristwatch. "We're supposed to meet my mother in a few minutes."

I turned around and kept walking backward up the hill. "Mrs. Duncan's up here someplace, too, but I'm not sure where they keep the women."

"Really?"

"And your mother said half an hour. We got plenty of time." I turned forward and climbed the roadway that circled behind the courthouse.

Marilyn glanced over her shoulder toward Main Street and then scampered after me. "This might be a bad idea. What if the killers break out and murder us?"

"Don't be silly. They're behind bars."

Marilyn caught up as we rounded the corner. "Mother says the nurse was buried alive."

"Maybe," I said. "We don't know for sure."

We stopped and stared at the flat-roofed three-story building standing at the edge of the parking lot behind the courthouse. Small barred windows lined the side of the menacing old structure.

Marilyn wrinkled her nose. "Something stinks."

The jail loomed above us, ominous, with dark stains running down the old crumbling stucco walls. A low rumble of men's voices, punctuated by high-pitched swearing, spewed from some third-story transom windows, hinged on the bottom, open on top. We couldn't see the prisoners through the bars and frosted glass, but they certainly saw us standing there in our pleated skirts and bobby sox.

"Hey, baby," a man hooted from above. "Get me outta here."

Are Olga's killers in there right now? Looking at us?

"Judi's father told us the kitchen is up there," I said. "That's why some of the windows are open a little, for air. I think they're supposed to bring Mr. Moya to this jail today. He might already be here."

Marilyn grabbed my hand. "I'm scared. Let's get out of here, before one of them gets out through one of the windows."

"What do you girls think you're doing?" boomed a voice from behind us. Marilyn and I jumped. She gasped and put her hand to her heart. I turned and saw a uniformed policeman standing a few feet away.

I stammered, "I w-w-was . . . looking for my father."

"He's in jail?"

A man screamed from a window: "Watch out, little girls! The cops are going to get you!" Someone else cackled.

"No, he works up here sometimes, reporting on trials and things . . . Bob Holt. Maybe you know him?"

"Uh-huh, I know Bob." He knitted his eyebrows and pressed his lips together with a slight frown. "Well, you've gone too far." He pointed back

the way we had come. "The main entrance to the courthouse is out front.
Is he expecting you?"

"No, it's a surprise."

Marilyn tugged on my arm. "We've got to go. My mother's expecting
us, and we don't want to be late."

"She's in the courtroom, too?"

"No, no, Jack Rose dress shop." Marilyn looked at her watch. "We gotta go."

"Help me!" a voice called out. "I'm melting, I'm melting. . . ."

The policeman jerked his face toward the jail. "Oh, what a world," he
hollered back. "What a world."

Marilyn and I hurried past the policeman. "Thanks for your help," I
called out over my shoulder.

We stopped at Main Street as thin wisps of fog floated over the pavement. A man at the newsstand across the street was selling the afternoon
edition of the paper. A handmade sign in big black letters was tacked to the
tattered awning over his stand: Lurid Murder Plot. There were a bunch
of newspapers stacked on a low shelf near the magazine racks. He held
one and shouted something as he waved the newspaper at passing cars and
pedestrians. I couldn't hear what he was saying over the sound of the traffic.

"Be right back," I said, and left Marilyn on the corner. I took off running.
A big blue Oldsmobile just missed me, brakes squealing and horn honking
as I darted into the street. I skidded to a stop at the wooden kiosk and read
from the paper on top of the stack. Husband of Slain Nurse Sought by
DA. Daddy's byline was printed underneath the headline. I could read it
clear as day. Bob Holt. *Officers from two counties sought to subpoena Frank
Duncan for the grand jury but . . .*

I dug into my purse, found a dime, and slapped it on the wooden counter.
"One, please."

I started reading the rest of the story as I stood there on the corner,
the mist growing thicker as it swirled around the newsstand, but Marilyn
called out, "Come on," from across the street. "My hair's getting frizzy,
and my mom's waiting."

A police car with two men wearing suits in the front seat slowed at the intersection and turned to go up the hill toward the jail. A dark-haired man sat slumped in the back seat behind the metal mesh. I watched as the car drove up California Street past the Father Serra statue and disappeared around the courthouse.

"Come on!" Marilyn yelled again.

I dashed back through the traffic and stepped onto the sidewalk, slightly out of breath. "I had to get a paper," I said as I followed Marilyn up the street and through the glass double doors of the Jack Rose shop. "Frank Duncan is missing!"

CHAPTER THIRTY-SIX

THE CLEAN BOY

Santa Barbara, California, December 23, 1958

S anta Barbara County sheriff John Ross stood outside the bars of Luis Moya's cell in the solitary confinement section of the jail. Moya sprawled across a chair, disheveled and unshaven, flicking cigarette ashes on the floor. He didn't look up.

Each day the sheriff left his office on the third floor to make his morning rounds. Lately, he had made a point of stopping to chat with Moya, hoping the young man would break down and confess.

"They found her . . . Olga," the sheriff said. He watched as Moya brought a cigarette to his lips to take another drag.

"Good," Moya said. "Happy for the family, I guess." He looked the sheriff in the eye. "But like I said before, nothing to do with me. Never met the woman."

The sheriff stared back into Moya's baby face and cold brown eyes. "Your amigo Baldonado says otherwise. Told the Ventura guys Mrs. Duncan hired him and you to kill Olga, and you took turns strangling her and then buried her up on Casitas Pass Road."

Moya pulled his lips together like a drawstring purse.

"Then your buddy showed them where she was buried." The sheriff gripped the bars of the cell and leaned closer. "They dug her up Sunday afternoon."

Luis shook his head. His "tough guy" face sagged. The stench of his unwashed body overpowered the foul-smelling air, ever-present in the poorly ventilated jail. "I told you. I'm innocent."

"Not what Baldonado says. Says you're the one who planned the whole thing. The kidnapping. The murder. You're the one who collected the money. He just went along for the ride."

"How could he say that?" Moya slapped his palm to his forehead. "Believe *me*. Believe *me*."

Both men were quiet for a few seconds. Moya stared at the floor. The sounds of the jail—shouting, wailing, deputies barking orders—echoed in the background.

"We need to get you cleaned up," the sheriff said. "Detectives from Ventura are on their way up here to talk to you." He motioned to the guard. "Take him down to the showers."

"I've got to call my mother in Texas again," Moya said as he stood. "She's trying to get the money for a lawyer for me."

"Not sure we'll have time," the sheriff said. "Maybe later."

Moya stuck his hands through a horizontal opening in the bars, and the guard put handcuffs on his wrists before unlocking the cell and sliding the door open. The sheriff took out a package of Juicy Fruit and slowly unwrapped a stick as he watched Moya lurch toward the showers, head bobbing from side to side. A scared man's walk.

Moya was freshly washed, dressed, and combed when the guard let Higgins and Henderson into his cell. Sheriff Ross didn't go in but stayed close, hand resting on the bars of the sliding door. Moya sat at a small table, trying to smile and look tough at the same time.

"He's a very clean boy," the sheriff said.

Moya grinned self-consciously. "After ten days in solitary with no shower, I'm kinda glad you guys decided to pay me a visit. Guess Sheriff Ross doesn't want you to know what a stinkhole jail he's got here in Santa Barbara."

Henderson smirked. "Then you should be happy to come with us to the Ventura jail. We can leave right now."

Moya's face clouded. "I ain't going nowhere. Ventura's got no reason to hold me."

Higgins loomed over him. "You can drop the innocent act. Baldonado told us everything."

Moya rocked in his chair. "Gus is a liar. You can't believe anything he says."

"Well," Higgins said, "yesterday he told us that we'd find Olga buried in a ravine out on Casitas Pass Road next to a drainage pipe. . . ."

". . . and that's where we found her," Henderson said.

"Nothing to do with me." Moya gave the detectives a hard, cold stare. No smiles now.

Higgins stared back, no longer the good cop. "Not what Baldonado told us. Says you lured Olga down to the car and then hit her on the head."

Moya was shaking his head before Higgins finished.

"No idea why Baldonado implicated you?" Henderson asked sarcastically.

"Other than everything comes out of his mouth is a fucking lie?" Moya reached for a small silver object lying at the corner of the table. His hands trembled as he fidgeted with it, turning it over and over in his long, smooth fingers, the nails bitten to the quick.

"What you got there?" Higgins asked.

Moya held out his hand to show a miniature wine goblet, smaller than the width of his palm, fashioned out of tinfoil. The bowl was smooth, the stem long, with intricate detail sculpted on the base. "I call this one 'Candlelight and Wine.'"

"Junior's got an artistic streak," the sheriff said from the door. "Uses the tinfoil out of his cigarette packs."

Neither detective took the tiny sculpture from Moya's outstretched hand, so he tossed his creation back on the table. "Nothin' else to do in this fucking place."

"You can make those down in Ventura as well," Henderson said.

"You got something to charge me with in Ventura?" Moya said. "You got nothing but some story from Gus trying to pin what he did on me."

The sheriff spoke up again. "Might want to think about it, Junior. I hate to admit it, but they got better accommodations down there. Plus, I can't keep you in these deluxe digs anymore. Got a child pervert being questioned as we speak. I'll need this cell for him." The sheriff smiled all around. "We'll have to move you to the tank with about twenty other assholes. Can't put the pervert in with them. No telling what they might do to a guy who hurts babies."

"'Course, Olga Duncan's baby got hurt, too," Henderson reminded the sheriff.

"That's true. . . ."

Moya rubbed his mouth. "They heard about me? All Gus's lies?"

"They got a radio. You're all over the news."

The sheriff turned to Henderson. "Right now, we're holding Junior on a state probation violation. I talked to the probation office, and they say we can transfer him down to Ventura whenever you want. I told Junior he can call his mother in Texas, then he's all yours. The whole sorry mess."

Henderson drove south on Highway 1 with Higgins in the passenger seat and Moya handcuffed and shackled in the back. Higgins stretched out his legs and thought about how little more than a week ago the Santa Barbara police had had nothing on this case. Then Mrs. Short spilled the beans to Charlie Thompson, and now they had a body and a confession.

The two-lane highway ran along a strip of land between brown, grass-covered coastal mountains and the Pacific Ocean. In the early spring, the rolling hills would turn gold with clouds of wild mustard. A wooden guardrail hugged the coastline, separating the asphalt from the beach a few feet below the road. A gray fog bank hung just offshore, two hundred yards or so beyond the cresting waves.

Moya stared out the window, watching the gray-blue water slam to the shore, breaking into foaming white water right next to the highway. Some of the waves sprayed the road when they crashed on the rocks below. Henderson had to put on the windshield wipers a couple of times.

Higgins glanced out his window as something dark and round bobbed up near rust-colored kelp floating beyond the shore break. *A head?* Seconds later, two more surfaced. Higgins heard Moya stir in the back seat.

"Seals," Higgins said. "Harbor seals."

A few seconds of silence followed before Moya spoke. "You ever go to Mugu Rock down there by Port Hueneme? Feed the seals?"

Higgins turned toward the back seat. "Yeah. I been there. There's a guy selling fish for people to throw to the seals."

Moya smiled. "That would be the life, huh? Being a seal. Lying around in the sun on the rocks watching the waves while people throw you your favorite meal?" He shook his head. "No one's ever given me nothin'."

"You say your mother's getting you the money for a lawyer."

"Maybe, if she can." Moya sank lower in the seat. "She's a good woman. Works hard. Raised four kids. I'm the only one in the family ever been in trouble."

"You know," Higgins said, "if you're innocent, you don't need a lawyer. Just talk to us and get it all straightened out."

"I'm innocent all right. I don't even know these people. These Duncans."

"Did you forget meeting them at the lineup?"

"Well, that's the first time I ever saw 'em," Moya said, staring out the window. The fog bank was getting closer. "And it was a lie, what they said. I never blackmailed anybody."

"They're *all* lying?" Higgins said. "Mrs. Duncan? Mrs. Esquivel?" He paused. "Gus Baldonado?"

Moya didn't answer.

"You got an alibi for the night Olga Duncan disappeared?" Higgins asked.

"Yeah, I got an alibi."

The detective waited, but Luis sat tight-lipped.

"Okay. Let's hear it, then," Higgins said.

"I'm only telling it to my lawyer."

"When your mother comes up with the dough for you to hire one?"

"Right."

"Could be a long wait."

There was a pause. The fog swept over the road. "What about a pastor?" Moya said. "I can talk to a pastor in the jail, right? That doesn't cost anything, does it?"

"You want to talk to a clergyman?" Henderson watched Moya through the rearview mirror. "I know a guy."

"A pastor? With a church and everything?"

"Yeah, Avenue Community Church. Reverend Floyd Gressett. He helps out inmates at the jail all the time."

"What do you want a pastor for?" Higgins said. "You find religion in the Santa Barbara jail?"

Moya blinked, his baby face in a pout. "I go to church . . . sometimes."

The fog drifted across Main Street as the police car slowed at an intersection. A little girl holding a newspaper turned her head to track the car all the way up the hill.

Henderson and Higgins walked the prisoner into the Ventura County jail side entrance. A deputy stood in the hallway with a handful of envelopes. "Subpoenas," he said, shaking the papers in Henderson's face. "Gustafson is calling fourteen witnesses for the grand jury on Friday." He pushed an envelope toward Moya. "Here's a little Christmas present for ya, buddy."

Moya didn't take it. His hands were cuffed behind his back. Henderson grabbed the envelope and stuffed it in his breast pocket. "I'll log it in."

The deputy stepped to the side as the detectives passed with the prisoner and called after them. "You hear about Frank Duncan?"

Higgins stopped. "I'll catch up," he said to Henderson and moved back to the deputy. "What about him?"

"Missing. Gustafson had someone try to call him after his wife's body was found, but his phone was disconnected, and when someone went to his apartment with a subpoena, Frank was nowhere to be found. Landlord said he came by Sunday night to tell him he was moving out. Didn't leave a forwarding address. You think he's on the run, like maybe he's involved?"

"Possible . . . or maybe he just wants to dodge the subpoena," Higgins said.

"Yeah, well, there's an all-points bulletin out on him. Got police in three counties trying to find him before Friday morning."

Higgins lifted his eyebrows.

"Officially, he's wanted as a witness in the grand jury investigation into the murder of his wife."

Right after they booked Moya, Henderson called his friend, the Reverend Gressett. "He wants God's help." But with Christmas only a couple of days away, the minister said he was too busy with church obligations to get to the jail before late Christmas night. Henderson was disappointed. The grand jury hearing to indict the three co-conspirators—Moya, Baldonado, and Mrs. Duncan—for kidnapping and murder was scheduled for Friday morning, December 26. He'd hoped the reverend would be able to add Moya's confession to the one Baldonado had already given, but that looked unlikely.

He and Higgins went to work on Moya in earnest the next day. They'd heard that the prisoner had had a poison oak rash on his back when he'd arrived at the Santa Barbara jail. Henderson thought that Moya might have touched the poison oak vines that grew around the grave site while burying Olga. When Moya refused to take off his shirt to let the officers check for the irritation, Henderson forcibly lifted the jail uniform. No rash. Moya, infuriated, refused to answer any more of Henderson's questions.

Henderson withdrew and left the interrogation to his partner. Higgins kept checking in to chat with Moya throughout Wednesday and Thursday, trying to understand the suspect's motivations. It became clear to Higgins during these talks that Henderson's instincts had been right: Moya might be convinced to tell the truth through religion.

"I want to see a minister," Moya said. "I pray every night. I'm relying on God to get me through this nightmare."

CHAPTER THIRTY-SEVEN

PRAY FOR US

Ventura, California, December 25, 1958

At eight o'clock on Christmas night, my grandparents backed out of our driveway, tires crunching walnuts as they inched their big Chrysler into the street.

"Thanks for the new Bible!" I called out.

We all waved like crazy as they drove off.

"Jesus, I thought they'd never leave," my father said.

Mother gave him a look as we walked across the lawn toward the house. The sound of our gravelly-voiced neighbor singing "Away in a Manger" drifted out from her kitchen window.

I climbed the stairs of our porch and waited for Daddy. "Reverend Ralston says the greatest joy at Christmas comes to those who know Jesus Christ our Savior."

Daddy stopped midstep. "You went to that church again? I thought you became a Baptist."

"I did, but I walked over there with Marilyn for the Christmas party Tuesday afternoon. Reverend Ralston said 'Christmas is Christ' and 'only Jesus can save our souls from hell.'"

Daddy opened the front door and stepped aside to let my mother and sister enter the house. "Yes, Jesus brought a message of peace and love, and it never hurts to have a little spiritual reflection on Christmas. But I don't think you're getting the right message from that reverend."

"But they had really good Christmas cookies and punch at the party."

"Yeah, well . . . I doubt that idiot reverend has a direct line to God. Maybe you should just stick with the Baptists." Daddy chuckled. "Ha . . . never thought I'd say that." He threw up his hands and walked through the door.

"Well, I think we need to pray more at Christmas," I called after him. "Get into the spirit and ask for salvation so we can all go to heaven." I followed him in. "Can't hurt."

Our little house was ablaze with lights. The Christmas tree in the corner of the living room twinkled and blinked. I put on my new Dodgers baseball cap that Daddy had gotten me for Christmas, picked up my Hula-Hoop that Santa brought, and twirled it around my waist, swinging my hips and counting the rotations out loud. "One, two, three, four . . ." The Dodgers cap slid over my ears.

Betsey headed for her new Happy Tunes record player, sitting on a side table in a jumble of torn bright wrapping paper and discarded ribbons. She turned it on, put the 45-rpm "Chipmunk Song" record on the turntable, and set the needle on the vinyl. Betsey turned up the volume.

"Christ, not that again. How many times does she have to play that god-awful record?" Daddy yelled to Mother, who was in the kitchen dealing with the new garbage disposal. It kept clogging up the drain. "Lois. Lois! Do something about Betsey and this damn record player your parents got her. She's driving me out of my mind.

Mother didn't answer.

"Santa brought me this record player from the North Pole," Betsey said as she put on her new Atomic Age robot hands and mask while the record blared. "On his sleigh."

High-pitched chipmunk voices filled the room.

". . . Twelve, thirteen . . ." I chanted.

"When are you going to take down the tree, Bob?" Mother called. "The needles are so dry, they're starting to shed. It's dangerous."

The tree had been up for two weeks, and my mother lived in constant fear that a string of bubble lights might short out, causing the tree to burst into flames. "The whole house might catch fire," she'd said many times, "killing us all as we sleep in our beds."

Daddy gritted his teeth and opened a big cardboard box next to the tree. He overturned it, and the metal parts for his new Weber Kettle barbecue fell in a heap at his feet.

The chipmunks sang on.

Mother rushed in from the kitchen when she heard the barbecue parts hit the hardwood floor. "What do you think you're doing, Bob? I thought we agreed you'd take the tree down tonight, before . . ."

"It's still Christmas. I want to get this thing together now. If I put it in the garage, I'll forget about it. It'll never get done."

She couldn't argue with that.

". . . Eighteen, nineteen, twenty . . ."

Mother glanced in my direction as she left the room. "Don't use that Hula-Hoop in the house, Debby. You'll knock the tree over, and the lights will explode."

I moved toward Daddy as I continued to spin the Hula-Hoop around my hips. "Twenty-one, twenty-two . . ."

"Get that thing out of here. You heard your mother. Can't you see that I'm trying to concentrate?" He swatted the hoop down.

Daddy's new red-and-green polka-dot bow tie that Santa had brought him dangled by one clip from the collar of his plaid shirt. "I'm doing this for the whole family. Everything will taste better with this cover over the barbecue." He held up the kettle cover and pointed at a pamphlet sticking out of the cardboard box. There was a drawing of a happy little chef with the words *Covered Cooking with Magic* printed across the top. He read out loud from the pamphlet. "Soon you will be performing feats of culinary magic that will amaze your family and friends!" His eyes sparkled.

Betsey swung the needle back to the beginning of the record. *"Let's sing it again. Yeah, let's sing it again . . ."*

Daddy pushed his Dodgers cap back from his forehead and dropped to his knees to begin organizing the barbecue parts on the floor. He dumped the screws and bolts from a small plastic bag and carefully lined them up. He scratched his head while he squinted at a diagram of the assembly instructions.

Betsey pushed her Atomic Age robot mask to the top of her head and leaned over his shoulder to look at the diagram. She pointed at one of the chrome-plated legs. "You need to . . ."

"Get out of here," he snapped, "before you mix everything up."

"I can put things together. I . . ." Her lower lip quivered. "I want to help."

Daddy pulled the tie off his shirt. "Here, then hold this."

"She's right, Daddy," I said. "Remember? She's good at fixing stuff. She got that flapper thing in the toilet tank back on after you tried for an hour and couldn't—"

He cut me off. "Yeah, yeah, okay, fine. If you want to help," he said to Betsey, "quit your sniveling and go get me my hammer and the Phillips screwdriver. I think, maybe . . ." He paused.

Betsey's face lit up. "I know where you put them," she called out as she scampered off. "They're in the clothes hamper . . . next to the toilet."

I stood beside Daddy as he examined one of the pieces of the barbecue. "We should have gone to midnight mass last night," I said.

"We're not Catholic," he said as he held the metal piece next to the diagram and turned it in different directions.

"Still, it would have been nice. I like the smell of the incense."

Betsey appeared with the tools. She had the tie clipped in her hair. "Here, Daddy," she said as she thrust the hammer and screwdriver into his hands.

He smiled at us. "Let's bow our heads, girls, and pray to God that Daddy can put this barbecue together. Pray for culinary magic!"

I moved the brim of my Dodgers cap to the side as I read from the cooking pamphlet. "Listen to this, Daddy. The cover prevents burnt food and eliminates flare-ups. Wow, that will be good. No burnt hotdogs. Maybe you could even make Dodger Dogs."

"Hmmm," he said as he tried to fit one of the legs into the small hole on the upside-down kettle.

Betsey restarted the record.

I swung the Hula-Hoop around my waist again but continued to read. "And it says here that you don't have to stand guard over the food. Just relax."

"I'm always relaxed," he said through clenched jaws, and he started singing along with the Chipmunks in a tight falsetto voice as he stuck a screw between his lips, held the leg in place, and picked up the screwdriver with the other hand. He switched from singing to very fast humming.

Mother called from the kitchen, "It's late. You girls need to get to bed."

"But there's no school tomorrow," Betsey wailed. "We're still on Christmas vacation." She waved her Atomic robot arms at Pinky Lee. The cat hissed and ducked under a table.

Mother returned to the living room. "Bob, why don't you finish that tomorrow? We're all exhausted."

"The goddamned grand jury meets tomorrow. I don't know when I'll be home."

I lost count of my Hula-Hoop rotations and let the hoop slide down around my ankles. "What about the grand jury? What do you think will happen?"

Betsey knelt next to the coffee table, squeezing the plastic robot hands open and shut around the cat's tail. Pinky Lee bolted across the floor and scrambled through the pile of parts, scattering the screws my father had neatly lined up.

Daddy flung his screwdriver across the room, hitting the Happy Tunes phonograph and sending the needle scraping over the record like a fingernail on a blackboard.

"You've scratched the chipmunks!" Betsey cried.

"Bob . . ." Mother wagged her head wearily. "Go to bed. You've got yourself all worked up again."

"I am not worked up." He kicked the jumble of barbecue parts. "No one around here appreciates the possibilities associated with culinary magic."

"You're agitated, Bob," Mother said before turning to my sister and me. "Get to bed, girls. It's late."

Betsey put the needle at the beginning of the record. *"Ready to si---g, boys? Al . . . in?"*

"Daddy ruined it," she wailed. Mother took her by the hand and led her off to the bedroom as the chipmunks hiccupped with every rotation of the turntable.

Daddy tried to push the larger barbecue pieces back into the box. "Son of a bitch . . ."

"What will happen at the grand jury?"

"Goddammit! I don't know." He let the box drop to the floor. "The DA's going to present witnesses to try to convince the grand jury members to indict Mrs. Duncan and her two henchmen for murder. The proceedings are held in secret, so we won't know what the witnesses say until the DA releases the transcripts. But we should know tomorrow night whether or not Ma Duncan, Gus Baldonado, and Luis Moya are going to stand trial."

"One of the men already confessed, right?"

"Yeah. Gus Baldonado led the police to the body." Daddy bent down to collect the screws. "That poor girl . . ." He threw a handful of screws across the wooden floor. "Just so goddamn senseless."

I plopped myself on the couch, shivering as I remembered the picture in the newspaper. *Olga's body in a black bag, being dragged up the embankment with a rope.* Mother said the photo was barbaric and should never have been printed.

I hugged myself, hands jammed into my armpits. "Do you think the others will confess?"

"Not Mrs. Duncan. That woman will go to her grave proclaiming her innocence."

"What about the other man, Mr. Moya? Will he tell what happened to Olga?"

The chipmunks had stopped singing. We listened to the crackling sound coming from the Happy Tunes record player as the needle skipped on the empty vinyl while Daddy scratched his head.

"God only knows, Debby," he said. "God only knows."

CHAPTER THIRTY-EIGHT

SPIRITUAL GUIDANCE

Ventura, California, December 25-26, 1958

Fifty-five-year-old Reverend Floyd Gressett finally arrived at the sheriff's office at 10:45 P.M. on Christmas night.

"We got a man here, Luis Moya, that says he needs help," Higgins told the pastor. "He's requested to speak to a clergyman for a little spiritual guidance, if you know what I mean."

Reverend Gressett, a longtime friend of law enforcement, nodded. "I understand. He needs to unburden his soul."

Higgins escorted the reverend into an interrogation room where Moya waited alone, hunched over a wooden table, his wrists handcuffed. After Higgins left the room, Gressett introduced himself.

Moya offered a tentative smile. "Thank you. I . . ." His face crumbled. He shrank further into his chair.

Gressett knew why Moya was in jail, even though Henderson hadn't said anything to him about it, and he'd made a point of not discussing it with Higgins either. The Duncan case had been all over the newspapers. But Gressett wasn't prepared for the big brown eyes staring back at him. Moya looked no more than a boy.

"How old are you, son?" the reverend asked.

"I'm twenty-two," Moya mumbled.

Gressett took an empty chair at the table. "I'm here to help you, Luis, if I can. Detective Higgins tells me there's something you need to get off your chest."

Luis dissolved into tears. "I'm so scared. Will you pray with me, Reverend? I want to tell God the truth."

"There is no need to tell God the truth, if you're going to lie to a man." Gressett tilted his head toward the door that separated them from the sheriff's office. "Lying without repentance and forgiveness only leads to 'a second death.'"

"I don't know what to do," Luis cried. "Can you get me a Bible?"

"There's no need of you reading the Bible. It won't help if you're still going to tell lies to the detectives."

Luis covered his head with his arms, rocking back and forth. "I'm going to quit lying. I even lied to you when I said I was twenty-two. I'm only twenty." Luis slid out of his chair and sat on the floor. "I've been praying. Praying night and day, but I don't get any answers. I don't think God hears me. I want to say I'm innocent because I'm worried about my parents. I don't want my mother to . . ." He started to sob.

"There is no forgiveness for the unrepentant," Gressett said softly.

Luis beat his handcuffed hands on the floor.

Gressett waited until Luis's sobs subsided and handed him his handkerchief. "If a man is a murderer, he will belong to his father, the devil, unless he repents."

Luis wiped his eyes. "I wish I could make things right. I'm so sorry for what I did. . . ."

"You need to tell the truth to men, and then you need to beg God for forgiveness."

"But I've never bowed down to anyone. . . ." Luis broke into tears again.

"Only God can save your soul." Gressett helped Luis onto his knees. "Are you ready?"

Luis sobbed, "I'm . . . I'm ready . . . to tell the truth about . . . everything."

"Then pray with me, son. Take my hand."

Luis closed his eyes, bowed his head, and clutched the reverend's hand in both of his.

Gustafson got the call at one A.M. on Christmas night.

"Moya confessed," Higgins said in an excited voice. "He sent word from his cell that he wanted to talk to me an hour after Gressett left."

Gustafson sputtered sounds of elation. "You got everything?"

"Signed and sealed. He corroborated Baldonado's story. They both say Elizabeth Duncan hired them to murder her daughter-in-law."

The district attorney stayed up the rest of the night, reworking his plans and revising the questions for the morning's hearing.

When the grand jury convened at nine A.M., Gustafson called fourteen witnesses, including Emma Short, Esperanza Esquivel, Gus Baldonado, and Luis Moya. Frank Duncan was the last witness on the list.

The missing Mr. Duncan had been located and subpoenaed early Christmas night at a Hollywood area apartment, where he'd registered under a different name. When asked by the press, Gustafson claimed he didn't know how the Los Angeles County sheriff, a friend of his, had managed to find the lawyer.

Before he testified, Frank held an impromptu news conference at the courthouse outside the grand jury room. Reporters asked him why he'd disappeared from Santa Barbara.

"I heard the news of the discovery of my wife's body over the radio Sunday night. Nobody had bothered to call me to tell me directly. I could do nothing. My wife was dead. I wanted to be alone."

"Were you surprised to get the subpoena?"

Frank shrugged. "Didn't matter. I'd already read about the hearing in the newspaper . . . planned to come here today anyway."

"What about Luis Moya and Augustine Baldonado, the men who have confessed to murdering Olga? You know them?"

Frank shook his head slowly. "I'd never heard of these boys . . . these monsters . . . until I read about them in the newspaper."

A reporter wearing a red-and-green polka-dot bow tie asked him if he thought his mother had anything to do with his wife's murder.

"It's impossible. I just don't believe my mother had anything to do with Olga's death. I don't recall her ever being cruel in any sense. Mother couldn't kill a chicken."

Nine hours later, the grand jury foreman opened the door into the corridor and signaled to the bailiff that the jurors had completed their deliberations. Roy Gustafson returned to the chamber to hear their decision. He was a bit nervous. They had deliberated for only fifteen minutes.

He needn't have worried. The grand jury had voted to indict Elizabeth Duncan and her two co-conspirators for the murder of her daughter-in-law. Gustafson thanked the jurors, dismissed them, and returned to his office to begin preparations for the trial, even though no trial date had yet been set.

CHAPTER THIRTY-NINE

MOTHER COULDN'T KILL A CHICKEN

Ventura, California, December 26, 1958

Daddy didn't get home until after eight o'clock that night. Mother made him a plate, and he took it directly to his den and closed the door. A few minutes later, I slipped into the room wearing my pajamas and curled up on the old couch next to his desk with a Nancy Drew book. Neither of us said anything. I liked to listen to him type. Sometimes I looked up from my book when the little bell sounded and he threw back the carriage return lever.

"What happened at the grand jury today?" I asked.

"The only thing I know right now"—he kept typing while he talked—"is that they voted to charge Mrs. Duncan and her two hired killers with first-degree murder."

I went back to reading about how Nancy and her friends were waiting out a storm drinking tea at a roadside inn. A tree had fallen on Nancy's blue Roadster.

The typing stopped, and Daddy ripped the page from the roller and added it to the pile on his desk. He smiled and pointed at my book. "Another mystery?"

"Uh-huh, *The Sign of the Twisted Candles*." I turned the book so he could see the cover picture. Nancy hid behind a tree watching a man dig a hole in the ground.

I pointed at the pages next to his typewriter. "Is that a new story about the murder?"

He shook his head. "I'm writing about an interview Frank Duncan gave to the press today."

"He should have protected Olga. Marilyn's mother says he's guilty as sin."

"I think he's guilty of being a very foolish, deluded young man," Daddy said.

"Well, he should have done something to stop his mother! You said she made threats against Olga."

Daddy picked up the article he'd finished typing. "I guess when you live your whole life with a crazy person always ranting and raving about something or somebody—"

"Ranting and raving . . . That's what Mother says you do."

He croaked out a laugh. "Hardly the same." He thumbed through his pages. "Frank says he never heard his mother threaten Olga with violence, and nobody ever told him she was threatening to kill his wife." Daddy crossed something out with his thick, soft-leaded pencil. "I don't think he took what his mother said seriously. Sometimes when a person is surrounded with constant yelling, they learn to tune it out."

"Like when you yell and I get scared and Mother says for me to just ignore it, that you're only blowing off steam and that you don't really mean anything by it?"

Daddy tousled my hair. "I'm sorry. I don't mean to scare you. I'm not really thinking straight when I do that. And Mother is right. I should be ignored when I'm on a tirade."

I watched his face intently for a moment and then smiled. "Don't worry, Daddy. I never pay too much attention to anything you say when you're yelling. If it gets really bad when we're around other people, I just pretend like I don't know you.".

He laughed. "Well, good. I imagine Frank Duncan's wishing that he didn't know his mother, either." He stood up. "You better get to bed, sweetheart. It's late."

I slipped my gold-tasseled Jesus bookmark between the pages of the Nancy Drew book. "So you don't think Frank Duncan knew his mother was going to kill Olga?"

"Today, at the courthouse, I asked him if he thought his mother had anything to do with his wife's murder. He said, 'Mother couldn't kill a chicken.'"

"A chicken?"

"Uh-huh. But the real question is whether she'd hire someone to do it for her."

CHAPTER FORTY

ASHAMED OF WHAT YOU DID?

Ventura, California, December 30, 1958

Four days after the grand jury indicted Elizabeth Duncan and her two co-conspirators for Olga's murder, Mrs. Duncan was arraigned in superior court on the charges. A crowd overflowed the courtroom, but Frank did not attend. He had not visited his mother since Olga's body had been discovered.

Mrs. Duncan was represented at the arraignment by famed Los Angeles criminal defense attorney Ward Sullivan. Moya and Baldonado also appeared but had their arraignments put off because they were not yet represented by attorneys. The judge appointed attorneys for them at the end of the hearing.

None of the three defendants showed any emotion during the brief proceedings. But afterward, when news photographers tried to get Mrs. Duncan to pose for pictures with Moya and Baldonado as the three were led back to county jail, she hung back. She grasped a windowsill as a female deputy tried to pull her along the courthouse corridor. Although Moya and Baldonado were both handcuffed, Mrs. Duncan was not, and she suddenly threw her arms over her face and scurried down the hallway.

She kept her face covered as Moya and Baldonado calmly smoked while the three waited for the jail elevator with their deputy escorts.

Baldonado turned to Mrs. Duncan and smirked. "What's the matter, you ashamed of what you did?"

At the exact moment of the arraignment, a private fifteen-minute funeral service was conducted for Olga across town at the Ted Mayr Mortuary. Cremation followed at Ivy Lawn Cemetery. Frank; Elias Kupczyk, Olga's father; her brother, William; and Mr. and Mrs. Stephen Woytko, Olga's LA friends from Vancouver, attended the simple service. Mr. Kupczyk and his son had taken a five-day train journey from Manitoba, Canada, to attend Olga's funeral and speak to local authorities about Olga's murder. Her mother was too ill with grief to make the trip. William and Mr. Kupczyk, a Canadian Railroad foreman, went home to Canada a few days later because Olga's father needed to go back to work. None of the family ever returned to Ventura. On the same day as the arraignment and Olga's service, Roy Gustafson released the transcript of the entire grand jury proceedings to the press. Moya and Baldonado had testified that they'd been hired by Mrs. Duncan to murder her daughter-in-law. Their testimony included gruesome details of how they'd kidnapped and killed Olga. Eighty-four-year-old Emma Short had testified about her friend's search to find a killer, and she added that she thought Mrs. Duncan and her son "lived as man and wife."

All of the grand jury witness testimony was printed, under banner headlines, in a daily series of newspaper articles before the trial began.

A week later, in a packed courtroom, Sullivan entered dual pleas to the charge against his client: "not guilty" and "not guilty by reason of insanity." He later explained to reporters that although his client completely denied guilt in the alleged murder-for-hire slaying of her daughter-in-law, she was leaving her options open. "My client has reviewed the grand jury transcripts with me, and she can't understand why those men would accuse her of asking them to kidnap and get rid of Olga. She never had any such intention," Sullivan said.

Soon afterward, the newly appointed attorneys for Moya and Baldonado entered pleas of "not guilty" and "not guilty by reason of insanity" for their clients as well. The three defense attorneys also made motions for a change of venue to have the trial moved to another county, charging that DA Roy Gustafson had made "inflammatory statements to the press, which prejudice the rights of the accused." The judge denied the change of venue motion and set jury selection for the trial to begin six weeks later, on February 16.

By then, Olga Duncan would have been dead for three months.

PART THREE

THE TRIAL

February 24, 1959–March 20, 1959

CHAPTER FORTY-ONE

FIRST DAY OF THE TRIAL

February 24, 1959

When I look back, Elizabeth Duncan's trial is linked inextricably in my mind to the sound of my father's voice—his dramatic, profanity-laced, sometimes humorous stories about witness testimony and crazy antics in the courtroom. Stories of blackmail, a Salvation Army man and a phony annulment, too many husbands to count, and Mrs. Duncan breathing fire to the end, often told in snatches between more chaotic attempts at home repair.

I read every word of his newspaper articles, and I scrutinized the front-page photos of all the trial participants. But his nightly accounts brought the bizarre and brutal characters involved in Olga Duncan's murder to life around our dining room table. I hung on every detail of his spellbinding tales, and although I'd never met any of these people, I knew them all very well.

The door at the back of Ventura Superior Courtroom One swung open, and a smiling, confident Elizabeth Duncan sashayed in like she owned the place. Her grand entrance was hindered only by the fact that she was cuffed to Mary Fogarty, a Ventura County deputy sheriff. Mrs. Duncan nodded and raised her fingertips to a few familiar faces in the press crowd that she'd come to know during the week-long jury selection process.

Reporters and photographers swarmed. "How about a few pictures before we start?" one of the newsmen called out. Mrs. Duncan's dapper little attorney, Ward Sullivan, nodded his permission and continued a conversation with his private investigator.

Deputy Fogarty, dressed in a brown skirt and jacket with a sheriff's star pinned on the front, unfastened the handcuffs. Mrs. Duncan stood next to her chair at the defense table and rubbed her wrist before turning toward the reporters. "Do you like my new outfit?" she asked as she fluffed the skirt of her two-piece, black-and-white dress with a Peter Pan–style, velveteen-trimmed collar. "Frank bought it for me." Flashbulbs popped.

The dark, mahogany-paneled courtroom, with its gleaming coffered ceilings, arched windows, and three beautiful stained-glass domed skylights, had been built as a public works project at the turn of the century. The judge sat at a raised desk at the front of the courtroom called the bench. The defense and prosecution tables faced the judge, with the witness stand and jury box to one side. Because of the large number of journalists covering the trial, a makeshift press section had been set up behind the counsel tables, inside the low wooden railing, called the bar, that separated the judge, jury, lawyers, and defendant from the ninety-eight-seat spectator gallery.

On most days, the atmosphere in Courtroom One was almost church-like. People instinctively lowered their voices as they entered. But on the opening day of the Duncan trial, an electric excitement spread throughout the building. Newsmen from all over the country descended on Ventura. Representatives of the wire services and national news magazines, photographers and reporters from all the major newspapers in the state, about thirty journalists in all, assembled in the press section to await the beginning of the trial.

Bob Holt sat in the first row of reporters chatting with Bennie Jo Colton*, a reporter from the *Los Angeles Daily Express** and the only female assigned to cover the trial. Miss Colton wore a well-cut light-gray suit with a tight skirt and a fitted, flared jacket. She shared reporting duties with her male colleague at the *Express*, Edd Flynn*.

"My little girl would love to be in your chair today," Bob said. "She tells me she wants to be my assistant cub reporter."

Bennie Jo gave him an icy smile. "I'm nobody's assistant."

Bob stammered. "Oh, no, no . . . didn't mean anything like that. . . . My daughter, Debby . . . she keeps saying that she wants to be a newspaper reporter when she grows up. She's dying to come to this trial."

Bennie Jo harrumphed. "It isn't easy. Women reporters usually are assigned to the society page . . . a lot of teas and fashion parades. Tell her she needs to sharpen her fingernails if she expects to cover any murder cases. I had to twist somebody's arm to get here today. Might have left a few scratch marks."

Bob leaned slightly backward as he watched her long, red-lacquered fingertips smooth her skirt over her knees. "Ha-ha . . . right. I'll pass it along."

Bennie Jo opened a notebook.

"So how do you and the other guy from the *Express*—Edd, is it?—split up the assignment?"

Bennie Jo glanced over her shoulder at her colleague, who sat slumped in a nearby chair reading the sports section of the *Times*. "Whenever he can, he lets me do all the work."

Bob chuckled as he watched reporters swarm the area where Mrs. Duncan held court. He took a pencil out of his coat pocket. "Looks like Mrs. D. is ready for her close-up."

He pushed through the crowd of reporters and photographers to get nearer to the defendant. Bennie Jo followed. "How are you holding up?" she called out to the defendant.

"I'm glad the trial is finally getting started," Mrs. Duncan said. "The food in the jail is terrible." She turned sideways. "Can't you tell? I've lost weight." More flashbulbs popped. "And it's impossible to sleep with all the noise those terrible women make. Frank got the judge to approve my sleeping pills; otherwise, I'd be up all night."

"Do you think you can get a fair trial?" Bob asked.

Mrs. Duncan held up both hands with her fingers crossed and pulled a rosary out of her pocket. "This is my good luck charm," she said as she clutched the beads to her breast. "Frank bought it for me. I pray every day, and I'm confident of winning the case."

Her Los Angeles lawyer, Ward Sullivan, finished his conversation with his investigator and stepped between the reporters and his client. "We said pictures, boys. Hold your questions. You'll get plenty of copy when the witnesses start testifying."

"How about one with you and your client, Mr. Sullivan?"

The attorney, never shy of the press, sidled up to Mrs. Duncan, straightened his trademark bow tie, and stayed for three or four shots before stepping away. The fifty-eight-year-old Sullivan was one of California's most respected criminal defense attorneys. By the time of the Duncan trial, he had handled seventy-five to eighty murder cases. The previous evening, Sullivan had been overheard in the dining room of the Pierpont Inn telling his companions, "We'll show these hicks how to put on a trial." Then he'd laughed. "That DA Roy Gustafson's just a big fish in a small pond."

The big wooden door at the back of the courtroom creaked open, and the rumble of voices in the overflowing public gallery intensified. Everyone turned to watch as Frank Duncan strode down the aisle toward his mother. She put out her arms.

"Let's get you in the picture, too," a reporter said as Frank gave his mother a peck on the cheek.

Frank stood next to his mother, his posture rigid, a stiff smile on his face.

"A little closer," another newsman called out.

Mrs. Duncan reached up and straightened her son's tie.

A question came from the back. "Frank, are you confident about your mother's case?"

Frank continued to smile as he spoke through clenched teeth. "My mother is innocent, but I'm only as confident as one can be when three of the jurors have admitted they believe that she's guilty based on newspaper accounts."

District attorney Roy Gustafson had quietly arrived in the courtroom and stood at the prosecution table taking papers out of his briefcase. He never looked up as he said, "Not exactly true. All the jurors have sworn that, in spite of any opinion they may have previously formed, they will base a verdict solely on the evidence presented in court."

Frank snorted. "We ran out of challenges. Would you want your mother tried by this jury?"

Mrs. Duncan would stand trial alone for Olga's murder. Moya and Baldonado had dropped their not-guilty pleas and agreed to testify against Mrs. Duncan. They pled guilty to the murder charges in order to get Gustafson to try them separately because both men's lawyers believed that would give them a better chance of avoiding the death penalty. Gustafson made no promises. Their sentencing trials were scheduled to begin in April after both testified against her.

"All rise," the clerk shouted above the din in the crowded courtroom. Everyone stood while eighty-three-year-old Judge Charles Blackstock slowly entered through a side door, directly from his private chamber. He used a cane to limp up the steps to his seat at the dais and with his good hand, picked up the gavel from the polished mahogany judicial bench with the words FIAT JUSTITIA engraved in the front panel. LET JUSTICE BE DONE.

Judge Blackstock presided from an elevated bench beneath the stained-glass domes depicting the three icons of justice—the sword, the scale, and the law book. He scowled down on the courtroom through thick, black-framed glasses, his balding head barely clearing the top of the worn leather chair behind the bench. The judge always wore a dark suit, some called it his funeral suit, while presiding at trial; he never wore judicial robes. After waiting for everyone to sit, he put down his gavel without so much as a single rap on the glistening wood surface. The judge nodded to the bailiff. "Bring in the jury."

Ventura County district attorney Roy Gustafson, dressed in a single-breasted gray suit and a dark tie, made a brief opening statement. He spoke in a matter-of-fact tone as he summarized the evidence that demonstrated Mrs. Duncan's unusual possessiveness of her son and her blind hatred of anyone who might take him away from her. Gustafson referred to the connection between Elizabeth Duncan and her son, Frank, as "a personal relationship that has existed for all of Frank's life, some twenty-nine or thirty years, staying with his mother always." The DA gave the jury a glance. "Wherever Frank was, Mother was with Frank, and they lived together until Frank married Olga."

The DA told the jury about Mrs. Duncan's campaign of threats and harassment against her new daughter-in-law and how she had impersonated Olga and hired someone to play the part of Frank in order to obtain an annulment of his marriage. When this didn't separate Frank from his wife, she looked for a killer.

Frank and his mother sat impassively as they listened to Gustafson speak. Frank had been granted permission to stay in the courtroom throughout the trial, even though he would later be called as a witness in his mother's defense, because Sullivan had argued that Frank was part of his mother's legal team and crucial to her overall defense. Gustafson had agreed to the plan as long as his prosecution witnesses were also allowed to remain in the courtroom to hear the testimony of the other witnesses.

Now Sullivan told the judge that he preferred to reserve his right to make an opening statement until later in the trial, at the beginning of the defense case.

In quick succession, Gustafson called three witnesses: Olga's dentist, Olga's friend Sylvia Butler, and the physician who had performed Olga's autopsy. The DA also introduced twelve crime scene photos into evidence. Sullivan objected to two of the photos as "particularly gruesome in nature and likely to appeal to the vice, passion, and prejudice of the jury."

Gustafson withdrew both photos.

The dentist, Dr. Richard Pagett, used dental charts to identify Olga's body. Sylvia Butler, one of Olga's friends who'd visited her the night she disappeared, followed Dr. Pagett to the stand.

"I will show you People's Exhibit 36, Miss Butler," Gustafson said. He held up the bloodstained, tattered robe that had been wrapped around the body. The display of the mud-caked pink nightclothes caused a collective gasp in the gallery. "I ask you whether you recognize these as the garments Olga was wearing the last time you saw her?"

"Yes, that's what she was wearing that night." Miss Butler put her hand over her mouth.

The next witness, Dr. D. Gordon Johnson, the autopsy surgeon, established the cause of death. He began by describing the condition of the body.

"The body was covered with dirt that we washed away to reveal the body of a young female, obviously pregnant. The facial features were fairly well destroyed by collapse of the nose and the ears, and some flesh was missing. There were many lacerations over the front half of the scalp. The hair was missing except—"

"Excuse me for interrupting, Doctor," Gustafson said. "I will show you these three pictures and ask you if they depict the condition of the scalp."

"Yes, sir, they do. Some of the lacerations reveal the skull, with hair particles carried deep into the depths of the wounds."

"And did you confirm your opinion that the deceased was pregnant during the autopsy?"

"Yes. We found a female fetus, forty-three centimeters crown-to-heel length, in the uterus."

The courtroom was silent as the doctor gave the autopsy pictures back to the DA, who handed them off to the court clerk to pass to the jury. Only the sound of crinkling photo paper broke the silence in the courtroom as steely-faced jurors examined the pictures.

Gustafson continued with the witness. "What is your opinion as to the cause of death?"

"The cause was one of three mechanisms: strangulation, brain damage, or suffocation."

"In other words, it could have been a blow to the head with a pistol, or actual strangulation, or . . . suffocation?"

"Yes, sir. Suffocation from being placed in an environment with no oxygen, such as being buried alive."

After Dr. Johnson left the stand, Gustafson turned to the defense. "You may cross-examine."

"I have no questions," Sullivan said without looking up.

Judge Blackstock scowled at the attorneys. "I assume the examination of the next witness is going to take some time?"

"Yes, Your Honor," Gustafson said.

The judge put his hand to his ear. "Speak up. Is that right? It will take quite a little while?"

"Yes, I believe so," Gustafson said in a louder voice. "Do you want a recess?"

"Yes. I guess it's a good time to take a break." The judge turned to the jury. "Do not discuss the case among yourselves or with anyone else. Do not form or express . . ."

In the press section, Bennie Jo turned to Bob. "Think the old codger needs a bathroom break?"

Bob finished writing something in his notebook. "Could be. He turned eighty-three a couple of months ago."

"What's wrong with him? I mean the cane, the limp arm? Is he competent?"

Bob chuckled. "He had a stroke last year, and he has a little trouble with his left arm and leg, but his mental faculties are fine. He's sharp as a tack."

Bennie Jo didn't look convinced. "What about his hearing?"

Bob rocked his hand to indicate "so-so."

"You're kidding me! And this guy gets assigned the biggest trial in county history?"

"We only have three judges, and he's the presiding judge."

Bennie widened her eyes. "So he assigned *himself*?"

Bob shrugged. "He's a fine judge. He usually handles the criminal cases, and he has a long history here. In fact, he was born a few feet from where we're sitting right now. His family home was torn down in 1912 to make room for this courthouse."

"That's a qualification?"

"Let me finish . . ." *Jeez, pushy broad. No wonder Edd keeps his distance.* "He was an unbeatable trial lawyer, the most sought-after criminal defense attorney in the county before he took a big pay cut to become a judge. Lots of folks thought he'd lean toward the defense." Bob smiled. "But it turns out Judge Blackstock doesn't have any maudlin sympathy for criminals."

"Can he even hear what's happening in the courtroom?"

"He knows what's going on. He never gets reversed by higher courts, unlike some of those Los Angeles judges I'm sure you're used to seeing." Bob glanced up as the judge made his way back into the courtroom. "A little gruff at times . . . and I'll admit, everyone needs to speak up in Judge Blackstock's courtroom."

Bennie Jo rolled her eyes. "He could keel over any minute."

After the break, Gustafson's next witness was Barbara Jean Reed, a young dark-haired woman wearing a white sheath dress with a matching bolero jacket and black gloves. She told the court that she had known the defendant, "Betty" Duncan, for many years; they had first met when Mrs. Duncan lived next door to her family in Ventura. After Mrs. Duncan moved away, Barbara Jean hadn't seen her for ten years until she started working as a carhop at the Blue Onion Drive-In in Santa Barbara. Mrs. Reed said Betty was a frequent customer and lived only a block away from the restaurant.

The DA turned a page of his yellow tablet. "Calling your attention to the month of July 1958, do you recall having any conversation with Mrs. Duncan at her residence?"

"Yes, I do. Betty called me. She said that she had a problem." The young woman glanced toward the defense table. "She asked me to come over to her apartment to talk."

Mrs. Duncan shook her head and whispered furiously to her attorney.

Gustafson kept his gaze on the witness. "Did you go there?"

Barbara Jean nodded as she looked down at her lap and removed her gloves. "She said that she had been receiving threats from some woman, and this woman was chasing around with her son, and she didn't want anything to happen to his career, nothing whatsoever."

Judge Blackstock leaned forward. "Could you speak a little louder, please?"

The witness raised her voice. "Then she started talking about Patsy. Patsy was her daughter, and she told me how much she missed her."

"Do you know her?"

"I went to school with Patsy." Barbara Jean twisted her gloves around her fingers. "But she died in 1948, when we were in high school."

The sound of sobbing filled the quiet courtroom. Mrs. Duncan sat slumped in her chair with both hands covering her face. When Frank got up to comfort her, she began to wail.

Sullivan stood up. "A moment, Your Honor?"

The judge glanced at the courtroom clock. "Five-minute recess," he barked.

Most people in the courtroom stayed in their seats. A low buzz of voices rose as the sobs quieted. Frank and Sullivan blocked Mrs. Duncan from view and patted her shoulders as they bent over her and spoke in soothing voices. Frank handed his mother his handkerchief.

Bennie Jo whispered to Bob, "A real sob sister, that one. Looks like crocodile tears to me."

Bob shook his head. "I think it's real. Patsy hit her head in a roller-skating accident when she was fourteen. And from what I've found out, Mrs. Duncan never recovered. She's been hooked on sleeping pills ever since."

Finally, Mrs. Duncan quieted, and Gustafson resumed his questioning of Mrs. Reed.

"What did Mrs. Duncan say about Patsy?"

"She said, 'Being as our Patsy isn't with us anymore, I want you to carry on for her.' I told her I would do anything for Patsy."

The sound of crying started again. The judge glared at Sullivan, who squeezed his client's arm.

"And then she started mentioning her problem with this girl again, a girl she called Olga." Mrs. Reed twisted her gloves some more. "She said that this girl had given her about enough trouble, and then she said, 'I'm not taking any more from that bitch.'"

Mrs. Duncan held her rosary to her breast, her face shiny with tears.

"What did she ask you to do about this girl named Olga?"

"She said she wanted me to go to the apartment that this girl lived in and take a bottle of acid and throw the acid in the girl's face, and that she would be directly behind me with a blanket soaked in chloroform and would throw it over the girl. And between the two of us, we could tie her up and throw her in the back seat of Frank's car, and then she wanted me to drive her up in the mountains and throw her over a cliff."

Mrs. Duncan bounced out of her chair and slammed her hand on the table. "Never!" The tears were gone. The room roared.

The judge banged his gavel as Sullivan pulled his client back into her chair. Frank remained in his seat, head bowed.

The judge banged his gavel three more times and yelled for the court to come to order. He leveled his eyes at Mrs. Duncan. "Your attorney speaks for you. If he has an objection, he makes it."

Mrs. Duncan leaned back, her mouth twisted into a pout and her arms folded across her chest.

The judge glowered at her through his thick, black-framed glasses for a moment before nodding at Gustafson to continue.

Barbara Jean told the court that Mrs. Duncan had promised her five hundred dollars if she would agree to the plan. She told Mrs. Duncan that she would "think about it," but instead, she'd called Frank the next day. "I didn't have the words within myself to come right out and tell him that his mother was planning a murder. I said, 'I think your mother has gone crazy. You better get this girl out of town before something serious happens.'"

Sullivan cross-examined Barbara Jean, asking detailed questions about where she had been sitting in the apartment while she was talking to Mrs. Duncan. When he asked what Frank's reaction had been to his mother's plan to "get rid of Olga," Barbara Jean testified that Frank had told her he would "take care of it."

Near the end of the cross-examination, Sullivan asked her, "Did you ever at any time report this incident to the police?"

"No, I didn't think anything like this would ever happen. Mrs. Duncan's always been . . . a little scatterbrained."

"You never told the police?" Sullivan repeated.

"No," Barbara Jean replied in a small voice.

Mrs. Barnett, manager of the Garden Street apartments, was the first witness called for the afternoon session. She shuffled down the aisle, leaning on the arm of an assistant DA. The sound of her shallow breathing was audible in the courtroom as the assistant helped her onto the witness stand. Mrs. Barnett had had a heart attack at Christmas, and her doctor had recommended bed rest. But she had insisted that she could testify. "I owe it to Olga," she'd told her friends.

After a few preliminary questions about her occupation, Gustafson asked Mrs. Barnett if she had gotten to know Olga Duncan.

"As much as it was possible to know my tenants without being too familiar, I did."

"Would you describe Olga Duncan's disposition as it appeared to you?"

Mrs. Barnett spoke in a strong voice. "Well, whenever I saw Olga, before all the trouble came up, of course, she was always very quiet, a very reserved girl. Quiet, a lovely disposition, very, very dedicated to her work as a nurse."

"And do you know the defendant, Mrs. Elizabeth Duncan?"

"Not personally. The only time I've seen her was when she came to the apartment house with her friend Mrs. Short while Olga was at work."

Mrs. Barnett went on to describe what had happened at the end of August 1958. "When Mrs. Duncan first arrived, she said that she wanted to rent an apartment. When I told her there weren't any apartments available, she changed her story and said that she was Frank Duncan's mother and wanted to be let into his apartment so she could surprise him. She showed me her driver's license and some pictures." Mrs. Barnett shook her head. "I knew it wasn't a good idea for me to let her into the apartment, but I did it anyway. I took her up there. She's a very convincing woman."

"Now, to the best of your recollection, Mrs. Barnett, what happened when you and the defendant went into the apartment?"

Frank Duncan leaned forward and tapped on Sullivan's chair.

Sullivan immediately stood. "We are going to object to this as incompetent, irrelevant, and immaterial and too remote and having no tendency to prove any of the issues in this case, Your Honor."

"Overruled."

"I will try to remember everything to the best of my ability." Mrs. Barnett flashed a dagger glare at Sullivan. "I opened Olga's door, and Mrs. Duncan flew right past me, straight back to the bedroom. She flung open the closet doors and became distraught. Then she pointed to the clothes and took hold of them and said, 'There, you see, none of Frank's clothes are here.' She repeated that several times. 'They are not married. Look at the bed. There is only one pillow.' I realized that I had made a very terrible mistake in letting her up there."

"Did Mrs. Duncan say anything else?"

"She screamed that they were not married and that he didn't stay at night with Olga. That's when I realized that he wasn't spending the night. I'd heard footsteps coming down the stairs around ten o'clock or so most nights." She shot Frank a disgusted look and shrugged. "I thought he was going out for a pack of cigarettes or something."

"Then you left the apartment?"

"Yes. I just wanted to get her out of there. 'Let's go back downstairs and let's talk about this,' I said, 'Why don't I make you a nice cup of tea?'"

"Was there further conversation downstairs?"

"Yes. She was still trying to tell me that they weren't married." Mrs. Barnett leaned forward. "And I didn't make her a cup of tea either. I just told her that because I wanted to get her out of the apartment."

Sullivan stood again. "May we interpose an objection, Your Honor, this testimony doesn't tend to prove or dispose any of the issues in the case and is too remote."

Judge Blackstock sat with his arms crossed over his chest, looking a little like the Great Buddha. "The objection is overruled."

"But, Your Honor . . ."

"Overruled."

Gustafson turned back to his witness. "Go ahead and tell us what the conversation was."

"She said that they were living in sin in my apartment house because the marriage had been annulled. She wanted me to put them out and told me that Olga had been married before, that she'd deserted her husband and two children, and that Olga was taking her boy Frank away from her. And that was the one thing that she was not going to stand for."

Gustafson moved closer. "Anything else?"

"She said that she wouldn't let anyone take her boy away from her." Mrs. Barnett put her hand to her breast. "That she would kill her first, if it was the last thing she did."

Murmurs filled the courtroom.

"Would you state for me the words, the exact words, as near as you can recall them, that the defendant, Elizabeth Duncan, said about killing Olga?"

"'She is not going to have my son. I will kill her if it's the last thing I do.'"

"You may cross-examine," Gustafson said.

"It's nearly four o'clock," Judge Blackstock said. "I think we better adjourn for the day."

Bob wound his way out of the courtroom through the lingering spectators. He made his motorboat sound as he descended the great marble staircase that led to the ornate iron gates at the front of the courthouse. Once outside, he switched to the fast, off-key humming of an unrecognizable tune as he passed the Father Serra statue and started down the steep sidewalk.

He stopped humming when he passed the open doorway of the Sportsman Bar and Grill. One of the guys from the *San Francisco Examiner* was heading through the door. "Hey, Bob. Come on in and join us."

Bob just gave him a backward wave and kept walking toward the newspaper office as he composed the headline for the day's story: JEALOUSY KILLED OLGA, THE DA SAYS. He smiled to himself. That about summed it up so far.

CHAPTER FORTY-TWO

SWIMMING WITH RICKY

February 24, 1959

Sometimes when I swam, I heard Ricky Nelson singing. The six-day-a-week swim team practices were long, hard, and repetitive. The beat of Ricky's guitar matched the rhythm of my pounding kick, although I didn't have control over which song reverberated through my brain. It seemed to depend on the timing of my strokes, the speed of my swimming. "Be-Bop Baby" frequently popped into my head for sprints.

The whistle blew. I ducked underwater, tucked my knees to my chest, and pushed off the wall with the other swimmers, kicking into a streamlined glide. Coach, his voice muffled through the water, yelled, "Pick it up. No dogging it!"

I swam faster, and Ricky sang faster, too. "Be-bop baby, be-bop baby . . ." My right arm swept downward as I caught the water, pushing it past my hips, while I lifted my left elbow and reached forward. Shadowy forms churned on either side. I flipped-turned at the wall, twisted out of the somersault, and pushed through the smooth, clear water to go back the other way.

On my right, Marilyn moved even with me. I put my head down and quickened my kick, but she cut through the water with her effortless stroke and surged ahead. The music stopped again when I spotted Betsey hiding out underwater, doing her "diver of the deep" impression. She was sitting lotus-style, floating below the surface in the far corner of the pool, opposite the coach, eyes wide open, cheeks puffed with air as she gently pushed her palms upward to keep herself underwater and out of sight. Betsey hated interval sprints.

I touched the wall and held on, breathing hard throughout the twenty-second rest as I watched my sister's upturned face barely break the surface for a quick gulp of air before slowly sinking again as swimmers from the second group splashed to the pool's edge.

The whistle blew. My group's turn again. "Get a move on!" Coach yelled.

After practice we pulled sweatshirts and sweatpants over our wet bathing suits and walked out to the street behind the Ventura High School pool. It was dark, so we stood under a streetlight. I shivered in my soggy sweat clothes.

"What's taking him so long?" Marilyn sat on a fire hydrant, whirling her arms around in a circle, trying to balance. "My mother hates it when I'm late."

Betsey searched for sow bugs in the grass.

Fifteen minutes later, Daddy finally pulled up to the curb in his old Chevy sedan. He'd recently had it painted robin's-egg blue at the Earl Scheib shop, but it didn't look much better than the original rusted white. Daddy leaned over the passenger seat, rolled down the window, and yelled, "Get in the damn car. We're late."

"But we've been waiting right here," I said, bewildered. I climbed into the back seat. "We weren't fooling around. We came out right after practice." I saw him squinting at me in the rearview mirror, his mouth scrunched and angry. I fiddled with a torn piece of upholstery.

"Goddamn assignment editor," he muttered. "I don't need help from some junior punk reporter with interviewing Frank Duncan or any other witness."

Marilyn and Betsey were still out on the lawn. Betsey threw sow bugs at Marilyn, who laughed and ran away, squealing across the grass.

Daddy opened his door and waved an arm wildly. "There's going to be hell to pay if you girls don't get into this car. Right now! Jesus H. Christ . . ."

All the laughing and squealing stopped, and the two hurried to the car. Betsey sat in the front seat. Marilyn got in beside me. She slammed the door. "Betsey's got sow bugs."

Daddy turned in his seat, breathing hard, his face blotched red. "Get those damned bugs out of this car!"

I sank into the seat and wrapped my towel over my head and across my mouth so that only my eyes were exposed. I watched him rub his hand furiously across his mouth. His face looked swollen and puffed out. Seething . . . like he might explode. "Agitated," my mother called it.

Betsey opened her door and threw out the bugs. She didn't even talk back. Daddy threw the car into gear, just as a blue Ford stopped alongside our car, blocking us.

A couple of high school boys in football uniforms and cleats were crossing over from the football field. The two girls in the Ford rolled down their windows, and the boys stopped in the street to talk to them.

"Son of a bitch!" Daddy exploded. "Punks blocking the road . . ."

Marilyn started to say something. I clamped a hand over her mouth.

Daddy was still looking at the Ford. "You goddamn blue bastard! Get out of the way, you imbeciles."

Betsey got up on her knees to look out the back window. "Daddy, you can back up and go around them."

He glanced back. "Well, goddammit. I don't want to back up. Why should I have to back up?" His voice shrill, he pounded on the steering wheel.

Marilyn pulled my hand off her mouth and whispered, "He's really having a cow."

Tears stung my eyes, the way they always did when Daddy got really angry in public. But at least my eyes were already red from the chlorine in the pool. Maybe he wouldn't notice.

The boys were bent over the Ford, leaning close to the windows and talking to the ponytailed girls.

Daddy knocked on his window and motioned. Spittle glistened at the side of his mouth. One of the boys turned our way and squinted at him. He probably thought Daddy was crazy, the way he was gesturing, his face all red and distorted, drool at the corners of his lips.

I moved the towel away from my mouth. "Daddy, I'm sorry we're late," I said.

Marilyn added, "My mother doesn't care that much what time I get home as long as she's not in a bad mood."

Daddy cracked his window open and motioned wildly at the students. "Son of a bitch!"

All four of them turned to stare.

I pulled the towel tighter around my head. "Don't worry, Daddy, everything will be—"

Betsey climbed up on her knees again. She reached in front of Daddy and hit the horn, really laid on it. Daddy let out a startled, strangled laugh. The boys jumped away from the Ford. One of them flung out his arms like, "What'd we do?" The girl driver waved at us, friendly-like, and fired up the engine. She moved into a space a little way up the road.

But one of the football players, number 54, had his hands on his hips. He lunged in our direction just as Daddy stepped on the gas and shot away, narrowly missing the kid.

"You showed those guys," Betsey said. She faced the back window and shook her fist at them.

When we got home, Mother was already in the kitchen. "Just in time," she said as she pulled a chicken out of the oven. Daddy grunted at her. He didn't like baked chicken, so he made himself a peanut-butter-and-jelly sandwich and stomped off to his office to eat. I didn't like chicken either, so I made myself a piece of toast. Mother didn't say anything. She was too tired from work.

Later, when Daddy came out of his office to take his plate back to the kitchen, Mother asked, "What's wrong with you?"

I stood in the hallway and peeked into the kitchen while they talked.

"I went by the office before I picked up the girls, and the assignment editor tells me he wants our new cub reporter, his nephew Jerry*"—Daddy made a face—"to try to interview some of the witnesses." He threw up his hands. "God almighty, that's all I need. I told him to keep his goofball nephew away from me and the witnesses."

"Bob, you didn't yell, did you?"

Daddy shrugged.

"Oh, Bob, not again."

"I don't need you grilling me." He paced back and forth.

Mother put her hand out. "Could you please sit down a minute? There's something I need to tell you."

"I don't need suggestions. I've already got enough pressure."

"This isn't about the trial. A call came into the switchboard at the hospital today. Some woman left a message, but not a name."

Daddy sat down.

Mother talked faster. "I don't really think it's anything to worry about, but it might have been Beth, my patient who took . . . care of Tweety and then . . ."

"Killed the bird!"

Mother closed her eyes momentarily. "We don't really know what happened."

A surge of adrenaline shot through my body. I squeezed my hand over my mouth. That crazy woman who murdered Tweety?

"I think it might have been Beth . . . could have been . . . The operator didn't understand everything, but she wrote down that the woman said, 'Tell Mrs. Holt that I know what that little girl and her bird were up to.' She thinks the woman also said, 'I'm not going to let her send thought waves . . . or maybe voices . . . to control my brain.' It was hard for the operator to understand because the woman was mumbling."

"What does she mean by 'let *her* send thought waves'?" Daddy said.

"I don't know. . . . Maybe she was talking about the bird."

"The bird's dead!" Daddy yelled. "I don't like this. I don't like this at all."

Mother shushed him. "Now don't get excited, Bob. Beth isn't violent. She's just a very sick paranoid schizophrenic who needs to be back in the hospital."

"Thank you, Dr. I've Got a Psycho Excuse for Everybody."

I slid down the wall, sat cross-legged next to the doorway, and peered into the kitchen while my parents discussed what should be done about this "possible" Beth situation. Mother made coffee.

"We don't want to overreact," Mother said. "Scare Debby for no reason."

"Make a mountain out of a molehill." Daddy took a sip of coffee. "You don't even know if it was Beth who made the call."

Mother nodded. "No sense jumping to conclusions. We'll tell Debby that if she sees Beth, she shouldn't talk to her, that she should run to the nearest house and call me."

"Because . . . ?"

Mother pondered a moment before saying, "Because Beth needs her medication, and I'll send someone from the hospital to pick her up and give it to her."

Beth's black-gloved hands flashed in my head. I closed my eyes and heard Ricky's soothing voice crooning the song: "There'll Never Be Anyone Else But You For Me."

Betsey burst into the hallway and pointed at me. "You're humming!"

"I am not!"

She bent over, still pointing at me, exaggerating her deep belly laugh. "You're humming Ricky Nelson."

As she turned to go, I jumped up and walloped her on the back.

She wailed.

Both parents appeared. Betsey tried to rub her back as she sobbed. "Debby hit me for no reason."

I looked away.

"She's in love with Ricky Nelson!" Betsey shouted. "She plays his records over and over again on the hi-fi after school."

My head whipped around. "I am not! I do not!"

Mother smiled. "That nice boy on *Ozzie and Harriet*?"

"Don't be ridiculous, Lois," Daddy snapped. "Debby doesn't go in for that mushy stuff. She's too smart for all that rock 'n' roll crap."

"Right. I'm not mushy, Daddy. I like important stuff! Like murder." I smiled up at his angry face. "Like you."

CHAPTER FORTY-THREE

GETTING RID OF OLGA

On the second day of the trial, Bob arrived early. He walked into the crowd in the hallway outside Courtroom One, greeting various court workers and attorneys with a friendly smile and a nod. A deputy blocked the doorway into the courtroom, arguing with one of the would-be spectators lined up outside the door.

"I'm sorry, ma'am, but there aren't any seats left."

The woman stomped her foot. "I drove all the way from Fillmore to see this trial. I've been here since four thirty this morning."

Bob raised his hand to the deputy as he ducked into the courtroom.

"Why's he getting in?" the woman from Fillmore complained.

"Press," the deputy said.

Someone else shouted, "Well, they don't need so many damn reporters! There must be forty of them taking up all those extra chairs."

Bob slid into the seat next to Bennie Jo.

"Did you hear the latest?" she whispered.

Bob gave her a quizzical look as he took out his notebook.

"Report going around that Mrs. Duncan and Frank got into a shouting match after court yesterday. Nobody seems to know what the fuss was about, but Sullivan had to shush them both up."

Bob looked toward the defense table, where Frank stood conferring with his mother, his hand resting on the back of her chair as he whispered in her ear. Bob raised his eyebrows. "Seem cordial enough now."

"Yeah," Bennie Jo said. "Looks like they kissed and made up."

Sullivan began his cross-examination of Olga's landlady, Mrs. Barnett, by asking details about the apartment building, the number of apartments, the number of tenants. He also wanted to know how and when the rent was paid. Finally, he got around to Mrs. Duncan's visit. "Was it while you were upstairs with Mrs. Duncan that she made the statement, 'She's not going to have him. I will kill her if it's the last thing I do?'"

Gustafson stopped taking notes and looked up in disbelief.

Mrs. Barnett said no, the conversation had taken place downstairs, in her apartment.

Sullivan repeated the threatening statement: "Was Mrs. Short present when Mrs. Duncan said, 'I will not let her have him. I will kill her if it's the last thing I do'? Is that right?"

The corners of Gustafson's lips edged a millimeter upward. *I will kill her if it's the last thing I do. How many times is he going to repeat those words?*

"Yes, Mrs. Short was present when she said she would kill Olga," the witness said.

"Did you speak to Olga Duncan about this threat?"

"Not at that time, I didn't, no. Mrs. Duncan asked me to please not say that she had been there. She didn't want her son worried. It might upset him. She asked me to say nothing." Mrs. Barnett looked around the courtroom. "Naturally, I thought that . . . I never dreamed she meant anything by it at all. So I agreed not to say anything."

Sullivan gave his head a disgusted shake. "You didn't make notes of this conversation you had with Mrs. Duncan when she came to the apartment building in August, did you?"

"No, sir, of course I didn't."

"In fact, you are endeavoring, as you sit here on the witness stand today, to rely on your memory. Is that correct?"

"Which is a pretty good one," Mrs. Barnett snapped.

Following Mrs. Barnett's testimony, Gustafson called a string of witnesses who had been approached by Mrs. Duncan to get rid of her troublesome daughter-in-law. Pretty, pregnant Diane Romero was the first to take the stand. She wore her dark hair pulled back in a ponytail and was dressed in a fuzzy yellow sweater over a brown maternity smock and skirt. Nineteen-year-old Diane hardly looked sixteen. She told the court that in September 1958, Mrs. Duncan had offered her fifteen hundred dollars to get rid of Olga.

The witness spoke in a nervous, quivering voice. "We met in the courtroom when her son Frank defended my husband, Rudy, on this phony narcotics charge. I think she always went to her son's trials. Sometimes me and Mrs. Duncan had lunch together, and I went to her apartment a couple of times. Well, we got to talking, and Mrs. Duncan started telling me about a woman named Olga who had been calling her up and bothering her. She said the woman was blackmailing Frank."

"Did she ask you to do anything about the situation?" Gustafson asked.

"She gave me five dollars to buy two cans of lye. I thought she wanted me to clean her bathroom with it, but then she told me that she wanted me to go to Olga's apartment, knock her over the head, put her in the bathtub, and then pour the lye over her."

Mrs. Duncan, looking very refined in a new black-and-brown English tweed outfit, let out an undignified snort.

Diane went on to testify that Mrs. Duncan asked her to go to an apartment on Garden Street. "She told me the woman named Olga was living there and was claiming to be her son's wife, but she wasn't because their marriage was annulled."

"Did Mrs. Duncan say why she wanted you to go to this apartment?"

Diane picked at some fuzzballs on the sleeve of her yellow sweater before continuing. "Uh-huh. . . . She wanted me to look the place over and see if I could get in there so I could get at Olga." Diane folded her hands on her pregnant belly. "To get rid of her."

"I see," Gustafson said. "Did she name the price?"

"First, she mentioned a thousand dollars. Then it was raised to fifteen hundred. Later on, she mentioned twenty-five hundred dollars."

Gustafson finished his examination of the witness, and the judge called a recess. Sullivan moved into the hallway and lit a cigar, which he would smoke at every opportunity throughout the trial. Reporters gathered around the affable attorney to ask a few questions. He made a point of making himself available to the press during trial breaks, often restating his unhappiness over Judge Blackstock's earlier refusal to grant a change of venue for his client's trial because of pretrial publicity.

"The district attorney did his best to prejudice the jury," he said. "Releasing a statement using this case as an argument in favor of capital punishment two months before the jury was even selected was a very obvious effort to influence the verdict."

A reporter countered. "But Gustafson points out that nowhere in his statement does he mention the names of any suspects. Says he was just stating his opinion on the death penalty as a private citizen."

Sullivan scoffed. "Moya and Baldonado had already confessed, and my client was in jail. The readers knew who he was talking about."

During his cross-examination of Mrs. Romero, Sullivan spent time having her rehash and clarify the testimony that Gustafson had already elicited. The defense lawyer asked her why she hadn't just told Mrs. Duncan that she didn't want anything to do with this plan to "get rid of Olga," and go to the police.

"Well, I had to play along with her. I didn't want her to be mad at me and get her son Frank to give up on my husband's case. He was on trial, and Mr. Duncan was his attorney."

"Did you ask her to give you half the money?"

Diane glanced toward the prosecution table. "Yes."

"You asked her for one thousand dollars, didn't you?"

"Yes," she said in a quivering voice.

"You would have taken it if she'd had it, wouldn't you?"

"Yes. I would have taken it if she'd given it to me. I wasn't planning to do anything for it, and she couldn't do anything to me if I took the money."

Bennie Jo whispered to Bob, "I don't get Sullivan's strategy. He goes over the same stuff Gustafson just asked. Sometimes the jury even gets to hear a few more damning details that the DA missed the first time around. He doesn't seem very well prepared."

Bob shrugged. "Yeah, well, he's playing without any cards. The man's got to say something, but he doesn't have a hell of a lot to work with."

Diane's husband, Rudy Romero, took the stand wearing an ill-fitting blue suit, his dark hair slicked back on his head. Rudy was an ex-convict and looked the part. But his matter-of-fact testimony had the ring of truth as he told the court a story almost identical to his wife's.

Sullivan's cross-examination of Romero ended quickly and failed to bring out any information favorable to Mrs. Duncan.

Gustafson continued questioning his string of would-be-killer witnesses. Next up was Bobby Huggins, a sailor that Mrs. Duncan had once dated, whom the DA called to show the defendant's hatred of Olga. Huggins was a reluctant witness who claimed that he remembered very little about what Mrs. Duncan had told him about Olga. Gustafson finally dragged out of him that Mrs. Duncan had been angry about a television set Frank had bought for Olga and upset about an insurance policy purchased by Frank with Olga as the beneficiary.

After much questioning, Huggins admitted that Mrs. Duncan proposed that he "beat up" Olga. When he declined, she suggested that he drive her by Olga's apartment so that she, Mrs. Duncan, could go inside and "take care of her."

Next the DA called Rebecca Diaz, a middle-aged Santa Barbara woman, who testified that Mrs. Duncan and Mrs. Short had showed up at her apartment in October.

"She asked me if I could use some money, and I said, 'Yes, I could.' And she said, 'Well, can you help me?' I said, 'It all depends.' Then she told me that she wanted to find somebody to get rid of a woman who had been threatening her and demanding money. I told her that I didn't want to get involved in anything like that. I said that I had to go to Oxnard for a few days, and she wanted me to look for somebody to help her there, but I didn't."

After Sullivan's brief cross-examination of Mrs. Diaz, Gustafson called the odd-job man from the Salvation Army. Ralph Winterstein, the tall, thin, twenty-six-year-old who had impersonated Frank Duncan at the phony annulment hearing, took the stand, wearing an open-collared shirt and a dark zip-up jacket.

"I came in contact with Mrs. Duncan last August through a fellow that worked at the Salvation Army who gave me her address. I needed the work, so I went to her house to talk to her."

Gustafson leaned nonchalantly on the lectern while looking toward the jury. "Will you tell us, Mr. Winterstein, what the conversation was about?"

Sullivan stood up. "Just a moment. We are going to object to testimony about this alleged annulment as incompetent, irrelevant, and immaterial."

"Overruled," the judge barked.

Gustafson nodded at his witness to continue.

"She brought me some coffee, and we chatted awhile about this and that before she got down to business. Then she told me she had a problem that her son was involved in. She said her son wanted an annulment, but he didn't have time to do it. She asked me how I would like to make one hundred dollars to help her get this annulment. She said she'd called a lawyer and made arrangements."

The witness testified that Mrs. Duncan had told him Olga was ruining her son's life, but Frank had put off getting an annulment. "She said, 'To hell with that bitch, if Frank won't get an annulment, I'll do it myself.' She said that her son's wife was a foreigner, too."

"You mentioned that Mrs. Duncan said she would pay you one hundred dollars to help her get this annulment," Gustafson said.

"That's right, sir."

"Did you get paid the one hundred dollars?"

"No, I did not."

During Ralph's testimony, Sullivan objected fifteen times about the admissibility of testimony concerning the annulment. The judged over-ruled every objection.

"Was there any other conversation between you and Mrs. Duncan at a later time?" Gustafson said.

"Well, once she hit her fists together." The witness demonstrated the fist pounding. "And she said, 'I'm so damn mad at that bitch that I could kill her.' And I told Mrs. Duncan, I says, 'Mrs. Duncan, that is no way to feel about the matter.'

"I tried to get her to understand that the best thing to do was to leave them alone, that she couldn't do anything about it, that it was their lives. And she was quiet, and she thought a while, and then she said, 'Ralph, how would you like to marry me?'"

There was snickering in the gallery again, killed by Judge Blackstock's glare.

Gustafson gazed at the jury. "She asked you, 'How would you like to marry me?'"

"Yes, she did, and I said, 'Mrs. Duncan, I have had experience in marriage before, and I'm not about to get married again.'"

On cross-examination Sullivan had only a couple of questions.

"Mr. Winterstein, have you ever been convicted of a felony?"

"Yes," Ralph said. "Twice."

"What felony?"

"Taking a stolen car across state lines."

"Any other felony?" Sullivan persisted.

Ralph furrowed his brow. "You mean the one now, down here in Ventura?"

"You pled guilty yesterday to a felony regarding this fraudulent annulment you've been telling us about, didn't you?"

Ralph cocked his head. "Because I swore that I was Frank Duncan . . . yes, sir."

"What felony was that?"

"Perjury, sir."

"Perjury? I see." Sullivan folded his arms across his chest. "You haven't been sentenced on that charge yet, have you?"

"No, sir, I have not."

"That is all," Sullivan said and sauntered back to the defense table.

Judge Blackstock roused himself and glanced at the clock. "I guess we better adjourn for the noon recess. It's already after twelve."

Bennie gathered up her purse and set it in her lap while she waited for the judge to finish the jury admonition. "We'll all be down at the Sportsman as usual, Bob. Sure you don't want to join us?"

Bob tucked his pencil in his shirt pocket. "Thanks, but I think I'll stick with the cheese-and-peanut-butter sandwich I got down at the office. Need to get a little work done."

"A break might do you good. Don't you want to hear what us out-of-towners think? Might get a different perspective."

Bob sucked air between his teeth. "Yeah, well. I need to check on an important source." He raised his eyebrows. "Go fish for a little information."

CHAPTER FORTY-FOUR

THE PIER

February 25, 1959

Judi and I had arrived at the pier with our fishing gear a little after noon that day. It was a minimum day at school, so we'd hitched a ride to the pier with Mrs. Alfred. She drove us north through Ventura on Thompson Boulevard, the old Highway 101, and turned left toward the ocean at California Street. I looked out the back window and stared at the big white courthouse perched on the hill as we drove the block to the beach. "My dad's up there." I pointed. "At Mrs. Duncan's trial. . . ." The car slowed as we crossed the railroad tracks.

A thin woman wearing a loose gray dress and a black scarf tied over her shoulder-length brown hair stood on the corner. *Oh no!* I turned around and got up on my knees to look out the back window so I could keep my eyes on her as she waited to cross the street.

Mother had told me the previous night about the mysterious phone call to the hospital that "might have been from Beth but probably wasn't." She said that there was nothing to worry about because she was sure that Beth had run off to Los Angeles. "And anyway," Mother said, "I don't think Beth has a car."

"Hey!" I pointed at the woman. "That might be . . ."

Judi looked around. "What?"

But the woman smiled and waved at someone across the street.

"Never mind," I mumbled as I turned around to face forward.

Mrs. Alfred steered the car onto Shore Drive and drove along the beach and under the pier. She stopped to let us out at the parking lot.

"Who were you pointing at?" Judi asked as we got out of the car.

"Oh, nobody. . . . Well, for a minute I thought it might be one of Mother's patients. The one who killed Tweety and said that he could read her mind."

Judi stopped short. "What?"

"I'm not supposed to talk about it. Mother doesn't want to scare the neighbors."

Judi stared at me, blank-faced.

"I get the creeps a little bit when I think about her." I laid my pole down and put on my new red jacket. "This lady's got skids-o-something. . . . She wears long black gloves every day."

"Gloves?" Judi looked back toward the road. "That sounds cuckoo."

I pulled on her arm. "Come on. Let's get out on the pier before all the big fish get caught."

Judi and I had been friends since before kindergarten. We had a lot in common, including an interest in churchgoing. Her family didn't belong to a church either, so she and I signed up for a lot of Vacation Bible Schools together. Judi liked the crafts.

We were also both keen about fishing off the pier, ever since we'd participated in the Ventura Recreation Department's Annual Fishing Derby the previous August. I'd won a ribbon for catching the smallest fish. I was hooked.

Judi came from a fishing family—her dad, Myron, had caught the giant sea bass—and she was very knowledgeable about the sport. She had her own tackle box with lots of important fishing stuff inside, like sinkers and hooks. She gave me a tattered hand-me-down fishing net to carry in my bucket. Her dad was a printer at the newspaper, and when we were done fishing, we were supposed to meet him so he could give us a ride home.

After stopping at the bait shop to buy a bag of anchovies, we headed down the pier. I watched the blue water and white foam through the planks. The pier shook every time a big wave rumbled between the pilings. When we stopped halfway out on the north side of the pier, Judi set the tackle box on a fish-gut-stained wooden bench, and I put the bucket down next to my feet. A seagull cried as it circled above our heads.

Judi held out the fishy-smelling bag to me. "It's your turn to bait the hooks."

We lowered our lines twenty feet down into the water. No casting anymore since the time I'd caught a nearby fisherman with my hook. The day was sunny with a stiff breeze blowing off the ocean. I leaned my pole against the pier and looked into the water, searching for fish. Nothing but a few little perch. Judi kept tilting her pole up and down as she watched her red-and-white float bob on the water's surface.

"Why do you keep doing that?" I asked.

"So the fish will think my bait is swimming. My dad says the fish like that."

I started moving my pole up and down too, but my hook flew out of the water and caught in the barnacles on the piling. I tried to jerk it free. "Oh, no . . ." I yanked again.

"Don't do that so hard," Judi said. "You'll—"

My line came loose.

"—break your line," Judi finished too late.

"Shoot," I said as I reeled in the empty fishing line. "Now I'll need another hook."

"And some more bait."

The words were no sooner out of my mouth than a seagull swooped down and grabbed the bag of anchovies in his beak.

"Hey, you!" I yelled as I watched the gull soar into the sky.

"Come back here, you big dodo bird!" Judi screamed.

Another gull followed and tried to snatch the bag away but only succeeded in knocking it loose. We watched as our bait dropped into the sea.

"Those seagulls steal everything," Judi said. "Now what are you going to do?"

I shrugged and leaned my elbows on the railing. After a while, I said, "I'm going to the Baptist church with Angela on Sunday."

"Again?" Judi kept jostling her pole as we talked.

"I like the bus," I said. "You can come. Anyone can ride it."

"I might go to the Jehovah's Witness hall with Lorraine's family."

"I thought you said you wouldn't go back after they washed that old lady's feet and you got really scared that you might be next."

Judi made a face. "That was at the Four Squares, not the Witnesses, and besides, Lorraine says we're going to learn about Armageddon and have chocolate cupcakes."

"I don't care if they have cupcakes or not. I'm never going there after what that teacher said at Vacation Bible School last summer . . . you know, about the shark."

"You mean when the boys swam out to the cruise ship to dive for the coins the passengers threw overboard?" Judi asked.

"Uh-huh. One of the boys kept grabbing more coins instead of swimming for shore, and then a shark came and bit off his arms and they sank to the bottom of the ocean, with his cut-off hands still holding all his coins. 'Greedy little hands,' the teacher said."

I stood listening to the ebb and flow of the ocean slapping at the pilings, staring at the swells as they rolled toward the shore.

Judi's pole jerked. We both squealed.

I grabbed the net from the bucket as she reeled in a tiny perch, wiggling and gleaming in the sunlight as it popped out of the water.

I put the net over the railing but accidently hit the fish with the metal rim of the net.

"Careful!" Judi said.

Too late. The fish slipped off the hook and fell back into the ocean.

"Sorry," I said as I looked over the railing. The fish was lying motionless in the water.

"It's okay," Judi said. "My dad told me not to bring home any more too-small fish." She swung her hook up and over the railing toward me.

I ducked out of the way of the hook and turned my gaze down the pier toward town. "Hey, look. Here comes my father." I ran as fast as I could to meet him. "Daddy!" I grabbed his hand. "Why are you here? What's happening at the trial?"

"Nothing," he said as we walked back toward Judi. "Just a lot of arguing." He smiled. "It's the lunch recess, and I thought I'd check on you girls. See if you've reeled in a giant sea bass yet."

When we reached Judi, I pointed to her fish floating belly-up in the ocean. "He got away."

"Doesn't look like he got very far," Daddy said.

I tugged on his coat. "You saw Mrs. Duncan? She's there, right?"

"Oh, yeah, she's there, big as life and breathing fire."

"Well, I'm tired of fishing, and a seagull stole our bait. How about you take us up to the courthouse to see Mrs. Duncan? She's handcuffed, right? With guards?"

"Are you kidding? Your mother would kill me."

"Just a peek, I don't want to get too close . . . but I need to see what she looks like in person. Then we'll leave. I promise."

Daddy shook his head. "No can do. I'm working. I'm only here to check the ocean temperature for the paper." He pointed to the winch at the end of the pier and fished some coins out of his pocket. "Go buy some more bait."

My lower lip started to quiver. "I've never seen a real murderer before. This is probably my last chance to see how one looks, so if I ever—"

Daddy cut me off. "No matter how much I tell you, you always keep angling for more. Nothing is ever enough with you."

"You think I'm greedy?"

"That's a good way to put it, Debby. Greedy for information." He patted my head. "But don't worry, you have plenty of time to see a murderer. It seems like they're all over the place these days, and by the time you grow up, murderers will be a dime a dozen. Someday you can just pop down to the courthouse to see the latest murder trial any old time you want."

"Really?"

Daddy waved goodbye as he hurried down the pier toward the winch.

I stared at the coins in my hand. "Want to go up to Woolworths and get some Cokes and an order of french fries? We've got plenty of time before we meet your father."

"But what if we see that cuckoo lady with the gloves?"

I opened the tackle box, smiled, and held up the rusty bait knife. "Just in case."

CHAPTER FORTY-FIVE

THE KILLERS

February 26, 1959

The next morning, Luis Moya, accompanied by two guards, entered the courtroom through the side entrance. People in the gallery strained their necks to catch a glimpse of the twenty-year-old confessed killer. Attired in a natty light-gray suit, white shirt, and blue tie, Moya looked as if he were dressed for a night on the town rather than a day on the stand confessing to a brutal murder. After the guard removed his handcuffs, he climbed into the witness chair, clenching and unclenching his hands and rubbing his wrists.

Although, before being appointed attorneys, Moya and Baldonado had confessed, to both the police and the grand jury, to kidnapping and murdering Olga Duncan, they had pled "not guilty" at their arraignment hearing. So had Mrs. Duncan. Based on those pleas, Gustafson had intended to prosecute the three defendants together in a single trial.

But after the arraignment hearing, the attorneys for Moya and Baldonado had met with the DA and asked if he would recommend life imprisonment instead of death if their clients pled guilty to first-degree murder. Gustafson's answer had been an unequivocal "No!"

Moya's lawyer had then requested another meeting with the DA. He believed that his client had a better chance of escaping the death penalty if he was tried separately from Mrs. Duncan. Gustafson would agree to a separate trial only if Moya testified against Mrs. Duncan at her trial. Even then, the DA refused to take the death penalty off the table. Still, Moya decided to take his chances with his own jury and withdrew his "not guilty" plea.

Baldonado's attorney advised his client to follow suit, and Baldonado did so. This left only a sanity and penalty trial for the two killers; it was scheduled for April after the completion of their testimony at Mrs. Duncan's trial.

Now Moya scanned the faces in the courtroom with a cool, pleasant expression. He raised his hand to Reverend Gressett, his spiritual confessor and religious advisor, who sat behind the prosecution table. Moya had told everyone he spoke to that he'd come clean with God and was ready to tell the truth in court.

Bennie Jo scooted her chair closer to Bob. "Doesn't look like he'd hurt a fly, does he?"

Bob watched Moya wave to a pretty, dark-haired young woman sitting in the back row. "Yeah, and Frank says Mom couldn't kill a chicken. See what you think after Baby Face finishes testifying."

"I know . . . I read the grand jury transcript. But look at that face."

"Right," Bob muttered. "Probably the last thing Olga saw . . . Moya's lying face."

Luis Moya, born in San Angelo, Texas, near the Mexican border, had grown up in a clapboard shack next door to a beer joint owned by his parents. Knifings and shootings were common in the neighborhood. His mother ran the bar while his father did odd jobs around town. As a child, Luis shined shoes in the bar. He was in and out of the family saloon most nights, talking to the patrons and joking with the prostitutes.

An average student in elementary school, Luis was well-liked by his teachers, popular with classmates, and a safety patrol captain. He was a member of the school's citywide championship basketball team, and a Cub Scout who played Little League baseball. Luis was a joiner, a pleaser, who very much wanted to belong to a group. One of his elementary school teachers was quoted as saying, at the time of his arrest for the murder, "To me he was just a sweet child. I ask myself, 'How could this happen?'"

The trouble that plagued Luis for much of his life started the summer between sixth and seventh grades. He began staying out all night, drinking alcohol, smoking marijuana, and committing petty crimes with a group of older friends he'd met hanging out behind the tortilla factory in his dilapidated neighborhood.

His parents were poor, hard-working Mexican immigrants struggling to raise their children in a crime-infested slum. None of Luis's four siblings were ever in trouble with the law, and neither of his parents had ever been arrested. But Luis chose a different path. School no longer interested him. Instead, he worked at becoming a convincing liar.

After talking his way out of many scrapes with the law, he was sent to reform school for the first time at age fourteen for burglary. His parents hoped the experience would straighten him out, but he spent the next six years in and out of reform schools and then jails. He served time on burglary and narcotics charges, but he'd never been charged with a violent crime.

Many people, including his boss at the Blue Onion, had kind words to say for Luis Moya. His landlord described him as "a very engaging young man. I used to lend him five dollars here and there, and he would always pay me back. The kid wasn't bad. I would have trusted him with anything."

The still-smiling, happy-go-lucky Luis had been on parole from Soledad State Prison for less than a year for narcotics crimes when he was arrested for Olga Duncan's murder. Moya later confided to Reverend Gressett that there was a "good Luis" and a "bad Luis," and that "bad Luis" was very, very bad.

The room grew silent as Gustafson approached the witness stand to face off with one of Olga Duncan's admitted killers. The DA pulled his normally stooped shoulders upright as he asked the young man his name.

"Luis Estrada Moya," he said proudly, nodding to the jurors, the spectators, and the judge.

After some preliminary questions about how Moya happened to move to Santa Barbara after being paroled from Soledad State Prison (a fellow prisoner had told him it was a nice place to live) and about his employment and rise to night manager at the Blue Onion Drive-In Restaurant, Gustafson moved on to the meeting with Elizabeth Duncan at the Tropical Café.

Moya said, "Mrs. Esquivel told me that this lady named Mrs. Duncan came to see her and wanted to know if she knew anyone who would do a job for her and get rid of her daughter-in-law."

"I see," Gustafson said. "And when you and Augustine Baldonado met with Mrs. Duncan the next day, what did the defendant say about Olga Duncan?"

"That she would like for somebody to get her daughter-in-law out of the way because the woman threatened to ruin her son's career." Moya glanced at Reverend Gressett. "Then, you know, we got down to brass tacks, and we started making suggestions of how much money it would be worth to eliminate her daughter-in-law, and when it would be paid, and there were suggestions made of how to get rid of her by both Mrs. Duncan and myself."

Moya spoke articulately, using his practiced, unaccented vocabulary. He described how Mrs. Duncan offered to pay them an immediate $3,000, with the same sum to be paid five or six months after the job was done.

"She seemed like a very trustworthy woman," Moya said. "I told her that we didn't have any money and we needed to get transportation, a weapon, and gloves and so forth to do the job. So she went out after all the arrangements were made and pawned her wedding rings for one hundred seventy-five dollars and gave the money to me."

Gustafson asked for more details about the "arrangements" that had been made.

For the first time, Moya looked toward the defendant. "Mrs. Duncan told me that she had some acid and rope and some sleeping pills which if, you know, we decided to put them to use, she would have them in her possession." He said it had been agreed that he and Baldonado would kidnap Olga from her apartment, knock her out, tie her up, and take some of her clothes to make it look like she had gone on vacation. They were supposed to drive her to San Diego and then cross the border to kill her in Tijuana.

"What was the method of disposing of her in Tijuana that was agreed upon?" Gustafson's gaze lingered on the jury.

"She left that up to us. We didn't know whether we were going to shoot her or give her an overdose of dope."

Gustafson walked to the prosecution table and poked around in a pile of folders. He took a legal-sized yellow piece of paper out of a file and went back to the lectern and led Moya through what happened next.

Moya and Baldonado had borrowed a gun and a car from friends, bought black leather gloves at Harris & Frank, and procured ammunition at a combination drug and gun store on State Street. They had cruised by Olga's apartment on Garden Street to find out exactly where she lived. On Saturday night at nine thirty or ten, they came back and went up to the door. The plan was to force their way into the apartment and kidnap the young nurse. "But nobody answered," Moya said, so they left and went back to the Tropical for a few drinks and to dance.

"So you didn't find her on Saturday, November 15th," Gustafson said. "Did you make any attempt on Sunday, November 16th?"

"No. Baldonado had to go to a wedding in Oxnard."

"What did you do on Monday, November 17th?"

"We drove back to the apartment that night. On the way there, I suggested that I try to get her to come downstairs to the car. I thought it would be the best thing to do, if I could accomplish it."

Moya went into the details of how he knocked on Olga's door and convinced her that her husband was downstairs in the car. "I told her, 'Well, I met him up here at a bar, and he's pretty drunk, and he has quite a large amount of money with him, and he told me to bring him home here. So I have him downstairs in the car, but I need help to get him up here.' And she said, 'Sure, I'll help you bring him up.' So she went downstairs with me." Moya patted his pants pocket. "I had the pistol with me also."

"I see," Gustafson said. "What happened next?"

Moya swallowed a couple of times. "So Baldonado was pretending that he was Mr. Duncan, passed out in the back seat of the car. When she opened the door of the car, I hit her on the back of the head with the gun to try to knock her out and force her inside."

"A hard blow?"

"It was a pretty hard blow, but it didn't knock her out. She screamed and . . ."

A sharp intake of breath cut through the silence of the packed courtroom. All heads turned toward the defense table. Frank Duncan scraped his chair backward across the wooden floor.

Mrs. Duncan reached toward him. "Frankie . . . please don't . . ." She half rose, but Sullivan grabbed her arm.

Frank strode up the aisle, holding his hand to his mouth. The sound of his muffled sobs filled the room. A rumble of voices rose as the giant wooden door banged shut.

"Quiet," Judge Blackstock barked. He rapped his gavel.

Moya finished telling how Baldonado had pulled Olga into the back seat of the car. Moya then drove toward Highway 101, but he had to pull into a parking lot near the beach because the engine was sputtering. "Plus, she was still screaming."

"Still screaming," Gustafson repeated.

"Uh-huh. Baldonado kept hitting her with the pistol while I drove, but he couldn't knock her out, either. So when I stopped the car, I told him to hold her and give me the pistol so I could hit her with some heavy blows on the head." Moya used the back of his hand to wipe his mouth. "She finally passed out, and Baldonado tied her hands up with the tape."

"Describe what happened as you left Santa Barbara," Gustafson said.

"The original plan to take her to Tijuana wasn't going to work due to the fact that there was something wrong with the car. Baldonado suggested, since he knew the Ojai territory pretty well, that we should dispose of her up there in the mountains." Sometimes Moya sounded like a homicide detective testifying about the crime. "I took the cutoff to Ojai on Highway 150 so we could find a nice little spot to bury her."

He folded his hands on the railing that surrounded the witness box. "And that's what happened. I stopped a few times on the side of the road before I saw what I thought would be a good place to hide the body. It was dark, so I couldn't see very well, but I didn't think she would be found there."

"But she was alive when you got there?" Gustafson said.

People stirred in their seats. Bennie Jo nudged Bob. "Look at Mrs. Duncan," she whispered. "Cold-hearted old bitch is mesmerized."

"Yes," Moya said, "she was still living."

"You dragged her down the side of the hill, down to the culvert?"

"Yes."

"What did you do at that place?"

"Well, I'd broken the pistol when I hit her the last time while we stopped down at the beach, you know. The handle was damaged so that we couldn't use it anymore. Gus had to hit her with his fist. So we decided to strangle her until she was dead. We took turns strangling her and digging a hole in the ground with our hands." Moya wiped a few beads of sweat from his forehead. "And then we hit her over the head with a rock to make sure she was dead."

The courtroom was very quiet.

"With a rock?" Gustafson looked at the jury. A man in the front row had gone pale. The woman next to him sat rigidly upright, slowly fanning herself with her hand. Sullivan watched from the defense table with a sour expression.

"After you hit her over the head with this rock and you took turns strangling her," Gustafson said, "did she ultimately cease to breathe?"

"After a while, she did, yes."

Gustafson focused on Mrs. Duncan's cold, flinty stare. "How did you know this?"

"Well, we felt her pulse and we couldn't feel anything, so we just took it for granted that she wasn't living, so we buried her."

Gustafson turned his head to follow the sound of murmurs coming from the public gallery. Judge Blackstock raised his gavel, and the room quieted.

"What did you do after you buried her?"

"We went back to Santa Barbara to Mrs. Esquivel's house to clean up."

"What was your condition at that time, Mr. Moya, your clothes and so forth?"

"Well, my clothes were full of blood. My hands also."

"Were Baldonado's clothes full of blood?"

"Yes."

"And what was the car like?"

Moya hung his head. "The same. Full of blood."

After Judge Blackstock called a recess, Moya was escorted off the stand. Some spectators stood, glancing furtively toward the door at the back of the courtroom, on the lookout for potential interlopers. They piled newspapers or other belongings on top of their chairs and conferred with neighbors about holding their places.

Bob had jumped out of his seat the second the gavel hit the bench. He bolted through the gate in the railing that separated the public gallery from the rest of the courtroom and fast-stepped down the center aisle.

After he pushed through the giant courtroom door, he looked toward the marble stairs that led to the main exit but turned in the opposite direction. He had a hunch.

Around the corner at the end of the dimly lit corridor, Frank Duncan sat slumped on a bench, head down, one leg crossed over the opposite knee, exposing a gray diamond pattern on his black argyle sock. One hand held a paper cup. The other hand was tucked in the pocket of his dark suit pants.

Bob stopped beside the bench but didn't say anything for a moment. He watched Frank move a hand to hide his red-rimmed eyes.

Bob cleared his throat. "I know it's got to be hard to watch that psycho-path come into the courtroom with his big innocent eyes and then talk like he's describing characters in a horror movie scene. I wouldn't stay in there either if it wasn't my job."

Frank snorted. "Job? Right. You gotta sell your newspapers with all the gory details of my beautiful girl's senseless killing." He looked up. "The more blood and gore the better. Right?"

"Maybe it doesn't look that way from where you sit, but I'm just interested in the truth." Bob glanced over his shoulder toward the increasing noise of voices spilling from the courtroom into the hallway around the corner. "Do you think Mr. Moya sounds believable?"

Frank waved a limp hand in front of his face. "I haven't got anything to say to you."

"It seems to me he's telling the truth. No reason to make it up. . . . Moya's not doing himself any good with this story."

"I just couldn't sit there and listen to those gruesome details." Frank swiped at the tears running down his cheeks. "What a cold-blooded animal. I'd like to lay my hands on that bastard."

"What about your mother?"

"It is inconceivable Mother would associate with a man like that." Frank turned his back. He pulled a handkerchief out of his pocket and blew his nose. "Surely if she had anything to do with this, it would be a frightful insanity."

Bob took his seat next to Bennie Jo as Judge Blackstock gaveled court back into session. Moya waited in the witness chair, wearing a guileless expres-sion as he watched spectators settle into their chairs.

Gustafson returned to the lectern and continued in a cool, dispassionate tone. "When did you next have any communication with or any contact with the defendant, Elizabeth Duncan?"

Moya testified that he had telephoned her two days after the murder and asked if she was going to hold up her end of the bargain. She replied that it was going to be hard because police officers had been up to her house inquiring about Olga's disappearance. They arranged to meet at the Blue Onion Drive-In.

Moya told a rambling story about how he and Baldonado drove Mrs. Esquivel to meet with Mrs. Duncan at the Blue Onion on November 21. After she offered only a two-hundred-dollar check, they met with her at various stores on State Street that same day trying to get cash. She finally gave them one hundred and fifty dollars.

Moya said he'd arranged to meet her at Jordan's Market on November 25 to get another payment. "But instead of bringing our money, she shows up with some mug shots that included pictures of me and Baldonado. She told me that the police had dropped them off. She said, 'The police find out about everything that goes on in Santa Barbara, and they think that the men in the photos have something to do with Olga's disappearance.'" Moya gave Gustafson a hangdog look. "Plus, she said that she didn't have any money anyway."

"Did you see her again?"

"I called her a couple of times in the next week and told her that I needed money, regardless of how much she had, and that she should put it in an envelope marked 'Dorothy' and leave it with the cashier at the Blue Onion." Moya smiled a little. "Dorothy was our code name."

"What was in the envelope?"

"Ten dollars."

"And this was the last payment you received from Mrs. Duncan? For doing . . . the job? Ten dollars?"

"Uh-huh. By that time, what with the mug shots and all, I figured it would be best to stay away as far as possible . . . to not get in contact with her anymore."

Gustafson looked at the jury. "And that was it? A grand total of three hundred and thirty-five dollars was all it cost to murder an innocent young woman and her unborn child?"

Moya flashed a dagger glare at the DA before continuing in an irritated tone. "She was supposed to get some money from Frisco, you know, said she would go there personally to get it, but . . . but yeah, that's all we got . . . three hundred and thirty-five."

During cross-examination, Sullivan tried to show that Mrs. Esquivel had helped Moya and Baldonado commit the crime. He also asked about Mrs. Short's presence during the planning of the crime and how she'd accompanied Mrs. Duncan during the various rendezvous along State Street when Moya was trying to collect payment for doing the job. Some jurors fidgeted in their seats during this rehash of Moya's previous testimony, but the press section was unusually still. Bob and Bennie held pencils poised above their notebooks as Sullivan asked his questions.

The defense attorney finished his cross-examination by asking Moya if he'd already pled guilty to the murder of Olga Duncan.

"Yes, sir, I have," Moya answered.

"You haven't been sentenced for that offense yet, have you?"

"No, sir."

"And your trial is pending, to determine your punishment. Is that right?"

"Yes." Moya looked down and bowed his head. "In two months . . . on April 20th."

Sullivan rocked back on his heels. He turned toward Gustafson. "I think that's all."

"It's noon," the judge said. "Court is adjourned until one thirty this afternoon."

During the noon recess, Bob wrote his story for the afternoon edition of the paper. He pounded the typewriter keys nonstop, retelling Luis Moya's account of the brutal kidnapping and murder of Olga Duncan.

> *The killers took turns choking the young pregnant woman, and when they couldn't feel a pulse, they concluded that she was dead. They buried her in a hole they'd dug with their own hands.*

Bob slammed the carriage return and ripped the last page out of the typewriter. Without a word, he stood, reached across the desk to where the city editor waited, and handed him the story. "Use the headline *Frank Duncan Weeps.*"

Bob pushed open the front doors of the newspaper building, checked his watch, and headed for the pier. Turning his face to the wind, he leaned on the white wooden railing, stared south, and inhaled the salty air as he watched the breakers roll to the shore. The pilings shook as a wave crashed underneath the pier. He thought about when Moya had smiled so innocently at Reverend Gressett in the courtroom that morning, how he'd stared at the jury with those wide, guileless eyes.

Frank Duncan is right. What a cold-blooded animal. I don't blame him for wanting to get his hands on the bastard.

Bob slumped lower against the railing. *What would I do if some monster hurt one of my daughters? And how would I feel about newspapers printing all the gory details?*

Later, out of breath from hurrying back up the hill to the courthouse, he slipped a half-eaten bag of peanuts into his pocket and took his seat as the judge called the afternoon session to order.

The court clerk called, "Augustine Baldonado, on behalf of the People."

Like Moya, the twenty-six-year-old man who had led investigators to Olga's body had agreed to testify against Mrs. Duncan in order to be tried separately. Baldonado took the witness stand, wearing a dark suit and tie, garbed and groomed as if going out on a date. Far from being the carefree, fun-loving boy described to reporters by his family and friends as always clowning around, he scowled and fidgeted in the chair. Although he was five years older than Moya, during the murder he had looked up to his buddy as the leader. He thought Moya was smart and knew what he was doing. His elementary school principal had described Gus as a "born follower."

Gustafson asked about the day he had met Mrs. Duncan at the Tropical Café, and Baldonado's testimony confirmed much of what Moya had said about the discussions of how to "get rid of Olga" But he added, "I brought up the question of . . . if it was possible for us to scare her out of town."

"What did Mrs. Duncan say to that?"

"She said no, that she had tried it."

"Did you hear any plans about taking Olga Duncan to Mexico?"

Long pause. "I believe I did."

"Any plans to shoot her when you got to the other side of the border?"

Baldonado fidgeted. "I don't recall."

Gustafson shifted to the night of the kidnapping and murder. Although Baldonado's halting testimony again substantiated Moya's story, it lacked his partner's cold-blooded matter-of-factness. He admitted to being with Moya and going to Olga's apartment to kidnap her but remained evasive about details.

When asked if he had held the pistol as they drove off with Olga in the back seat of the car, he said, "I don't remember."

"Did you hit her with your fist?"

"I can't recall."

"Well, you remember your fist was swollen the next day, don't you?"

Baldonado shrugged. "Just a little."

"Sore from hitting her?"

"I can't recall."

"Wasn't it true, Mr. Baldonado, that it was agreed between you and Mr. Moya that you were going to be the one to shoot her?"

"I can't say."

Gustafson raised his voice. "You can't remember?"

"No, I can't."

"Well, at any rate, you were the one that suggested, when the car was giving you trouble, that instead of going to Mexico you would go up in the mountains near Ojai. And Luis stopped the car two or three times along the way looking for a place to do the job until you finally pulled over above the culvert near the pipe?"

"Yes, we did," Baldonado said in a monotone.

"Now, at this point, was it necessary for you and Luis Moya to drag Olga out of the car?"

"Yes, it was."

"She was still struggling?"

"I don't recall."

The DA looked at the jury. "But you took her down the hill into the culvert . . . fifteen or twenty feet down the embankment?"

"Yes."

"And according to your grand jury testimony, she struggled so hard you told Luis that you couldn't hold her any longer and that he had better hold her while you dug the hole."

"Something of that sort."

"And then you came back, that is, you quit digging and held her again while Luis dug?"

"I can't recall."

Gustafson pulled his glasses down his nose and peered over the rims. "According to your grand jury testimony, you were holding her with your arm around her neck, strangling her, weren't you?"

"I can't recall."

"Well, that is what you were trying to do, wasn't it, kill her?"

Baldonado leaned his elbows on the railing surrounding the witness chair. "Yes. Yes, it was."

Gustafson nodded to the jury and faced the defense table. "You may cross-examine."

Bob stopped writing and watched Baldonado slouch in his chair, mouth slightly open. The now not-so-cocky punk dropped his chin to his chest as he waited for Sullivan's questions.

"What a cold-blooded bastard," Bob muttered under his breath. He shook his head as if he were trying to clear it. Dots of light flickered at the edges of his field of vision. . . . Just a twinkle at first, but the flashes quickly increased in brightness and intensity. He squeezed his eyes shut, put his fingers to his right temple, and rubbed. He groaned softly. *Oh Jesus, not this.*

He took a bottle of aspirin out of his coat pocket and popped a couple of tablets into his mouth. He angled the side of his hand against his forehead to shade his eyes from the overhead lights as he watched Sullivan step to the lectern.

As he had done with Moya, Sullivan concentrated his cross-examination on Baldonado's knowledge of Mrs. Esquivel's role in the planning of the crime and the collecting of the payment from Mrs. Duncan. The attorney clearly wanted to emphasize, for future appellate courts, should his client be found guilty, that Mrs. Esquivel had acted as Mrs. Duncan's accomplice.

Again, Gus Baldonado's memory was poor. "I don't remember" and "I don't recall" were the most frequent responses to questions.

Toward the end of the cross-examination, Sullivan asked the young man, "You have heretofore admitted in this court your guilt in the murder of Olga Duncan, haven't you?"

Baldonado's tongue flicked across his dry lips. "Not to my knowledge."

Sullivan pulled his head back. "You haven't?"

"No. I withdrew a plea of not guilty, but I didn't plead to anything else."

"But you withdrew your plea of not guilty?"

"Yes, I did."

Sullivan frowned. "Well, didn't you understand, when you withdrew a plea of not guilty, that you were admitting your guilt?"

Baldonado shook his head. "No, no, I didn't mean that."

"But didn't anybody tell you the effect of withdrawing that not-guilty plea was admitting that you are guilty of first-degree murder?"

"I don't recall," Baldonado mumbled.

"What?"

"I don't recall." Baldonado's Adam's apple bobbed as he swallowed. "I don't understand that part very good."

All eyes followed Baldonado as he was escorted out of the quiet courtroom by two deputies. After the door thudded shut, the judge glanced at the clock. "I guess we better adjourn for the day. It's already five o'clock, and the next—"

Sullivan interrupted. "A moment, Your Honor. I'd like to approach the bench to request some leeway in scheduling an additional psychiatric evaluation for my client."

CHAPTER FORTY-SIX

CRAZY BISCUIT EATERS

February 26, 1959

We'd just started dinner, and I was on my second biscuit when Daddy dragged himself through the front door, holding his head.

"I spent the whole goddamn day listening to a couple of cold-blooded bastards regurgitate every excruciating detail of how they beat and strangled . . ." He threw his newspaper onto an empty chair and rubbed his temple. "I think I'm getting one of my headaches."

"Sit down and eat something," Mother said. "You'll feel better." She walked to the stove to get the plate she'd been warming in the oven and set it on the table in front of him.

"Not fish sticks again," he groaned.

"What's cold-blooded?" I asked.

"Goddamn pieces of shit who murder innocent young women and their unborn babies."

"Bob, that's enough. We're eating dinner," Mother said. "You're scaring the children."

Daddy scowled at her as he rummaged through his jacket pocket looking for his aspirin bottle.

"I thought I saw Beth today . . ." I said. "This lady in a car . . . on the way home from school. . . . It was really scary."

Both my parents turned toward me with identical stricken, wide-eyed expressions.

"Jesusss . . ." Daddy moaned.

"Judi and I were walking on the trail on the hill when I noticed a lady with stringy brown hair in a car waiting at the top of our street, and—"

Mother cut in. "What do you mean? What happened?"

"We hid behind a tree and stood really straight to try to make ourselves disappear behind the trunk." I demonstrated by squeezing my arms to my body and sucking in my breath.

"Oh dear." Mother put her hand to her mouth.

"You think it was Beth?" Daddy asked. "How can she possibly—"

I let out my breath. "I'm not sure. I know I'm supposed to run to the nearest house and tell them to call you, but I was afraid. It was really scary. . . . My hands were shaking."

Daddy patted my arm. "What happened? Did she . . ."

I told them about how I peeked out from behind the tree and could see that the lady wasn't wearing any long black gloves and how Mrs. Gottlieb ran down the front steps of her house carrying a cake.

"Mrs. Gottlieb got in the car with the lady, and they drove away." I sucked in my breath again and blew it out. "So I guess it wasn't, you know, Beth driving the car, but my heart was beating really fast."

Daddy patted my arm again and popped a couple of aspirin tablets into his mouth.

Mother sat down beside me. "Oh, Debby, what have I done? I feel terrible about Tweety . . . and that I got you involved in my patient's troubles."

"Goddammit, Lois. That hospital needs to do something. . . . We can't have—"

"Pull yourself together, Bob. Beth is harmless. I don't even think she has a car. We think she may have taken a bus to LA."

"Talk about scaring the children . . ." Daddy mumbled.

I tried to smile. "It's okay. I'm being careful. Better safe than sorry, that's what Grandma always says. I don't want to disappear like Olga."

No one said anything for what seemed like a long time while we pushed fish sticks around our plates.

"Something important came up today," Daddy finally said in a jolly sort of tone. "Sullivan wants Mrs. Duncan to have another psychiatric evaluation." He slathered ketchup all over his sticks. "And when he hung around after court talking to the press, we asked him about that brain wave test Mrs. Duncan took a few days ago." Daddy stopped chewing and looked at Mother. "You know anything about that? They took her over to Camarillo for the test."

"Your hospital, Mother?" I held half a fish stick under the table and wagged it back and forth for Pinky Lee. "Did you know Mrs. Duncan had her brain tested?"

"I think they might have taken her up to the neurology floor early on Washington's birthday. The day before the trial started." She got up from her chair and spooned more macaroni onto my sister's plate and then held up the bowl. "Macaroni, anyone?"

I shook my head, but she plopped down a spoonful anyway. I slid my hand under my chair with the other half of the fish stick and patted Pinky Lee's head when he took it out of my fingers.

Mother stomped her foot to shoo Pinky Lee away. "Eat your dinner, Debby."

I scooped up three macaroni noodles with my spoon and moved them toward my mouth as I watched Betsey's nimble little fingers inch their way over to the basket in the middle of the table and snatch another biscuit. There were very few foods in the world that my father, my sister, and I would all eat for dinner except for Mother's rolled Bisquick biscuits.

"Seems like there's crazy people all over the place," I said.

"Mentally ill," Mother corrected.

Daddy reached for the empty biscuit basket. "Frank wanted his mother to have the test. He says she was in a coma for a few days after she took that overdose of sleeping pills two years ago. He thinks the pills might have made her even wackier than she already was."

Mother shrugged. "An overdose of barbiturates could cause severe damage."

Daddy put down the basket. "Sullivan admitted tonight that the test results showed no unusual brain activity."

"You aren't eating your fish sticks, Debby," Mother said. "We agreed that you would eat three tonight."

I held up one finger. "I ate—"

"The one you gave the cat doesn't count."

Daddy peered into the empty biscuit basket again and ate one of the crumbs. He scowled at my sister. "Goddammit. How many did you eat?"

"I ate four fish sticks." Betsey slid off her chair smugly. "Can I watch *I Love Lucy* now?"

Neither of my parents said no.

"How many biscuits did you eat, Debby?" Daddy said.

I shrugged. I really couldn't remember if it was two or three.

Daddy switched his gaze to Mother. "I got no biscuits. Not one."

Mother stood up as she gathered Betsey's empty plate. "I'll make more, but Debby, you have to eat the rest of your fish sticks."

Daddy filled my milk glass after she went into the kitchen. "Just wash them down." He offered me the bottle of ketchup, too.

"No thanks." I pinched my nose, shoved the fork holding a tiny piece of fish into my mouth, and took a big gulp of milk. I had to clamp my hand over my lips to keep from gagging. I repeated the process five more times to finish one stick. "I can't eat any more," I whimpered.

Daddy glanced over his shoulder toward the kitchen and used his fork to spear the last fish stick off my plate. He ate it in one bite. No ketchup. His eyes bugged out as he chewed.

I giggled. "So what made Mrs. Duncan do it if her brain's all right?"

Mother arrived at the table holding a baking sheet in her scorched oven mitt and dumped the biscuits into the basket. "Be careful. They're still hot."

"Smells delicious," Daddy said as he scooped three of the biscuits onto his plate. I reached for one, too.

"You ate your fish sticks, Debby?" Mother asked.

I looked at Daddy, but he was busy buttering. I crossed my fingers behind my back. "Uh-huh. They're all gone."

"Well, good." Mother glanced over at Pinky Lee, sleeping on a pile of newspapers in the corner. "Now that wasn't so bad, was it?"

I made a sad face and shook my head a little as I helped myself to another biscuit. "It sure seems like there are an awful lot of mentally ill people in the world," I said between bites.

"Not so many," Mother said. "And we're trying to help as many as possible at the hospital."

"Like Beth?" I said. "But she's still mentally ill."

"Well . . . she quit taking her medication, but when we find her, we'll try again."

I stopped chewing. "Why didn't somebody help Mrs. Duncan so she didn't kill Olga? Daddy said that she'd have to be insane to think that she could get away with murder."

Daddy cut in. "That was just a figure of speech. Her actions were . . ." He hesitated.

"Cuckoo?"

"Exactly. That's a highly underused psychiatric diagnosis, but Mrs. Duncan is very cuckoo, and unfortunately for her, cuckoo doesn't meet the legal definition of insanity. She didn't think of Olga as a human being. Just something that got in the way of what she wanted." Daddy finished his last biscuit. "Mrs. Duncan's a psychopath."

"A psycho . . . ? But she looks so normal. Her hair is nice, and she doesn't wear weird long black gloves like Beth."

"Psychopaths are hard to spot," Mother said. "Faces hide secrets."

CHAPTER FORTY-SEVEN

MRS. ESQUIVEL

February 27, 1959

By 9:45 A.M. the next morning, Bennie Jo and Bob were seated in their usual spots in the press section. Bennie Jo was reading yesterday's edition of the *Star-Free Press*. She folded the paper and turned to Bob. "So you get a byline on your stories every day?"

"Yeah, of course. It's the biggest story in years. Probably the biggest trial in county history." Bob raised an eyebrow. "You don't?"

"Never." Her lips formed a tight smile. "Don't think the paper wants the readers to know that a woman is covering a sordid murder trial."

Bob laughed. "Gee, the murder mastermind is a woman, and so is the victim. Think the readers might appreciate a woman's touch to the articles." He winked at her but gave her an empathetic sigh. "I thought the *Express* was all about human interest."

Bennie Jo smiled for real this time. "Nice try, but I don't think it works that way."

"All rise," the clerk called out. Chairs scraped the wooden floor as everyone in the courtroom rose to their feet.

Gustafson whispered to an assistant hovering at the prosecution table to hurry and then faced the judge. "Sorry, Your Honor, almost ready. Mrs. Esquivel is just down the hallway."

"Probably have to get her out of the ambulance," Bob told Bennie Jo. "Gustafson had her registered under an alias and hidden over on the isolation ward at General Hospital. Tuberculosis, I think."

"*Tuberculosis?*"

"Not contagious now, they say. But anyway, he's got to get her testimony on the record while he can." They both knew that Mrs. Esquivel would be a crucial witness for Gustafson. In order to prove that Mrs. Duncan was as guilty of murder as Moya and Baldonado, the DA needed to corroborate that she had advised and encouraged the two men in killing Olga. That corroboration would come from the ailing owner of the Tropical Café.

When Esperanza Esquivel finally entered the courtroom, a deputy had to help her into the witness chair. Her clothes appeared to be a couple of sizes too big for her frail, sickly body.

Gustafson began his questioning. In a halting voice, Mrs. Esquivel testified that Mrs. Duncan, accompanied by her friend Mrs. Short, had shown up at the café one afternoon the previous November and introduced herself as the mother of Frank Duncan, the lawyer who had represented Mrs. Esquivel's husband on a burglary charge. After a little small talk, Mrs. Duncan got to the point: Did Mrs. Esquivel have any friends that could help her get her "no good" daughter-in-law "out of the way"? The girl was blackmailing her, Mrs. Duncan said, and had threatened to throw acid in her son's face.

"What did you say, Mrs. Esquivel?" Gustafson asked.

"I want to help her," Mrs. Esquivel murmured in her dense accent. "Her son is my husband's lawyer, and I want him to get Marciano probation. So I say there were some boys, but I don' know if they wanna talk to her or not."

"Did you talk to Luis Moya and Augustine Baldonado about this?"

Mrs. Esquivel cleared her throat. "Yes. They come in late in the afternoon and I tell . . ." She took a jagged breath. "I tell them there is a lady that wants to talk to them, that she has a job for them and will come back the nex' day."

When Mrs. Esquivel described the meeting the following afternoon, she downplayed her own role. She said she had been busy working around the bar and heard only snatches of what was said. "Mrs. Duncan was saying something about three thousand dollars, and would it be all right, and that she had some sleeping pills, and if they don' have a car, she had a car." Mrs. Esquivel coughed behind her hand. "If it is necessary, Mrs. Duncan said, she will go with them to do the job."

There was something else Gustafson wanted to get on the record. "And all during this conversation," he said, "Mrs. Short was sitting at another table, she wasn't part of this conversation?"

"Yes, sir."

The DA moved on to the early morning of November 18 and asked Mrs. Esquivel if she'd seen Moya and Baldonado at that time.

"I worked until two o'clock in the morning. I think I got home sometime after two thirty. I went to bed. Early in the morning, I heard a noise in the back room, and I got up. I went back to see who it was, and it was Moya and Baldonado." Mrs. Esquivel stared into her lap. "They had blood on their clothes and tol' me that they had to get some clothes and take the car back."

"Did you hear one of them say that 'Mrs. Duncan's job is done'?"

"Yes, sir."

"What did you do then?"

"I went back to bed because I was tired, and I had to get up at five thirty in the morning to cook breakfast at the café, an' I was supposed to go to court to see what was going to happen to my husband. That day was the day that they were going to sentence him."

"That is all," Gustafson said and resisted the urge to wipe his brow.

Judge Blackstock called for the lunch recess.

Unlike Gustafson, Sullivan always made a habit of seeking out the press. Before court had begun that day, he told reporters, "One of my main arguments will be that all the testimony against Mrs. Duncan is coming from people who are admitted accomplices in the crime. In spite of what our esteemed district attorney may have to say, I intend to show that Mrs. Short and Mrs. Esquivel are, in fact, part of the conspiracy. The law requires independent, corroborative evidence from people not directly involved with committing the crime. I plan to hammer the point hard."

But Sullivan began his cross-examination by asking Mrs. Esquivel questions designed to bolster Mrs. Duncan's story that she had had nothing to do with Olga Duncan's murder.

"During the fall of 1958, your husband was represented by Frank Duncan. Is that right?"

"Yes, sir."

"And your husband was not granted probation, was he?"

"No, sir."

"You were dissatisfied with that, weren't you?"

"No, sir."

"Never at any time?"

"No, sir." Mrs. Esquivel set her mouth in a straight line. Through several more rounds of questioning on the subject, she stubbornly insisted that she had never been unhappy with Frank Duncan's representation of her husband. She also denied that she had ever tried to blackmail Elizabeth Duncan.

Sullivan eyed the witness for a moment before moving on to questions about Mrs. Esquivel's role in the meetings at the Tropical Café that led to Olga's murder.

"Did she say why she wanted to meet friends of yours?"

Mrs. Esquivel hesitated. She glanced toward the prosecution table.

"I didn't hear your answer, Mrs. Esquivel."

"That she had a job for them." Her voice trembled. "She wants to get rid of her daughter-in-law."

Sullivan put his hands on the lectern. "Did you believe it?"

"No," she said softly.

"Did you tell Moya and Baldonado that Mrs. Duncan wanted somebody to get rid of her daughter-in-law?"

Mrs. Esquivel cowered into her chair and coughed. "She was the one that explained everything to them. She was the one that talked to them."

Sullivan moved on to questions about the morning of November 18, when Mrs. Esquivel woke up and heard the boys in her house.

"Well, when you heard them, you got up?"

"Yes."

"And you saw the blood on their clothes?"

A long pause. "That is right."

Sullivan snorted. "You weren't at all concerned about how the blood got there?"

"No."

"But you knew from the conversation that you had with Mrs. Duncan that she wanted the boys to get rid of her daughter-in-law."

"But I didn't know if they was going to do it or not."

Sullivan asked her about the meetings after Olga was dead, when she went with Moya and Baldonado to try to collect money from Mrs. Duncan. She said that the woman wanted to give her a check instead of cash.

"I tol' her I didn't have nothing to do with her business, that she had to talk to the boys."

Sullivan smiled malevolently at the quivering woman. "You didn't even know what this money was being paid for?"

"For the job that she wanted done," the witness mumbled.

"So after you learned that Olga Duncan, Mrs. Duncan's daughter-in-law, was missing, did you ever go to the police department to report any of this?"

Mrs. Esquivel hesitated again. "No."

"Of course not," Sullivan said, an ugly twist to his lips. "Incidentally, you haven't been charged as a defendant in this murder case, have you?"

"No, sir."

"Did anyone ever tell you that you would not be charged if you would be willing to be a witness in this case?"

"No, they told me just to tell the truth."

Sullivan sighed noisily. "That is all."

At Sullivan's request, Judge Blackstock dismissed court early. Most of the reporters, including Bob, followed Gustafson into the hallway. A reporter from the *San Francisco Examiner* pushed his way to the front of the pack and called out a question.

"Sullivan wants Mrs. Esquivel charged as an accomplice. Isn't that right?"

Gustafson kept walking.

Another reporter followed up. "That Esquivel woman sure sounds like she had a part in the murder of Olga Duncan. She found Mrs. Duncan her killers. Any comment?"

Gustafson stopped and slowly pivoted to face the journalists. "Mrs. Esquivel is a *witness*, not an accomplice or an accessory to murder."

"How do you figure that?" another reporter called out. "She helped these guys every step of the way."

Gustafson put up both hands. "That's not going to work. Based on the evidence, she had no criminal intent when she told the men Mrs. Duncan wanted to meet them."

Bob scratched his head. "Well, what did she think they were going to do to 'get rid' of Olga? And when she saw all the blood, why didn't she go to the police?"

Gustafson was already shaking his head. "Mrs. Esquivel is in this country illegally. She was afraid to go to the police." He gave Bob an icy stare. "I can't charge Mrs. Esquivel with the murder of Olga Duncan based on any evidence we've uncovered. She was a sick, desperate woman with her husband in jail awaiting sentencing and afraid that if she wasn't nice to her husband's lawyer, he might not work hard to keep him out of prison. Therefore, she isn't an accomplice or an accessory."

"Guess she's just a witness who happened to help with the arrangements," Bob mumbled as Gustafson walked away.

"Quit worrying about it," Bennie Jo said. "You told me yourself that Gustafson's considered a legal scholar in the state."

"Uh-huh, and sometimes as a legal manipulator in this county."

During the afternoon session, Gustafson called a number of witnesses to corroborate details from earlier testimony. Employees of the Blue Onion restaurant testified that Mrs. Short had left an envelope marked "Dorothy" at the register and that Luis Moya had picked it up later the same day.

Harold Cohen, the owner of the pawn shop on State Street where Mrs. Duncan had pawned her diamond rings to make the down payment on Olga's murder, was the final witness of the day. He told the court that he'd known Mrs. Duncan for three or four years and that she'd been a customer at his shop many times.

After asking Mr. Cohen the date of the transaction and details about how much money he gave her for her rings, Gustafson asked the witness, "What was Mrs. Duncan's appearance at that time?"

"You mean what was she dressed in?"

"Her demeanor," Gustafson said.

"Well, she was as calm as she has ever been whenever she is in my store. Mrs. Duncan is always pleasant."

At 3:55 P.M., Judge Blackstock adjourned court for the weekend.

CHAPTER FORTY-EIGHT

SUNDAY DUTY
March 1, 1959

I was crouching in the back seat of Daddy's old Chevy sedan as he swung his camera and the case holding flashbulbs and extra film onto the passenger seat. He slid in and started fumbling in his pocket for the keys. When I put my hand on his shoulder, he jumped. "Jesus Christ. What are you doing here?"

"I told Mother I was going with you for Sunday duty."

"No, you're not. . . ."

"Mother says it's okay with her if it's okay with you . . . but don't tell Betsey because she'll have a fit and want to come too, and you know what a problem she can be. She's not old enough to go to the police station." I glanced sideways out the car window. Mother was watching us from the kitchen. I waved and then smiled hopefully at Daddy in his rearview mirror. "I promise to keep quiet, and I'll carry your camera bag and flashbulbs in case we need to take pictures for any big stories."

He rested his forehead on the steering wheel momentarily, mumbling unintelligibly, and backed the car down the driveway. Mother, still standing at the window, smiled. He gave her a little salute. Mother had outranked him when they'd met in the army during World War II. I ducked lower in the back seat to avoid Betsey's snoopy eyes.

When we pulled into the empty parking lot of the Ventura Police Department, I opened my pink plastic Pony Tail purse to make sure that my little notebook, the one just like Daddy's, was tucked inside.

"Do you think there might've been any murders last night?" I asked.

Daddy gave me a pained look as he opened the car door. He headed for the entrance to the station. I ran to catch up.

"Hi, Sarge," Daddy said as we walked through the double glass doors. I hovered next to him, my hand on his pants leg, suddenly self-conscious as I gazed at pictures of wanted criminals on the bulletin board behind the tall wooden counter.

"Hey, Bob." A man in a navy-blue uniform with a badge pinned to his chest scanned the room behind us. "What happened to Jerry? They got you doing the Sunday beat again?"

"Yeah, well. Jerry got . . . transferred. Everybody's taking turns again." Daddy smiled unhappily. "So, anything going on?"

Sarge pulled out a big open ledger from under the counter and set it in front of Daddy and peered at me. "This is the city, Ventura, California," he said in his best Sergeant Friday voice. "I'm a cop. I carry a badge . . . Dum de dum-dum."

I giggled.

Sarge spun the ledger around so Daddy could read it. "Here's the arrest log. Pretty quiet night."

Daddy got out his notebook. I opened my purse to take out my notebook, too. I stood on my tiptoes, trying to get a look at the log, but my chin barely reached the countertop.

"Four drunk drivers. Two of them ran into each other out on the Avenue. We also arrested a warehouse burglar at the wharf. Caught him red-handed with a pickup full of chicken feed." Sarge handed Daddy a slim manila folder. "Here's the arrest report."

"Fascinating," Daddy said unenthusiastically.

Next, we drove to the fire department to check on any overnight "conflagrations," as Daddy called them, but nothing doing except for a small kitchen grease fire out on Bristol Road.

Our last stop was the sheriff's office behind the courthouse. As we drove, I picked up a three-day-old newspaper from the floor and stared at the headline above Daddy's byline: Moya Tells How Olga Was Slain. . . . *Mrs. Duncan sat impassively through Moya's whole recital of . . .*

"Can we see where they're having the trial while we're here?" I turned to get a better look at the huge pillared white building as Daddy entered a driveway marked Official Cars Only. I swiveled my head forward again. "Are we official?"

"Official enough," Daddy said. "Nobody cares on a Sunday."

"Well, what about seeing the courtroom?"

Daddy shook his head as he pulled the car into a space marked Reserved. "Nope. That part of the building is all locked up on Sundays."

"But if we're official . . ."

"Yeah, well, not that official."

As we walked through the parking lot, I heard inmates yelling from the third-story windows of the jail. I stuck close to Daddy. "Do you think Mr. Baldonado and Mr. Moya are up there making all that noise?"

"Probably not them," he said as he held a side door marked No Entry open for me. "I think they're keeping them all by themselves in special cells on one of the lower floors."

We headed down a dreary hallway and got in the elevator. "What about Mrs. Duncan? Where's she staying?"

"Not anywhere we're going." When the elevator stopped, Daddy pushed me out real fast, but the door closed on his arm before he could get out of the way. "Goddammit," he said as he pushed the door open. "Can't they get this door fixed?"

Daddy was still rubbing his arm when we stepped into a room at the end of another hallway. He rang the bell on the counter. No one came. We could hear laughter coming from a back room. After a few moments,

I reached up and whacked the bell myself. Daddy grabbed my wrist. "Slow down . . . they'll be here. Probably got something going on with a new prisoner."

A smiling man in a brown uniform, sipping from a coffee mug, sauntered into the room. "Keep your shirt on."

"Sorry. My assistant here"—Daddy cocked his head at me—"gets a little impatient when we're on the trail of a big story."

"Looks like you got yourself a regular Girl Friday there, Bob."

"Oh, yeah," Daddy said. "And Saturday, Sunday, Monday . . ."

The deputy winked at me. "You must be here to check on the big news out of Oxnard connected to the Duncan trial."

Daddy's head snapped back. We reached for our notebooks.

"What's the story?" Daddy asked.

The deputy trailed his hand through the air above his head as he gazed up into space. "I can see the headline now . . . Roy Gustafson Outmaneuvered by a Cat."

"Huh?" we both said.

The deputy slapped his knee. "One of our deputies was just telling me that Roy Gustafson had to call the Oxnard police last night to get his cat off his roof. Poor animal had been up there since Friday. Roy's wife, Edna, was giving him hell when the patrolmen arrived because Roy wouldn't climb up on the roof to get the cat down himself. He told the missus that it would come down when it got hungry."

I whipped my head around to look at my father. "Wow, called the police? We should have done that when Cinderella got lost."

"Shh," Daddy said and turned back to the deputy. "So the Oxnard police rescued the cat?"

"Yep. A Siamese named Ting-A-Ling. One of the officers got Roy's ladder and coaxed the cat with some canned tuna."

"That's good," I said. "Because sometimes cats don't come home when they get hungry."

"Shh," Daddy said again.

The deputy gave me another wink. "You two can probably interview some eyewitnesses, Bob, if you want to drive over to Oxnard. Bunch of the neighbors who'd listened to the cat meowing for twenty-four hours gave the officer a big round of applause. Don't think Roy's the most popular guy in the neighborhood. Ever hear an unhappy, hungry Siamese?"

Daddy smirked as he wrote in his notebook. "I'll give Oxnard PD a call when I get to the office. Little human-interest story while the trial's going on. . . ."

"But the cat's all right?" I interrupted.

"Jim Dandy," the deputy said.

"Anything else?" Daddy asked. "Maybe a little criminal activity?"

The deputy took a small stack of papers out of a manila folder and pulled a pair of glasses out of his pocket. "Let's see what we got . . . Vandals in the cemetery again. Couple of headstones toppled. Probably kids. Beer cans and cigarette butts strewn around. . . ." He moved the report so Daddy could read it. I stood on my toes.

The deputy pushed the rest of the reports toward Daddy. "Only other thing you might want to check up on is some horse by the name of Trigger—not Roy's—got loose up in Oak View yesterday. Galloped down Highway 33 'til Barney Stone, old guy lives by the road in that tar shack, finally jumped on his horse and roped it. Snarled traffic pretty bad but don't think they wrote up an official report. Might be another one of your human interests."

"Is the horse okay?" I asked.

"Just fine," the deputy said. "Safe and sound back in his corral."

I tugged on Daddy's jacket. "We should've called the police when Cinderella got lost."

Daddy laughed nervously. "But, honey, Cinderella wasn't actually lost. She was, well, in the backyard."

My lip quivered as I gazed into the deputy's friendly face. "She died," I said. "By the geraniums."

"I'm sorry to hear that, sweetie."

"And my bird, Tweety, got murdered by one of Mother's crazy patients."

Daddy groaned and shook his head at the deputy. "Don't ask," he mumbled.

The deputy furrowed his brow a moment and rummaged around under the counter. "Seems like we had some lollipops around here for lost kids . . . but I'm afraid the sergeant sometimes"—he came up empty-handed—"eats them himself."

"That's okay," I said. "Cinderella died a long time ago. Last April."

"I know what," the deputy said in a too-cheerful voice. "How would you like me to take a mug shot of you?"

I broke into a huge grin. "With the mug shot camera? Really? Just like you do with the criminals?"

He looked at Daddy for the "okay" and swung open the little wooden gate through the counter as he swept his arm in the direction of a doorway that led to the back room. Daddy followed, carrying the reports and his notebook with him. The deputy took my hand as we walked.

"Do you know Mrs. Duncan?" I asked.

He did a double take. "Thankfully, no. She stays in the women's jail."

I scanned the small room, taking in an empty metal desk and a big camera on a tripod that was set up in the corner in front of a wall with black lines to measure feet and inches. "I might be a policewoman when I grow up, too, so that I can arrest murderers and put them in jail."

"Oh, you don't want to do that, sweetie."

I shrugged. "I started a Helpful Club. . . . Is the women's jail near here?"

"Uh, upstairs. . . . Now you just stand on those marks on the floor and look at the camera." He squinted into the viewfinder. "Say 'cheese.'"

The flash blinded me.

"How about Mr. Moya and Baldonado?" I asked as I blinked wildly to get rid of the ghostly black spots floating in front of my face. "Do you know them?"

The deputy glanced sideways at Daddy, but he was busy at the desk taking notes.

"Uh . . . now don't you worry your pretty little head about those two goons. They're locked up tighter than a preacher's . . . a . . ." He harrumphed. "And they're going to be throwing away the key."

When Daddy and I got to the empty *Star-Free Press* office, I twirled around in the city editor's chair while Daddy typed up stories about quadruple drunk-driving arrests, the chicken feed thief, the grease fire, the cemetery vandalism, the horse, and all that other stuff. "I'm saving the 'Cat Caper' story for last," he mumbled under his breath. "I got to talk to Oxnard PD first." He wasn't talking to me. Daddy sometimes talked to himself as he typed.

I was taking another whirl on the city editor's chair when I heard one of the teletype machines cranking out a story from a distant city. "I'll check the wire," I called as I headed for the little room with the Associated Press and the United Press machines. "Could be important."

Paper rolled out of one of the machines. Invisible keys magically typed the report, clicking and beeping as I read the print. "Hmmm . . ." I stuck my head outside the door. "Hey, this says the Dodgers are getting a player named Wally Moon from the Cardinals. Says he's a good hitter." The Dodgers had moved to LA the previous season, and Daddy had taken me to a couple of games at the Coliseum. He was teaching me the "official way" to keep score in order to keep me "out of his hair" and help me keep my mind on the game. "Oh my gosh," I called out. "It says Wally's an All-Star!" No response. Daddy was on the phone with the Oxnard police, laughing with someone about what he was now calling the "Great Saturday Night Cat Caper."

Daddy didn't notice when I snuck back to the room where the linotype machines made the metal slugs of type that were used to print the newspaper on the Big Press.

Judi's father, Myron, operated one of the linotype machines. Once Myron had shown me how he took pages of a story that Daddy had written on his typewriter and typed the words into his machine to cast small metal slugs imprinted with the type. The small slugs were somehow linked together to use on the Big Press.

After collecting a few of the discarded slugs from the concrete floor under the machines, I tiptoed into the next room to take a peek at the Big Press. The gigantic iron machine was as tall as the high-ceilinged room. Its wheels, complicated belts, and pulleys that spun the huge spools and rollers to feed paper through the printing process stood eerily still.

Daddy had taken me to see the Big Press when it was running. I shuddered at the memory of the thundering noise it made when the enormous roll of newsprint threaded up, over and down the printing cylinders. I'd covered my ears and stood as far away as possible.

Men with black-smudged fingers—wearing overalls, T-shirts stained with ink, and paper hats of folded newsprint—had watched from below, ready to turn off the press in case of mechanical breakdowns or if the paper went haywire winding through the rollers. Amazingly, the Big Press not only printed, it also cut and folded the newspapers and sent them down a little conveyer belt to be stacked by a man with some missing fingers. Daddy had said that he'd mangled his hand in the rollers, but I wasn't sure if he was kidding.

As we drove home, I thumbed through the pages of my little notebook and sighed. I'd hardly written anything. I picked up the old newspaper again. "So that lady, Mrs. Short, is going to testify tomorrow, right?"

Daddy blasted the horn at a woman in a car lingering at the stop sign in front of us. "Come on, come on . . ."

"I wonder why she didn't try to help Olga?" I said.

Daddy honked again. "Stupid old woman."

CHAPTER FORTY-NINE

THE SIDEKICK
March 2, 1959

Eighty-four-year-old Emma Short, attired in a black wool dress and jacket with polka-dot-trimmed satin cuffs and a matching collar, looked small and shriveled sitting on the witness stand. She gazed nervously in every direction except the defense table, where her longtime friend Elizabeth Duncan sat.

Gustafson said a silent prayer before he began to question the witness. "Mrs. Short, do you know the defendant, Elizabeth Duncan?"

Mrs. Short looked up nervously. "Pardon me?"

"Do you know Mrs. Elizabeth Duncan?"

"Yes, sir, I do. I met her at the Penguin Shop, the secondhand clothing shop I used to operate twenty years ago."

"Did you see Mrs. Duncan frequently?"

"Yes. When she moved to the same apartment building a few doors from me two years ago, she recognized me one morning and came to visit. After that I saw her almost every day."

"Who was living with her, if anyone, at that time?"

"Her son was living with her."

"Now, did you have any conversations with Mrs. Duncan with respect to her son, Frank Duncan?"

"Well, she said to me many times that . . ." Mrs. Short glanced sideways at the jury. "In what respect do you mean? With respect to . . ."

"With respect to Frank's girlfriends, if any."

Elizabeth and Frank Duncan both stared at the witness.

Mrs. Short focused on the district attorney's face as she talked. "Yes, she spoke many times about how she would like to have Frank stay with her and not marry anyone. Nearly every day she would remark about that. She wanted him to be with her, live with her, and she said she would make it rather disagreeable if he went out with young ladies."

"Did you occasionally see Frank Duncan in the apartment he shared with his mother?"

"Yes, when he would leave in the morning. When he would come home at night."

Gustafson glanced at his notes. "There were two bedrooms in the apartment?"

"Yes, sir."

Gustafson paused, cocking his head as if considering the next question. "Did Mrs. Duncan ever say to you what the sleeping arrangements were?"

Sullivan scrambled to his feet. "Objection . . . immaterial."

"Well, I don't know whether it is immaterial or not." The judge stroked his chin. "But it is a leading question. The objection on that ground is sustained."

Gustafson turned back to the witness. "Did you ever see Frank in bed in that apartment?"

"Yes," Mrs. Short said.

Sullivan was back on his feet. "We object. What difference does it make if Frank ever went to bed? We assume he did once in a while."

Gustafson smiled. "Then what's your objection?"

"Well, it's . . . it's . . . immaterial."

People in the gallery laughed.

Judge Blackstock banged his gavel. "Be quiet!"

Gustafson said he would reframe the question and turned back to Mrs. Short. "Did you ever see Frank Duncan in bed at a time when the defendant, Elizabeth Duncan, made some comment about Frank?"

Sullivan was still half standing. He slapped his hand on the defense table. "I object to that as immaterial. If he wants to have her testify as to some comment that she made about Frank, I have no objection to that."

Gustafson held out his hands, palms up. "Well, that's all I'm asking."

"Well, the part of it about whether he was in bed, that's immaterial," the judge said.

Gustafson shook his head. "No, Your Honor, I'm pegging the time. I'm asking, did she have a conversation with Mrs. Duncan at that time?"

Judge Blackstock glowered at the DA. "At what time?"

"When Frank was in bed," Gustafson said.

"All right, overruled."

Sullivan sank into his chair.

Mrs. Short answered the question. "One morning I went into the apartment, and Frank was lying in her bed. She came out and said, 'Isn't he beautiful?'"

Snickers burst forth again. Frank kept his head down. Mrs. Duncan crossed her legs and kicked her foot slightly.

Because of Mrs. Short's somewhat confused state of mind, Gustafson was careful to identify dates for her and to ask questions about events in chronological order.

"Mrs. Short, do you remember an incident in the early part of November 1957 when Mrs. Duncan argued with Frank because she'd bought a beauty parlor without consulting him?"

Mrs. Short tilted her head to one side. "Why, yes. I went to see her, and she told me she had an argument with her son and that he'd told her to leave that night, to get out. She said that she'd asked him if she could at least stay the night and leave in the morning. He told her, 'Yes, you can stay tonight.' So she did, and then she took all those sleeping pills, and that's how she ended up in the hospital."

Gustafson glanced at the jury. All eyes were focused on the witness. One juror was nodding encouragingly.

"And this took place in November of 1957, a year before Olga disappeared?"

"Yes."

"And Mrs. Duncan later told you the reason she took the sleeping tablets was because her son ordered her out of the house?"

"That's right."

"After she returned to her apartment, did you have any further conversation with her regarding her stay at the hospital?"

"She didn't like her nurse that waited on her. She wasn't at all satisfied because she didn't get the treatment she thought she should have."

"Now, later on after that, did Mrs. Duncan have any conversation with you with reference to this nurse?"

"Well, she thought that Frank was going out with her, and she objected very much. She said she would break it up if she could."

"Did she ever tell you anything about Frank having the nurse come over to their apartment?"

Mrs. Short cleared her throat. "Yes, she said the nurse named Olga came there the following Sunday after Mrs. Duncan returned home from the hospital, and as she went down the stairs, Mrs. Duncan said, 'I would like to trip her so she would break her leg.'"

Mrs. Short testified that Mrs. Duncan knew where Olga lived and had called her many times and told Olga to leave her son alone. "'You are not a fit person to be with my son.' That's what Betty told her."

Gustafson looked over his shoulder at the sound of a muffled hissing. Mrs. Duncan had grabbed her attorney's arm to pull him close as she furiously whispered in his ear. Mrs. Short twisted a loose strand of hair and took a keen interest in the stained-glass ceiling dome. Sullivan hushed his client.

Gustafson turned back to his witness. "Did she say anything else?"

Mrs. Short blinked a couple of times before responding. "She said, 'If you don't leave him alone, I'll kill you.'"

A collective gasp reverberated through the courtroom.

Mrs. Duncan jumped out of her chair. "You liar!"

Sullivan grabbed his client by one arm, Frank took the other, and together they managed to get her to sit down. Even then she kept twisting, trying to wrench herself free. "You're lying, Emma!" she spat, her face contorted in rage.

Mrs. Short sank lower in the witness chair, eyes moving rapidly.

Throughout the commotion, Judge Blackstock hammered his gavel. "Mr. Sullivan, control your client," he said, and he called for a five-minute break.

Bob scribbled notes as he watched Elizabeth Duncan wipe tears from her eyes while Frank patted her back.

"A nice little courtroom outburst always makes good copy," Bennie Jo said. "Let's see . . . I think I'll lead with, 'If you don't leave him alone, I'll kill you.' I swear to God, these people are writing the stories for me." Bennie Jo kept her eyes on Mrs. Duncan and sighed theatrically. "I almost feel sorry for her. Guess it's not easy when even your best friend turns on you."

The reporters continued to watch while Frank rubbed his mother's shoulders and talked quietly in her ear. Mrs. Duncan smiled bravely and rested her cheek on her son's hand.

Bob cocked his head. "Yeah, well, she'll always have Frank."

When the courtroom quieted again and the defendant settled, Gustafson asked his witness how often Mrs. Duncan had made telephone calls to Olga.

"Nearly every day she would call her and have something to say about leaving her son alone. 'You are a foreigner, and I'll see that you go back.'"

"Go back where?"

"To Canada where she came from."

When asked if Mrs. Duncan ever said anything to her about Frank possibly marrying Olga, Mrs. Short said, "Yes. She was afraid Frank would marry her, but Frank had told her many times that he would never marry

Olga." Mrs. Short nodded solemnly. "'I'll always live with you, Mother. I'll never leave you.'"

Frank crossed his arms and shook his head.

"Did you ever observe whether or not Mrs. Elizabeth Duncan waited on Frank Duncan in bed?"

"Yes, she gave him his breakfast."

"Every morning?"

"Every morning."

"Anything else that she did for him that you observed?"

"She just gave him his breakfast and got his clothes out for him."

"Arranged his clothes for him to wear?"

"Well, on a chair, his suit or something."

Gustafson paused a moment to check a small calendar he kept on the lectern. "Calling your attention to the date of June 20, 1958, do you recall what happened on that date?"

Mrs. Short squinted. "Twentieth of June?"

"Yes. Do you recall what Elizabeth Duncan said, if anything, to you about Frank and Olga getting married?"

"Oh yes, she said she called Olga up and she said to Olga, 'If you don't stop going with my son, I'll kill you,' again, and Olga said—"

Sullivan put his hands on the table and pushed himself to his feet. "Just a moment, just a moment!"

Gustafson put his hand out toward Sullivan, turned back to the witness, and informed her that she could only repeat what she had heard firsthand.

"Oh, she did. . . . Mrs. Duncan told me that Olga said, 'We are going to be married.' And then Mrs. Duncan said, 'You'll never marry my son. I'll kill you first.'"

Sullivan held on to his client's arm to keep her in her chair. Gustafson moved on to the topic of Frank and Olga's marriage.

"She told me Frank came home, and she asked him, 'Are you married?' and Frank said, 'No. I'll never marry Olga.' But then he went out the next day and married her anyway."

"Did Mrs. Duncan tell you where Frank and Olga went after they were married?"

"Yes, she said that they were married at the courthouse, and then Frank came home on the night of his wedding."

People in the gallery rustled around and whispered. The judge picked up his gavel and held it until silence returned.

Mrs. Short testified that three weeks after the wedding, Mrs. Duncan went to Olga's apartment when Frank was there. "He said, 'What are you doing here?' I can't recall all that went on because I wasn't there, but Mrs. Duncan said that she and Olga had a disagreement and they pushed each other around. The landlady came in and got hold of Olga and tried to pacify her because they had quite a few words, and then Frank said to his mother, 'Come on, doll, let's go home.' So they went home."

"'Come on, doll?' Had you heard Frank use that term, 'doll,' in talking to his mother before?"

"Yes, I had, many times."

Gustafson asked if Mrs. Short had continued to overhear the defendant make phone calls to Olga.

"Many times. Nearly every time she would talk to Olga, she would remark about wanting to kill her if she didn't leave Frankie alone."

Gustafson glanced innocently toward the defense table. "Did Mrs. Duncan tell you that she talked to Frankie about this matter?"

Sullivan bolted out of his chair. "His name is Frank!" he thundered.

Gustafson turned to the witness. "Did Mrs. Duncan refer to her son as Frank or Frankie?"

"Frankie," Mrs. Short said in a small voice.

"Continue," Judge Blackstock said.

"Did Mrs. Duncan tell you that she had talked to Frankie about this matter?" Gustafson repeated.

Frank Duncan sat clenching his jaw and glaring at the DA.

"About his marriage?" Mrs. Short asked.

"Yes. What did she tell you that Frankie said?"

"Frankie said many times to leave well enough alone, let nature take care of itself and . . ."

"And what happened then?"

"She called an attorney in Ventura and made an appointment to get Frank's marriage annulled."

Mrs. Short told the jury about Mrs. Duncan hiring the man from the Salvation Army to impersonate Frank and going to Ventura to get the annulment.

"Were you introduced to the lawyer?" Gustafson asked.

"Yes, I was introduced, but not as . . . I was . . . the aunt . . . Betty's Aunt Anne. But I didn't do anything or sign anything."

"Mr. District Attorney . . ." Judge Blackstock looked up at the courtroom clock. "I think we better take a short break."

Mrs. Duncan leaned back in her chair. Frank squeezed his mother's shoulder before he headed down the aisle toward the door.

Gustafson walked to the railing of the witness stand. "You can go out for a few minutes if you need to," he told Mrs. Short. "Just make sure you come right back."

"Thank you. I'll only take a minute to go to the ladies'."

Bob followed in a line of reporters as Mrs. Short picked her way toward the aisle through the standing reporters and court personnel. As she passed the defense table, Mrs. Duncan leaned forward and pointed at her. "Bitch. She's wearing my clothes. I gave her that suit."

Mrs. Short ducked her head, putting a hand up to block her face.

A deputy moved behind Mrs. Duncan and touched the handcuffs on his belt.

"And that pearl necklace?" Mrs. Duncan shouted at Mrs. Short as she scurried by. "It's mine, too! You took it out of my apartment!"

Bob moved with Bennie Jo and the other reporters toward the defense table, eager to hear more. Mrs. Duncan obliged.

"Look at her. She's a thief!" Mrs. Duncan cried. "That woman's wearing my dress, and she's lying!"

Sullivan, who had been in deep conversation with his investigator, closed his eyes momentarily and reached over and grabbed his client by the arm. "That's enough," he said through clenched teeth.

Mrs. Duncan shook loose. "I feel like ripping that dress right off her back."

"Great copy," Bennie Jo murmured as she wrote. "Love that woman. . . ."

After the break, Mrs. Short testified at length about how Mrs. Duncan had tried to hire Diane and Rudy Romero, Barbara Reed, and Rebecca Diaz to "get rid of Olga."

"Becky Diaz said she was going to Oxnard and would find someone to do the job for her, but I could tell that she wasn't going to do it."

Then she recounted the meeting at the Tropical Café.

"Did you hear the conversation that went on between the men and Mrs. Duncan at the café?" Gustafson asked.

"No, I sat at a different table, but I saw Mrs. Duncan give the boys something when she got back from the pawn shop. She told me when she came back to my table, 'They're going to do it. They're going to take her to Mexico.'"

"Did she say they were going to kill Olga?"

"She said that the boys told her, 'You will never know when or how it will be done.'"

"Did Mrs. Duncan ever say anything to you about Olga having disappeared?"

"She said that Olga was gone. That she was gone and that she didn't think that she would be back."

The only noise in the courtroom was the sound of Gustafson shuffling papers as he turned to the last page of his notes. Everyone continued to watch the old lady fidgeting in the witness chair.

"Now, do you recollect the day that Frank Duncan went to the police station in Santa Barbara to report that his mother was being blackmailed?"

"Yes, I do."

"What did Frank Duncan say to his mother when he returned from the police station?"

"When he came in, he was angry, and he said to his mother, 'I don't understand what this is all about, that this matter should come up at the same time that Olga disappeared.'" Mrs. Short glanced sideways toward the defense table and quickly refocused on the DA. "He said to his mother, 'You're as guilty as you can be.' And then they had quite a heated discussion about it."

Gustafson kept his voice steady. "The next morning, did you talk to Mrs. Duncan about what Frankie had said to her?"

"Yes."

"What did she say?"

"She said, 'I think Frank thinks I'm guilty. I know he thinks I'm guilty.'"

The jury members shifted in their seats and turned their heads in unison toward Frank Duncan, sitting in his usual place behind his mother at the defense table. He refused to meet their eyes. Elizabeth Duncan folded her arms across her chest and shifted her murderous gaze to the back of the district attorney's stooped shoulders, twisting her mouth into a scornful sneer.

"That is all," the DA said. He turned to Sullivan. "You may cross-examine."

"It's already four o'clock, Mr. Sullivan," Judge Blackstock said. "Would you rather recess for the day, or start now?"

"I would prefer to begin my cross-examination tomorrow, Your Honor."

Judge Blackstock nodded. "Court is adjourned until ten o'clock tomorrow morning."

Bob watched as two burly sheriff's deputies led Mrs. Short out of the courtroom. Mrs. Duncan craned her neck, trying to give her former friend one more death stare. "That dress looked better on me," she muttered.

"Good grief!" Bennie Jo used her notebook to fan her face. "What a day. Just when you think it can't get any more theatrical."

Bob shook his head. "Good God, Mrs. Duncan's facing the death penalty, and she goes into histrionics because someone wears her old dress?"

Bennie Jo buttoned her jacket and slipped her purse strap over her shoulder. "For a minute there, I thought we might see a good old-fashioned hair-pulling match."

CHAPTER FIFTY

NAUGHTY GIRLS

March 2, 1959

After school, I lingered over my snack to put off practicing my accordion. I'd taken up the instrument after a door-to-door accordion lesson salesman came to our house offering a good deal on six months' worth of lessons at Frank Umbro's Accordion Studio. I'd begged my parents to let me play and promised to practice every day.

Mrs. Alfred was sitting at our red Formica table, her usual babysitting command post. When I put my cereal bowl and chocolate milk glass in the sink, Mrs. Alfred looked up and turned on her hearing aid. A high-pitched squeal came from the side of her head. She adjusted the volume and placed her latest paperback novel facedown on the table as she reached for the smoldering cigarette in the ashtray. "Time to practice."

I twisted my head to get a better look at the cover of her book. A young woman in a nurse's uniform, with long, flowing blonde hair, eyes closed, red lips slightly parted, leaned into the chest of a big-shouldered man standing behind her. I read the bold black letters printed above the picture. *Naughty Student Nurses.*

Mrs. Alfred took a long drag off her cigarette and hacked a couple of times. "You better hurry up, dear. You have to get ready for swim team soon."

I left the kitchen for the bedroom, threw my math book on the bottom bunk, shut the door, and sat down on the bed to think about telling Mother about *Naughty Student Nurses*.

It was a strategic matter. Mother was very against all forms of hanky-panky. If I told her about the book, she might get rid of Mrs. Alfred and hire a more competent babysitter with high moral standards. I sighed deeply. *I can't risk that.* Mrs. Alfred and I had reached an unstated "I won't bother you if you don't bother me" arrangement. A new babysitter might make me clean my room, and worse . . . she would probably have good hearing. Because of Mrs. Alfred's hearing loss, she didn't know if I was actually practicing, because she couldn't hear anything from her spot in the kitchen.

I wasted another fifteen minutes sitting around reading a Nancy Drew book. I'd just lifted the accordion out of its case and hoisted its straps over my shoulders when I heard Betsey yelling.

"You get back here this minute, Pinky Lee! You can't wear that outside."

Wear what *outside?*

I stormed down the hallway. My accordion, still strapped over my shoulders, bounced against my body as I lumbered into the living room. Betsey was gripping the squirming cat by his hind legs. Pinky, dressed in a pink satin dress, pawed the hardwood floor trying to get traction.

As my hands slipped off the keys of the accordion, the bellows opened, drooping downward with an unmelodious racket of discordant notes. Pinky yowled as he thrashed around on the floor, trying to get away from my sister and the psychotic accordion noise.

"You dressed Pinky Lee in my . . . my evening gown!" I stomped my foot. "Grandma made that dress for my doll." The accordion kept playing off-key horror-movie music on its own, the bellows jiggling up and down as I whirled back and forth indignantly. "You stole that dress out of my doll case."

Betsey's lips trembled. "I just borrowed it. . . ." She yanked harder on the cat's legs, trying to pull him closer, but the dress was snagged under the leg of the couch.

"Wait!" I cried. "The dress is . . . Stop before you . . ."

Pinky Lee bit Betsey on the wrist. She screamed and let go. Pinky scrambled to his feet, pulling the snagged dress until it ripped loose from under the couch. The gown tangled in the paws of the terrified cat momentarily before he crouched low and zigzagged out of the room like a soldier dodging a barrage of bullets, the torn pink dress trailing behind.

"It's all your fault. You scared him with your yelling," Betsey whimpered. "He thought you were mad at him . . . and that crazy accordion . . ." She started to cry. "Poor Pinky."

I slipped the straps of my accordion off my shoulders and let the instrument fall to the floor with another bellow of clashing chords and knelt to get the piece of torn fabric out from under the couch leg. I waved it in my sister's face. "You, you . . . crazy girl," I snarled. "Look what you did." I grabbed her hair and pulled.

Betsey grabbed a handful of my hair and yanked as hard as she could. I let go of her when she pinched my arm. She scooted backward, her arms and legs jerking in an awkward crablike motion, until she turned over to grip the couch to pull herself up. I walloped her on her back.

"I wish you'd disappeared instead of Olga!"

"I'm going to tell!" she wailed. "You're not supposed to say that to me."

Our screams finally penetrated the circuits of Mrs. Alfred's hearing aid, forcing her to leave the comfort of her chair in the kitchen and hurry to the living room. "Stop, stop," she said in her raspy little voice. She wrung her fingers and moaned, "You'll kill yourselves."

Out of breath, I picked up my accordion. Betsey wiped her eyes and stood up.

"I don't know how you girls can act so ugly," Mrs. Alfred said as she turned, shoulders hunched, hands aflutter, to retreat to the kitchen. As she passed the front door, it burst open with the sound of Daddy's off-key humming. Mrs. Alfred jumped out of the way and hovered behind a lamp. The shade hid her face.

Daddy stopped when he saw Betsey wiping tears from her eyes. "What's going on here?"

Betsey held up her wrist where the cat had bitten her. "Debby hit meeeee. . . ."

I picked a few *possible* hairs from my shoulder. "Betsey pulled my hair right out of my head and . . ." I held up the torn piece of satin. "And she stole my evening gown, the one Grandma made for my doll." Tears streamed down my cheeks.

"And she said she wished I'd disappeared like Olga . . . *again*."

"She's lying," I sobbed.

"Control yourselves!" Daddy shouted. "Jesus H. Christ. I've had enough female drama for one day." His eyes flashed fury. "I need a gavel to keep order in this circus."

Betsey and I yelled simultaneously, "BUT SHE—"

Daddy picked up a magazine, rolled it up, and slammed it on the coffee table. "If you two can't be quiet, I'll have to clear the room." He beat the magazine on the table again. "Do I make myself perfectly clear? I will not tolerate this behavior in my . . . house." He slapped the magazine against the palm of his hand.

"It's Mother's house, too," Betsey sniveled.

He glared at her as he slapped the magazine again. "You're out of order."

Mrs. Alfred stepped from behind the lampshade and squeaked, "Pardon me, Mr. Holt," her eyes blinking wildly. "I was just going to say, girls, you need to change into your bathing suits. It's time to leave for swim practice." Her whole body twitched as she wrung her hands.

Daddy shuffled back a step or two. His head turned to focus on Mrs. Alfred as if she'd just materialized out of thin air. "Swim practice?"

"We better hurry," I said, "or we're going to be late."

"Fine." He made a big sweeping motion with his arm. "Clear the living room!"

Betsey and I ran for the bedroom.

When I returned to the kitchen a few minutes later, Daddy was just removing his head from the refrigerator. "Goddammit. Why can't anybody leave me any Jell-O?"

"Betsey ate it all," I said.

My sister huffed in behind me, carrying a sweatshirt. She swatted me with it.

"I will not tolerate any more outbursts in this house," Daddy yelled. "Do you understand?"

I nodded. Betsey stuck her finger in her mouth and turned toward Mrs. Alfred. She fingered the *Naughty Nurses* paperback stuck in the front pocket of the babysitter's purse.

"Keep your snoopy eyes off of Mrs. Alfred's things," I scolded my sister.

Mrs. Alfred pulled her purse away and laughed nervously.

Daddy pounded his fist on the kitchen counter. "Goddammit! Stop it, Debby. Leave Betsey alone. You girls keep acting like this, fighting over a dress, and I hate to think what might become of you."

"Sorr-ry," I mumbled.

"Thank you." Daddy swept his arm across the room. "Proceed. Now take a swim break and pull yourselves together."

Mrs. Alfred opened the front door for us but then looked back to my father. "Such lovely girls, Mr. Holt. Really, such lovely girls."

CHAPTER FIFTY-ONE

CONFUSING MRS. SHORT

March 3, 1959

A s people streamed into the courtroom early the next morning to hear
Sullivan grill Mrs. Short, Bob followed Bennie Jo through the little
gate in the bar to a seat in the press section. He scribbled a few words in
his notebook with a question mark next to them. "I still find it hard to
believe that Mrs. Short and Mrs. Esquivel aren't considered co-conspirators
instead of witnesses."

"Gustafson says his case is bulletproof," Bennie Jo said. "The judge
already ruled that they're witnesses."

"I'm not talking about Judge Blackstock. I'm thinking about what an
appeals court might say if it gets that far."

Ward Sullivan began the cross-examination of Mrs. Short in a pleasant,
friendly voice, asking her about how Frank and Mrs. Duncan had first met
Olga. Mrs. Short repeated the story about Mrs. Duncan being admitted
to the hospital for taking an overdose of sleeping pills and how she wasn't
satisfied with the care she got from a nurse named Olga. "She complained
that Olga hurt her with some of the injections that she had to give to

her . . . and she just did not approve of foreigners waiting on her. She was very much disgusted."

"And when did Mrs. Duncan next see Olga?"

"I think it was a few days after leaving the hospital—on a Sunday—that Frank brought Olga to see his mother."

Sullivan smiled benevolently. "And when did this all take place? The approximate date that you think Olga came to the apartment?"

Mrs. Short furrowed her brow.

"I think you told Mr. Gustafson that it was around October or November," Sullivan said helpfully.

"No." Mrs. Short cocked her head. "About June the 16th."

Gustafson tensed.

"June? Okay, June of what year?"

"Let's see . . . 1958?"

"June 1958?" Sullivan squished his eyebrows together. He turned toward the jury. "Hmmm . . . You're pretty sure of that date? That is the best your memory serves you?"

"That's right, I believe . . ." She bit her lip.

Gustafson bounced his knee up and down under the prosecution table.

"As you sit on the witness stand today?"

"Correct."

"Yet when you testified yesterday, you agreed with Mr. Gustafson that all this—Mrs. Duncan's hospitalization, meeting Olga—took place in November 1957."

Mrs. Short blinked around the room. "Did I? I don't know. . . ."

Sullivan watched the jury as he flipped to his next page of questions. "All right. Do you know when Olga and Frank got married?"

"I can't tell you the date exactly."

"What month was it?"

Mrs. Short put her fingers to her lips for a moment. "Well, it was about a month after this happened." She fluttered her hands. "No, it wouldn't be a month after that. A few weeks after that? Would it have been the 18th?" Mrs. Short looked to the prosecution table. Gustafson avoided her eyes.

"Mrs. Short?" Sullivan waited for the witness to look his way. "Well, if I were to tell you that they were married on June 20, 1958, would that refresh your recollection as to the date?"

"It would be July."

Sullivan's head flinched back slightly. "What?"

"It would be in July."

"You think they got married in July?"

"Would you repeat the question again?"

Gustafson ran his fingers through his hair with one hand as he leafed through a manila folder on the table in front of him.

Sullivan repeated his question. "I asked you, 'If I were to tell you that Frank and Olga Duncan were married on June 20, 1958, would that refresh your recollection as to the date' that they were married?"

Mrs. Short smiled. "Yes, it would."

"Well, do you recall that it was about June 20th that they were married?"

"I think so." Mrs. Short narrowed her eyes again. "Yes, June . . . 1957."

Gustafson closed the folder and picked at something on the sleeve of his jacket.

Sullivan twisted his mouth to suppress a smile. "Nineteen fifty-seven?" He stroked his chin. "I see. You're saying that they got married about ten days after the date you told us that Mrs. Duncan came home from the hospital. Is that right?"

Mrs. Short nodded rapidly. "That would be right."

"That would be your best recollection?"

"It would be," Mrs. Short said emphatically.

Sullivan looked pointedly at the jury. "And during this ten-day interval, from the time Mrs. Duncan returned from the hospital until Frank and Olga got married, you were at Mrs. Duncan's apartment, and you heard her phone Olga?"

"Yes . . ." Mrs. Short's expression clouded. "I-I . . . don't . . ."

Judge Blackstock picked up his gavel as he stared down at the waffling witness. "I'm going to call a short recess at this time."

"Your . . . Your Honor . . ." Sullivan sputtered.

The judge tapped his gavel on the bench. "Take fifteen minutes."

"Now, Mrs. Short, I was just about to ask you how many times, between the time that Mrs. Duncan returned from the hospital and the time that Frank married Olga, did you hear Mrs. Duncan phone Olga?"

Mrs. Short leaned forward. "Yes, I did."

Sullivan shook his head. "How many times did you hear her call Olga?"

"Every day for ten days she told me that she phoned Olga."

"She *told* you? Well, you testified a few minutes ago that you were at the apartment when she made these calls. Yesterday you told Mr. Gustafson that you *heard* Mrs. Duncan make these calls to Olga."

"No, I have never been at the house when she called Olga on the phone . . ." Mrs. Short touched her throat. ". . . Personally, myself. Mrs. Duncan would tell me about what she said the next morning."

Gustafson's face flushed bright red as he picked through crime scene photos.

"So you never heard Mrs. Duncan call Olga and threaten to kill her?"

Gustafson held his breath. He'd been dreading this moment all morning. He didn't believe that Mrs. Short had deliberately lied, but the old woman couldn't distinguish between what she'd seen and heard herself and what someone else had told her.

She stared blank-faced at Sullivan for a moment. "I . . . I . . . heard her say that . . . she said it."

"You heard her say it on the phone?"

Mrs. Short blinked several times. "Maybe not on the phone . . . but she said, 'I'm going to kill her' many times."

"Were you confused when you were answering Mr. Gustafson's questions?"

"A little."

Gustafson closed his eyes. *For the love of God, let this be over. . . .*

"Are you confused now?"

Mrs. Short straightened her shoulders. "No, I am not."

"You had a discussion with Mr. Gustafson during the recess, didn't you?"

"I asked him to help me on some dates," Mrs. Short said in a huffy tone.

Sullivan stared pointedly at the DA. "And did he help you?"

"The date of the marriage, I wasn't quite sure of."

"What did he say?"

"He helped me. He told me the date of the marriage."

"Did you ask him about any other dates?"

"Nothing else."

"You remembered all the other dates that you testified to here on the witness stand? You remembered those dates?"

"I'm not real sure of them."

"You didn't need your memory refreshed?"

Mrs. Short did not respond.

"Your answer is no?"

"I am mistaken on dates sometimes."

"And all of these things that you have been telling us about what took place between yourself and Mrs. Duncan, you didn't make notes on those conversations?"

"No, but my memories are very accurate about that." Mrs. Short perked up. "Dates are the only thing that I fall down on."

The cross-examination continued, Sullivan hammering away at Mrs. Short's memories: the Blue Onion meeting with "the boys"; the exact nature of the threats against Olga, if any; even whether or not Mrs. Short had personally heard Mrs. Duncan receiving any blackmail threats—always, always pressing the old woman for exact dates. Mrs. Short's responses became increasingly muddled.

"You believed that Moya and Baldonado were trying to extort money from Mrs. Duncan, that they were blackmailing her. Is that right?"

Mrs. Short's hand trembled as she put her fingers to her chest. "Well, I don't really know what I thought. I can't tell you."

"Did Mrs. Duncan ever ask you, Mrs. Short, to do anything with respect to helping her with Olga?"

"She made a lot of suggestions, but I disapproved of everything, of course."

"What did she suggest?"

"She asked me if I would go over to Olga's apartment and get her to come to my place to take care of someone who was very ill. Have her sit down in a chair in front of my closet, and Betty would jump out and put a rope around her neck and choke her and throw poison in her eyes and cut off her hair."

"Mrs. Duncan would do that?"

"Yes, she would do that. And break every bone in her body, if she could."

Sullivan leaned forward on the lectern. "Anything else?"

"She wanted to hang her up in my closet until evening. Then later, when it got dark, she would put a blanket around her, tie her with a rope, and put a stone to the rope, and then take her to the beach in a taxi and throw her off the wharf."

"In a taxi?" Sullivan scoffed.

"Well, I objected to it, most definitely, that it was a horrible thing to think of. 'Do you realize what you are trying to do?' I said. I told her, 'She will never stay in my apartment and hang there in my closet all day.'" Mrs. Short gazed indignantly around the courtroom, although she avoided the defense table and the eyes of her former friend.

Gustafson put his face in his hands. He knew that Mrs. Duncan had concocted some wild schemes, but even he doubted that she had proposed to drag a bag containing the body of a full-grown woman into a taxi for a trip to the wharf without the taxi driver becoming slightly suspicious.

Sullivan smirked as he turned the last page of his notes facedown. "I think that is all."

The district attorney exchanged places with the defense attorney and gently asked Mrs. Short a few questions on redirect about details in conversations with Mrs. Duncan that differed from her answers in earlier testimony. In particular, he wanted to clarify the matter of Mrs. Duncan's blackmail story. He wanted the jury to have no doubt that that had been a fabrication intended only to mislead Frank about his missing typewriter money. This time Mrs. Short was explicit about what Mrs. Duncan had told her.

"Mrs. Duncan turned to me, and she said, 'The only way I can get the money from Frank to pay these boys is to call it blackmail.'"

Gustafson exhaled. "Thank you. Now, Mrs. Short, you've seen and talked to Mrs. Duncan and visited her on many occasions from the time Mrs. Duncan left the hospital to shortly before Olga's body was discovered, haven't you?"

Mrs. Short flashed a disapproving glance toward Sullivan. "Yes, that is right."

"Well, Mrs. Short, you've passed your eightieth birthday, haven't you? And your memory is not nearly as good as it used to be, especially for dates?"

"Hardly." Mrs. Short chuckled.

"And it is somewhat true, isn't it, Mrs. Short, that you have a difficult time trying to distinguish in your mind between what Mrs. Duncan told you were the facts and what you yourself observed as the facts?"

Mrs. Short nodded.

"But you believed that Olga Duncan would be killed, that there were plans to kill her, long before this meeting at the Tropical Café with Moya and Baldonado."

"Yes."

"Why didn't you go to the police at those times?"

"Because Mrs. Duncan told me, 'I will cut out your tongue, and you know that it will be the electric chair for you if you say anything.'"

"Gas chamber," Bob mumbled to himself.

After six days of testimony against Elizabeth Duncan, the district attorney excused his final prosecution witness. Gustafson turned to face the judge at four o'clock Tuesday afternoon. "That is all. At this point, Your Honor, the People rest."

CHAPTER FIFTY-TWO

WHO KILLED THE CAR?

March 4, 1959

Wednesday morning, the day Mrs. Duncan was to begin testifying in her own defense, I awoke from a dream about Beth trying to grab me with her black-gloved hands. While reassuring myself that it was "only a dream," I heard shouts from the kitchen.

"Somebody killed the car!"

I slid down the ladder and got to the kitchen just in time to see Daddy storm out the front door, waving around what looked like a black rope with metal clothespins on the ends.

"Somebody stole my other cable," he bellowed as he stomped down the porch stairs. "Goddamned thieves . . ."

Mother stood at the kitchen sink, looking out the window, sipping a cup of coffee. I stuck my head through the kitchen doorway. "The car's dead?"

"The battery's dead," Mother said as she took another sip. "You don't happen to know where the other jumper cable might be, do you?"

"Better ask Betsey," I said. "She's the wagon master."

Mother turned to look at me. "You and your friends weren't playing in Daddy's car again, were you, after you quit selling lemonade for your

Helpful Club?" She narrowed her eyes. "Fiddling with the radio, listening to the Top 40 countdown, hmmm?"

I pushed my lips into a circle. "Ohhhh . . ." *Playing the radio can wear down the battery?*

I slipped out the front door and ran to the curb, where Daddy fiddled with the car's hood, trying to find the release lever. "Maybe your car is out of gas," I said helpfully.

"The damn battery is dead," he snapped as he lifted the hood. "You wouldn't know anything about that, would you?"

I paused for a moment like I was thinking. "How does the gas chamber work? Do they use the same kind of gas you put in your car?"

Daddy struggled to get the metal prop pole into the right groove, trying to get the hood to stay up.

"No," he said impatiently. "They use potassium cyanide pellets and drop them into sulfuric acid. The gas fumes kill the person." He wheeled around to face me, and the hood of his car slammed shut.

"Jesus! Go in the house. You're not helping."

"Does it hurt . . . you know, when they breathe the gas? Will Mrs. Duncan feel any pain if she gets executed?"

Profanities spewed from his mouth as he lifted the car hood again and slammed the metal pole into place. "She'll just go to sleep," he said in an exasperated tone.

"How do you know that?"

Daddy ran his hand down his face. "Because that's what the governor says. Well, not this governor. The last one said it was just like being given anesthetic for an operation."

"Like when Betsey got her appendix out? But she—"

"Get in the house!" he screamed.

I got as far as the porch, but I stopped when I heard a woman's voice.

"What the hell's going on here, Bob?" Marilyn's mother, Florence, had crossed the street wearing her flowered housecoat and holding a coffee mug with the words *Go Jump in the Lake* printed on the side.

"You're going to wake up the whole damn neighborhood." She took a sip of coffee.

Daddy held his one jumper cable and gestured so wildly the clamp on the end almost wacked Florence in the head. "Mrs. Duncan is testifying today, and I *cannot* be late," he shouted. "Now this shit happens."

Florence grabbed the cable as it swung past again, pulled it out of his hand, and tossed it onto the grass. "You can't do anything with one cable." She peered into the engine compartment. "You probably left the radio on. I'll get Gene." She jabbed her *Go Jump in the Lake* mug at him as she backed away. "And don't touch nothing 'til he gets here and tells you what to do."

As soon as she was gone, Daddy raced Mother's station wagon down the driveway and into the street. He was punching the gas pedal to speed forward, in order to line up the front of Mother's car with his old Chevy, just as Florence and Gene arrived.

"Stop!" Florence shouted as she pushed her hands at Daddy's car. "You're going to smash the bumpers."

The brakes squealed. Gene stood to the side, a cigarette dangling from his mouth as he untangled his jumper cables. Daddy got out of the car and leaned over the engine compartment again, scratching his head as he peered inside.

Our next-door neighbor, Charles, a stooped, shriveled furniture store owner, joined the group to offer advice. "You get those cables mixed up, Bob, you can melt your battery."

Charles walked around Daddy's old Chevy, idly kicking the tires. "The back driver's side's a little low," he called out. Then he looked under the car and spotted fresh oil on the asphalt. "Doesn't look good, Bob. This baby might throw a rod any day now. . . ."

Other neighbors, some still in their robes, stood on their porches to watch. Daddy always drew a crowd. Nothing like a little drama at the Holt house to start the day.

Daddy paced around his car while he hummed a toneless tune at breakneck speed. "How you doing there, Gene?" he asked. He kept humming really fast in between talking. "Court starts in half an hour." He climbed into his car. "Ma Duncan will be breathing fire, telling the world that she's the innocent victim in this mess."

Charles opened the door of the station wagon. "I'll start this one up when you're ready."

Gene wiped his hands on a rag he'd pulled from his pocket and leaned into my father's window. "Put it in neutral and don't touch that key till I say so." He moved back and forth between the two cars, wiggling the cables with his free hand. He took a last drag on his cigarette before throwing it to the pavement. "All set, Bob. Don't want to keep the old broad waiting." He put his hand up like he was holding a stop sign out to my father as he nodded to Charles.

Charles fired up the station wagon and revved the engine. Gene was still holding up his hand, but Daddy turned the key anyway, grinding the starter.

"Hey!" Gene yelled, stepping out of the way when the engine caught. Daddy smiled and nodded through the windshield.

Gene walked back to the station wagon to remove the jumper cables as Daddy popped out of his car to slam the hood shut. The engine almost died before he could get back inside to put his foot back on the gas.

All three neighbors yelled, "Hold it!" But Daddy was revving the engine and didn't hear their shouts to wait. He threw the car into gear and roared away.

The hood popped up again before he'd driven half a block because he'd closed it on the jumper cables. He slammed on the brakes but continued to rev the engine to keep the car from stalling, causing the clips on the cables to rattle against the car's grill.

Gene hustled down the street and undid the cables from the battery and slammed the hood shut. "Give 'em hell, Bob," he called out as Daddy roared away again, waving a cheery goodbye out his window.

Florence poured what was left of her coffee on Charles's lawn. "Poor bastard. Best damn reporter I ever read but doesn't have sense enough to turn off his radio when he parks his car."

Charles shook his head sadly. "Yeah, well, what are you gonna do? He's Bob. . . ."

Everybody laughed.

I looked up and down the street for any signs of Beth and slipped back into the house. *Yeah, what are you gonna do?*

CHAPTER FIFTY-THREE

STAR WITNESS

March 4, 1959

At 9:20, Bob pushed his way through the throng outside the courtroom. "'Scuse me, 'scuse me." He held up his press pass as one of the deputies carved a path for him. The largest crowd, so far, in the week-long trial had descended to hear what Elizabeth Duncan had to say for herself.

"Running a little late on the big day, aren't we, Bob?" the deputy chuckled. "Oversleep this morning?"

"Automotive crisis," Bob said with a grim twist to his mouth. "Terrible situation."

He swung the courtroom door open and huffed down the aisle to the press section to hear the defense present their case.

Sullivan declined to make an opening statement. "We are ready to proceed with the evidence, Your Honor."

Elizabeth Duncan, dressed primly in a black-and-white wool dress with a rounded, black-trimmed collar, took the stand to tell her side of things to the jury. She swore her oath to tell the truth and primped her hair as she waited.

Ward Sullivan, standing five-five and weighing only 120 pounds, stepped to the lectern in a well-tailored, impeccably pressed suit and a red bow tie to begin the defense's case. After a few preliminary questions to put his client at ease, Sullivan asked her what had led up to the suicide attempt that landed her in the hospital where Frank met Olga.

"I got mad at Frank. We had a big argument, and he told me to move out."

"What did you write in the suicide note that you left for Frank?"

"I told him that I loved him, but I wanted to die because if I had to live alone, I'd become petrified. All my life I've been afraid of being alone."

"You were in a coma for days. Is that right?"

"Yes, I took a lot of my Seconal pills. I'm not sure how many."

"And Frank met Olga because she was one of your nurses in the hospital after your suicide attempt. Is that right?"

"Yes," Mrs. Duncan responded in a flat tone.

A few of the jury members shifted in their seats.

The defense attorney attempted to lead his client, step by step, through her version of events after Frank married Olga, but she quickly veered off the narrative, adding information of her own choosing: how she thought Frank couldn't afford to get married and the things Frank had said about the situation. Gustafson fidgeted as he listened but let it go on for a while. He knew that juries resented being deprived of the opportunity to hear the full story.

Mrs. Duncan said that on June 19, she'd talked with Frank about whether he planned to marry Olga. "Frank promised me that he wouldn't marry her. I asked him what kind of a girl she was, because I had explained to him—"

Gustafson finally stood up. "Your Honor, I'm sorry, but I'm going to have to object to all this hearsay now. I haven't heretofore objected—"

Mrs. Duncan spoke in an indignant tone. "It's not hearsay."

Gustafson ignored her. "What she said to Frank is hearsay, and I object. Frank Duncan is not on the stand. I can't cross-examine him about what his mother *says* he said."

Judge Blackstock nodded. "The objection is sustained."

Sullivan turned back to his client. "Well, you had some further discussion with Frank that night, and he told you his girl's name was Olga Kupczyk?"

"He just called her Ollie."

"After you learned her name, did you endeavor to communicate with her in any way?"

Mrs. Duncan folded her hands in her lap. She lifted her chin. "First I want to tell my story."

Sullivan shook his head. "You can't relate the conversation you had with Frank that evening because His Honor has held that that is hearsay testimony. I want to know now what you did to communicate with Olga after you learned her name from Frank the evening of June 19, 1958."

Mrs. Duncan glared. "You mean I can't say what I said to Frank?"

"No, you can't."

Gustafson stood again. "I ask the court to admonish the witness to answer the question. Mr. Sullivan has asked the question three times, and the witness insists on talking about something else."

"Please answer the question," the judge said.

Mrs. Duncan shot the DA another disgusted look, but for a while she confined herself to direct responses to the questions. She admitted to calling Olga after her conversation with Frank and saying, "'Ollie, Frankie has just told me about you and him, and he's been spending several nights away from home, and I don't approve of my son marrying a woman of that kind.'"

"What did she say to you, if anything?"

"She said that she was marrying Frank, regardless if I liked it or not."

"And how did you learn that Frank was married?"

"Well, I was so disturbed from what Frank said, and then from talking to Olga, that I took my sleeping pills and went to bed. The next morning, Frank called me and said that he wouldn't be home to dinner that night, as he'd promised he would."

Gustafson stood up. "I will move to strike that entire answer as nonresponsive."

"Motion is granted," the judge said.

After being admonished again to confine her answers to the question itself, Mrs. Duncan huffed, "I called the hospital where Olga worked. One of the nurses told me that Olga had gotten married to the attorney that she had been going with and that his mother had been a patient at the hospital. I knew that it couldn't be no one else but Frank."

"When did you next see Frank?"

"He came home later that morning, and I asked him, 'Frank, did you marry that girl?' and he said that he did."

"What happened next?"

"I was just in hysterics. I really was."

When Sullivan tried to lead her through the confrontations she had had with Frank and Olga at their apartment, the defendant continued to volunteer details and give hearsay evidence.

"Did you resent that Frank removed his clothes from your shared home?" Sullivan asked.

"I was just lonesome for him," Mrs. Duncan said.

Sullivan tried again. "Well, did you resent the fact that he had moved some of his clothing from your home?"

"I just missed him, that's all."

"Yes, but did you resent that he'd moved out?"

"I just know that I wanted him home. That's all."

Gustafson stood. "Your Honor, I object. She's not—"

Mrs. Duncan burst into tears. "I was so lonesome for Frank." She wiped her eyes with a handkerchief supplied by Sullivan.

After she had regained her composure, the judge again reminded her to only answer the questions. Sullivan asked her about her confrontation with Olga and Frank at the Bath Street apartment a week after they got married.

Mrs. Duncan insisted that Olga had started everything. "She pushed me, and she yelled at me, 'Get out of the house. You're not wanted here.'"

When questioned about her visit with Mrs. Barnett, the landlady at the Garden Street apartments, she said, "I only went to the apartment to see if Frank was living there . . . to see if his clothes were there, that's all. I never threatened anyone."

Again, Mrs. Duncan kept volunteering information that hadn't been asked for. Gustafson grew more and more exasperated. She could be quite the charmer as she rambled on with her answers, and he worried that some of the jury members might be taken in by her con artist persona. He watched as they listened thoughtfully to her testimony, smiling at times at her retorts to his objections.

Sullivan spent the rest of the morning asking his client about her interactions with Mrs. Short, Barbara Reed, Rebecca Diaz, and the Romeros. Mrs. Duncan denied emphatically the testimony from all these witnesses that she'd ever tried to hire anybody to kill Olga. She admitted that while, yes, she was unhappy with her son's marriage, "Lots of mothers don't approve of their sons' wives." But she insisted that all these witnesses were lying. "I never wanted anyone to kill my daughter-in-law," she said.

Sullivan asked her if she had ever tried to get Diane Romero to go to Olga's apartment to knock her over the head, put her in the bathtub, and throw lye on her.

Mrs. Duncan put a hand to her heart as she vehemently shook her head. "That was never mentioned, never."

Sullivan continued to attack the damning evidence presented by the prosecution over the previous six days. Mrs. Duncan told the court that she had only asked Barbara Reed to help her *kidnap* Frank. "I told her that I thought Frankie had flipped his lid, and I wanted to tie him up and take him to Los Angeles and let him think about this thing, and then maybe we could come to an understanding." Mrs. Duncan looked around the courtroom with a sheepish grin. "I know it was foolish, but that is what I said, and she agreed that she would help me."

"Did you tell Frank about this plan?"

"Heavens no!"

"And did you try to do this, to tie Frank up and take him to Los Angeles?"

"I changed my mind after Frank came home and went to bed. I decided to let him work this out himself."

After a lunch recess, Sullivan turned to impeaching Mrs. Short's testimony.

"Did you ever have any conversation with Mrs. Short in which you asked her to try and get Olga to come over to her place and have her sit in front of a closet, and that you would be in the closet with a rope?"

"Nooo. I couldn't sit in there," Mrs. Duncan said scornfully. "There's no ventilation in that closet."

"Well, did you say that you would put a rope around Olga's neck and choke her, cut off her hair, and hang her until evening, and then you would put a blanket around her, tie her with a rope, put a stone on it, and take her down and throw her off the wharf?"

"I couldn't very well do that, Mr. Sullivan. For one thing, I had a stroke in my left arm, and I couldn't lift Olga, and I wouldn't ask such a thing anyway. . . . No, I did not do it." She rubbed her healthy-looking left arm.

"Wait a minute, wait a minute." Gustafson stood. "I move to strike all portions of the answer except the words *I did not do it.*"

"The jury are directed to disregard the part stricken," the judge said in an exasperated tone.

Sullivan raised his face to the heavens above. "Mrs. Duncan, try, try to confine your answers to the question that is asked of you, will you please?"

Mrs. Duncan smiled contritely. "All right."

Sullivan moved on. "When was the first time that you ever talked to Mrs. Esquivel?"

"Mrs. Short and I were planning to look at apartments near the beach, and we wanted to have lunch at the Barbara Hotel on the way, but it was closed. We kept walking down State Street. . . ."

Gustafson rolled his eyes.

"I didn't know Mrs. Esquivel's place from a hole in the wall. But when we got to the front of the Tropical Café, she was standing in the doorway sweeping. She said to me, 'Aren't you Mrs. Duncan, and isn't your son the lawyer that is representing my husband?' And I said, 'Yes, I am. I am very proud of my son.' And then she said, 'Why don't you come in and have some coffee?' And so Mrs. Short and I went inside and had a cup of coffee and talked to Mrs. Esquivel for a while."

"And what did you talk about that day?"

"We talked about her husband, and let's see . . ." Mrs. Duncan furrowed her brow. "I told her how I wanted to find an apartment near the beach . . . how I thought that I would enjoy living at the beach in the summer months."

"Anything else?"

"No, no. We went out very good friends, I thought."

"And this was November 12th."

"Yes."

"When did you see her again?"

"The next day. It was on our way home from looking at apartments again. I wasn't at all satisfied with the apartment on Mason Street. We looked at a few other places. It was getting along about three or four, and we started home. . . ."

Sullivan glanced toward the prosecution table, where Gustafson now sat nonchalantly doodling in his notebook.

"The buses don't run but every hour, so we just kept walking up State Street. We got right to the door, and Moya and this other fellow and Mrs. Esquivel were standing there."

Mrs. Duncan testified that Mrs. Esquivel asked her to come in, and when she refused, Moya grabbed her by the wrist and pulled her into the café.

"Mrs. Esquivel told me that she didn't like the way that my son handled her husband's case, and she wanted her money back. She said that she was broke, and she wanted the $500 fee back that my son charged. She said she wanted it immediately, or my son and myself would be killed."

Sullivan did his best to look shocked. "What did you say?"

"Well, I was frightened, and Moya said, 'Give me your purse.' He jerked my purse open and said, 'How much money do you have?' And I said, 'Ten dollars.' And of course it wasn't enough, but I did have my diamond rings on and my diamond watch. Moya said that I should go up to the pawnshop in the next block and pawn my jewelry so that I could give Mrs. Esquivel some money right away before I left."

"And did you?"

Mrs. Duncan nodded. "I walked up to Mr. Cohen's pawnshop, and the other one followed me. I got $175 for the rings, and Mr. Cohen said to keep my watch. Moya and Mrs. Esquivel were waiting for us when we got back to the café."

"And Mrs. Short?"

"Yes. She was there, sitting by herself at the back, drinking a cup of coffee."

"What next?"

"I gave Mrs. Esquivel the $175, but Moya couldn't believe that that was all I got for my rings. I showed him the pawn ticket to prove it."

"Anything else?"

"Moya said, 'You'll hear from us later. We want the full $500 back, and Mrs. Esquivel said, 'You better not tell your son about this, or the police.' Which I didn't because Moya threatened to kill Frankie and me if we told anybody."

"Did you have any conversation about all this with Mrs. Short in the taxicab on the way home from the café that day, on November 13th?"

Gustafson stopped writing and peered over the top of his glasses at the defense attorney. *Are you nuts? Please keep repeating that date for the blackmail meeting: November 13th, November 13th.*

"I'm not sure of the exact day, but I told Mrs. Short that they had demanded Frank's fee back because Mr. Esquivel had been sentenced to prison and not sent back to Mexico as they'd hoped."

"Well, you've testified earlier that at the meeting at the Tropical, when Moya grabbed your wrist and pulled you inside, it was the day that you pawned your rings and gave Mrs. Esquivel $175. Is that right?"

"That's correct."

Sullivan held a small piece of paper toward his witness. "Now, referring to the People's Exhibit 42, do you notice the little notation on the margin, '11-13-58' and '$175' with the letters 'B.D.'?"

"Yes."

"And are those your initials, B.D.?"

"They are, sir."

"And does that refresh your recollection that it was November 13, 1958, that you paid this $175 to Moya?"

"Yes."

Gustafson's jaw dropped. Sullivan just kept hammering on that assertion that the blackmail meeting had occurred on November 13. But Mrs. Esquivel's husband hadn't been sentenced to prison until November 18. Surely a hotshot lawyer from LA like Ward Sullivan must have figured out that his client could not have been blackmailed on November 13 for a sentence that was not passed down until five days later.

Gustafson realized that Sullivan was looking at him, noticing his self-satisfied smile. Sullivan's forehead wrinkled.

That's right, hotshot. You've got a problem, a really big problem.

Sullivan returned to questioning his client in a halting voice. "And you say . . . that Mrs. Esquivel told you . . . that she wanted her fee back . . ." The flaw in Mrs. Duncan's story seemed to dawn on the attorney. "because . . ." He put his hand to his forehead and stared down at the lectern.

From the witness stand, Mrs. Duncan looked at Frank, who was ever so slightly shaking his head, a troubled expression spreading across his face.

"You know," Mrs. Duncan said, "she either said her husband had been sent to prison or she found out he was going to be sent, one or the other. I have forgotten. But whatever it was, she wasn't happy."

A flush of adrenaline tingled through the DA's body. *Here's a new element! Now she's saying that Mrs. Esquivel knew what the judge was going to do before the judge knew it himself.*

Sullivan plowed ahead. "And you say that you told Mrs. Short that they demanded the payment of the fee back. That is, the fee that had been paid to your son, Frank, for defending Mr. Esquivel, because he'd been sent to prison?"

"I think they demanded the fee back the day that Moya pulled me into the Tropical," Mrs. Duncan said in a hesitant voice.

Gustafson set his pen down and leaned back in his chair. *Thank you. Nothing could help my case more.*

Sullivan pressed Mrs. Duncan, taking her through her attempts to pay off Moya and Baldonado. Her story about meeting in stores along State Street and sending an envelope with ten dollars to the Blue Onion jibed with the testimony of Mrs. Esquivel, Luis Moya, and Mrs. Short. She also agreed with the previous witnesses' tally of $335 in payments. The difference was that Mrs. Duncan insisted she was making blackmail payments, not subsidizing the murder of her daughter-in-law.

Sullivan moved closer to his witness. "Did you ever at any time enter into any scheme, plan, or design with Luis Moya, Augustine Baldonado, Mrs. Esquivel, Mrs. Short, Barbara Reed, Rudy Romero, Diane Romero, Mrs. Diaz, or any other person whatsoever to kidnap Olga Duncan?"

"I did not."

"Or cause Olga Duncan any harm of any kind or nature whatsoever?"

"No, I did not."

"Did you ever at any time in your mind and heart plan to kill and murder Olga Duncan?"

"Certainly not."

"You've told us that you didn't approve of the marriage?"

"That is true." Mrs. Duncan folded her hands in her lap.

"Did you want the . . . marriage . . ." Sullivan looked away from his client. He hesitated a moment before saying, "I withdraw the question." He stepped back to the lectern and picked up his notes. "That is all."

Gustafson jerked his head up from his note-taking. *That was abrupt.* He scrambled to his feet. "Your Honor, I would prefer to begin my cross-examination of Mrs. Duncan in the morning."

Judge Blackstock adjourned court at two thirty P.M.

CHAPTER FIFTY-FOUR

FALLEN ANGEL

March 4, 1959

Daddy got home early that afternoon, changed into his yard clothes, and wandered out to the garage. After finishing reading the afternoon paper, I went outside to jump on my new pogo stick, but I got tired.

I called up to him as he stood atop the stepladder, humming "Davey Crocket," his head in the rafters. "I read in your story that Mrs. Duncan testified that all the witnesses against her are making it all up. I'm worried that the jury might believe her."

"I think," Daddy muttered, "everyone in the courtroom has figured out . . ." He tugged on something in the rafters that I couldn't see. ". . . that everything that comes out of that woman's mouth is a lie." The ladder rocked a little. "Goddammit . . . who put all this stuff up here?"

"What are you doing?"

"Getting down this old vacuum cleaner." He grunted again as he yanked on some camping equipment. "Goddammit," he grumbled. "Your mother broke the new one." More grunting.

I held the shaft of my new pogo stick with one hand and put my other hand out to steady the ladder. "Can I help?"

"Son of a bitch. Who jammed these damned things in like this and then put the luggage rack on top?"

I craned my neck to look. Tent stakes, pieces of carpet, the croquet set, and a plastic camp cooler were all precariously balanced across the rafters. I saw the wings of plastic angels and Santa's black boot peeking out from under our car luggage rack.

"I think you did, Daddy. Remember . . ."

He cut me a look, his face red, his Dodgers cap askew. "I did no such thing. No one in their right mind would—"

I heard a rumble and scraping as something came loose on the makeshift plywood shelf.

"Watch out!" Daddy screamed. He lost his grip, and his weight shifted backward.

My pogo stick clattered to the cement floor as I ducked and covered my head. Daddy stumbled and slid down the ladder, followed by tent stakes and the cooler. A three-foot-tall plastic angel flew past my face and nicked my father's arm. She landed with a loud thud in the middle of the garage floor.

"Son of a bitch." Daddy rubbed his arm.

"Oh no," I wailed. "The angel."

"Nothing to worry about," Daddy snapped. "Just a little accident . . . of a religious nature," he mumbled under his breath.

I knelt by the fallen angel. "She's my favorite." Her head had come off and slid across the concrete floor, and one of her wings was broken. Her electric cord snaked out from under the damaged body. I stared at the jagged plastic edges of her broken neck and touched her plain white dress, then crawled over to the lawnmower and reached around it to pick up the head. She was still smiling.

"Don't worry, I'll resurrect her." Daddy scratched his head. "Now, where's my quick-drying cement?"

I held the broken wingtip and the angel's head while he rummaged through an old chest of drawers in the corner of the garage where he stored a lot of his fixit junk. He pulled out a tube and began reading the directions.

"Hmmm." A big smile spread across his face. "For repair of wood, china, cloth, metal, *plastic*. . . ." He looked up. "Doesn't say anything about angel's wings, but worth a try, don't you think?"

I nodded solemnly. Daddy knelt, standing the angel's body up in front of him. He took the broken wing piece from my fingers and turned it round and round in his hands. Once he'd figured out which end was up, he spread the colorless liquid along the edges of the break and fitted the pieces together. He held them in place for a moment before saying, "You take over. I need to check the directions again."

I bent down and held the pieces together as tightly as I could while he looked at the glue tube. He moved his ball cap back on his head as he read. "Only takes a minute." He grinned at me. "Just a little more 'laying on of the hands' here," he said as he rubbed his finger along the repaired edges and glanced at his watch. "Okay. You can let go."

At first, the glue seemed to be holding. We both held our breath. But in a moment, the broken wing tip started to droop.

"Oh, shit. This may require a more complicated miracle than I first thought." He scratched his head again and turned the angel over. "Might have to take the whole wing off so we can lay it flat." He sighed. "No rest for the wicked."

He lifted his glasses and peered at the angel's back. "Looks like the wings are attached with a screw. I expected something a little more ethereal, like, say, a rivet. But we must work with what we have."

I was used to not completely following my father's line of thinking, so I made no comment.

"Find me the Phillips," he said, holding out his hand like a surgeon waiting for an instrument.

I found the screwdriver in a drawer and slapped it in his palm.

After much grumbling and swearing, he managed to loosen the screw and take the wing off, placing it and the broken tip on a hastily cleared spot on his workbench. He reapplied the glue to the broken edges. I sat on a stool and held the pieces together while he laid the angel's body on the floor and glued on her head.

We pressed our broken pieces together while we waited for the glue to set. "Let's give it five minutes this time," he said.

He screwed the repaired wing back on the angel and stood it upright on the workbench. "Looks pretty good," he said. Her angelic expression was unchanged, but she had a smudge on her nose.

"I think the wing is still drooping a little bit," I said.

He waved his hand. "Well, she's an angel. These heavenly beings are always a little tenuous. Ephemeral, you know." He picked up the cord and plugged it in. "Ah, pure light," he said. "At least the light bulb didn't break in the fall."

"You fixed her, Daddy." I threw my arms around him. "A miracle!"

He patted me on the head. "A good deed in a naughty world."

CHAPTER FIFTY-FIVE

LYING LIPS

March 5, 1958

C rowds of would-be spectators eager to hear Roy Gustafson's cross-examination of Elizabeth Duncan congregated in the hallway, sitting on the floor, leaning against the wall as they munched breakfast foods out of lunch boxes. Ropes restrained the line to keep a clear path to the courtroom doors. A United Press International news team interviewed two women from the nearby rural town of Oak View.

"We got here at five thirty this morning so we could be first in line," one of the women complained. "But there were fifty people already here ahead of us."

Inside the courtroom, Roy Gustafson huddled with his secretary, conferring in low voices as Gustafson thumbed through typewritten pages. Bob watched the little powwow from his chair in the press section. He felt that Gustafson's prosecution witnesses had been solid, except that the most important ones—those who had testified about the threats or the plot to kill Olga—were not the most credible people in the world. Moya and Baldonado had already admitted to murdering Olga. Mrs. Esquivel had an arrest record. Rudy Romero was an ex-convict, and Mrs. Short was a confused old woman. Mrs. Duncan, on the other hand, had turned on the charm, smiling warmly at the jury and presenting herself as an innocent woman unjustly accused.

And Bob knew Gustafson must have another concern: reasonable doubt. As Luis Moya had testified, Elizabeth Duncan was a very convincing woman, and it only took one waffling juror to hang a jury. Unfortunately, because it was not evidence related to this particular crime, Gustafson couldn't present testimony about Mrs. Duncan's con-artist background: how she'd repeatedly tried to make a buck by bamboozling men into marrying her or fast-talked herself into apartments with some sob story, telling landlords that the money was "on the way," and then lived there rent-free for months before skipping out to dupe the next sucker.

Gustafson studied the faces of the jurors as they filed into the courtroom. *I need to get her angry enough to show the jury her true disposition. Let everyone see that this respectable, ladylike façade is just an act. I can't tell them myself, so she'll have to do it for me . . . her and Frankie.*

"All rise," the bailiff called.

Judge Blackstock gave his strongest warning of the trial. He pointed his gavel at the gallery and raised his voice. "Now, remember, I don't want any demonstration of any kind from this audience. Be careful. Otherwise, I will clear the courtroom."

"This should be good," Bob whispered to Bennie Jo. "Roy Gustafson takes no prisoners in court . . . real killer instinct. I think Sullivan's way underestimated our 'small-town DA.'"

Mrs. Duncan flounced to the witness stand like a princess taking her throne. The DA stood at the lectern, hands behind his back as he waited for her to settle into the chair. Then he began: "Mrs. Duncan, I want to talk about some matters that Mr. Sullivan went over with you yesterday."

"Yes, sir," the defendant said in a pleasant tone.

"You are nervous, are you?" Gustafson asked in an equally agreeable voice.

Mrs. Duncan smiled sweetly. "No, I'm not nervous at all."

Her first few answers to questions about her age and where she was born were answered with a patient attitude, conveying the sense that all of this questioning was quite unnecessary.

"Did you say yesterday that you are fifty-four years old?"

"I did," Mrs. Duncan said.

"What year were you born?"

Mrs. Duncan thought a moment. "Nineteen oh four."

"Is that so?"

The defendant bristled. "Yes, it is."

"Your maiden name was Nigh?"

"That's right."

"Elizabeth Ann Nigh?"

"No, it was not." She folded her arms across her chest. "I had my name changed later."

"What was your name before you changed it?"

She scowled at the judge. "Do I have to answer that? I'd rather not."

"Certainly," Judge Blackstock said. "Answer the question."

The witness huffed. "All right, if you must know, my name is Hazel."

"Hazel Sinclaira Nigh?" the DA continued.

"That's right," Mrs. Duncan snapped.

At the defense table, Frank tried to catch his mother's eye. He held his hand near his lap, making a "calm down" motion.

Gustafson smiled to himself. *The sugar coating is already beginning to melt.*

"When and where did you have your name changed?" he asked.

"I just changed it myself."

"I see . . ." Gustafson moved on. "Now, as I understood your testimony yesterday, you certainly never did have any intention of killing Olga Duncan, did you?"

"No, sir, I did not."

"So, you didn't ever tell anybody that you were trying to have Olga killed?"

"I never told anyone, and I didn't do it, either." Mrs. Duncan folded her arms.

"You said yesterday that you disapproved of the marriage of Frankie and Olga. Is that correct?"

Frank Duncan jumped out of his chair, his face contorted in anger. "Mr. Gustafson, just one moment. My name is Frank. It is not Frankie. When you refer to me—"

Gustafson wheeled around. "Will you please sit down? Your Honor, I will ask that this man be ejected."

Judge Blackstock wiggled his gavel at Frank. "Don't make any moves like that again."

"Well, his name *is* Frank, Your Honor," Mrs. Duncan sputtered.

Sullivan got to his feet. "Will the court request Mr. Gustafson that when he speaks of Frank to call him Frank or Mr. Duncan?"

Gustafson shook his head. "Your Honor, the transcript of yesterday's testimony shows this witness, Mrs. Duncan, referring to him more often as Frankie than as Frank, and there is already evidence that that is what he is called by this witness. I have a perfect right to refer to him as Frankie."

"You can have some respect for him," Sullivan said.

Gustafson cocked his head. "Why?"

"And refer to him by his right name," Sullivan continued.

"Frank and Frankie aren't very far apart." The judge thought a moment and turned toward Gustafson. "You can call him either one you want."

"Well, I won't answer if he uses the name Frankie," Mrs. Duncan snarled.

People in the gallery tittered. A few of the jury members tried to suppress smiles.

Gustafson stepped back to the lectern. "Did you tell anyone that the baby that Olga was carrying wasn't Frankie's child?"

Mrs. Duncan eyed Gustafson with a chilly glint and did not reply.

Judge Blackstock leaned across his bench toward the witness. "See here, you have to answer the questions, Mrs. Duncan."

She balled her hands into fists. "I didn't say it wasn't Frankie's . . . Frank's child. I didn't know anything about it until after all this came out in the newspaper."

"So you didn't say anything to anybody that it wasn't Frankie's child?"

"I said that I didn't see how it could be his because he had been ill when he was a child. He had the mumps, and the doctor told us that he could never have children."

"Ahhhh . . . I see."

"Mr. Gustafson, Olga told me that the reason she wanted to marry Frank was because she'd been sleeping with him."

"And you told her that you wanted him to marry a woman with a character at least as good as yours?"

"I wanted someone to like me, and she didn't like me. She told me when I called her on the phone that she thought I was very possessive . . . and she called me a dirty name."

"What was the dirty name she called you?"

Her face hardened. "I'm not going to repeat the name she called me."

Gustafson raised his eyebrows. "Yes, you are."

"Oh, no, I won't."

"Oh, yes, you are."

Mrs. Duncan folded her arms across her chest. "You make me."

"All right." Gustafson turned toward the judge, who seemed to have been listening to the testimony with his eyes shut. The DA cleared his throat loudly. "Your Honor, ask her to repeat the name."

Judge Blackstock started. "What?" he said as he put his hand to his ear.

Gustafson raised his voice. "The witness refuses to state the name that she alleges that Olga Duncan called her."

"Well, what did Olga Duncan call you?" The judge stifled a yawn with the back of his hand. "You said she called you something. What did she call you?"

Mrs. Duncan chewed on her lower lip a moment before speaking. "That woman is dead. I don't want to discuss what that woman . . . what happened."

"You are on the witness stand now under cross-examination. Answer that question," the judge growled.

Sullivan rose from his chair and addressed his client. "You will have to tell them."

Mrs. Duncan flounced her hair. "She said I was crazy."

Laughter arose from the gallery. Gustafson bit his lip to suppress a smile. "Crazy? That was the bad name she used?"

"Yes."

"I see. Well, now, you told Olga, did you not, about the type of girl you wanted your son to marry, and that you wanted that girl to be of a character at least as good as yours, didn't you?"

Sullivan stood up. "Just a moment. This is assuming facts not in evidence."

Gustafson whirled around to face Sullivan. "I am cross-examining her and asking her did she say it. Now she can say yes or no."

Mrs. Duncan answered the question. "No, sir."

"Thank you." Gustafson put his hands on his hips. "My goodness, Mr. Sullivan certainly knows that I'm entitled to ask the witness on cross-examination anything pertaining to this subject."

Sullivan opened his mouth as if to say something but seemed to think better of it and fixed an icy glare on Gustafson as he took his seat.

"So, back to that telephone conversation you had with Olga on the night before she and Frank got married . . . the conversation that Mrs. Short testified about when she said that you threatened to kill Olga if she didn't leave Frank alone."

"Yes, but I never threatened to kill anyone," she said, and went on to insist that she hadn't even told Mrs. Short about any conversation she had with Olga.

"Do you have any idea of how Mrs. Short learned about this conversation?" Gustafson asked.

"Mrs. Short only knows what you and your investigator have told her about it."

"Do you know how we learned about this conversation?"

"Well, I think I must have told one of your detectives."

"Did you tell one of the detectives that during that conversation you threatened to kill Olga?"

Mrs. Duncan slammed her fist on the witness stand railing. "I never threatened to kill Olga!"

"Then Mrs. Short couldn't have learned about that part of it from the detective."

Mrs. Duncan didn't respond.

"Now, yesterday, I believe you told us about an incident after the marriage where you had contemplated tying Frankie up?"

"Tie *Frank* up, Mr. Gustafson."

"I think it would be much easier if you don't worry about what name I call your son."

"Frank is an attorney, the same as you are, and I think you should show him some respect." Mrs. Duncan looked lovingly toward her son where he sat stiff-backed in his chair, his face pinched and flushed. "I want you to show some respect for my son," she snapped. "Do it."

Gustafson cocked his head. "Yes, ma'am," he responded sarcastically.

"Well, start in then."

"Now, Mrs. Duncan, when you abandoned the idea of tying Frankie up and taking him to—"

"I can't understand you. If you say Frankie, I won't understand the question."

Gustafson took a deep breath. "Now, Mrs. Duncan, when you abandoned the idea of tying Frankie up and taking him to an apartment in Los Angeles, did you decide to let him work his problems out for himself?"

Mrs. Duncan turned away. "I don't understand a thing you're saying. I don't understand the question." She looked up at the judge. "If he says 'Frank' and rephrases the question, I will understand it."

Judge Blackstock narrowed his eyes at the defendant. "Listen. There is nothing disrespectful about 'Frankie.'"

"It is disrespectful," Mrs. Duncan retorted.

"That's what you think," the judge barked.

"I do, sir." Mrs. Duncan pointed at Gustafson. "And he's doing it for meanness."

The judge rubbed the back of his neck. "Where were we?"

"I asked her why she'd abandoned the idea of tying her son up so she could take him to Los Angeles. Had she decided to let him work things out for himself?"

Mrs. Duncan sighed dramatically. "That is right, sir. I abandoned that idea."

"And you didn't thereafter do anything further to interfere with the marriage relationship?"

"Well, I would talk to him and try to get him to stay home. I did do that."

"I believe that several times, Mrs. Duncan, you told people that Frankie was not living with Olga."

"Frank was not living with Olga, Mr. Gustafson . . . or, what is your first name? I might call you that."

The DA smiled sweetly at the witness. "You may call me anything you choose." He turned to his next page of questions. "Didn't you tell Mrs. Barnett, Olga's landlady at the Garden Street apartments, that Frank and Olga were not married because, in fact, an annulment of that marriage had been obtained in Ventura? And didn't you tell Mrs. Barnett that she could come to Ventura and check the records?"

"I never told Mrs. Barnett that, no."

"Are you saying that she was lying when she said that on the stand?"

"Well, I didn't tell her that."

Sullivan stood up. "We are going to object to that as improper cross-examination, Your Honor."

Mrs. Duncan wrinkled her nose. "I would like to oppose this whole thing."

The courtroom erupted in laughter.

"Objection overruled." The judge banged his gavel. "And we will adjourn for our morning recess."

Gustafson headed up the aisle to get a drink of water from the fountain in the hallway. As he passed the defense table, Mrs. Duncan half rose from her chair.

"You son of a bitch," she hissed.

Gustafson turned around. "Pardon me?"

Sullivan jumped out of his chair and pulled his client back into her seat.

Bob glanced over his shoulder at Bennie Jo. "Well, he did tell her that she could call him anything she wanted."

When court resumed, Gustafson continued to ask questions about the annulment, and Sullivan continued to object. The judge overruled all of his objections. Mrs. Duncan pretended not to understand Gustafson's questions whenever he used the name Frankie.

The DA finally moved on to other subjects. He tried to confirm that November 13 was the date on which Mrs. Duncan had met with Baldonado, Moya, and Mrs. Esquivel at the Tropical Café.

"Mrs. Esquivel told you that she was displeased because she didn't like the way Frank had handled her husband's case because he'd been sent to prison?"

"No, I didn't say that. I said I didn't know for sure if Mr. Esquivel had been sent to prison." Mrs. Duncan took a sideways look at her son. Frank slumped in his usual chair, his legs and arms crossed, his shoulders hunched, and his lips pinched closed. His squinty gaze shifted between the jury, the judge, and his lap.

Gustafson suppressed another smile. *I see one of these legal geniuses has finally told her that there's a problem with the date she says she was blackmailed.*

"What did Mrs. Esquivel tell you, exactly?" he asked.

"She said that she didn't like it because she knew that her husband was going to be sent to prison, and he wasn't going to go back to Mexico as they previously had planned."

"Did you ask her how she knew this?"

"Yes, she said that she had talked to Frank about probation, and he had told her that it was doubtful that the judge would give probation to him."

"Oh, that was it?" Gustafson said sarcastically.

"Yes, that was it," Mrs. Duncan answered with cool distaste.

"Yesterday you testified that when you were riding home from the Tropical in a taxi with Mrs. Short, they had demanded the fee back because Mr. Esquivel had been *sent* to prison . . ."

"No, I didn't!" Mrs. Duncan resettled herself in her chair and continued in a softer tone. "If I said that, I didn't mean that. What I said is that he was *going* to be sent to prison."

"You want to correct that, then?"

Mrs. Duncan nodded. "Yes, I would like to, yes. . . . I meant that he was going to be sent to prison."

"And she wanted the $500 back whether he was sent to prison or not, even if he got probation?"

"She said that she'd just got through talking to my son, and he had told her that there was no chance for probation."

"Well, today on this witness stand is the first time, is it not, that you ever said that Mrs. Esquivel had told you that she was unhappy because her husband *might* get sent to prison?"

"No, sir."

"Isn't it true that you told the officers in Santa Barbara and my investigator, Mr. Osborne, that Mrs. Esquivel said that she was sore because her husband *had been sent* to prison?"

Gustafson eyed the witness as he waited for a response. Both he and Mrs. Duncan knew that an interview with Osborne had been recorded, but only Gustafson knew that the recorder had malfunctioned, failing to record the questions and answers about her meeting with Mrs. Esquivel at the Tropical Café. Mrs. Duncan glanced toward the defense table. Frank and Sullivan stared back, stony-faced.

Gustafson started to repeat the question. "Isn't it true that . . ."

"I'm not denying that I said that, but I don't think he had been sent to prison at the time I first saw her."

"Absolutely, of course, he hadn't been sent to prison, and you found that out subsequently, and now you had to change your story, didn't you?"

"I did not. I did not. That's a lie!"

"But you didn't tell anybody that Mrs. Esquivel only *thought* her husband might be sentenced to prison until you testified in this court today. Isn't it true? This is the first time you ever said that?"

Mrs. Duncan turned toward the court reporter. "Would you read that? He talks so fast I can't even understand him."

"Well, suppose I withdraw it."

"I wish you would."

"You made up this story about the blackmail, and then it dawned on you—"

"Don't you dare say that to me." Mrs. Duncan balled her fists on the railing in front of the witness chair. "That's a lie."

"So you changed your story to fit the dates."

"That is a lie. My son was living at home all this time, and I knew, and I could keep track of everything if I wanted to, and that was not necessary."

"But you didn't keep track."

She began to snivel. "I don't know. It is just awful. I have been in jail, and I don't know, and I just . . . I just don't know. . . ."

The DA ignored the crying and reviewed the rendezvous Mrs. Duncan had had with Moya and Baldonado at stores on State Street when she'd cashed Frank's $200 typewriter check at a bank and gave them a $150 installment on the blackmail demand.

"Now, when Frank wanted to see a receipt for the typewriter payment, you told him that you were being blackmailed. Is that right?"

"That's right."

"And when Frank asked, 'Why didn't you tell me about that payment that you made at the Tropical Café when you pawned your rings?' you told

Frank that you didn't want to worry him because of Olga's disappearance. Isn't that true?"

"I guess I did."

Gustafson cocked his head. "Even though Olga hadn't disappeared until November 17th?"

"Well, how could I tell him that?" Mrs. Duncan snapped.

"You did tell him that. You just got through saying it."

The formerly charming Elizabeth Duncan squeezed her lips into a thin, hateful pucker.

Sullivan sat at the defense table staring unseeingly at his client, his lips curved into a humorless smile.

After lunch, Gustafson reviewed Mrs. Duncan's visit to the Garden Street apartments the day she'd talked Mrs. Barnett into letting her into Olga's apartment.

"Was there another time, other than the day you talked to Mrs. Barnett, that you went over to the Garden Street apartments?"

"Yes, there was."

"This was the time when Frank and Olga were in the apartment, and they wouldn't open the door for you?"

"Yes."

"And you beat on the door and asked that it be opened."

"No, sir. I wouldn't beat on the door. I knocked on it."

"You knocked on it pretty hard?"

"Well, if you call using my fist 'pretty hard.'"

"And you hollered at them to let you in?"

"No, sir, I never hollered."

"You called out that you knew that they were in there, didn't you?" he said bitingly.

"I did not. I did not. I knocked on the door. I tried to be a lady." Mrs. Duncan smoothed the skirt of her dress.

"Well, you knew they were in there?"

"I thought they were because I saw Frank's car out front."

"And that is why you hollered at them to let you in, that you knew they were there?"

"I did not holler, Mr. Gustafson."

"And they would not open the door?"

"Mr. Gustafson, I did not holler! Let's get that straight right now," the witness shouted. "I knocked on the door. That is what I did."

"But they didn't open the door for you?"

"No." Mrs. Duncan shook her head sadly. "No."

"We talked earlier today about you changing your name from Hazel to Elizabeth. Do you remember that?"

"Yes."

"When you told me that your name was Hazel Sinclaira Nigh, you omitted something."

Mrs. Duncan looked away in disgust. "Why go over all that?"

"I'm just trying to find out what your name is. That's all."

"My name is Elizabeth."

"But you call yourself Lucille in the phone book."

"Yes, I do, for good reasons. Do you want to know why?"

Gustafson's expression perked up. "Yes, sure."

"I was married to a man, and I didn't want him to know where I was at."

"What man was that?"

"I'm not going to tell you that. I don't think that is quite necessary, do you? I told you that much."

Gustafson mentally rubbed his hands together. *Yes, you did. Bless you, Mrs. Duncan, you old fool. You brought up the marriage.* The DA looked to the judge. "She asked to volunteer this information and—"

Judge Blackstock nodded. "You'll have to answer the question, Mrs. Duncan."

Gustafson continued. "And having done so—volunteered this information—I submit, Your Honor, that she has to answer other pertinent questions about it."

Mrs. Duncan shot a worried look toward the defense table. "All right. I was married to a man by the name of Gillis when I lived in San Francisco, and I didn't want him to know where I was. The marriage had been annulled, but he'd been bothering me."

"I see." Gustafson paced in front of the witness stand. "But later, you never changed the listing? You kept using the name Lucille Duncan in the phone book all the time you've been living in Santa Barbara?"

"Yes. I have."

Gustafson looked at his notes. "From November 7, 1928—the day your son Frank was born—until December 13, 1958—the day you were arrested—except for three months when he was living at his college fraternity house, he constantly lived with you?"

"No. When we lived in San Francisco, when he was in law school, we had two small apartments. And I would say that was about a period of a year and a half."

"Well, now, your relationship with your son Frank was one of a great deal of love and devotion by you to him, was it not?"

Mrs. Duncan looked the DA straight in the eye. "I love my son very much. I always have."

"You love Frank the most of all of your six children?"

"I wouldn't say that. . . ." She picked at something on her skirt. "Well, yes . . . I think I will say that . . ." Her head shot up. She did a double take. "Six children?"

"Yeeeeeesss," Gustafson said in an exaggerated, drawn-out voice.

A burst of laughter erupted in the back of the courtroom.

Mrs. Duncan glared at the DA for a full fifteen seconds. "Well, I think you're a—" She sputtered and then shook her head. "Yes, I guess that's right."

"That's correct, isn't it, six children?"

She furrowed her brow. "I have to think."

"Pardon?"

"Yes, that's right. There may be ten after a while."

"Ten? Well, maybe so. Let's find out who they are."

Sullivan stood. "Just a moment. We are going to object to that question as incompetent, irrelevant, and immaterial, Your Honor."

"Well, I'm certainly entitled to show the nature of her devotion and relationship with her son Frank Duncan as compared with her other five children. And now she's raised the question about the number of children. She said that there may be ten, and I would like—"

"Oh, I was kidding." Mrs. Duncan flapped a hand in front of her face. "I didn't mean that."

The DA let out an exaggerated sigh. "Okay. Just six." He walked to the prosecution table and retrieved a typewritten list of names. Dates were handwritten in red ink beside each name. His investigator, Tommy Osborne, had been searching records and compiling the information for weeks. Gustafson referred to it as the List of Fools.

"Now, Mrs. Duncan, I believe that you told us that at the time Frank was born, on November 7, 1928, you were married to Frank Lowe, was it? And that you named Frank after his father, Mr. Lowe?"

"That's right."

"Well, as a matter of fact, at the time that Frank was born, you weren't married to Frank Lowe, were you?"

Sullivan wearily placed both hands on the defense table and pushed himself to a half-standing position. "Just a moment. We are going to object to this as incompetent, irrelevant . . . He's going back more than thirty years here. It doesn't tend to prove or disprove any of the issues in this case, Your Honor."

"Your Honor," Gustafson said, "this matter was brought out by Mr. Sullivan's questioning of Mrs. Duncan, and I submit that if he's had his witness state something that isn't true, I should have the opportunity to impeach the witness on that fact."

"All right, the objection is overruled."

"When were you married to Frank Lowe?" Gustafson asked Mrs. Duncan.

"July 12, 1928."

"But at that time, you knew that your former husband, Edward James Lynchberg, was still living, didn't you?"

Mrs. Duncan scrunched her face up. "Lynchberg? I never married any Lynchberg."

"The name doesn't ring a bell with you?"

"It doesn't ring any bell because I don't have any bells in my head to ring." Mrs. Duncan smiled all around the room. "And I don't know of a Lynchberg."

"I see," the DA deadpanned. "Well, you knew, did you not, at the time you went through the ceremony with Frank Lowe, that your husband, Dewey Tessier, was still living and you had not been divorced from him?"

Sullivan stood again. "I object."

"Overruled."

"Dewey was divorced from me. He went to Mexico and got a divorce. He married another lady after he got the divorce."

"Did you ever see any papers?"

"No, but I know he got it. He married that other lady."

"And you also had three children with Mr. Tessier that you abandoned?"

This time Sullivan flew out of his seat. "Objection!"

"I withdraw the question, Your Honor."

Gustafson turned back to the witness. "When you married Mr. Lowe, weren't you aware of the fact that your husband, Mr. Mitchell, was still living?"

"Objection."

"Overruled."

Mrs. Duncan folded her arms. "I don't know if he was alive or not. He got us a divorce."

"What year?" Gustafson said.

"I don't know."

"You didn't get the divorce."

"No, I didn't. What's that got to do with this case, anyway? I was married to Frank Lowe legally. And that's all you need to know."

"You said in answer to Mr. Sullivan's question that you were married to Frank P. Duncan at the time that Patricia was born."

"I was."

"You weren't married to him legally, were you?"

"I certainly was."

"Well, Mrs. Duncan, I am going to show you a copy of a complaint for the annulment of your marriage in a case brought by your son's stepfather, Frank Duncan."

"To which I object," Sullivan interjected.

"Overruled."

"Your Honor," Sullivan said, "just so that I won't have to keep interrupting Mr. Gustafson's questioning of this witness, may it be understood that my objections go to the entire questioning upon this subject matter?"

"All right," the judge said.

Gustafson handed Mrs. Duncan the copy of the complaint. "And in this complaint, it is alleged that at the time of the marriage ceremony between Frank Duncan Sr. and Betty Duncan, the marriage between Betty Duncan and a former husband was still in force."

"Mr. Lowe wrote and told me he had gotten a divorce. He was not my husband at the time I married Frank Duncan."

"Which man was your husband at the time that you married Frank Duncan?"

"I didn't figure I had a husband at the time I married Frank Duncan."

Gustafson continued in a biting, sarcastic tone. "Well, in 1952, at the time Frank Duncan Sr. got an annulment from you on the grounds that you still had a husband when you married him, you made no objection to that, so you must have figured you had a husband at the time."

"I did not want to answer him back because I wasn't interested in him. If he wanted to get an annulment, let him get it. I didn't care."

Gustafson nodded. "I believe we have established that for most of your son's life, he has always lived with you. Is that right?"

"That is right."

"And he continued to live with you while you were married to Frank Craig?"

"I never lived with Frank Craig. What's this got to do with all of this?"

The judge cut in. "Never mind what it has to do with all this."

"Well, I certainly do," the witness shot back.

The judge gave Mrs. Duncan a look designed to peel the hide of the most recalcitrant of defendants. "You are only to answer the questions."

"And Frank Duncan, your son, continued to live with you while you were married to Harry Irwin?"

"Objection."

"This is terrible," Mrs. Duncan interjected.

Sullivan slapped his hand down on the table. "She already told you the times that her son Frank lived with her and the only times that he didn't live with her. These questions are asked only to degrade her and prejudice the jury."

"And to degrade my son," Mrs. Duncan added.

"The objection is overruled."

"Now, did your son continue to live with you during the time that you were married to Joseph Gold?"

"Your honor," Sullivan said. "Objection. This is an appeal to the bias and prejudice of this jury, and upon further grounds, that question has already been asked and answered."

"Overruled."

"I will answer all of it. My son has always lived with me except the times that I have told you about, Mr. Gustafson."

"In other words, all the time that you were married to George Satriano?"

A few more giggles came from the back rows.

"I told you."

Gustafson moved his finger down to the next name on the list. "How about when you were married to Benjamin Cogbill?"

The gallery erupted in laughter. The judge banged his gavel.

"My son lived with me at all times, except what I told you," the defendant said through gritted teeth.

"And that would include while you were married to Stephen Gillis?"

"Objection!" Sullivan called out.

Judge Blackstock shifted his gaze to Gustafson. "Well, she said her son lived with her at all times. That takes in everything."

"All right, I will withdraw that and go at it the other way then." Gustafson turned back to Mrs. Duncan. "Frank was living with you at all times. And when you were married to Leonard Sollenne, Mr. Sollenne did not live with you and Frank, did he?"

Sullivan banged his fist on the table. "Objection. How is that going to prove or disprove any issue in this case?"

Judge Blackstock scowled at the DA. "I don't think it proves anything. The objection is sustained."

"Thank you, Your Honor," Sullivan said softly as he took his seat.

Gustafson waited a moment, frowning at his List of Fools. "All right." *That leaves me hanging. No more questions on the marriages* . . . He took off his glasses. "You said, Mrs. Duncan, in answer to Mr. Sullivan's question, that you are fifty-four years old."

"I did."

"And you say that you were born on April 16, 1904."

"That is correct."

"But actually, that isn't the date of your birth, is it?" The DA picked up a piece of paper from the lectern. "Because on July 13, 1929, you swore that you were twenty-four years old when in fact you were twenty-five years old."

Sullivan stood. "Just a moment. I'd like to see this documentation Mr. Gustafson refers to. . . . Let's see what it is."

"All right, I will offer it. . . . This marriage certificate of Frank Lowe and Hazel Elizabeth Nigh." Gustafson handed the paper to the judge.

"It seems to me that what you have stated is purely argumentative," Judge Blackstock said as he read the document.

"Pardon?" Gustafson said.

Sullivan said, "May I glance at this document, Your Honor, before Your Honor rules on its admission as evidence?"

The judge passed it over. The defense attorney studied it for a few moments. "We object on the grounds that it is an attempt to impeach her on an immaterial matter, probably a few months' difference in age."

"The objection is"—Judge Blackstock scratched his head—"overruled." He gazed around the courtroom. "It is half past four. Court will adjourn until tomorrow morning at ten o'clock."

"But I'm right in the middle of . . ." Gustafson sputtered. "It will only take . . ."

Judge Blackstock shook his head and turned toward the jurors to give the admonition.

Bennie Jo gathered her coat and handbag as the judge and jury left the courtroom. She stuffed her notebook in the side pocket of her purse while Bob finished writing his notes for the session.

"I count ten husbands," she said. "How about you?"

Bob flipped his notebook open. "I got eleven husbands—don't forget Lynchberg."

"Oh yeah, Lynchberg, the one she couldn't remember." Bennie Jo scoffed. "Eleven! That's a lot of husbands."

"Well, she got an early start. She married the first one when she was fifteen."

As Bob got up from his chair, he noticed Gustafson standing at the back-exit door, staring glassy-eyed toward the judge's empty bench.

Sullivan passed in front of the two reporters on his way to the main aisle and gave them a jaunty little wave.

"He seems to be in a good mood," Bennie Jo commented. "That's weird. Didn't think his client did all that well today."

The DA gave the door a hard push and disappeared into the hallway.

"Probably something to do with an appeal if he needs one," Bob said.

An assistant district attorney was hovering in front of Gustafson's secretary's desk when the DA burst through the door.

"Hey, great cross, boss. . . . I caught some of the testimony between my hearings. . . ."

Gustafson stormed into his office but didn't close the door. The assistant DA followed his boss inside.

Gustafson gazed despondently around his office. "I'm worried that I might have ruined the case," he said.

"How?"

"Because of the questions I asked about the husbands. I was on solid ground until Blackstock sustained one of Sullivan's objections before I could make my point about why the subject was relevant. I could have tied everything up in a nice legal knot, but now . . ." He shook his head.

The assistant DA slid his eyes sideways. *The boss is admitting a mistake?*

Gustafson stared out his window. "It's Judge Blackstock's fault. He should have never allowed the questions in the first place if he was going to cut me off partway through. I needed to show that Mrs. Duncan continued to live with Frank rather than with the men she married." Gustafson turned around in his chair to face his assistant. "I thought there was a very strong inference from these facts that Mrs. Duncan was totally unwilling to face life unless she, and she alone, could live with her son. This could have helped explain her hostility toward Olga."

"Agreed, boss. Important point."

Gustafson picked up a pencil from his desk and twiddled it between his fingers. "So I asked her the questions about why she refused to live with them . . . Craig, Irwin, Gold, Satriano . . . and Gillis . . . that poor slob."

"Gillis was Frank's law school classmate, right? The one she claimed fathered mystery child number six, right?"

"Yeah, when she was forty-nine. I think that's why she balked when I said six children. She forgot about the baby she made up to bilk Gillis."

"Unbelievable."

"It is unbelievable because it isn't true," Gustafson said. "She never actually produced a child for anyone to see, but all the same, she got a little money out of Gillis. Just one more of her con jobs." Gustafson swept his hand through the air. "But, alas, all irrelevant and immaterial to this case according to Sullivan and now Judge Blackstock."

"Relevance . . . sort of a fine line."

"Not a fine line with me. Sullivan objected to every one of the questions about the husbands and was overruled every time. Then, before I could connect it all to the case, Judge Blackstock changes his mind and sustains an objection. I couldn't ask Mrs. Duncan any more questions on the subject." He threw his pencil on the desk. "I'm a little afraid of what an appellate court might say if it gets that far. The judge left me with everything in midair."

"Midair," the assistant repeated. "Not a good place to be."

CHAPTER FIFTY-SIX

GET AWAY FROM ME

March 6, 1959

The next morning, while spectators jostled in line to get seats in the gallery, Sullivan and Gustafson were meeting with Judge Blackstock in his chambers. Sullivan sat in a chair next to the DA, his legs crossed and a foot gently swinging up and down as he contemplated his fingernails.

Gustafson cleared his throat. "Yesterday, near the close of session, I asked a series of questions about the defendant living with her son instead of the men she'd married. My purpose was to show that her relationship with her son was so unusually close that she continued to live with Frank even though he was a grown man, in preference to her various husbands."

The judge leaned forward in his chair. "I now feel that these marriages are really immaterial to the issue of this case."

"You think?" Sullivan muttered under his breath.

Gustafson took paperwork out of his briefcase. "I'd like to propose a solution to this situation." He handed documents to Sullivan and the judge. "The jury must be told to disregard that testimony."

Sullivan scanned the paperwork. "This is all right with me."

Judge Blackstock nodded as he read the pages. "All I need to do is read this to the jury?"

"I think that will take care of it, Your Honor."

Sullivan smoothed his hand over the back of his head. *Right you are! And the appeals court will take care of both of you.*

"All rise."

Sullivan held the door for Judge Blackstock. Gustafson followed them both into the courtroom.

"Something's up." Bob nudged Bennie Jo. "Look at Sullivan's smug expression."

Judge Blackstock summarized Mrs. Duncan's testimony regarding her many husbands and directed the jurors to disregard much of what they had heard about these marriages. "All testimony about marriages subsequent to her marriage to Frank Duncan Sr. is to be expunged from the record. None of this matters or has any bearing on the issues of this trial. You are to disregard all of this testimony during deliberations."

The courtroom buzzed. Sullivan asked the judge for five minutes to consult with his client before she went back on the witness stand.

"Gee," Bennie Jo said. "So the jury is supposed to forget all about the eleven husbands?"

"Judge says it has no bearing. . . . You'd think he could have figured that out before he let Gustafson ask all those questions." Bob wrote a few words in his notebook. "No wonder Sullivan had that smirk on his face. This might be a problem for the prosecution if there's an appeal."

"Don't see how the jury will forget about those husbands," Bennie Jo pondered. "That train has left the station."

"The ship has sailed," Bob agreed.

"Can't unring the bell. Or turn back the clock."

"Nope. And you can't put the cat back in the bag, either." Bob moved the cuff of his sleeve to reveal a scar on his wrist. A talisman from the dearly departed Cinderella.

On his way to his lectern to continue his cross-examination, the DA gave Sullivan an arrogant one-shouldered shrug as he walked past the defense table. Sullivan flashed the prosecutor a challenging stare. *Double dare.*

Gustafson turned toward the defendant. "Mrs. Duncan, I believe you testified that you and your son did not occupy any bed together. Is that correct?"

The courtroom hummed. Judge Blackstock glared the room silent.

"That's right."

"Well, you lived with your son in San Francisco at 825 Geary Street in apartment 501, did you not?"

"Yes, sir."

"That was a one-bedroom apartment, wasn't it?"

"That's right, sir."

"And it only had one bed in it, and no pull-down, no davenport in the living room . . . nothing except one bed in it?"

"That's right."

"And you and Frank stayed in that bed together, did you not?" Gustafson said in a loud, challenging tone.

More low buzzing from the audience.

"We did not," Mrs. Duncan said calmly. "Don't be ridiculous."

"Where did Frank sleep?"

"Well, this apartment had a very large closet, almost a little room, with a rollaway bed, and Frank stayed home only every other night, as he worked some nights at the school. The rollaway bed was his." Mrs. Duncan turned toward the jury. "I guess you ladies and gentlemen have seen those portable beds that can be all folded up in the daytime. That's where my son slept." She turned back toward the DA and smiled sweetly.

Gustafson's face clouded. "I just got through asking you, 'There was no pull-down,' and you said that was true. Have you changed your mind?"

"I didn't understand the question. I didn't understand you to say that. It was a rollaway."

"Oh, so you are pretty sure of this, that there was another bed in the apartment?" Gustafson asked suspiciously.

"Yes, sir. You can go take a picture of it." Mrs. Duncan smiled out over the audience.

"Well, we'll see about that, Mrs. Duncan," Gustafson grumbled. "Now, on the night prior to Frank's marriage, that is, June 19, 1958, isn't it true that you said to Mrs. Short, 'She will never marry my boy. I will kill her first?'"

"No, that is not the truth. Absolutely not."

Gustafson picked up a newspaper clipping from the lectern and waved it at the witness. "And as soon as you discovered the marriage on June 21st, you trotted down to the newspaper and put an ad in the paper saying that Frank wouldn't be responsible for—"

"You don't have to show that. I admit it. I did it . . . and I didn't trot. I walked." She made a grab for the clipping.

"Look out," Judge Blackstock warned the defendant.

Gustafson read the ad out loud to the court. "I will not be responsible for debt contracted by anybody other than myself and my mother, Elizabeth Duncan. . . ."

"I did it. I said I did," Mrs. Duncan pouted.

"Did Frank tell you to do that?"

"No."

"But you signed Frank's name to it."

"I signed it." Mrs. Duncan made a so-what gesture with her hand. "You are asking stupid questions."

"So already you were starting this chain of harassing Olga, were you not?"

"I did not like Olga. I did not. I admit it."

"This girl whom you had seen once in your home."

"That's right."

"You didn't like her?"

"Just like someone else may not like me, I just didn't like her." She gazed into Gustafson's face with a challenging sneer. "Undoubtedly, you don't like me."

The courtroom burst into howls of laughter. Mrs. Duncan grinned at the crowd.

"Look out, now," the judge shouted at the gallery. "No demonstrations or I'll clear the courtroom."

The laughter immediately cut off.

"You conceived of a plan to lure Olga into a trap and throw acid in her face and put a chloroformed blanket over her and take her to the mountains? Isn't that the plan you proposed to Barbara Reed?"

"No. I would have chloroformed myself. You can't carry a chloroformed blanket. Any intelligent person would know that. Where is your intelligence? I would have chloroformed myself and everyone else in the car. . . . Ridiculous!"

Gustafson shook his head and turned a page of his notes. "You testified here yesterday that after you abandoned the idea of tying up Frank and kidnapping him, you said, 'Well, I'm going to let Frankie work things out for himself, and I'm not going to interfere.'"

"That is right."

"But only a few weeks elapsed between that time and the time that you did interfere. You went about getting his marriage annulled."

"Maybe I changed my mind."

Gustafson took a step closer. "I think that is exactly it, and maybe that is what we need to find out. You not only interfered by getting the annulment, but you later interfered by hiring two men to kill Olga Duncan. Isn't that true?"

Mrs. Duncan half rose from her chair. "That is a lie! That is a lie! That is an absolute lie!"

"Maybe you had another change of mind."

"I didn't have any change of mind," she spat.

"Well, first you said after the proposed kidnapping that you decided that you wouldn't interfere with the marriage, and then you had a change of mind and decided that you would interfere with the marriage."

"You talk so damn fast. I couldn't understand that."

Judge Blackstock put up his hand. "Calm down a little bit."

"Calm down?" she screamed. "How can I, when you sit there and overrule everything?"

The judge shook his head disgustedly. "Never mind."

Gustafson sighed. "I withdraw that last question, Mr. Court Reporter." He walked back to the lectern and checked his notes. "By the way, Mrs. Duncan, just about a week before you finally found the two men at the Tropical Café that would do the job for you, you got even more angry at Olga, didn't you?"

"I did not."

"So much so that when you discovered a wallet in Frank's car that Olga had given to him for his birthday, you cut it into shreds, didn't you?"

"I didn't cut up the wallet."

"Who did?"

"Mrs. Short cut it up."

Gustafson stepped to the table of exhibits and picked up a clear evidence bag with the cut-up wallet inside.

Mrs. Duncan shook her head. "I don't want to look at it. I already saw it."

"Why did you give the wallet to Mrs. Short?"

"I told her to give it to one of her boyfriends because I didn't want Frank to have it."

Gustafson walked to the witness stand as he fingered the pieces of wallet through the plastic bag. "Why?"

"Because I just didn't."

"Why?"

"How do I know?" she snapped. "Don't stand so close to me, either, when you talk like that." She raised her hand to the district attorney as if she were going to hit him. "I'm telling you. You better get away from me."

The DA looked toward the gallery with an amused half smile on his lips. "I will." He walked to the end of the jury box, about twenty feet away.

"That's the best place for you, right up there," she snarled.

"I will agree," Gustafson shot back as he put a hand on the jury box railing. "It was because of your extreme jealousy of Olga that you cut up the wallet that Olga had given to Frank for his birthday, wasn't it?"

"I knew you would say that."

"Really?"

Gustafson returned to the lectern, looked at his notes, and ran his finger down the page. "So far as you knew on November 12th and 13th, when you met with Luis Moya and Gus Baldonado at the Tropical Café, they didn't even know Olga Duncan, did they?"

"I don't know that."

"And so far as you knew on November 12th and 13th, and so far as you know now, Esperanza Esquivel didn't know anything about Olga Duncan?"

"I certainly do not."

"And you know of no reason why Moya or Baldonado would kill Olga Duncan, do you?"

"No, I do not."

Sullivan stood up. "Just a minute."

The judge raised his eyebrows.

The defense attorney stared at his client for a moment and then mumbled something inaudible. He sat back down.

Gustafson led Mrs. Duncan through another series of questions on the payments she'd made to Moya and Baldonado after the murder, including the ten dollars she had put in a blue envelope with *Dorothy* written on the front for Mrs. Short to leave for Moya at the Blue Onion.

"This ten-dollar payment was made after the police put the machine on your phone to record any more blackmail demands," Gustafson said. "You were supposed to report to the police if you heard from Moya again. Isn't that right?"

"I really don't remember."

"You paid them ten dollars on November 28th, and you had every intention in the world of not having the police or Frank know anything about any payment that you made to these men, because you were paying off the debt that you owed them for killing Olga. Isn't that right?"

"That is not the truth. You are a liar."

Judge Blackstock pointed his gavel at the witness. "Listen. You can't talk that way. He's the district attorney."

"I don't care who he is."

"He has a right to ask you questions," the judge continued in a harsh tone.

"He shouldn't accuse me of something that he knows nothing about."

Gustafson picked up his notes from the lectern. "You felt pretty sure that you would get away with this sort of thing because your son is a lawyer and he would get you out of anything."

"Objection!" Sullivan shouted.

"Sustained."

"On November 13, 1958, did you, in your mind, desire anything more than you desired to have Olga killed? Yes or no?"

"I never wanted Olga killed, ever in my life. Not then, or ever, or anyone else. I lost my own daughter, and I know what that means. No, I did not want Olga killed. I didn't want harm to come to anyone."

Gustafson nodded to the jury with the trace of a smile. "That is all."

Mrs. Duncan immediately got up from the witness chair.

"Wait a minute. Wait a minute. Wait until your attorney gets through." The judge turned to Sullivan. "Any questions?"

Sullivan stood. "No redirect, Your Honor, and I request that we adjourn for the day." He glanced over his shoulder at Frank Duncan, who sat staring at nothing in particular. "I'll call my next witness Monday morning."

CHAPTER FIFTY-SEVEN

THE ORANGE BITCH

March 7, 1959

On Saturday morning, the day Daddy said would have been Olga's birthday, I sat on the living room floor and dumped a paper cup full of coins onto the previous day's newspaper. The money scattered on top of the front-page picture of Mrs. Duncan sitting on the witness stand, lips pressed, angry eyes shifted to the side. The headline read: GET AWAY FROM ME, MRS. DUNCAN TELLS DA above Daddy's byline.

My friends and I had earned the coins at the Helpful Club lemonade stand over the previous few weeks. Twenty-one dimes, eighteen nickels, eight quarters, and ninety-five pennies. Five dollars and twenty-five cents. We'd sold lemonade every weekend so that we could buy a doll for Cathy, a little girl who lived at Camarillo State Hospital, where Mother worked. But sometimes when sales were slow, we got bored and drank a lot of the lemonade. I think Daddy must have slipped extra coins into the cup when I wasn't looking.

I put the money back in the cup and turned to an inside page of the newspaper to skim through the continuation of the story on the trial.

Mrs. Duncan Admits to 11 Husbands, 6 Children

After the court session was over, Sullivan consulted with his client and then gave out a list of the six children and eleven husbands to the press. . . . Dr. Louis Nash, a psychiatrist appointed by the court to evaluate the defendant's sanity, was in court observing Mrs. Duncan's demeanor. . . .

Her de-mean-er? Wonder what that is? "She had eleven husbands, Pinky. Gosh. Eleven husbands! If that's not proof that she's crazy, then I don't know what is."

Pinky purred.

Later that afternoon, I was lying on the front lawn with Pinky Lee, watching the clouds shape-shift through the air as I thought about what Mother had told me about Beth the previous night.

"She's safe," Mother had said. "I'm so relieved. We can't have mentally ill people wandering around on the streets. It's not safe for them. Thank God, she's living with her sister in Los Angeles now, and she has a field social worker assisting her. Checking in with her every week."

Beth's safe? Great. But what about Tweety?

Stretching my arms and legs as far as I could reach, I made grass angels on the lawn and listened to the sounds of the neighborhood: a barking dog, rhythmic pounding of a hammer off in the distance, the melodic chords of Marilyn practicing the piano coming from across the street. . . .

Pinky and I turned our heads simultaneously when we heard Daddy humming and singing, "*Beep-beep, beep-beep. His horn went beep-beep-beep,*" as he strutted down the driveway, pushing his new bright orange gas-powered lawn mower. He wheeled the mower to a stop at the edge of the lawn near where I was making the grass angels.

"Let's get this baby fired up." He gave me a big grin. "I'm thinking of calling it the 'Mrs. D.' since I used my overtime check to buy it."

I got up from the grass and looked at the mower, its blades hidden under the shiny orange cover. I folded my arms across my chest. Pinky Lee hid under our matching orange station wagon in the driveway.

"I've been thinking about your story in the paper." I twisted the tassel on the sleeve of my blouse. "You know, about the doctor from Mother's hospital coming to court to see if Mrs. Duncan is crazy or not."

"Yes . . ." Daddy said absently as he scanned the instruction manual for the mower and tossed it onto the driveway.

"What's *de-mean-er* mean, anyway?"

"*Demeanor?* It means how she acts and what she looks like," Daddy said. "Dr. Nash already evaluated her sanity at the hospital, but I guess he wanted to see Mrs. Duncan in action. Experience her firsthand, so to speak."

"But she looks normal. She's not going to get off, is she?"

Daddy hunched over the lawn mower and reached for the pull cord. "Stand back, Debby. This is dangerous business if you don't know what you're doing."

"Wait," I called out. "Do you think Mrs. Duncan is crazy?"

Daddy pushed his ball cap back on his head. "Like a fox."

"But not mentally ill crazy, like Beth? Not officially crazy."

"I'm no psychiatrist, but I think Mrs. Duncan is sane, all right. She knew exactly what she was doing when she had Olga murdered." Daddy shrugged. "She's devious, unrepentant, dangerous, a very convincing liar. . . ."

"She looks normal in the newspaper pictures. You can't tell she's dangerous. Nice clothes, and no long black gloves or crazy blank face like Beth. But Beth's . . . *de-mean-or* is terrible. She looks scary. Mother says she isn't dangerous, just very, very sick."

"Uh-huh, your mother knows these things."

"Even though Beth killed Tweety?" I mumbled.

"Yeah, well . . . we really don't know how Tweety died. And anyway, when Mrs. Duncan opens her mouth"—Daddy bent over and grabbed the cord—"her comportment, shall we say, changes." He gave the little rope a tentative yank. Nothing happened. "Shit's sake!"

I took a giant step backward. Mother came out onto the front porch, wiping her hands on a dishrag. "Be careful, Bob." She glanced in my direction. "Get up here with me, Debby. Your father doesn't know what he's doing."

Daddy glared at her. He pulled on the little rope again, harder. The engine made a coughing sound and fell silent.

"Maybe you should get Gene over here," Mother said. "Get some help."

"Goddammit, I don't need any help . . . just a little elbow grease." Daddy planted his feet on the grass and bent his knees. He grabbed the end of the rope with both hands and yanked it with all of his might, grunting like a Russian weightlifter on *Wide World of Sports*. The engine roared to life.

I applauded wildly. "Yay, Daddy. You did it!"

"Watch your feet!" Mother yelled over the engine noise as Daddy and the mower glided effortlessly across the lawn.

Mother and I watched while Daddy made his first pass over the grass, his face set in steely concentration, his gaze riveted on the lawn. He stopped on the other side of the yard and scowled at the path he'd covered. The mower hadn't cut a single blade of grass.

"You're going to have to set the blades lower, Bob," Mother shouted over the mower noise, "if you actually want to cut any grass."

"I know . . . I know that!" Daddy yelled back. "This is just a little test run to check the engine." He looked glumly at the mower before reluctantly hitting the off switch. The engine sputtered and died. Daddy turned toward me. "Get the wrench, Debby. It's somewhere . . ." He made a big sweeping motion toward the house.

Daddy was polishing a spot on the mower with his handkerchief when I came back carrying two wrenches that I'd found on the floor in a corner of the garage. Mother was gone.

I handed him the smaller wrench first. He squinted as he turned it this way and that, then shook his head and tossed it into the grass. I handed him the bigger wrench. He smacked the palm of his hand with it a couple of times, nodded at me, and then bent down on one knee next to the mower.

After much fumbling with the tool, he managed to lower the blades to a level barely off the ground.

"That ought to do it," he muttered.

It took four pulls and a lot of bad words to get the engine restarted. I clapped again. A cloud of dust sprayed in all directions as the rotating blades dug into the grass. Daddy had to push the handle really hard to move the mower across the lawn.

After he'd gone only a few feet, there was a terrible clanging, grinding noise. The little wrench he'd tossed into the grass flew from under the mower and smacked his hand before landing in the flower bed. The engine stopped with a resounding thud.

Daddy rubbed a red spot on his hand. "Goddamn . . . orange . . . BITCH!"

Mother stepped back onto the porch. "Bob, that's enough. . . . The neighbors . . ." She gazed at the small swath of gouged lawn he'd just finished mowing. "Looks like you got the only combination mower/plow in the neighborhood. . . . Cuts everything off just below ground level."

Daddy leaned over the flower bed, pushing plant stems and leaves aside in all directions as he searched for the wrench. He glanced over his shoulder at the gouged lawn. "Goddamn grass killer. That stupid machine is a menace, just like the original Mrs. D."

"Maybe it's a bad sign, Daddy. Because you named it 'the Mrs. D.'" I took another backward step as the mower's engine cooled. "I think I hear it ticking. . . ."

Finally, he straightened up holding the wrench and shook it. "Lucky I wasn't killed when she flung this wrench at me. . . . Goddamn *orange bitch*." His demeanor looked very bad.

CHAPTER FIFTY-EIGHT

FRANKIE

March 9, 1959

"Y oo-hoo, Frankie, going to see Mama?"

Frank Duncan stalked down the hallway in the courthouse, tight-lipped, past the line of spectators waiting for a seat.

Another voice came from the back of the crowd: "How you doin', mama's boy?"

Popping flashbulbs greeted Frank at the big double doors as he ducked into the courtroom. His mother, seated at the defense table, turned when the wooden doors opened. She beamed at her son and flapped her hand impatiently for him to come to her. Frank took his time. When he reached the table, his mother grabbed his coat to pull him closer so she could whisper into his ear.

Frank Duncan took the stand wearing a dark suit, a white shirt, and a thin dark tie. He'd brushed his thick, wavy dark hair back, Tony Curtis–style. He looked a little like the actor but with much thinner lips.

Ward Sullivan began the questioning by asking him about his profession, his age, and if Mrs. Duncan was his mother.

"Have you resided with your mother practically all of your life?"

"I have. I am proud to say so."

Gustafson leaned back in his chair. "I move that the last portion be stricken as a nonresponsive, volunteered statement."

"The motion is granted."

Sullivan asked Frank a series of questions about the years he had lived with his mother during high school, college, and law school.

"Did your mother voice objections to you keeping company with young ladies?"

"Never. If anything, she encouraged it."

"During your residence in San Francisco during law school, did you ever live in any apartment or any other type of residence or dwelling where you slept in the same bed with your mother?"

"Absolutely not."

"Has there ever been any occasion during your adolescent years, during your young boyhood, or your manhood when you ever slept in the same bed with your mother?" Sullivan asked.

"Never," Frank replied in a strong, steady voice. "Never!"

Sullivan moved on to Frank's engagement to Olga. "Did you have some reason why you did not tell your mother about your engagement to Olga?"

Frank nodded. "My mother has always been petrified of being alone. She couldn't stand to be alone, and well, I was always there for her. It became more difficult . . . this fear . . . after my stepfather left seven years ago." Frank looked to the jurors. "I would come home for my dinner every night, and . . . Well, Mother has always been very proud of me . . . and I suppose I was the apple of my mother's eye, you might say." He brushed some hair off his forehead. "I knew that news of my engagement to Olga would hurt her, upset her. I knew that she did not want to lose me."

"When did you finally tell your mother that you were married to Olga?"

"The day after Olga and I were married, I returned briefly to my mother's apartment to tell her, but she'd already guessed that the marriage had taken place."

"Tell the jury what happened with your mother at the apartment," Sullivan said.

"She was crying, uncontrollable hysteria, and I tried the best I could to console her. It wasn't really anger; it was just like a panic that my mother was in." Frank shook his head despondently. "I left her there and returned to my wife."

"Did you reside with Olga in her apartment on Bath Street?"

Frank bit his lip. "Not all of the time. I resided there continuously for about three weeks."

"Something occurred at that time?"

"Yes," Frank said. "One might describe it as a donnybrook. My mother came up to the door—we had a screen door there—and she rapped on the door and said, 'Let me in. I want you to come home.' And an argument started, a very heated argument. It was mostly between my mother and myself. My wife really didn't engage in it."

"Did you hear your mother make any threats to kill Olga?"

"I did not."

"Did you leave with your mother?"

"I did."

"At the time you left with your mother, did you say to her, 'Come on, doll, let's go home'?"

"Not hardly." Frank folded his arms across his chest. "I was furious with my mother. I wasn't about to call her 'doll' or any other term of affection."

"Did you move back in to live with your mother?"

"Yes. I had my clothes somewhat split up. Most of my things were still at my mother's home. Quite frankly, I was going back and forth like a yo-yo."

"You moved your wife to a new apartment soon after this . . . donnybrook?"

"Yes."

"Did you tell your mother your new address?"

"No, I didn't."

"And after Olga moved over to the new apartment, did you resume your residence with your wife?"

"Yes, I did . . . part-time. As I say, I was going back and forth. I was trying to keep two women happy."

"Did your mother ever come to this apartment while you and Olga were there?"

"On one occasion, she knocked on the door, which was a sliding glass door, and said, 'Let me in. I know you're in there. I see your car out front.' My wife and I were in the bedroom. We didn't let her in. A few minutes later, my mother left. She could not have been there more than two or three minutes."

"Did you hear her make any threats to Olga?"

"None at all."

"Well, now, after you moved into the Garden Street apartment, what was the situation with respect to your living either at home or with Olga?"

"I was living with my mother at that time." Frank hesitated. "But I very frequently would go over to my wife's after eating dinner with my mother and spend the evening there, and I spent some weekends with my wife there in the Garden Street apartment, and some nights. That is, overnight."

"Were you in love with your wife?"

"I was, sir."

"What was the reason that you resided at home with your mother at this time?"

A pained expression spread across Frank's face. He resettled himself in the witness chair. "My mother, of course, opposed me getting married, and she had no particular liking for my wife. I loved my mother and I love her still, and I loved my wife, also. I felt that if I could keep some type of peace with my mother and my wife until the baby was born that my mother would see the baby and, well, she would come around, and it would be a happy affair." Frank laced his fingers together in his lap. "I felt that I could accomplish this. I tried my very best."

"Did she ever talk about you ending your marriage to Olga?"

"Well, she wanted me to secure an annulment from my wife. But I refused. I told her it was my business who I was married to. I loved my wife and had absolutely no intention of severing that relationship."

"What did she do or say when you told her that?"

"I believe she cried."

Sullivan flipped through some notes. "Do you remember the witness, Barbara Reed, that testified here?"

"Yes, I believe that she was an acquaintance of my sister's. I never liked her."

"Did Barbara Reed call you and say that she wanted to talk to you?"

"Yes, she asked me to come by the Blue Onion, where she worked. She said it was important."

"What did she say when you met with her?"

"I believe her opening words were, 'Is your mother crazy, Frank?' She told me that my mother tried to get her to kidnap my wife. I couldn't believe it. It sounded so preposterous. I said that I would take care of it. I'm sure the conversation did not take ninety seconds."

"Did you talk to your mother about this conversation?"

"I went right home. I related my conversation with Barbara Reed. My mother said, 'That girl is lying. I know it sounds crazy, but I was going to kidnap *you*.' She told me how she was going to tie me up and take me to Los Angeles until I came to my senses." Frank scoffed. "I just blew my top. I was extremely angry, and it seemed such a stupid thing."

"Did your mother say anything more?'"

"No, because I was so mad, I wouldn't let her, and I concluded that Miss Reed had either made a mistake or was not telling the truth."

Sullivan next asked questions about how Frank had learned about the blackmail scheme. Frank said it all came out when he asked to see the receipt for the typewriter payment.

"I was extremely angry. I told my mother that I was not going to be blackmailed and that I intended to go immediately to the Tropical and get the money back." He turned up the palm of one hand. "She talked me into going to the police station instead."

"When did you first learn of your wife's disappearance?"

"Approximately 12:15 in the afternoon on November 18, 1958. I'd been at court that day on the matter of Mr. Esquivel. I was told that I needed to call my office, that it was an emergency. I went to the clerk's office to make the call." He cleared his throat. "Mrs. Barnett, Olga's landlady, had left a message for me at the office to call her immediately. Olga was missing, and her door had been left open. I told Mrs. Barnett that I would come right over."

"Did you call the police?"

"Yes, I made that report, it must have been, no later than one thirty on the afternoon of the 18th. The police undoubtedly have the time and date."

"Did you talk to your mother about Olga's disappearance?"

"I told her when I got home that Ollie was missing under rather strange circumstances. I told her about the sliding glass door being open and that her purse was there and that all of her clothing was still there and that there appeared to be no signs of violence. I said that I was very worried."

"What did your mother say?"

"She said, 'Well, maybe she stayed overnight with a friend or something and she'd forgotten her purse and had forgotten to lock the door.'"

Gustafson watched from the prosecution table, his elbows on the table and his fingers pressed together.

"When was the last date that you saw Olga?"

"On the morning of November 8th."

"And on that occasion, your relationship was a friendly one between you and your wife?"

"It was."

"Between the 8th of November and the 17th of November, did you talk to Olga on the telephone?"

Frank shifted in his chair. "I must say, sir, that I did not."

"But you were in court on the morning of November 18, 1958, representing Mr. Esquivel at his sentencing hearing on the burglary charge when you heard of your wife's disappearance?"

"That is correct, the hearing on whether Mr. Esquivel would get probation."

When Gustafson heard these words, he sat up straight. That morning before court, he had told his secretary, "I'm dying to hear how Frankie's going to spin the story about how Mrs. Esquivel was mad because her husband didn't get probation . . . before she actually knew that he didn't get probation."

"You were in court with the Esquivels the morning your wife disappeared," Sullivan said.

"Yes."

"On November 18th. During this hearing, was your client, Mr. Esquivel, granted probation?"

"He was not. He was sentenced to state prison."

"Did Mrs. Esquivel appear to be agitated?"

"Well, she was crying. I had previously told her about remarks that were made by the probation officer, Mr. Weitekamp, and from the impression I received from the judge, I felt that probation would be denied. There was no doubt in my mind about that."

"When was it that you first learned what the recommendation of the probation department would be insofar as Mr. Esquivel was concerned?"

Gustafson leaned forward. *Okay, Frank, this is the crux of the whole defense.*

Frank tilted his head as he thought. "It was the week before the 17th. Yes, it would have been no earlier than the 10th of November and no later than November 14th. . . . My recollection is that I found out the recommendation of the probation officer on November 12th."

The 12th . . . How helpful for the defense. The day before Moya supposedly pulls Mom into the Tropical and threatens to kill her if Mrs. Esquivel doesn't get her money back.

Mrs. Duncan sat back in her chair and smiled all around.

"And when you talked to Mrs. Esquivel on November 12th, did you tell her that her husband wouldn't get probation, that he was going to go to prison?"

"Yes, I told her that I felt that the judge would follow the recommendation of the probation officer, which is done nine times out of ten." Frank's eyes slid away from Sullivan.

Uh-huh, Frankie boy; we'll see what the probation officer has to say about that.

"Now, has your mother ever at any time, insofar as you are concerned, said or done anything that would cause you to believe that she contemplated any kind of physical harm being inflicted on your wife, Olga Duncan?"

"Positively no."

"I have no further questions." Sullivan bent slightly at the waist as he pivoted away from the witness.

"It's time for our afternoon recess," Judge Blackstock barked. Then, to Gustafson: "You may start your cross-examination of this witness when court resumes." He glared out over the courtroom. "Keep your seats and keep quiet until the jury gets out of here."

"Judge seems in a fine mood," Bennie Jo said as the room began to empty. "Maybe he's disgusted with the loving husband who'd say *anything* to help his mother."

"For all his bravado, I believe that Frank Duncan is a very naïve young man. He thinks it's him and Ma against the world and Roy Gustafson," Bob said. "And now he's trying to keep his mother out of the gas chamber."

Bennie Jo faced Bob. "You'd think he'd want to stand up for his wife and unborn child."

"Maybe Frank sees Gustafson as not fighting fair," Bob said. "He's probably furious with all the innuendo about incest. And he knows that getting at least one juror to believe his mother's cockamamie blackmail story is her only chance to avoid the gas chamber. And that hope rests squarely on Frank's testimony that he already knew Marciano Esquivel wasn't getting probation before November 13th and that he told Mrs. Esquivel about it before that meeting at the Tropical. Otherwise, the blackmail story doesn't hold water."

"He knows she's guilty. Maybe he was in on it from the beginning."

"I doubt that," Bob said. "The authorities would have never solved the case if Frank hadn't insisted that his mother talk to the police about the supposed blackmail. He practically dragged her down to the station."

Bennie Jo stared at the empty jury box. "Do you think the jury believed him?"

After the recess, Frank looked confidently around the courtroom as he waited in the witness chair for the cross-examination to begin.

Gustafson strode to the lectern, all business. "You discussed the possibility of Mr. Esquivel getting probation with the probation officer, Mr. Weitekamp?"

"That is correct. He told me that he'd recommended that Mr. Esquivel not be granted probation."

"I see. Did you have the report in hand when you discussed the possibilities with Mrs. Esquivel?"

Frank scowled. "No, I did not."

"So it is your recollection that you had this telephone conversation before you saw the report?"

"Yes. It seems that Mrs. Esquivel dropped in sometime during the week of November 10th to see if I had heard from the probation office, and while she was there, I said that I would call Mr. Weitekamp, and I did so."

Gustafson moved the narrative forward to the blackmail story. Quoting from the grand jury transcript, he read the testimony aloud.

"Question: Did your mother tell you, at the time that you reported the blackmail to the police, why she hadn't told you of this payment at the time she made it at the Tropical Café?

"Answer: She stated that she knew I had these other worries, and she was afraid for my life, too, and I must say that I was extremely worried at this time.

"Question: Because of Olga's disappearance?

"Answer: Because of the disappearance, that is correct.

"Question: And your mother explained to you that the reason that she hadn't told you about the payment of this money that she had obtained from pawning her jewelry at the time it was done was because you were too worried about Olga's disappearance?

"Answer: She knew that I did have that worry, and she didn't want to give me an additional burden of worry."

Gustafson looked up from the transcript. "Were these the questions asked and the answers given by you at the time of the grand jury hearing on December 26, 1958?"

Frank nodded.

Gustafson repeated the question in a louder voice: "Were these the questions asked and were these the answers given at the grand jury hearing?"

"Yes," Frank said in a monotone.

Gustafson picked up an item from the evidence table. "Now, you received this wallet on your birthday on November 7, 1958?"

"I did," Frank said.

"At that time, you were still in love with Olga?"

"I was."

"You were so devoted to your wife that you threw the wallet in the back seat of your car and never thought about it again for a couple of months. Isn't that right?"

Mrs. Duncan shot out of her chair and jabbed her finger at the DA. "You're a liar!"

Gustafson wheeled around. "You be quiet!"

Sullivan reached across the table and tugged on his client's arm until she sat back down. "Your Honor, we object. What Mr. Duncan did in regard to the wallet doesn't tend to prove or disprove any of the issues."

"Oh, yes it does," Gustafson sputtered. "Mr. Sullivan had this witness testifying time and time again how much love and devotion he had for his wife."

Mrs. Duncan jumped up again. "Liar!"

"Mrs. Duncan, Mrs. Duncan, you have a good lawyer there," Judge Blackstock said, "and you better take some advice from him."

She pointed at Gustafson. "Well, then make him stop—"

Judge Blackstock raised his voice. "You are in contempt of court when you do that."

Mrs. Duncan flounced back into her chair.

"Now," Gustafson continued, "prior to the time that you last saw Olga on November 7, 1958, were you aware that she was having illness in the form of neuritis in her hand?"

"I was."

"And by then she was quite late along in her pregnancy, was she not?"

"She was."

"She was nervous, worried, and upset?"

"I would say no, not the last time I saw her, no. Quite frankly, I felt she was serene that last evening I spent with her."

"And that was November 7th, your birthday . . . the day she gave you the wallet?"

"It would have been the morning of November 8th, having spent the evening of November 7th at the apartment."

"You never saw her again?"

"That is correct."

"Never talked to her again?"

"That is correct."

"Did you have a fight with her that night?"

"I did not."

"Why didn't you call her on the phone in the subsequent weeks?"

Sullivan jumped to his feet. "I object. It's irrelevant."

"Objection sustained."

"And why didn't you go to see her at any time after the 7th?"

Sullivan shot back up. "Objection. Mr. Duncan is not on trial."

"Sustained."

Gustafson looked down at the lectern a moment and then raised his chin. He put his hands behind his back and stared directly into Frank Duncan's face. "Isn't it true, Mr. Duncan, that the entire reason why you never saw Olga after November 7th is that by that time, her physical condition by reason of her pregnancy was such that you could no longer have sexual intercourse with her, so that you didn't care to see her anymore?"

Sullivan was up on his feet again and genuinely angry. "We will object to that upon the same grounds, immaterial and argumentative."

The judge shook his head. "The objection is overruled."

"That is a lie!" Frank yelled.

The judge turned toward him. "What do you mean by that? Will you answer the question, sir?"

"The answer is no, positively no." Frank raked his fingers through his thick, wavy hair.

"Was there a compelling cause for you to leave Santa Barbara for a trip to San Francisco when your wife was still missing?" Gustafson asked.

"Yes. I had to leave my employment at the law firm because of all the publicity at the end of November. I needed to look for work. I felt that—" Again, Frank dragged his fingertips through his Tony Curtis hair. "I was certainly hoping that Olga would reappear, but I felt that it was probably time . . . because this had all come up . . . and it seemed to do no good just to sit around Santa Barbara, and I hoped to secure another position because I did not have any large savings whatsoever and I depended upon working. . . ." His voice petered out.

"And you were still quite concerned about Olga's disappearance?"

"I was."

"You still loved her and were hoping that she would be found well and alive?"

"Of course."

"And you would have gone back to her as her husband had she been found?"

"I certainly would have."

"But didn't you have a date with a young woman named Catherine Covington on December 10, 1958, in San Francisco? Three weeks after Olga disappeared?"

Frank's face flushed. "I did take her out to dinner."

"And you didn't tell her you were married, did you?"

He crossed his legs. "I did not."

"And isn't it a fact that you didn't tell Catherine Covington that you were married because you knew in your mind that you weren't married because you knew that your wife had . . . that your mother had already had your wife killed?"

Frank narrowed his eyes to crinkled slits. "That is not correct."

Gustafson looked toward the jurors. One woman in the front row slowly shook her head as she stared at Frank Duncan.

The DA continued in a sarcastic tone. "And you still felt all the love and affection in the world toward Olga at the time you appeared for your mother in court here in Ventura on this annulment matter on December 17, 1958, didn't you?"

"I loved my wife."

"Didn't you make a public statement to the press on the stairs outside this courtroom after your mother's hearing on the annulment charge that your wife was just doing this to give you . . . unpleasant publicity?"

"The comment was taken out of context."

"Mr. Duncan, going back to when your mother had told you about the phone calls she received on the blackmail, did you report it to the police that your mother had received such a call?"

Frank rubbed his chin. "I, quite frankly, cannot recall, as I have stated."

"Did you ever tell the police that your mother had made arrangements to have meetings with these men and to send money to these men without having notified the police?"

"No, I did not."

"When those events occurred, didn't you believe that the blackmail story that your mother was telling was a complete fabrication?"

"I did not." Frank squeezed his mouth into an angry circle.

Gustafson looked around the courtroom and then focused an unwavering, disgusted gaze on Frank Duncan. *Everyone in this room knows you're lying through your teeth to protect Mama.* He picked up his papers from the lectern and nodded to the jury. "That is all," he said and headed for his seat at the prosecution table.

After some short questions on redirect and re-cross-examination, Sullivan told the judge that he had a motion to take up with the court in the absence of the jury. "It won't be over ten or fifteen minutes, Your Honor."

After Judge Blackstock dismissed the jury for the day, Sullivan stood at the defense table and said, "May it please Your Honor, at this time and before the defendant rests, I desire to move the court to declare a mistrial"— low murmuring emanated from the gallery—"upon the grounds that the district attorney has brought into evidence matters which are extraneous to the issue but were presented for the sole purpose of biasing and prejudicing my client and to degrade and debase her in the minds of the jury."

Sullivan stated he was referring to Gustafson's questions to Mrs. Duncan about her many marriages and whether or not she had legally divorced these husbands.

"Now, I realize, Your Honor, that the district attorney came into court the following day and asked you to strike this evidence from the record and instruct the jury to disregard it, which Your Honor did do. But I think Your Honor will agree with me that there is nothing that this Court can do that can erase this information from the minds of the jury."

Sullivan's second reason for requesting a mistrial was that the judge had allowed Gustafson to question Mrs. Duncan about getting a fraudulent annulment for her son's marriage when she had been charged for that crime in another court and the case had not yet been adjudicated. Sullivan complained that over his objections, the annulment had been introduced as evidence in the murder trial for the purpose of biasing and prejudicing Mrs. Duncan in the minds of the jury.

When Sullivan finished, Gustafson stood up and said that he had brought up all the husbands only to show the jury that Mrs. Duncan was not legally married to Frank Duncan Sr. and to impeach the truthfulness of her testimony. He argued strenuously that he had been rightly allowed to bring up the fraudulent annulment that Mrs. Duncan obtained because it showed the defendant's hatred and ill will toward the victim of the murder, Olga Duncan.

Also, Gustafson argued, although Mrs. Duncan had testified that she'd done nothing to interfere with her son's marriage after July, when she'd given up on the idea of tying Frank up and taking him to Los Angeles, she had in fact obtained the fake annulment in August.

"I respectfully submit, Your Honor, that there is no basis for a motion for a mistrial and that the motion should be denied."

"Is that all?" the judge asked both men.

Sullivan stood. "Yes, Your Honor."

"The motion for a mistrial is denied," Judge Blackstock said.

The courtroom burst into applause.

CHAPTER FIFTY-NINE

A DOLL FOR CATHY

March 9, 1959

That afternoon, I missed swim practice so I could deliver the doll that the Helpful Club had bought for the nine-year-old girl at Mother's mental hospital. Mother came home from work early to pick me up and drive back to Camarillo State Hospital with the baby doll.

I fidgeted as we left the highway at Lewis Drive and drove through farm fields and then up the broad sweep of the tree-lined road toward the hospital.

"I think this will help you understand that you don't need to be afraid of people with mental illness," Mother said.

I smoothed the doll's hair as I held her in my arms, wrapped in a little pink blanket. "Why is Cathy mentally ill?"

"They call it childhood schizophrenia, but no one knows for sure what causes it. I hope I live long enough to learn the answer." Mother made a sad smile. "Surely, they'll find a cure in your lifetime."

"Schiz-o-phrenia? That's what Beth has, right?"

"Yes, but Cathy has the childhood type. It's uncommon in children."

We entered the main gate of the parklike hospital grounds. Buildings of white adobe with red-tiled roofs sprawled across acres of lawns and trees. Patients with passes from their wards roamed the grounds freely.

"It's a hospital, not a prison," Mother had told me many times.

I craned my neck as we drove past the main buildings. "Where did Beth live?"

She pointed vaguely toward a huge rectangular building. "You don't need to worry about Beth anymore. Remember? She's staying with her sister in Los Angeles, taking her medication, and she's doing much better."

I stared at the big building's mesh-screened windows as we passed. "I don't think anyone would want to live here if they didn't have to."

"Most of our patients are here because a judge has decided that they're severely mentally ill and need to be in the hospital. Sometimes their families are so worried about them that they go to court to get them committed." Mother smiled a little. "I admit that this place has a lot of problems, but at least the patients get treatment."

"But does it really work? Look what happened with Beth."

"It's far from perfect, but many of our patients get better . . . go home . . . get jobs."

"Like at the Coca-Cola bottling plant?"

She sighed. "It's a start."

"Well, Cathy doesn't need a job. Why does she have to live in such a terrible place? Where are her parents?"

"Cathy isn't on any of these wards, dear. She's in the children's unit, where they have their own school, a gym, and even a swimming pool. There aren't many schools available for children with Cathy's problems. Her parents don't know what to do. They just want her to get help."

We parked at a newer-looking stucco building behind the main hospital campus. Only ten or so cars clustered near the front. A wide, well-manicured lawn surrounded the building. A chain-link fenced area with playground equipment sat empty off to the side.

"Where's the swimming pool?" I mumbled.

Mother and I climbed out of the car and walked toward the entrance. It was so quiet I could hear birds squawking in a nearby tree. No moaning or crying coming from the building like it did where we waited sometimes for Mother after her Sunday duty.

I carried the doll in one arm and lugged a small red doll trunk in the other.

"You stay here on the porch, dear," Mother said, "while I stick my head inside and let the front desk know we're here. I'll be right back. Cathy's social worker is expecting us."

A faint whiff of stale, rancid air mixed with lemon cleaner escaped as Mother opened the door. I patted the doll on my shoulder as I waited, telling her not to worry, that everything would be all right.

Soon Mother and the social worker emerged from the front entrance. Mrs. Mildred Gable held the hand of a small blonde girl with short tangled hair, wearing a cotton dress a size too big. The girl looked like she'd just woken up. We all sat on the grass, near a tree.

"It's so nice to meet you," Mother said to the girl. "Mrs. Gable has told me so much about you . . . how well you're doing."

I set the little trunk on the ground and cradled the doll in my arms.

The social worker spoke to the girl in a happy tone. "This is Mrs. Holt's daughter Debby." She turned to me. "And Debby, this is Cathy."

I looked to Mother's encouraging face for an instant and said, "Nice to meet you."

Cathy stared at the grass while she rocked back and forth at the waist.

"This doll is for you." I held the doll out to her, but she didn't look at it. "My friends and I have a Helpful Club, and my mother told us that you need a doll. . . ."

Cathy shifted her dull gray eyes in my direction momentarily as she continued to rock, but then her gaze skipped past me.

I patted the little doll trunk. "There's extra clothes in here."

Cathy dropped her chin. She twisted her fingers together.

Mother and I watched while Mrs. Gable whispered something in Cathy's ear and put her hand on the girl's shoulder to steady the rocking.

After a few moments of silence, I asked, "Where is the swimming pool?"

Cathy smiled over her shoulder toward the tree and whispered, "Stop it, Rodney."

Mrs. Gable pointed at a tall stucco enclosure. "The pool is behind the wall, Debby."

"Oh." I craned my neck to see if someone was hiding behind the tree. Mother shook her head at me.

Mrs. Gable took the doll from me and turned to Cathy. Mother leaned in from the girl's other side and gently spread Cathy's hands so that the social worker could put the doll in her arms.

Cathy made a little mewing sound, pulled the doll to her chest, and held on tight. She nuzzled her face into the baby doll's neck as she gently rocked her in her arms.

"I think she likes her!" I said.

Mother and Mrs. Gable smiled.

I opened the doll case and took out an extra blanket and some tiny booties. "You can use these when you put her to bed, and"—I rummaged through the trunk—"this dress is . . ."

Cathy kissed her new doll over and over and stroked her hair as I chattered on about the doll's wardrobe.

The social worker smiled at me. "Thank you, Debby, and please thank your friends, too. Your gift is very appreciated and very . . . helpful."

I got onto my knees and leaned closer to Cathy. "Do you want me to show you how to comb her hair?" I held up a tiny brush and comb.

Cathy lifted her head and focused her lifeless eyes in my direction.

"Because you don't want to brush too hard and make her hair fall out like my sister did to her—"

Cathy's eyes slid toward the tree again. She whispered, "Rodney."

"We don't want to tire Cathy," Mother said. "We should be going, dear."

Mrs. Gable looked at her watch. "Yes. It's time for her medication."

"Who was she talking to, anyway? Who's Rodney?" I asked as we retraced our path through the farm fields on our drive back to the highway.

"Cathy has hallucinations sometimes," Mother said. "She sees people who aren't really there. Mildred told me she's getting better, but some days . . ." Mother sighed. "The doctors are trying to get her medications adjusted to the right level."

"So that's what mental illness is like?"

"Sometimes, but saying a person has a mental illness is like saying that someone has cancer. There are lots of different types, and some are much more serious than others."

"Cathy doesn't seem dangerous." I turned toward Mother. "Maybe Beth didn't mean to hurt Tweety, either."

Mother nodded.

I folded my arms across my chest. "They're not like Mrs. Duncan at all."

"I'm afraid Mrs. Duncan is a psychopath. Selfish, manipulative, willing to do anything to get her own way. She knows what's going on, but she's still a very sick woman."

"She's bad. She should get thrown into the lake of fire." I kicked at the bottom of the dashboard.

Mother glanced at me.

"And I don't see how living in that smelly hospital with a bunch of other mentally ill children can help Cathy. It doesn't seem like the medicine is doing any good."

Mother shook her head sadly. "I'm afraid most of the medicine the doctors prescribe is to keep her calm, and sometimes it's hard to get the technicians to follow instructions for the right dose. They have a lot to do, with so many children on the ward. . . ." Her voice trailed off, and we rode in silence until she turned off the highway onto the frontage road by Korb's.

"Do you think Cathy can fit the trunk under her bed so she can keep all the doll's new clothes safe?"

Mother bit her lip.

"Wait . . . where will she keep her doll?"

Mother focused her eyes on the road. "All the girls on her ward share their toys. The technicians don't have time to keep who owns what straight. You know, the children learn to share. . . ." Mother sighed.

"What?"

We pulled into the driveway. "It was a lovely gesture, Debby, what you and your friends did," Mother said in a gentle tone. "A lot of little girls at the hospital will benefit. You and your friends should be proud of yourselves."

"So it won't really be Cathy's doll?"

Mother shook her head. "I'm sorry. I didn't know that until last week."

I cried while mother searched her purse for a tissue. She finally found a crumpled, lipstick-stained one and handed it to me. I blew my nose.

"I might not be a reporter or a policewoman when I grow up." I sniffled. "I want to help children like Cathy so they can stay at home with their mothers and have their own toys."

We shut the car doors and walked toward the house. I bent to pick up the afternoon paper from the lawn and unfolded it to read the front-page headline, and all thoughts of Cathy and her doll were immediately pushed out of my head:

FRANK DUNCAN SUPPORTS MOTHER'S STORY
Love For Wife A Lie, Says Gustafson

CHAPTER SIXTY

REBUTTAL AND ARGUMENTS

March 10-11, 1959

When the trial resumed Tuesday morning, Gustafson began his rebuttal to defense witness testimony by calling probation officer Lawrence Weitekamp to the stand to establish the time and date on which Weitekamp had informed Frank Duncan about his recommendation that Marciano Esquivel not be put on probation. This was crucial, because Frank had testified that he'd passed the information on to Esperanza Esquivel on November 12—the day *before* the alleged blackmail meeting at the Tropical Café.

But Weitekamp's testimony, confirmed by his secretary, was that he had not told Frank about his probation recommendation until November 14.

For further support, Gustafson called Esperanza Esquivel to the stand and asked her only one question: "Did you at any time ever talk to Frank Duncan in person or by telephone about what the recommendation would be of the probation officer on your husband's sentence?"

"No, sir."

"You may cross-examine."

Sullivan bustled to the lectern, all business.

"You never asked Mr. Duncan about the recommendation in the probation report?"

"No."

"You were interested in what was going to happen to your husband,
weren't you?"

"Yes, but I was waiting for the day of the sentence. I thought they
wouldn't say it until the day of the sentencing on November 18th."

Gustafson took nothing for granted. Throughout Tuesday and most of
Wednesday he continued calling rebuttal witnesses to refute the testimony of Mrs. Duncan and her son. On cross-examination, Sullivan asked
detailed questions about events and dates, trying to shake the witnesses,
but most emerged unscathed.

On Wednesday afternoon, after his last witness left the stand, Gustafson
faced the judge. "The People rest."

"We have no rebuttal, Your Honor," Sullivan said, "no more witnesses.
We likewise rest."

March 12, 1959

At 10:40 A.M. on Thursday morning, after sixteen days of testimony from
thirty-one witnesses, stretching over three weeks, with almost four thousand
pages of accumulated transcript, Roy Gustafson began his summation to
the jury. The courtroom was packed, the gallery electric with anticipation.

"Olga Duncan's marriage certificate, in truth and in fact, turned out to
be her death certificate," he said. "One of the pities of this case is that the
girl who was so brutally murdered on the night of November 17th might
have been any other girl. This might have been anybody's sister, anybody's
daughter. Any girl could have been Elizabeth Duncan's murder victim if
she happened to marry her son Frank."

Speaking like a college professor, he explained to the jury that first-
degree murder, by legal definition, is "a killing committed with malice
aforethought."

"Now, *malice aforethought* is a legal term, which in essence means 'a wicked, evil heart.'" Gustafson looked toward the defense table. "And of course, we've got that here . . . wickedness of heart."

The DA took the rest of the day to summarize the evidence and relevant laws, step by step. He told the jury that Mrs. Duncan had either hired Moya and Baldonado to murder Olga, or she hadn't done so. If she had, then she was guilty of first-degree murder. He recapitulated Moya's and Baldonado's confessions on the stand. "Both men have admitted in excruciating detail that they committed the murder and that Mrs. Duncan told them that she wanted to get rid of her daughter-in-law and pay them $6,000 for doing the job. Now I ask you, when Moya and Baldonado took Olga Duncan out of that apartment on November 17th, what earthly reason would they have for doing that, except that they'd been hired by Mrs. Duncan to do it? They didn't know the girl. They didn't have anything to do with her.

"Mrs. Duncan's story of blackmail was a story she told to Frank that got out of hand. She had to give Frank some reason why she'd used his two-hundred-dollar check, meant for a payment on a typewriter, to pay Moya and Baldonado instead. That, of course, was her undoing. The solution of this murder case was the fact that she told this story to Frank about being blackmailed, and instead of his just accepting it, he went to the police. The events that happened after that unraveled the whole tale."

The DA went through the many steps Mrs. Duncan had taken to have her daughter-in-law kidnapped and murdered. "Have you ever seen anybody who shows less remorse over the death of a poor young girl than this defendant, with all of her preening and smiling and laughing and giggling and so forth? Does she have any concern over the fact that this is a murder trial in which the victim is her daughter-in-law? No, she doesn't. She is glad that Olga is gone."

Gustafson held up a photo of Olga, young and smiling in her crisp white nurse's uniform. "This is what she looked like before Elizabeth Duncan got on the scene. This is the girl, Olga Duncan, lovely, sweet. By every standard in the world a wonderful, wonderful girl."

He passed the picture to a juror in the first row, returned to the folder, and then took a few steps back toward the jury box with a crime scene photo extended in his hand. One juror covered her mouth as the DA pointed to the image of Olga's decomposing body curled in a fetal position in her impromptu grave. "*This*," he thundered, "is the consequence of this young woman having crossed the path of Elizabeth Duncan. There she is in the hole in the ground where she ended up as a result of the machinations of this vicious woman that is on trial here now."

Gustafson returned the pictures to the folder and turned his notes facedown on the lectern. He'd hardly used them at all during his lengthy summation. "Ladies and gentlemen, I think that the evidence in this case not only proves beyond a reasonable doubt, it proves beyond any doubt whatsoever, it proves to a degree that hardly has been shown before inside a courtroom, that the defendant, Elizabeth Duncan, is guilty of the murder of Olga Duncan. I ask you to please, for the people of California, return a verdict of guilty. Thank you."

Judge Blackstock adjourned court for the day and excused the jurors. As the spectators filed out of the courtroom, Sullivan and Frank were still sitting at the defense table, their heads bent close in a hushed, animated conversation.

Mrs. Duncan rested her chin on her hand and stared at the empty jury box. She looked around only when Gustafson scraped his chair on the floor at the next table and stood up. She leaned toward him, behind her attorney. "You're a lying son of a bitch," she said in a low hiss.

"What did you say?" the DA responded.

Frank stood over his mother. "She didn't say anything."

"Good. Glad to hear it," Gustafson said in a tone dripping with sarcasm.

"Did you catch that?" Bob asked Bennie Jo as they left the press section.

"Partly. I think she called him a son of a bitch again."

Edd, Bennie Jo's colleague from the *Daily Express*, came up beside her. "No. She called him a 'lying son of a bitch' this time."

The three reporters stood back as the matron cuffed Mrs. Duncan to take her to the jail. Frank patted his mother's shoulder as she left.

"If you look carefully, you can still see the umbilical cord," Edd sneered.

March 13, 1959

When court resumed the next morning, Friday the 13th, Bob scanned the room and said, "Look, some of the seats are empty."

"I think people made up their minds before the trial ever started," Bennie Jo said as the jury filed in. "Don't want to hear any more lies."

Judge Blackstock took his seat and gaveled the room to order. Ward Sullivan stepped to the front of the courtroom wearing a black suit, suspenders, and his signature red bow tie.

"May it please Your Honor, Mr. Gustafson, ladies and gentlemen of the jury?" The dapper little defense attorney nodded all around. "We have now reached this phase of the trial of Elizabeth Duncan where it becomes my duty to come before you and plead her cause. At the outset, let me put you straight about one thing." He smiled at the jury. "I am no Perry Mason, and I'm not going to pull any tricks out of a hat." He coughed, then patted his lips with a handkerchief. He had a cold.

He then launched into an attempt to show that Mrs. Short and Mrs. Esquivel were actually accomplices in the crime, negating their testimony against Mrs. Duncan because it had not been corroborated by others outside the conspiracy. He insisted that the prosecution's case rested principally on a rogue's gallery of the Santa Barbara underworld, including Rudy and Diane Romero, Barbara Reed, Ralph Winterstein, Mrs. Short, and Mrs. Esquivel. Sullivan tried to convince the jury to judge the testimony of those witnesses with skepticism.

He also wanted them to view the DA's tactics with distrust. In contrast to Gustafson's mostly matter-of-fact delivery, Sullivan raised his voice to almost a shout when he said, "The prosecution tried to infer an unnatural relationship between Mrs. Duncan and Frank. They failed totally. They tried to create an impression in your minds, but they never presented any evidence. This was an effort by the prosecution to create bias and prejudice in the minds of the jury members."

He walked to the back of the defense table, stood between Elizabeth and Frank Duncan, and put a hand on each chair. "Is there anything wrong with Mrs. Duncan having an intense love for her son? Mrs. Duncan admitted on the witness stand that of her six children, she loved Frank the most.

"As to Mrs. Duncan, you saw her on the witness stand. I'll grant you that at times she was erratic. You see the type of individual she is. She is impetuous, she is sarcastic, she even argued with the district attorney. One time she argued with His Honor. Frankly, I marveled at the court's patience with her while she was on the witness stand. I don't excuse her conduct in that respect, but it doesn't mean because she acted that way on the witness stand that she wasn't telling the truth.

"The one thing throughout this entire trial, and even before that, she has continuously protested is her innocence of the kidnapping and murder of Olga Duncan, and there isn't a word of testimony that she has ever admitted that she had anything to do with this crime. She admits that some of her actions were wrong, but she vehemently denies that she had anything to do with Olga's murder."

Sullivan tried to convince the jury of a plausible reason why Moya and Baldonado would kill Olga. He theorized that Moya and Baldonado had concocted a scheme to get money from Frank instead of Mrs. Duncan.

"Moya is too smart a man to go out and commit murder for the paltry $175 that Mrs. Duncan raised by pawning her rings. . . . After Mrs. Duncan agreed to pay back Frank's $500 legal fee, the boys got greedy. They believed the lawyer Frank Duncan was a wealthy man and that they could get a lot of cash by kidnapping his wife."

Sullivan coughed again. "They wanted bigger money, so they conceived of the idea of kidnapping Olga. I don't think they intended at that time to kill her. I think that they were going to hold her for ransom and demand money from Frank. But the whole plot failed because Olga resisted, and instead of a victim that they could hold for money, they had a corpse on their hands. So they went back to Mrs. Duncan with the blackmail demands, this time upping it to $2,000. And then they got angry with her because she had them arrested on the extortion charge." Sullivan shrugged. "So they implicated her."

He wiped his nose with his handkerchief while the jurors stared at him blank-faced.

"And you must be careful," he went on. "View the testimony of accomplices in a crime with caution. The law will not allow you to convict Mrs. Duncan solely on the testimony of these accomplices." His voice rose again. "You may believe every word of their testimony, but the law says that you must reject it standing alone!" He slammed his fist in the palm of his hand. "It is your sworn duty as jurors to return a verdict of *not* guilty." He was losing his voice. "You must of necessity come to the conclusion that there is no legal corroboration and, therefore, the evidence is legally insufficient upon which to base a conviction. I'm going to ask," he croaked, "that you return into this courtroom with a verdict of not guilty."

The courtroom was silent.

After the noon recess, Gustafson faced the jury again. Since the prosecution has the burden of proof in a criminal case, it gets the last opportunity to make its case. Gustafson began by explaining why Mrs. Esquivel and Mrs. Short should not be considered accomplices.

"Mr. Sullivan is very eloquent and very clever in his argument. He says it all in a very loud voice. But I ask you—would you convict Mrs. Esquivel of Olga Duncan's murder on November 17th because of her activities on November 13th? Or convict Mrs. Short because she sat in the Tropical Café by the jukebox that day?"

Gustafson wandered closer to the jury and switched to the topic of Mrs. Duncan's relationship with her son. "Elizabeth Duncan admitted that there was only one bed in an apartment she shared with her son in San Francisco."

Sullivan immediately stood. "Your Honor, just a moment. My recollection is that Mrs. Duncan testified that there was a rollaway bed in the closet—a large closet. . . . The district attorney hasn't presented any—"

"Perhaps so, Mr. Sullivan," Gustafson said. "I didn't mean to misstate that, if that is the evidence. Anyway, it doesn't make any difference. That isn't pertinent here. In case there is any doubt in your mind, let me clarify it right now. I didn't ever say I was seeking to show any *unnatural* relationship between Mrs. Duncan and her son, meaning sexual relations between the two. No, I sought to show that there was an *abnormal* relationship between Frank and his mother. Of course, we didn't prove that there was any unnatural relationship, if you are talking about sex. We didn't prove it because we didn't try to prove it."

Sullivan sat down.

The DA turned back to the jury and commenced to ridicule the kidnap-for-ransom theory that Sullivan had introduced in his final argument. It was, he said, "a fantastic, weird, and unbelievable story. Those two men confessed on the stand to Olga Duncan's murder in graphic detail, and they are scheduled to stand trial here next month on whether they shall live or die. I would guess that under the evidence that you heard them testify to in this courtroom, each of them will be sentenced to the gas chamber."

Finally, Gustafson closed his final argument with a stirring appeal. "I don't have a client sitting over there." He pointed to the empty prosecution table. "I represent the People of the State of California, and I have a judicial responsibility to try this case on behalf of society for the murder of an innocent young woman." He moved closer to the jury. "Do not shirk your duty. Quickly return a verdict of first-degree murder for the killing of Olga Duncan." He nodded. "Thank you."

The room was quiet as Gustafson returned to his chair. All three people at the defense table looked toward the judge, faces inscrutable.

"Ladies and gentlemen of the jury," Judge Blackstock said, "it is about a quarter to three." He pointed out that reading the jury deliberation instructions would push the day to at least three thirty. "All of you who would rather I read the instructions now, hold up your hands."

Nobody held up a hand.

"All of you who would rather I read the instructions Monday morning, hold up your hands."

Twelve hands shot up.

"All right. I'll read them at ten o'clock Monday morning when court resumes. Court is adjourned."

Bob left the courthouse humming a frenzied, toneless tune as he fast-walked the three blocks to the newspaper office. Without a word of greeting to his colleagues, he grabbed a stack of blank newsprint from a drawer and rolled the first sheet into his typewriter. He typed furiously.

> *"Anybody's sister, anybody's daughter would have been Elizabeth Duncan's victim if they happened to marry her son Frank," District Attorney Roy Gustafson told the Duncan murder case jury today. . . .*

CHAPTER SIXTY-ONE

THE VERDICT

March 16, 1959

E lizabeth Duncan entered the courtroom Monday morning looking cheerful in a blue dress with a white sailor collar. She murmured "Good morning" to a few regular spectators and smiled at passing reporters as the matron removed her handcuffs.

Bob pointed out two men muscling through the crowd. One had a young, pretty woman on his arm. "That's Detective Charlie Thompson and his partner Jim Hansen from Santa Barbara," he told Bennie Jo. "We wouldn't be here if it wasn't for the hard work they put in."

Hansen flashed his badge and cut in front of the line of people looking for seats. He grabbed the last two spots in the third row for himself and the brunette. Charlie Thompson found a seat near the back.

At ten A.M., Judge Blackstock called court to order.

"Ladies and gentlemen of the jury, it becomes my duty to instruct you concerning the law applicable to this case, and it is your duty as jurors to follow the law as I shall state it to you."

He put on his glasses and proceeded to read the instructions in a loud, clear voice that echoed in the quiet courtroom. One of the most important instructions concerned the definition of "guilt" as it applied to this case: if the jury believed beyond a reasonable doubt that Elizabeth Duncan had "encouraged or advised" Luis Moya and Augustine Baldonado to kill Olga Duncan, then Mrs. Duncan must be considered as guilty as the men, even if she had not been physically present during the commission of the crime.

As for "reasonable doubt," Judge Blackstock explained that the term did not refer to absolute certainty but "only that degree of proof which convinces the mind and directs and satisfies the conscience of those who are bound to act conscientiously upon it."

He explained a few other issues, after which the eight women and four men of the jury—six housewives, a bank secretary, a female hospital worker, a farmer, a rancher, an accountant, and an outdoor-sign business owner, ranging in ages from twenty-two to fifty-six—filed out of the courtroom to determine Elizabeth Duncan's fate.

It was 10:35 A.M.

The courtroom remained silent until the bailiff closed the door behind the last juror. Then the room erupted into excited conversation.

A group of reporters gathered around the defense table as Mrs. Duncan stood and put her wrists out for the handcuffs.

"How do you feel about the case, now that all the evidence is in?" one of the reporters asked.

She held up her hands, fingers crossed. "I just don't know how to answer. I hope it's all right."

Nobody in the gallery got up. Spectators discussed estimates of how long the jury deliberations might take. The consensus was for a verdict the next day.

"They got to spend a little time at it," one veteran court observer opined. "Gotta make it look like they did their duty and went over all the evidence, give her the benefit of the doubt, you know?"

Eventually many of the spectators, after conferring with seatmates about saving their places, picked up belongings and headed for the door.

Detective Charlie Thompson sat down next to Bob. "What do you think?"

Bob turned his mouth down with a considering expression. "Couple of hours. Sometime after lunch, I would think. Certainly not before lunch. Don't think the jury members are going to give up a free restaurant meal."

"Guilty?" Charlie asked.

Bob shrugged. "It only takes one."

Charlie scanned the courtroom. "Looks like Hansen took his new girlfriend to lunch." He chuckled. "One of Olga's nurse friends. Ever since she showed up at the station asking Hansen for an update, she's been leading him around by the nose. He even let her drive his pristine classic coupe." Charlie chuckled again. "Want to go get a bite to eat?"

Bob pulled a bag of peanuts out of his pocket. "Think I'll stay around the courthouse. I don't think the jurors want to spend the night in a hotel. What about you?"

Charlie shrugged. "I can wait here all night if I have to. I got no place to go. Eleanor threw me out again."

At 4:45 P.M., Sullivan and Gustafson were in conference in Judge Blackstock's chambers, discussing whether the jury should be permitted to deliberate after dinner, when the intercom on the judge's desk buzzed. Judge Blackstock pushed the button on the black box.

"We have a verdict," his secretary said.

"Call the jail," the judge barked into the box. "Tell them to bring her down immediately. I want everybody in court in ten minutes."

Sullivan looked at his watch as he slowly got to his feet. "That was fast."

Without a word, Gustafson swung his long legs around from his chair and took a giant step toward the door.

Bob was downstairs milling around outside the makeshift pressroom in the city clerk's office, telling anyone who'd listen how last year's seventh-place Dodgers were going to win the World Series next season, when the bailiff called out over the din: "Judge says ten minutes!"

Reporters dashed through the hallways. Spectators scrambled into the courtroom to claim seats. Bob hummed at a hundred miles an hour as he raced up the elegant marble stairs.

As he took his seat, he scanned the courtroom for Cliff McNair, the *Star-Free Press* photographer. Bob nodded when he spotted his colleague kneeling at the front of the press section. Cliff raised his camera to Bob. The Santa Barbara detectives were seated toward the back, talking to Higgins and Osborne, their Ventura counterparts. Gustafson's investigator, Clarence Henderson, sat behind the prosecution table.

Bennie Jo arrived, out of breath.

"I told you not to go anywhere." Bob looked at his watch. "Jesus, they deliberated less than five hours."

Voices quieted to a low buzz as Judge Blackstock hobbled into the courtroom, climbed the steps to his seat on the bench, and picked up his gavel. "There will be no demonstrations."

The buzzing stopped as Mrs. Duncan entered through the back door, flanked by her entourage of sheriff's deputies. The defendant looked pale, but she grinned around the silent room and gave a little wave to someone in the crowd. She walked briskly to the counsel table and cast a side-glance and a smile at her grim-faced son, seated as always just behind.

"Hello," she said to Frank in a loud whisper.

He mouthed the words, "Hi, Mom."

Mrs. Duncan handed him a note. He unfolded the paper, glanced at it, and then shook his head at his mother as he gave her a wry smile.

Mrs. Duncan turned and fixed her eyes on the stony-faced jurors as they filed into the room. Bob noticed that a few of them briefly returned the defendant's gaze.

"Ladies and gentlemen of the jury, have you arrived at a verdict?" Judge Blackstock asked in a booming voice.

The newly selected jury foreman, Paul Gosney, the forty-eight-year-old outdoor advertising sign businessman, stood. "We have." He handed the written verdict to the bailiff, who delivered it to the judge. Judge

Blackstock read it to himself and handed it to the court clerk to read aloud.

Mrs. Duncan, her hands folded on the defense table, sat smiling and calm.

"We the jury . . . find the defendant, Elizabeth Duncan . . . guilty of murder in the first degree."

A sound, something like a sigh, ran through the courtroom, but the spectators followed the judge's strong warning against demonstrations.

Mrs. Duncan received the verdict without a flicker of emotion, a slight smile still curving the corners of her mouth. Frank put his face in his hands. Gustafson blew out his breath.

Sullivan asked that the jury be polled. Each juror was asked, "Is this your verdict?" by the clerk. Mrs. Duncan's expression never changed as each juror answered in the affirmative.

"Now, ladies and gentlemen of the jury," Judge Blackstock said, "this has only been the first stage of the trial. You will have to pass judgment on the question of penalty next, and I admonish you seriously, do not discuss this case . . ."

When the judge finished the admonition, Gustafson stood. "Your Honor, I suggest that this jury be instructed to return tomorrow at ten A.M. to start the penalty trial."

"That is satisfactory, Your Honor," Sullivan said.

"All right," Judge Blackstock agreed. "Court is adjourned until tomorrow morning at ten o'clock." He leveled his eyes at the jury. "If anyone tries to talk to you about the trial, notify the court."

Mrs. Duncan stood and turned to her ashen-faced son as the matron handcuffed her wrists. "Don't worry too much, Frank." She squeezed his forearm and leaned close to Sullivan and whispered something into his ear. Frank Duncan huddled close to listen.

A minute later Mrs. Duncan was walking rapidly, her head bowed, across the room on her way back to her jail cell. "You run interference," she said flippantly to her six-foot-four-inch sheriff's deputy escort. "I'll follow."

Reporters crowded in.

"Is that the verdict you expected?" one of the reporters called out.

Mrs. Duncan looked over her shoulder. "I didn't expect the jury would do that to me. I didn't do it."

Behind her, another group of reporters crowded around Frank.

"I knew it was coming," he said, "but you can't prepare yourself for that. It's like death."

CHAPTER SIXTY-TWO

EXTRA, EXTRA, READ ALL ABOUT IT

March 16, 1959

I bent the Venetian blinds to get a better look at our empty driveway. "What's taking so long? Everyone knows she's guilty."

"Debby," Mother said in a stern voice.

"That's what Daddy says," I pouted.

"The jury decides on guilt or innocence. Not your father."

"Even Grandma says there's 'no doubt' she's guilty. She's been reading stories in the *LA Times*."

"Come away from the window," Mother pleaded. "Finish your homework."

I flounced back to the dining room table and flipped through pages in my math book. "What's taking Daddy so long?"

Mother opened the oven door, where she had his dinner warming, then adjusted the temperature knob. "He's at the courthouse if the jury's still out. And if the jury already brought back a verdict, he's probably writing his story for tomorrow's paper. Or maybe's he's over at the Sportsman with all the out-of-town reporters, reliving the trial." She pressed her lips together. She didn't think much of the big-city reporters. She'd called them "a sketchy lot."

Headlights shone through the window and swept across the walls of the room.

"Daddy!" I cried as I jumped out of my chair and ran for the front door.

"Wait," Mother said, but I was already bounding down the porch steps.

"Extra, extra, read all about it!" Daddy called out as he climbed from the car.

When I reached him, I snatched the newspaper out of his hands. "Guilty! Wow! We should celebrate."

"I'm starved," he said in a tired voice.

Over dinner, Daddy told us what had happened in court. How calmly Mrs. Duncan had taken the news. How Frank had seemed more upset than his mother.

I scrutinized the photos on the front page of the "Extra" edition newspaper. . . . Mrs. Duncan and Frank conferring with each other before the verdict was read. . . . Solemn-faced jurors listening as the court clerk read the verdict as Mrs. Duncan looked on from the defense table. . . . I glanced up. "How did the district attorney look? Happy?"

Daddy rested his chin on his palm. "Tired. Relieved, I think."

"It says here that the jury only took four hours and fifty-one minutes to come back with a verdict. What took you so long to get home?"

"Getting the newspaper out. This is the first Extra edition we've published since World War II. I had to get my story in fast. Wrote it out longhand right there in the courtroom and then ran all the way down California Street to the office."

"Ran?" Mother said.

Daddy pointed to the picture of the jury and Mrs. Duncan. "Cliff got some good shots. We had to wait for him to develop his pictures. Then I went to the press room and watched while the paper was printed." He pointed to the paper I held. "That's the first one off the press."

"Really?" I held the paper to my chest. "Can I keep it?"

CHAPTER SIXTY-THREE

THE PENALTY PHASE

March 17–20

A small group of reporters caught up with the district attorney in the courthouse hallway before court began.

"What do you think about trying your first penalty phase under the law you coauthored?" Bob asked as he trotted along, attempting to keep up with Gustafson's long-legged strides.

"This is the type of case I had in mind when we wrote the legislation." Gustafson paused as he reached for the courtroom door. "Even though the jurors found her guilty of a despicable crime, they might be under the impression that she is otherwise a kindly, gentle lady who was merely too possessive of her son, as Mr. Sullivan suggested." The DA hauled open the door. "Now they will hear the truth."

The sole issue of a penalty trial is for the jury to decide whether the defendant should receive life imprisonment or the death penalty. Considerations like mitigating circumstances, background, remorse, and the possibility of rehabilitation are all considered relevant.

Now, at last, Gustafson could present witnesses and information he had not been free to bring forward during the criminal phase.

The first witness, a San Francisco vice squad officer, informed the jury that Mrs. Duncan had been convicted in 1953 of keeping a house of prostitution. That was lurid enough, but next came the long parade of Mrs. Duncan's disgruntled ex-husbands that Gustafson had alluded to during the guilt phase of the trial. It soon became clear that she had told each man a similar story: that she was entitled to an inheritance, but only if she was married. She had promised each man she would give him a sum of money from the inheritance if he would marry her. But after the wedding took place, not only did no inheritance appear, but the new bride tried to extort money from her partner before she would agree to end the marriage.

The cavalcade of resentful exes—some of whom Mrs. Duncan had married, some of whom she had not—went on for most of two days.

Leonard Joseph Sollenne had been promised a cut of the $196,000 his new bride said she would receive from the estate of a deceased prior husband. Sollenne soon realized that no such money existed, but when he filed for an annulment, he discovered that Betty had already gone to court to request alimony from him.

Although bus driver Robert Luigi D'Amato had never married Betty, after having three "motel dates" with her, he got served with a separate maintenance suit from "Betty D'Amato" demanding financial support.

At age forty-nine, Mrs. Duncan convinced Frank's twenty-six-year-old law school classmate Stephen Gillis to marry her so that she could, she said, collect a big trust payout. His promised cut: $50,000. His actual paycheck: $10,000. Which bounced. Then his loving bride promised to ruin his career with accusations and inuendoes if he caused any trouble about it. Later, when he joined the Marine Corps, his commanding officer received a letter claiming that his wife, "Elizabeth Gillis," was destitute, eight months pregnant, and in need of financial support. Which was remarkable, given that the marriage had never been consummated.

Real estate agent A.P. Williams received a $50,000 personal check from Mrs. Duncan as down payment on a $255,000 apartment house, although her bank account contained only $28.20 at the time.

As the parade of aggrieved men continued, Sullivan kept objecting that most of the testimony had no bearing on the matter of penalty. Judge Blackstock constantly overruled him. Mrs. Duncan sat unsmiling and composed at the defense table, her manner much more subdued than the animated, cheerful demeanor she had displayed before the guilty verdict the previous day.

Until her last ex-husband took the stand. George Satriano, an outgoing, dark-haired typewriter salesman, would prove to be a favorite of the gallery. He told essentially the same story as had Stephen Gillis and Leonard Sollenne—but with more style.

"I met her at the Avalon Ballroom in San Francisco. I asked her . . . Oh, wait a minute. Hold the phone. *She* asked *me* to dance, and a discussion followed." He uncrossed and recrossed his legs. "It was just before Christmas, and some way or another the discussion of my mother came up. I told her I was going to send my mother a twenty-five-dollar check for Christmas. In the course of the evening, Betty painted quite a picture for me. She said, 'Why don't you marry me? I'll give your mother a thousand dollars for Christmas.'"

Someone in the back of the courtroom snickered.

"And among other things, she said, 'I'll set you up in business. We'll go on a trip to Europe.' It's pretty hard stuff to refuse. I'm a salesman myself." Mr. Satriano shook his head. "And I was getting sold right up the line."

Laughter filled the courtroom. Judge Blackstock glared the room quiet.

"And you agreed to marry her?" Gustafson asked.

"I'm afraid I did. Married her three days later . . . sort of spur-of-the-moment thing, you know."

He testified that he and the defendant had bought a Cadillac in San Francisco one day.

Gustafson asked, "And what became of the car?"

"She hid it in the . . ." Satriano began laughing. He laughed so hard that he couldn't finish the sentence. Hilarity spread throughout the courtroom. Mrs. Duncan threw back her head and laughed the loudest. Her infectious laughter nearly broke up the proceedings meant to determine whether she would live or die. Judge Blackstock had to call a ten-minute recess so that everybody could compose themselves.

Afterward, Gustafson resumed questioning Mr. Satriano. "And what were the circumstances under which you left Mrs. Duncan?"

"I have a habit of having a little shot of bourbon every night. I used to buy these little half pints of Early Times. Anyway, one night I had a drink and left the bourbon on the drain board. I told her to fix dinner while I read the paper.

"When I came back for another shot, the bottle was empty. She told me she'd poured it down the sink." The witness scowled toward the defense table.

Mrs. Duncan smiled back coyly.

Satriano continued, "Of course, these things started to get my goat. It wasn't worth it."

"So you left?"

"Here's the way I left. I was pushed out. Frank dispossessed me, clothes and all. He took everything I owned and dumped it off at a hotel near where I work and then sent a cab driver to deliver a note to tell me what he'd done." Mr. Satriano smiled around the courtroom. "Well, that was a godsend. At least I was out."

More tittering from the spectator gallery.

"One night a private detective came to warn me that my wife had tried to hire him to throw acid in my face. He said she'd offered him five hundred dollars to do the job. After that I was scared of her. I'd see her loitering outside my place of business some nights."

"What did you do?"

"I would lock the front door at closing and climb out a back window. From there, I'd run across the street to the railroad tracks, and down the tracks I'd go."

"So you ran from her?"

"As fast as I could go." Mr. Satriano chuckled but stopped abruptly. "I was scared all the time."

Not only men had been victimized by Elizabeth Duncan. In the afternoon, Gustafson called Mrs. Betty Lou Brantley to the stand. All eyes turned toward a buxom, bleached-blonde woman wearing a tight black sweater and bright red lipstick as she strutted up the aisle to the witness box.

Mrs. Brantley testified that Mrs. Duncan had tricked her into giving up her three children for adoption to a childless Oxnard dentist and his wife. She said she hadn't been able to work and take care of them, so Mrs. Duncan had offered to help her find someone to care for her children. Mrs. Brantley told the jury that she didn't understand when she signed the paperwork that the children would actually be adopted.

"Later, after my children were placed, I moved to Santa Barbara, and one day Mrs. Duncan asked me to drive her to Stockton because she wanted to see her son Dewey Tessier Jr. that she hadn't seen in many years. So I drove her to Stockton."

"Did you stay overnight?"

"Yes. In a motel."

"Who stayed in the motel?"

"Mrs. Duncan, Mr. Tessier, and myself."

Gustafson glanced toward the jury. "What were the sleeping arrangements?"

"The motel was a four-room apartment. There was a big living room, a small kitchen, and two little bedrooms on either side of the living room. I slept in the living room."

Gustafson moved closer to his witness. "What happened later that evening?"

"I couldn't sleep very well, and I was awakened by Mrs. Duncan going into Dewey's room."

A hushed gasp circulated in the courtroom.

"You see, Mrs. Duncan had made remarks before that, earlier in the day . . ." The witness hesitated and then stared into Gustafson's face. "She said that, given time, she could have Dewey doing just exactly like she had Frank doing."

Mrs. Duncan slapped the defense table with a bang. Sullivan grabbed her arm. "Objection! This has no bearing on the issue of penalty."

"Overruled."

"And what happened then?" Gustafson asked.

"Mrs. Duncan went into Dewey's bedroom." Mrs. Brantley pressed her fingers to her scarlet lips, leaving a slight smudge of lipstick at the corner of her mouth. "Later on, you could hear the ruckus clear into the living room. It made me sick, and I got up and went into the kitchen."

The whole courtroom sucked air. Frank groaned and waved his hand toward the back of Sullivan's chair as if trying to get the attorney's attention.

Mrs. Duncan shook her fist at the witness as she hissed, "*No.*"

"And did Mrs. Duncan later come out of Dewey Tessier's bedroom?" Gustafson said.

Mrs. Brantley nodded. "I asked her, when she came into the kitchen, what the idea was, and she just laughed."

Mrs. Duncan watched the witness through beady rat eyes with a murderous gleam. Frank sat behind her, shaking his bowed head. The courtroom was silent.

Sullivan's cross-examination of Mrs. Brantley elicited testimony to show that she had willingly given up her children for adoption. She admitted that she had met with a social worker about the adoptions but that later she was furious with Mrs. Duncan because she'd changed her mind and wanted her children back. Sullivan tried to show the jury that Mrs. Brantley was a "bad woman," sleeping around while her navy husband was stationed overseas, and that she had reasons to lie about Mrs. Duncan to get back at her.

Gustafson ended by putting into evidence ten certificates that documented some of Mrs. Duncan's many marriages, along with records of her various annulments and divorces. He hoped that the sum of the evidence he'd presented to the jury about Mrs. Duncan's past, combined with the callous, heinous murder-for-hire of her son's pregnant wife, would be enough to convince the jury to impose the death penalty.

Judge Blackstock adjourned court for the day, leaving Sullivan to contemplate the impossible task before him. How could he counteract the devastating portrayal of Mrs. Duncan as a lying, cheating con artist and murderess?

In the end, Sullivan called only two witnesses to try to convince the jury that his client's life should be spared: Mrs. Duncan herself and her son Frank. There was no one else to testify to her good character, but the defense attorney was desperate to define his client as more than a conniving bunko artist and incestuous, bigamous woman. He needed her many marriages to somehow sound reasonable to the jury.

"Do you recall how many times you've been married?" he asked her.

"No. I'm afraid to count them."

Laughter erupted in the courtroom. Some of the jurors smiled. Judge Blackstock picked up his gavel.

"In other words, you may have had some marriages that you don't even recall?"

Mrs. Duncan shrugged. "They didn't mean that much to me."

Sullivan looked up from his list of husbands. "Why did you go through so many marriage ceremonies?"

"I don't know. I think I was seeking something, and I don't know what." She sighed. Deeply. "After I married them, I didn't want them at all."

Sullivan changed the subject to Betty Lou Brantley, whom Mrs. Duncan had met in Oxnard in 1956 while working in the Salvation Army thrift store. "She used to come to the Salvation Army store every day for some reason or another, and one day she came in all worried because her mother had told her that she had to come up to Stockton and get her children.

"Betty Lou told me she couldn't take care of the children anymore. And I said that I knew a nice dentist and his wife who wanted to adopt the children. So we placed the kids with them. Frank did some paperwork. I thought Betty Lou was happy about it."

"Now," Sullivan said, "when Betty Lou drove you to Stockton in Frank's car to visit your son Dewey Tessier Jr., and you all stayed in the motel . . ."

"I didn't do what she—"

Sullivan put up his hand to stop his client. "Was there ever an occasion when you got up in the early hours and went . . . ?"

Mrs. Duncan was already shaking her head.

". . . and you went into Dewey's bedroom?"

"There was never anything like that. Nothing."

"You heard Mrs. Brantley testify that you went into Dewey's bedroom, and while you were in there, she heard a ruckus. Do you remember that testimony?"

"Yes."

"Was there ever an occasion when such a thing happened?"

"The ruckus was me yelling and jerking her off my son. I went in there and found her in bed with Dewey. I jerked her out because I didn't think that she was the type of person I wanted in bed with my son." Mrs. Duncan folded her arms across her chest. "That was the ruckus."

Next Sullivan called Frank Duncan.

"Mr. Duncan," Sullivan began, "you have resided with your mother practically all of your life?"

"Yes, I have," Frank answered.

"Has she always been a good mother to you?"

Frank smiled at Mrs. Duncan. "An extremely fine mother, Mr. Sullivan."

Mrs. Duncan beamed at her son.

"Do you remember having any discussion with your mother about her marriage to Mr. Sollenne or Mr. Gillis, who were young men around your own age?"

"I must confess, Mr. Sullivan, I found these things extremely unpleasant. My personality is such that at the time, I certainly didn't want to discuss those marriages." Frank shifted in his seat and crossed his legs. "Certain people like to discuss, perhaps, their problems, but I am not one of them. I like to close it up, and I discussed it really very little with my mother."

"You have had to on occasion through the years observe your mother's manner and demeanor and conduct, have you?" Sullivan asked.

"Yes, I have."

"From your observation of her, has she appeared to be a woman who could exercise good judgment?"

"No. She cannot."

Mrs. Duncan shuffled through some papers on the defense table.

Sullivan said, "How would you describe her conduct generally, and her actions and so forth?"

"My mother has always been an impetuous person. She can, I believe, be the warmest person that I have ever known." Frank looked fondly in his mother's direction. "She can charm you out of your boots."

A few members of the gallery laughed.

"As a child, there was one thing that I always knew." Frank continued to gaze at his mother. "I always knew that I was loved. My mother has been generous to a fault. I think she has—in fact, I know she has—a tendency to love friends immediately after having just met people."

"She has had a lot of friends?" Sullivan encouraged.

"Well, she has a difficult time getting along with people after a while. But I've never known her to really hurt anyone." Frank turned back to look at the attorney. "It is difficult, of course, to talk about one's mother, but in all sincerity, despite all of this . . ." Frank waved his arm around the courtroom. "If I had a choice for a mother, as much as I've been humiliated and hurt, I would still pick the same mother."

Mrs. Duncan covered her face with her hanky and began to sob.

Sullivan watched his client as she wiped her tears and then asked Frank if his mother appeared to be strong-willed.

"Yes."

"Is she the type of individual with whom you could reason?"

Frank shook his head sadly. "Absolutely impossible to reason with my mother, Mr. Sullivan. It is like talking to a block of granite."

"Is that the way she dealt with her various husbands?"

"That's right. With everyone, in fact. That's one of the reasons she had a difficult time getting along with people. She had to have her own way."

Sullivan made a little bow toward Frank. "I think that is all."

"So what's Sullivan's strategy?" Bennie Jo asked as the crowd dissipated for the lunch recess. "He gets Frank to say she was a great mom. To Frank at least. Maybe a little impulsive. What's the point?"

"I think Sullivan's trying to humanize her enough to convince at least one member of the jury to vote against the death penalty," Bob said, keeping an eye on Mrs. Duncan at the defense table. She was tugging at the tails of her attorney's jacket. "He doesn't have a lot to work with."

"She was a great mom but a really bad grandmother since she murdered her unborn grandchild."

Bob nodded. "Hard to forget."

Mrs. Duncan had managed to get Sullivan's attention. She pointed energetically toward the back of the courtroom, where George Satriano, her favorite ex-husband, was talking to a shapely blonde. His hand rested on her arm.

Bob eased closer to the defense table.

Mrs. Duncan was still pointing. "Look over there," she implored her attorney. "That's Betty Lou Brantley with George. They're both witnesses. They aren't supposed to be fraternizing."

Sullivan glanced over at Betty Lou, who was smiling warmly at George. Then the attorney looked back at his client and shook his head.

Mrs. Duncan stomped her foot. "Somebody needs to get that hussy away from him. . . ."

Next up were the psychiatrists.

When she had first been arraigned on the charge of murder, Mrs. Duncan had also entered a plea of "not guilty by reason of insanity."

Defense attorneys file such a motion almost as a matter of course in capital cases for the simple reason that most people, upon hearing about some particularly atrocious act, tend to say that the perpetrator "must have been crazy to do something like that." The testimony of psychiatrists about a defendant's mental state is normally presented during a sanity hearing, which would follow the jury pronouncing sentence. But Sullivan had read the psychiatric reports and knew that his client did not meet the legal criteria for a diagnosis of "legally insane." Mrs. Duncan had clearly understood the difference between right and wrong at the time Olga was murdered. Still, Sullivan hoped the jurors would consider her mental illness, and her inability to exercise good judgment, as mitigating factors and choose the lesser of the two possible sentences.

To this end, on Thursday afternoon, Sullivan called Dr. Louis R. Nash to the stand. The psychiatrist, an assistant superintendent at Camarillo State Hospital, had been appointed by Judge Blackstock to conduct a psychiatric examination of Mrs. Duncan before the trial began.

Standing to the side of the witness stand so that he could face both Dr. Nash and the jurors, Sullivan began his last-ditch effort to save his client's life.

"As a result of your examination of Mrs. Duncan, Doctor, and your observations of her testimony, did you come to any conclusions about the personality of the defendant?"

"I found Mrs. Duncan to be a maladjusted, impulsive, egocentric, and emotionally immature individual. The defendant particularly has been unable to stand frustrations or maintain her emotional equilibrium and independence during major or minor stresses."

Mrs. Duncan sat sideways in her chair with a sour expression on her face while she watched the psychiatrist describe her maladjusted personality.

"In connection with the history of Mrs. Duncan's past life and the examinations which you made, did you learn that she was addicted to the excessive use of sleeping pills?"

"I did. I learned from her that in 1948, after the death of her daughter, she had a very stormy emotional period when she resorted to the use of barbiturates in the form of Seconal. She related to me that she took this seda-tive, increasing it in dosage until, at the time I examined her, she told me that she had been taking a very large amount—eight capsules every night."

When asked how such abuse might affect the defendant, Dr. Nash said, "Any drug that has an effect on the brain that will cause sedation, such as a barbiturate, will affect judgment, memory, and the ability of a person to think."

"Thank you, Doctor. Nothing further." Sullivan turned to the DA. "You may cross-examine."

Gustafson didn't even wait for the defense attorney to get back to his seat before he asked his first question. "Doctor, saying that she has a mental disorder or trait, which you describe under the label of psychopathic per-sonality, is not the equivalent of saying that she is insane, is it?"

"It is not. I did not find her to be insane."

"And the type of personality that you have described in your report as being one that Mrs. Duncan has, one which affects the person's ability to exercise judgment"—he read from his notes—"a maladjusted, egocen-tric, emotionally immature, impulsive individual called a psychopathic personality—is the type that most criminals have, isn't it?"

"Yes."

"Many of the people who come in conflict with the law, and because of it are in jails and prisons, fit into this category, yes?"

"Correct. A psychopathic personality is a social misfit who causes prob-lems for themselves and the world they live in. They actually use the society where they exist as a battleground to act out their own inner tensions in an antisocial manner."

"And if this person who is a psychopathic personality is confined in an institution, isn't it true that under stresses, major or minor stresses, that the person might have the same type of reaction—that is, acts of violence or impulsiveness, possibly even killings?"

Dr. Nash nodded. "Yes, their pattern of behavior would be the same."

"Thank you," Gustafson said. "That's all."

March 20, 1959

The next morning, March 20, Sullivan called his last witness, another psychiatrist, Dr. Bruno Birlinski, to the stand. Dr. Birlinski had been hired by the defense. He told the courtroom that he believed Mrs. Duncan's mental condition was aggravated by the death of her daughter, menopause, and possible brain damage caused by an overdose of barbiturates when she attempted suicide in 1957.

"She was in a coma for three days," he said as he pulled on his earlobe. "Mrs. Duncan has only a fourth-grade education. She felt inferior as a child and never fit in with other children. As a result of this, she has felt suspicious of people all of her life."

Dr. Birlinski said he had administered a myriad of psychological tests during his examination of Mrs. Duncan. He explained to the jury that she had little ability to conceptualize, she was unable to interpret many proverbs, and she didn't know that Canada was north of the United States. She thought Lincoln was the first president.

"Mrs. Duncan is not a well woman."

"When you say that Mrs. Duncan is 'not a well woman,' do you mean that she is mentally ill?" Sullivan asked.

"Yes, you can use that term."

The doctor also testified about a memory test he'd administered to the defendant. "She was able to remember and repeat six numbers forward, but only three backwards." He fussed with the cuff of his shirtsleeve. "Her memory appeared to be a little spotty."

When it was Gustafson's turn to question the psychiatrist, he set out to discredit the doctor.

"Are you board-certified in psychiatry or neurology?" Gustafson asked.

"No, not certified. I was a psychiatrist in the army for five years, and I have held other positions in the field."

"And the total time you spent examining the defendant was about two and a half hours?"

Dr. Birlinski shifted in his chair. "I believe that is right, but I also researched background information."

"Like what?"

Dr. Birlinski stroked his chin as if he were in deep thought. "I perused newspaper articles and such . . . yes, excerpts from the newspapers."

"I see. And, Doctor, with respect to the number memory test you gave her, do I understand this correctly? You would say, for example, "Seven, four, nine, two, five, eight" to the patient and ask her to repeat those numbers and then to repeat them starting the other way, backwards?"

"Yes," the psychiatrist said in a haughty tone.

"All right," Gustafson said. "Tell me what the numbers are backwards."

"That you just told me?" Dr. Birlinski asked incredulously.

"Yes."

After a painful silence, the doctor stammered, "Well, uh . . . I wasn't paying attention to the numbers you said."

The courtroom howled.

"So you don't really have to be mentally ill not to be able to repeat a six digit number backwards, do you?"

"Of course not," the doctor snapped.

Gustafson gave the doctor a condescending smile. "One more question, Doctor. In your opinion, is Mrs. Duncan legally sane?"

"I believe that she is a sociopathic personality and that she is mentally ill."

"But is she *legally* sane?"

Dr. Birlinski huffed. "Yes."

Gustafson picked up his papers from the lectern. "That's all. Plaintiff rests."

"The defense rests, also, Your Honor," Sullivan said in a tired voice.

Closing arguments began immediately after lunch.

"You know what the death penalty is," Gustafson told the jury, "but you may not know what life imprisonment is. In California, 'life imprisonment' is *not* life imprisonment." He shook his head. "If the defendant is given life imprisonment as a sentence, she will be eligible to be paroled after she has served only seven years."

After a pause to allow jurors to contemplate the early release of Elizabeth Duncan, Gustafson continued. "What have we shown in this penalty phase of the trial? Well, in the first place, we've shown that the defendant is a liar in just about everything she's ever said."

He jabbed his finger on the lectern. "She is as guilty as anybody can be. I don't know how many witnesses we have presented at this trial—possibly over fifty all told, including the penalty phase witnesses—and everything that any person has said from this witness stand that has been harmful to her, she has denied. Everybody else is a liar.

"But each of you must decide for yourselves, and if you don't think she's defrauded some of her husbands or obtained a fraudulent annulment for her son's marriage"—Gustafson shrugged—"it doesn't matter. And if some of you don't think that she committed incest with her son Dewey Tessier, I don't care. That's all right with me. The important thing is that she *did* commit murder, and you must decide her penalty."

Gustafson moved closer to the jury. "During this portion of the trial, Mrs. Duncan is entitled to show her goodness, her background, anything that will put her in a good light to convince you people that the appropriate penalty should be life imprisonment with the possibility of being paroled after seven years, rather than the death penalty."

Gustafson shot a glance toward the defendant. "Now, I listened hard, and I didn't hear one word of evidence of how good she was, about anything that she ever did to benefit any human being on the face of this earth." Gustafson focused on the faces of the jurors. "And I certainly don't want you to forget the most important evidence of all . . . the brutal crime. Even if Mrs. Duncan had done nothing else in her life that was bad, this case would call for the death penalty on the basis of her cunning, planning, and scheming to have her daughter-in-law murdered."

He looked toward Mrs. Duncan with disgust. She returned a flinty gaze.

"Here was a lovely, innocent young girl who hadn't done anything to harm Mrs. Duncan," Gustafson said, "who just asked, begged, and prayed to be left in peace to try to work out her marriage to this man whom, unfortunately, Olga fell in love with."

Frank Duncan stared at the floor.

"And what was the consequence of that?" Gustafson thundered. "She was dragged from her apartment on the night of November 17th, brutally beaten over the head, her wrists taped up, taken on that road into Casitas Pass, hit over the head many times with a pistol, and then finally strangled to death and buried in that shallow grave."

Gustafson took a breath. He lowered his voice. "Don't forget, that is what you are punishing her for. I can't in my mind imagine what kind of murder would be worse than this one, and if this crime doesn't deserve the death penalty, then no crime does." He balled his fist and rapped the lectern. "I demand of you, in the name of the People of California, that you go out and vote that Elizabeth Duncan be sentenced to death."

Gustafson snatched his notes off the lectern. "Thank you."

The courtroom was silent as Sullivan walked to the lectern with deliberate steps.

"I have seen the prosecution build a wall of hate for you in order to appeal to your bias and prejudice, so that you may satisfy the craving of the prosecution for the infliction of the death penalty on Elizabeth Duncan." He took a deep breath. "There is nothing good that can be said about Elizabeth Duncan. Her friends, her relatives, her brothers, her sister have all deserted her. She sits alone here today supported by the one person who loves her, her son Frank."

Frank sat in his usual seat behind his mother, his chin now raised high.

"And it is because he has displayed this love and has been loyal and faithful to her that the prosecution has vilified him.

"You have been told that 'life imprisonment' does not mean life imprisonment. Yes, but it doesn't necessarily follow that after being sentenced for first-degree murder you will be paroled at the end of seven years just because you are eligible. I believe from my experience that the shortest time which one serving such a sentence might have hope, just a hope, to be paroled, would be somewhere from fifteen to twenty years.

"The evidence in this case shows that today she is fifty-four, fifty-five years old. Should you choose in this case to impose life imprisonment as the appropriate penalty, if she is ever paroled, she will be an old lady, a very old lady. To her, a sentence of life in prison means exactly what it says. You may rest assured that Elizabeth Duncan will never leave the confines of her prison alive."

Sullivan went on to accuse the prosecution of throwing "practically the entire penal code at the defendant." He moved closer to the jury box. "Take her marriage to Mr. Satriano, for example. I have no doubt that at the time Elizabeth Duncan married Mr. Satriano, she represented to him that she was coming into an inheritance. I think at that time she was actually suffering from delusions of grandeur, and she wanted to impress him with the fact she had money.

"And then there was the supposed incest. . . ." Sullivan gave a disgusted shake of his head. "They tried all through the first phase of this trial, *repeatedly* tried to establish an incestuous relationship between Mrs. Duncan and her son Frank, and they utterly failed, failed completely." The defense attorney swept his arm toward the prosecution table. "And then during this portion of the trial, they put Betty Lou Brantley on the stand, and she tells some cockamamie story about Mrs. Duncan and her son Dewey. Mrs. Brantley, a proven liar, who testified under oath that she never agreed to have her children adopted but then had to change her tune when she was confronted with paperwork from the adoption file. Oh yes, she had to admit that she did give her consent."

Sullivan folded his arms across his chest. "My client has done a lot of weird things in her life, I'll grant you that, but is there some reason she does these things? Is she as responsible for her conduct as you and I would be, or isn't there something in her makeup? She is still a human being, endowed with body and soul, made in the likeness and image of her creator. Can't you find something in this evidence that will mitigate in some small way her conduct?"

He straightened his small frame and raised his voice. "The doctors said she is sane, but she is ill." He made an imploring gesture as he enunciated each word. "She is mentally ill, and sometimes this mental illness will cause a person to do things that a normal individual would not do under any circumstances. According to the psychiatrist's report, you are dealing with a woman unable to control her conduct. It just doesn't measure up to normalcy, and that is something you need to take into the jury room.

"Mr. Gustafson has told you that in this case, you should invoke the law 'an eye for an eye, a tooth for a tooth, a life for a life,' but Christianity was born in this country with a doctrine of forgiveness." He softened his tone. "Olga has gone to her eternal reward. Perhaps where Olga is now, where all is forgiven, if she could raise her hand to direct you in your deliberations, she would say, 'Don't take the life of Elizabeth Duncan. Spare her life but put her where she belongs, away from society and in prison.'"

A soft sound of in-taking breath emanated from the gallery. At the prosecution table, Gustafson bit his lip, his face red, disapproval glinting from his eyes.

"You hold the life of this woman in your hands." Sullivan lifted his arms to the heavens. "Ask your creator to guide you in your deliberations, and I am sure that you will find that the appropriate punishment in this case is that of life imprisonment."

He let his arms fall and dipped his head. "Thank you."

Frank Duncan patted his mother's back. Mrs. Duncan, her mouth a grim slash, glanced at her attorney as he settled himself beside her at the table. They did not make eye contact.

Again, as in the first phase of the trial, the prosecution would have the last word.

"I don't pretend to be the equal of Mr. Sullivan in that kind of emotional plea." Gustafson flashed a cold smile toward the defense table. "But luckily, I think I have the facts on my side, and I have the law on my side. I submit to you that Mr. Sullivan has admitted that there isn't one good thing that can be said about Elizabeth Duncan, nothing. There's nobody to say a word for her other than Frank. So even if you wanted to cross off from your mind all of these other items of criminality in her background"—Gustafson held up his fingers to count—"fraud, solicitation of prostitution, adultery, obtaining money under false pretenses, perjury, extortion, conspiracy, bribery, forgery, grand theft"—he ran out of fingers—"bigamy, fictitious checks . . . all these crimes strewn six ways to Sunday . . . you would still be faced with the fact that here is a cold-blooded murderess about which there is not one good word to say."

A deep furrow of concern creased Gustafson's brow. "Mr. Sullivan said, 'Olga has gone to her eternal reward.' Well, I wonder whether Olga thought it was any great reward to go in the fashion she went. Certainly, that wasn't any favor that Mrs. Duncan did for Olga. I certainly hope that I'm not rewarded in a fashion of that kind for anything I have ever done."

Mrs. Duncan narrowed a feline glare at Gustafson. He ignored her and fixed his angry gaze on the jury. "Consider the horrible nature of this crime. Not only did she hire men to kill her daughter-in-law, she had her unborn grandchild murdered as well. Mrs. Duncan had no more feeling for that child than she had for Olga."

He slowly scanned the jurors' faces. "If this crime doesn't carry the death penalty, no crime carries it. I realize that this isn't a pleasant duty. Mr. Sullivan says that you hold the life of Elizabeth Duncan in your hands. True, in a way you do, but don't forget that Mrs. Duncan put her life in your hands by virtue of murdering Olga Duncan. She earned the death penalty by what she did, and she deserves to get what she earned.

"In the name of the People of the State of California, I ask and demand that you return a unanimous verdict of death. Thank you."

Judge Blackstock read a short list of instructions to the jurors, and at four thirty, they retired for deliberations. Reporters and spectators lingered in the courtroom, talking in quiet voices. None of the excitement that had accompanied the wait for the verdict on guilt or innocence simmered in the room.

CHAPTER SIXTY-FOUR

A MISERABLE EXCUSE
FOR A HUMAN BEING

March 20, 1959

That night, Mother sent Betsey and me to bed right after *Zorro* ended. I climbed into the top bunk, put my palms together, and whispered my usual prayer: "Now I lay me down . . . if I should die before I wake . . . but please, God, not tonight. I'll be good. . . ." But afterward, I didn't go to sleep. I couldn't. Daddy had called after dinner to tell Mother he didn't know when he'd be home. The jury was out.

After Betsey's breathing changed rhythm, I used my flashlight to read Nancy Drew for a while, but I put the book away when I heard mother turn on the TV. Quietly, I lowered myself from the top bunk, propped my flashlight up in one of Betsey's tennis shoes, and stretched out on my stomach across the area rug with a pile of paper dolls. Pinky Lee slipped through the crack of the slightly opened door and curled up on top of the paper-doll evening gowns.

"Move," I whispered. "The Alameda girls have to get ready for a party." Pinky purred as he washed his face.

I'm not sure what time I nodded off. When I awoke, the room was cold, my flashlight dead, and the house dark. I heard the sound of clicking typewriter keys.

I sat up, wide awake. *He's home.*

Tiptoeing to my bedroom door, I peered into the hallway. Light seeped under the door of Daddy's study. I crept to his door, silently turned the handle, and pushed it open a few inches.

Daddy scowled as he pounded his fingers across the typewriter keys, his mouth set. He pushed the carriage return lever hard, and the bell dinged. He stopped typing and stared at the page, cracking his knuckles. I hovered in the doorway as he grabbed the piece of paper and ripped it out of the typewriter.

"Goddammit," he mumbled as he crumpled the page into a ball and tossed it on the floor next to a half dozen other wadded-up pages. He put his elbows on the desk and his fingers at his temples as he stared at the empty typewriter.

"Is she going to die?" I asked quietly.

Daddy whirled around, making a strangled noise in his throat. "Jesus. What are you doing up?"

"I've been waiting for you." I pushed the door the rest of the way open and scooted inside. I smiled hopefully. "Did she get the gas?"

Daddy rolled another page into the typewriter. "Not tonight."

"I mean did the jury say she's getting the death penalty?"

"I know what you mean." He took a deep breath and released it in a long drawn-out hiss. "Yes. The jury voted for death. Happy?" he said in an angry tone as he began to type again.

My lower lip trembled. "I thought you said Mrs. Duncan should die for what she did to Olga. Did you change your mind? Do you think the death penalty is wrong, like Mother?"

"Not really. I'm just tired." He shook his head sadly. "If a nation is willing to sacrifice millions of our best young men in war in the name of self-protection, I guess we can put a few murderers to death in the name of self-protection, but . . ." He didn't finish.

"What did Mrs. Duncan say when she heard?"

"Not a word. Just stared straight ahead. But Frank had plenty to say after court. He insisted that the appeal will not fail because three of the jurors said they already believed his mother was guilty before the trial ever started."

"But everyone knows—"

"My head's pounding. I'm not up to a bunch of questions tonight. Why the hell are you still up, anyway? Can't your mother put you to bed on time?" He shot me a disapproving look. "Go on. Get out of here. I've got to finish this damn column." He pounded the keyboard for a few more minutes, but I didn't move.

My eyes welled. "I thought we'd be happy if the jury said 'death'—"

He cut me off. "There's no jubilation in something like this."

My voice broke. "But what she did . . . to Olga and the baby."

Daddy closed his eyes. "Oh, sweetheart," he said softly. He opened his arms, and I leaned into him. He held me tight as I cried quietly into his shoulder. "You shouldn't be thinking about executions. I don't know how you got so interested in all this."

I blinked back my tears. "I read all your stories in the newspaper every day. I want to know all about bad people so they don't hurt me."

Daddy patted my back. "Aren't you supposed to be going to the Coca-Cola bottling plant with your Girl Scout troop tomorrow? It's past midnight. You need to get some sleep."

I swirled my head around. "I won't be too tired. Judi says we'll get free Cokes right off the assembly line. And Beth doesn't work there anymore, you know. She lives in Los Angeles, and Mother says she's doing better."

"Well, good." Daddy made a half attempt at a smile. "That's . . . something."

I bent down to pick up one of the crumpled pages from the floor and smoothed it open. "Why are you throwing away your story?"

"I already wrote my story about the verdict at the office before I came home." He glanced at me and took the page out of my hands, then wadded it up again. "I'm trying to write about the death penalty being a deterrent to murder." He shrugged. "But Elizabeth Duncan's execution isn't going to do anything to protect the next murder victim. Even Roy Gustafson concedes that point."

"But she murdered Olga. It's her punishment. She's getting what she deserves, right?"

"Maybe justice will be done, but it won't bring Olga back. And I guess nobody wants to risk Mrs. Duncan conning her way past the parole board in seven years," he said wearily. "Gustafson calls capital punishment 'retribution' for a few of the worst killers, the ones he calls 'unsalvageable' . . . an eye for an eye, a life for a life."

"That's what Reverend Ralston says, too."

He raked his fingers through his short, spiky hair. "Her attorney told the jury that she should be spared because she's still a human being, endowed with body and soul . . . Sullivan said Olga would forgive Mrs. Duncan."

"What! That woman murdered Olga's baby! Even Olga isn't that good."

"Nobody believes Sullivan, Sweetie. He's just grasping at straws." Daddy looked down at his typewriter keys. "Elizabeth Duncan is a miserable excuse for a human being who committed a terrible, heartless crime, but when you've seen someone every day, talked to"—he gave me a sideways glance—"laughed with them . . . it makes you think."

"Laughed with them?"

"Like Sullivan said, 'She's a human being.'"

"But a miserable excuse," I mumbled as he typed the number *-30-* at the end of the page.

"Why do you always do that at the end? Type thirty?"

"So the typesetter will know that the story is finished."

"The end!" I said emphatically.

Daddy shook his head. "I'm afraid this isn't the end of the story. There'll be an appeal. Sullivan believes his client's civil rights have been violated and that there's 'more glaring errors' in this trial record than any case he's ever tried."

"But what about Olga? The jury said Mrs. Duncan should die for what she did to her." I searched his face. "She won't get off, will she?"

"Mrs. Duncan's lawyer will try to get her off. He'll tell the higher courts that she didn't get a fair trial. He says that Gustafson tried the case in the press before the real trial even started. Poisoned the jury pool." Daddy rubbed the back of his neck. "I think Sullivan plans to use some of my stories to make his case."

My voice quivered. "Well, she shouldn't have murdered Olga. Then you wouldn't have had to write about all that bad stuff she did. And anyway, you only wrote the truth, and there's nothing wrong with that, right? Just the facts."

"I can't forget the expression on Frank Duncan's face when the clerk read the verdict that his mother was going to die. He says Gustafson's climbing over his mother's body to get to the governor's office." Daddy fiddled with the lever on his typewriter. "And he's been calling the press coverage sensationalism, yellow journalism."

"Yellow?" I pointed to a copy of the *Star-Free Press* he'd tossed on the side of his desk. "That newspaper is black and white."

Daddy put his arm around me. "I guess the Supreme Court will decide if there's anything wrong with the color of my journalism."

PART FOUR

THE AFTERMATH

April 1959–September 1962

CHAPTER SIXTY-FIVE

FINAL JUSTICE

April 6, 1959–August 9, 1962

Roy Gustafson had made no promises to Luis Moya and Augustine Baldonado before they confessed to Olga's murder, but he did agree to try the men separately if they testified against Elizabeth Duncan at her trial. Therefore, after she was sentenced to death, separate penalty trials began for the admitted killers to determine their fates: life in prison or the death penalty.

Gustafson prosecuted each penalty trial before a new jury. The defendants were represented by local attorneys Burt Henson and John Dench, both experienced defense attorneys appointed by Judge Blackstock.

Baldonado's trial began two weeks after Elizabeth Duncan's trial ended and lasted four days. The verdict was death.

Moya's trial started ten days later and lasted eight days. His attorney, Burt Henson, made an impassioned and compelling plea for his client to be granted a new trial or to be sentenced to life in prison. He argued that Moya had not received a fair trial because of pretrial publicity. Gustafson worried about a hung jury, but after five hours of deliberations, the verdict for Moya was also death.

Under the law, Judge Blackstock had the authority to reduce the punishments to life imprisonment at the final sentencing hearings. He did not. The eighty-three-year-old judge, who had never before pronounced a death verdict, said, "If anyone imagines I have not thought about this case night and day and at midnight and at all times, they are mistaken. But if you are going to be a judge, you have to be a judge."

California law provides an automatic appeal to the California Supreme Court for all death penalty sentences. The attorneys representing the appellants all cited the same reasons for the court to overturn the guilty verdicts: inflammatory pretrial newspaper coverage and numerous procedural errors during the trials themselves.

Roy Gustafson personally prepared the prosecution's briefs and appeared before the court to argue the case for the People. Despite Sullivan's confidence during the trial, in January of 1960 the California Supreme Court unanimously affirmed the guilty verdicts and death penalties. The court stated that there was "abundant evidence of guilt," and the justices were satisfied from examination of the entire record that there was "no miscarriage of justice." An execution date for all three was set for April 14, 1960.

The attorneys for Mrs. Duncan, Moya, and Baldonado all filed additional briefs in federal court requesting new trials. The appeals progressed through the system all the way to the United States Supreme Court, where the trial judgments were unanimously affirmed on March 11, 1960. A new execution date was set for June, but the executions were stayed again when the American Civil Liberties Union injected itself into the case on behalf of all three defendants.

The ACLU's principal contention accused Roy Gustafson of misconduct for deliberately attempting to inflame the community and poison the jury pool. They contended that the Ventura County district attorney's "vitriolic" pretrial public statements to the press had "prejudicially violated" the defendants' right to a fair trial.

Gustafson called the claims "hogwash" and complained that he was being subjected to a "bitter personal attack" by the ACLU. He admitted to bone tiredness, telling colleagues that he couldn't stand to go through the case again during the new appeals.

On July 2, 1960, as the federal appeals court considered this new argument, Moya, Baldonado, and four other prisoners tried to break out of San Quentin State Prison. Someone had smuggled a hacksaw onto Death Row, and the inmates used it to saw through their bars. Once out of their cells, they jammed several toilets. When a guard went to investigate the running water, he was hit over the head with an iron pipe. His guns—a pistol and a twelve-gauge shotgun—were taken by the prisoners. Another guard was held hostage when he arrived to check on his partner. Moya used the telephone and tried to disguise his voice as the injured man to lure more guards to the cell block, but the injured guard yelled into the phone, "There's trouble here!"

The warden ordered tear gas lobbed into the cells, which quickly ended the endeavor. He later told the press, "The escape try was hopeless. They never had a ghost of a chance of gaining freedom." All the prisoners involved in the plot were placed in solitary confinement.

Roy Gustafson resigned as Ventura County district attorney effective January 1, 1961, and went into private practice. Assistant DA Woodruff J. Deem was appointed to serve out his term. Many more execution dates were set and then revised as the ACLU appeal wound through state and federal courts. After two years, the case was finally heard by the United States Supreme Court for a second time. The court issued an unusually short one-sentence opinion stating that "the facts failed to support the accusation made by the defendants."

A judge in Ventura Superior Court set a new execution date: August 8, 1962.

The only remaining hope of halting these executions was to convince California governor Edmund G. (Pat) Brown to commute the death sentences.

Governor Brown held a clemency hearing in Sacramento on August 1, 1962. Frank, his new wife, Elinor Chandler Duncan, and Ward Sullivan took turns describing Mrs. Duncan as a kindly person.

"My mother lives in a dream world and has never done anything seriously wrong," Frank told the governor. "She is the best mother a man could ever have. She gave me life. I'm asking you to give her the rest of hers."

Frank's second wife, herself an attorney, said that during her visits with Mrs. Duncan at Corona women's prison, she had found her mother-in-law to be a very warm and good-natured person. "Mrs. Duncan would have been the first to come to Olga's rescue if she'd known Olga was being attacked," the new Mrs. Frank Duncan insisted.

In response, newly elected Ventura DA Woodruff Deem detailed for the governor Elizabeth Duncan's part in the horrific crime. He described some of her more shocking activities, such as getting the fake annulment of her son's marriage. Several times, the governor turned to Frank and said, "Is this true?" Each time, Frank admitted that it was.

The attorneys for Moya and Baldonado, along with friends and relatives of the two men, also pleaded their case for clemency, citing examples of good works and claiming that "they never had a chance" because of their early troubled lives.

At the conclusion of the hearing, Deem left behind color pictures of the murdered Olga and her unborn child for the governor to review. "The photos reveal the extent of the atrocity and torture inflicted by the murderers," he said. "These particular pictures were never shown to the jury because anyone who sees them either becomes enraged or is made violently ill." He asked that the governor not release the pictures to the press.

Governor Brown, well known for his anti-death-penalty views, rendered his decision the following morning: "I have reviewed in great detail the evidence and the arguments presented for clemency for Elizabeth Duncan, Luis Moya, and Augustine Baldonado. I am unable to find circumstances to warrant commutation. I will not intervene in these cases."

On the morning of August 7, 1962, at the California women's prison in Corona, Elizabeth Duncan stepped into an unmarked car, accompanied by two guards and a nurse, for the four-hundred-mile drive north to the gas chamber at San Quentin State Prison. The superintendent said Mrs. Duncan had appeared to be "at ease" that morning after being comforted by the prison's Catholic chaplain. A small group of correctional personnel said their goodbyes at the door of the prison's release room. As she left the prison, Mrs. Duncan covered her head with an olive-colored jacket to prevent photographers from taking her picture. One of the matrons who had guarded her during her three-year incarceration at Corona teared up as the car pulled away for the long drive north.

That night, Frank visited with his mother in her small cell near the gas chamber. He had filed one last, long-shot writ of habeas corpus in federal court on August 1, 1962, claiming that his mother had been so drugged by medication administered at the Ventura County jail that she had been unable to fully cooperate with her defense during her trial.

During this last meeting with her son, Mrs. Duncan said that she had confidence that "her very good boy" would get another reprieve for her at the hearing, which was scheduled for the following morning. "I'll see you tomorrow," she told Frank before returning to her cell to take a sedative and go to sleep.

The next morning, August 8, Mrs. Duncan received communion and then repeatedly asked her guards, "Where's Frank? Where's Frank?"

Frank was in San Francisco making the last-ditch plea to get her execution delayed. In case the court granted another stay, Governor Brown was waiting near an open phone line connecting the prison to his summer house in Los Angeles.

Fifty-seven witnesses gathered in the observation room to see Mrs. Duncan die, including members of law enforcement, the press, and politicians from throughout the state. Three of the men—sheriff's deputy Ray Higgins, who had persuaded Augustine Baldonado to confess and lead police to Olga's body; the Reverend Floyd Gressett, Moya's spiritual advisor; and Bob Holt, the only reporter who had attended all sessions of the trials for all three defendants—waited next to the heavy glass windows of the gas chamber. They stood so close to the death chamber that if one had extended his hand toward Mrs. Duncan and she had extended hers, they could have easily touched if not for the glass and steel between them. The chamber itself was so small that there was room inside for little more than its two metal chairs.

Supporters and family of the condemned were also allowed to witness the executions, but Mrs. Duncan had no friends or family present. Frank was still at the appeals court ten miles south in San Francisco.

Bob Holt's firsthand account of the execution appeared in the *Ventura County Star-Free Press* in the afternoon edition on the same day. More articles would follow over the next six days of August 1962.

At 10:02 A.M., after telling the warden one last time, "I am innocent," Mrs. Duncan walked quietly into the gas chamber, wearing a pink-and-white striped prison smock, her graying hair pulled into a tight bun. Her glasses and false teeth had been removed. She appeared to have gained considerable weight during her three-year prison stay.

Three guards accompanied Mrs. Duncan into the small green octagonal room, its thick walls studded with bolts. They strapped her into the chair. One of them patted her on the shoulder as they left the chamber.

Mrs. Duncan kept her eyes closed and her lips pressed together. At 10:04, the warden gave the signal to pull the lever that dropped the cyanide pellets into a vat of acid under Mrs. Duncan's chair. No gas fumes were visible to the spectators crowded into the observation room, but soon Mrs. Duncan began struggling to breathe and strained against the straps. Slowly her head dropped backwards onto the green-metal chair's backrest; her sightless eyes stared at the ceiling. Her lips moved one last time. If she said anything, no one heard.

The prison doctor, clipboard in hand, was visible through slatted windows beyond the death chamber. Through a stethoscope taped to Mrs. Duncan's chest, he listened until her heartbeat ceased at 10:12 A.M., eight minutes after the pellets dropped.

While his mother was inhaling the cyanide gas, Frank Duncan stood defeated outside the federal court building in San Francisco, his last-chance plea to the court rejected.

"They won't listen," he told reporters. "It's a most barbaric thing. The son of a bitches are going to kill her."

Following Elizabeth Duncan's gassing, pumps and a tall chimney cleared the deadly cyanide from the double-seated chamber to make it ready for the simultaneous executions of Olga's other two killers. At one P.M., Augustine Baldonado, wearing a jaunty smile, entered the small green eight-sided room. His last words to the warden were, "Be sure to shut that door tight."

Following on his heels was a pale and resigned-looking Luis Moya. During the murder of Olga Duncan and its aftermath, Moya had been the leader, with Baldonado relying upon him for guidance. But on this day, it was Moya who seemed to look to the older man for courage as they faced death.

Among the witnesses outside the heavy glass windows were Baldonado's brother and brother-in-law. When Baldonado saw them, he smiled and waved. Meanwhile, Moya was being strapped into the chair where Elizabeth Duncan had died three hours earlier.

Although the gas chamber was assumed to be soundproof, some of Baldonado's remarks were semi-audible. When his brother began to weep, Baldonado winked and said, "It's okay." As a guard tightened the straps on his ankles, Baldonado called out, "Visit my kids!" Then the guards left, and the hatch-like door closed with a thud.

The start of the one o'clock execution had been slightly delayed because of an appeal filed by a San Francisco attorney on the grounds that the two condemned men were too simple-minded to know what they had done. Both Moya and Baldonado had asked the attorney not to make this final appeal, but the prison warden waited by the phone. When the appeal was rejected, at 1:05 P.M., the pellets dropped.

As the cyanide fumes began to rise, Baldonado shouted, "It's down! I can smell it, and it doesn't smell good!"

Moya looked out at his longtime spiritual advisor, Floyd Gressett, and mouthed the words, "Goodbye, Reverend."

Baldonado laughed and joked. The two men smiled at each other and for a while engaged in animated conversation. Both wore white shirts, open at the throat, and dark trousers for their death uniforms, with stethoscopes attached under the shirts.

Soon the banter ended. Both men fell unconscious, their heads sinking onto their chests. The only sounds in the observation room were the sobs of Baldonado's brother.

Moya was pronounced dead at 1:14, Baldonado at 1:15. Moya's body was immediately taken to Stanford Medical Center so that his eyes could be donated to the eye bank there.

Following the executions, the San Quentin warden held a press conference. He was asked, "Do you think the murder rate in California will fall off as a result of this triple execution?"

"No," he said. "I think the death penalty has very little deterrent effect. However, I think that there are some people who must be put to death for the protection of society."

When asked if the Duncan murderers were in this category, the warden said, "I'd rather not comment. But remember, we're carrying out these executions for you, the people of California. Nobody here wants to do it."

After I finished reading my dad's front-page story, I sat silently at our modern glass-topped dining room table, still wearing my new two-piece bathing suit after a day of body surfing with my teenage girlfriends. Marilyn had driven us to the "cool kids'" beach by the pier and to Fosters Freeze afterward for deep-fried corn burritos.

I read the headline again—TRIO DIES IN GAS CHAMBER. MA GOES QUIETLY, ACCOMPLICES JOKE—and waited to feel something. Relief? . . . Satisfaction? . . . Safer?

They removed Mrs. Duncan's false teeth. . . . Good.

Resting my chin in my hands, I stared at the crystal vase filled with wilting pink, yellow, and white roses that had been cut from my mother's prized bushes in the backyard. I picked up a brown-edged petal, closed my eyes, and inhaled its sweet fragrance.

The deadly fumes began to rise. . . . Slowly her head dropped backward. . . . Her sightless eyes stared at the ceiling.

I hadn't thought about Olga and Mrs. Duncan very often in the three years since the trials had ended. The killers were all awaiting execution, and the sensational newspaper stories had disappeared from the headlines. Gradually my attention had turned to the complexities of junior high social life.

The little bird in the clock on the wall above me shot from its door, calling out, "Cuckoo, cuckoo, cuckoo, cuckoo." I slammed my hand to my heart. *Oooh.* Time to get ready for swim practice. Big open ocean water swim in three weeks. *Don't think about the sharks.*

I folded the newspaper to take to my bedroom and reread what the warden had said. *The death penalty has very little deterrent effect.* Then a small headline below the fold caught my attention:

KIDNAP MURDER SUSPECT SOUGHT

The kidnapping and murder of an 18-year-old student shot after being abducted with his 16-year-old girlfriend while on a swim outing at a lake touched off an intense man hunt. . . . The boy's body was found in a plum orchard last night. The girl . . .

CHAPTER SIXTY-SIX

LIFE GOES ON

Thursday, September 27, 1962:
Seven weeks after the executions

After changing into a green pullover sweater and rolled-cuff jeans in the pool bathroom, I carefully combed my wet hair, parting it to better show off the streaks, and went outside to wait for my dad. Betsey and Marilyn hadn't gone to practice that day. My sister had started complaining that her throat hurt right about the time she remembered we would be swimming the mile for time. Marilyn, a junior in high school, was with her boyfriend, Mike, cruising Main Street in his Model A Ford hot rod.

"Hop in," my father called from his new beige Dodge Dart with red vinyl upholstery. A big improvement over his embarrassing old Chevy.

I slammed the car door, and he shot away from the curb, narrowly missing a couple of football players who were crossing the street on their way to the locker room. I ducked lower in the seat. My father didn't seem to notice one of the players shaking his fist. Daddy was excited.

"You should see that new freeway," he said gleefully. "Well, the first four and a half miles of it, anyway. Dedication ceremony today. The mayor called the freeway opening 'an event of more significance than the building of the railway to Ventura in 1886.'" He passed a hand through the air. "It doesn't officially open to the public until Monday."

I gazed out the window.

"The high school band played. Lots of political speeches." He glanced at me. "Not too long, thank God. Sports cars carrying beauty queens, and the antique car club led the motorcade." He waved his hand around again and accidently whacked it against the door. "Son of a bitch!" he yelled and shook his wrist. "A navy helicopter flew overhead as we drove north along the completed stretch from Lemon Grove Avenue to California Street. Very impressive."

"Hmmm. Only four and a half miles?" I said as I reached for the radio dial. "Can I turn on some music?"

"Someday, when it's all finished, it will connect us to Los Angeles and run all the way north to the Rincon in Santa Barbara County. He sucked a little on his sore hand as he glanced at me again. "What happened to your hair?"

"Linda trimmed my bangs . . . a little."

"I mean the color."

I smoothed my hand over the golden streaks. "Lemon juice. . . . We sit in the sun. . . . Linda says it—"

"God, you're too young for all that hair stuff." He sighed deeply.

I flipped on the radio to Shelly Fabares singing "Johnny Angel."

Daddy turned it down. "So, what do the Baptists think about hair lightening?"

"I quit the Baptists. A man at the church told us that people who aren't official Baptists can't be saved. Methodists, Lutherans, Presbyterians, Catholics. None of them. All going to hell." I gave him a disgusted look. "Anyway, I'm not official."

"Really? Why?"

"'Cause you have to get baptized by the Baptists. Dunked in a river. Even Reverend Ralston's out. I know you don't like him, but he's trying to help people live a good life. Doesn't seem right."

"Hmmm," Daddy said.

"Judi and I are thinking about trying the Episcopal church."

He smiled. "Good idea. I believe the Episcopalians are quite liberal about hair and such."

While we sat at the stoplight at Five Points, he pulled his little notebook out of his pocket and jotted something down.

"Hey, you're not thinking of writing a column about . . . my hair?"

He shoved his notebook into his pocket and mumbled something unintelligible.

"Because I don't want you to write any more columns about me. Ever." I crossed my arms. "I already told Mother to tell you."

He shrugged. "I guess she might have mentioned some little problem you had about . . . something or other."

"Little problem? It was the most embarrassing day of my life. That creepy art teacher told the whole class, 'We hear you've been shaving your legs with your father's razor,' and then he snickered out of the side of his mouth. Everybody turned and stared at me."

Daddy squinted like he didn't know what I was talking about. Somebody honked their horn after the light turned green, and we pulled away from the intersection.

"You remember, you wrote a column last week called 'How Are Your Blades Fixed'? You said that you'd cut a big gash in your chin and that it was my fault because I changed the setting on the razor to ten when I shaved my legs."

He formed an O shape with his lips and then laughed a little. "I don't think I wrote it quite like that. Just a little family humor. . . ."

I glared. "There've been lots of other times. You wrote about the Father-Daughter Banquet at school and how I told you not to talk loud or be conspicuous and . . . how we danced and you said I was, I was . . . PRETTY!" I burst into tears.

"Pretty? That's a compliment!"

"Some of the popular girls whispered about it in gym class, and they laughed. Angela told me."

He tried to jolly me up. "Who cares about some silly girls, right?"

"They know what *pretty* is. You don't know anything!" I wailed.

Daddy pulled the car out of traffic and parked along the curb on Telegraph Road. He turned off the radio. "Honey, I'm sorry. . . . I never thought about it that way."

"Junior high is like church. The girls have a lot of different rules that keep popping up. You just have to figure it out for yourself. It's easy to make a mistake without even knowing," I said.

"Indeed."

"And the lady at the dentist's office laughed her head off when I had my teeth cleaned after you wrote about our family having 'a toothpaste tube squeezing crisis,'" I sniveled. "You exaggerate!"

"People love my stories about the family. Readers send me letters all the time."

"I don't want to be that little girl in your column that people laugh about anymore. Someday I'll move away from here and be whoever I want to be."

He handed me his handkerchief.

"In eight months, I'll be fifteen and a half, and then I can get my learner's permit."

He made a sour face. "Jeez. Eight months?"

I nodded. "I'll be driving on that new freeway pretty soon."

He stared at the steering wheel for a moment and then brightened. "I've got a great idea. Why don't we take a little spin on the new freeway, right now? Give you a glimpse of the future."

"We'll get in trouble. You said the public's not supposed to drive on it until next week."

He waved me off. "I've been on it twice this week already—at the dedication ceremony today, and I rode in the governor's caravan when he paid the county a little visit on Tuesday." Daddy gave me a devilish grin. "Maybe I need to go back out there to check on something for my column."

I shot him a sideways glance.

"Since the hair stuff is out," he mumbled.

We drove past the newly graded construction site for the Broadway department store and shopping center and entered the freeway through an entrance boldly marked CLOSED TO TRAFFIC. DO NOT ENTER. I sat straight in my seat as he maneuvered the car around the barrier.

Daddy stepped on the gas and accelerated up the ramp. We burst onto a pristine strip of concrete, heading north through orchards and farmland, with rows of eucalyptus trees blocking the fields from wind and erosion.

"Wow," I marveled. "It's humongous."

"Vast," Daddy agreed. "We're like pioneers."

He zigzagged the car across the newly painted white lines and sometimes straddled the lane markings as the new Dart zipped along the wide, empty roadway. Once, he swerved near the shoulder, where hay had been strewn on the freshly planted ground cover, and corrected back toward the center divider.

"Slow down," I said. "You're going too fast. We might get in an accident." I gripped the sides of the red vinyl seat and craned my neck to look for cars behind us. Nothing but empty road.

He glanced at the speedometer. "I'm only going . . ." He slowed then abruptly made a U-turn to head back the way we had come. He picked up speed again, giving me another mischievous laugh.

"Stop! You're going the wrong way!"

"There is no wrong way today. We can go any way we want. Live a little!"

"Daddy, please. Let's get out of here before somebody sees us."

"Honey, who cares if somebody sees us?"

"Don't write about this in your column."

He slowed, made another U-turn, and headed north again at a more moderate speed. I caught a glimpse of the ocean as the freeway swept down the bluffs at Pierpont Bay. A line of waves crested, white foam surging to shore. "Wow! We'll be able to get to the beach really fast on the freeway."

To the east, we passed white ranch houses with friendly porches and tall trees nestled among citrus groves. Bigger homes dotted the brown hills above the city. A church with a bell-shaped tower and white steeple stood out against the dusky hillside. *Maybe I'll try that church sometime, see if . . .* I studied the church for a moment as we passed by and then faced straight ahead. The new thread of roadway disappeared toward Santa Barbara, where Olga Duncan had lived.

What if one of those witnesses had told police that Mrs. Duncan was asking them to help her get rid of Olga? Or warned Olga about it? What if Frank hadn't moved out of the apartment to go home to his mother? What if . . . I let out a big sigh.

The new pavement ended, and we took the ramp up to California Street. I craned my neck to see the courthouse perched on the hillside above the city. *Olga would've liked living here. She could have been a nurse at our hospital, and maybe—*

"Goddammit," Daddy grumbled at the big wooden barriers completely blocking our exit to the street. He punched the reverse button on the car's dash, backed down the ramp too fast, and made another U-turn. We headed south, going the wrong way again in the northbound lanes. The southbound side of the freeway still wasn't finished.

"We'll go back to where we got on." Daddy sounded like he was getting tired of our freeway adventure.

I looked over my shoulder to try to see the courthouse again. "I read your story about Mrs. Duncan getting killed in the gas chamber."

He stared ahead. "You read about the executions?"

"Uh-huh."

"Well, it was a . . . terrible thing to witness. Just awful."

"Olga's murder was awful, too. She'll never get to drive on the new freeway or anything."

"A senseless, brutal, cold-blooded act," Daddy agreed.

We watched the darkening horizon to the west as the sun slipped lower in the sky.

"I know the reverend at that Episcopal church you were talking about, Reverend Gilbert," Daddy said. "He's very anti–death penalty."

"The warden said it doesn't do any good anyway." I shrugged. "There's still lots of bad things happening every day . . . more killings and kidnappings. Why even have the death penalty if it doesn't do any good?"

"Good question. The district attorney says 'retribution.'"

"Revenge? Do you think that's right?"

"I think the voters of California should stand where I stood that morning last month and then do it again in the afternoon for two more executions. It would be interesting to see how many people changed their minds about capital punishment."

"But they should have to see the pictures of Olga and her dead baby, too, before they decide." I turned and pressed my hand on the window, watching the sun flatten against the sea. "I thought I'd be happier when Mrs. Duncan died, but I keep reading about all the other killers out there. A whole family got murdered in their beds in the middle of the night in Kansas. Why does God let these things happen?"

"I don't think God has anything to do with it. Olga's murder was caused by bad luck and bad people."

"I guess there's too much going on for God to take care of everything. I'll have to watch out for myself."

"We all have to look out for each other."

I turned away from the sunset to face him. "I don't think Olga did anything to deserve what happened to her. Do you?"

"Honey, I think if Olga were here, she'd tell you to enjoy your life. You can't waste your time worrying about what *might* happen." He pointed at the freeway. "Look. Progress. You've got your whole life ahead of you. Why, just last week President Kennedy promised to put a man on the moon by the end of the decade. Maybe you'll fly to the moon one day."

"I don't want to fly to the moon."

Daddy turned on the headlights and illuminated a wide-open stretch of the new freeway.

"Things keep changing, but how do you know everything's going to be all right?"

"It's progress, honey."

"I just want to go away to college and have fun." I glanced at him out of the corner of my eye and mumbled, "Maybe I'll be a writer someday . . . like you."

Daddy moved his hand toward my head.

I pulled away. "Don't mess up my hair."

He chuckled and turned the radio to the news. "Military authorities said today that the construction of a Soviet port in Cuba appears to be part of a worldwide plan to position the Russians—" I twisted the dial and stopped when I found Chubby Checker singing. "Let's Twist Again Like We Did Last Summer."

Daddy punched the gas pedal. "We gotta get home. I have to finish a story about the school board agenda before the Dodgers come on tonight. Big game."

"We're tied for first place with those stink-o Giants, right?" The sun slipped below the horizon. Purple-gray clouds tinged with pink blew in from the ocean. "I like to listen to Vin Scully," I said.

Daddy began humming "Take Me Out to the Ball Game." Headlights flickered in the distance where cars had stopped at an intersection on a surface street. Daddy gestured at the empty six-lane highway ahead of us. "This freeway system's going to work out great. When it's all finished, it'll be clear sailing in the 'fast lane' all the way to Los Angeles. No traffic!"

As we exited through the partially blocked entrance where we'd started, I glanced over my shoulder toward the unlit ribbon of roadway connecting us to the dark, wide world beyond.

"When I leave here," I said, "I'm going in the slow lane."

Daddy threw his head back and laughed. "You can go any way you want, sweetheart, and still get where you want to go. It's not a race."

"But don't worry, I'll come back and visit you sometimes."

He resumed humming "Take Me Out to the Ball Game," tugged out his shirt pocket, and took a quick peek inside. I saw something white with red numbers printed on it poking out. I squealed in a breath. "We're going to Dodger Stadium on Sunday! You got the tickets?"

He patted his chest. "Right here."

I slapped my cheeks. "Oh my gosh. The last home game of the season . . . in the NEW stadium."

"Only six games left to see who goes to the World Series."

"I'll keep score for you in the program," I chattered as he turned onto the street that led to our neighborhood. "You know, the official way you taught me, in case you need to check any details for a column . . . and don't worry, I'll make sure to write down all the Ks and Bs . . . and we can each get two Dodger Dogs, first inning and seventh." I hardly noticed when he eased the car to a stop in front of our house. "I really hope Sandy's pitching and Wally hits a moon shot. . . ."

Epilogue

The Attorneys

During the appeals of the Duncan murder convictions to state and federal courts, Ventura County district attorney **Roy Gustafson** began to experience fatigue, intermittent numbness in his hand, and occasional blurred vision. Within a year, he was diagnosed with multiple sclerosis. He never ran for governor; both his health and the times were against him. Gustafson was a Republican in a period when Democrats ruled California. In November 1960, he would run unsuccessfully for superior court judge in Ventura County.

He resigned as the Ventura County district attorney effective January 1, 1961, while the American Civil Liberties Union's challenges to the Duncan case verdicts were still winding through the federal appeals courts. He entered private practice and became one of the highest-paid trial lawyers in Ventura County. In 1968, Governor Ronald Reagan appointed Gustafson to a superior court judgeship in Ventura, and the year after that promoted him to the California Court of Appeal, District 1. Gustafson retired in 1970 following a heart attack but continued to go to his office regularly to write articles for legal reviews.

On June 27, 1972, ten years after the executions of Mrs. Duncan, Luis Moya, and Augustine Baldonado, Roy Gustafson died in his sleep at the age of fifty-three. The cause of death was attributed to a heart attack and complications from MS.

Bob Holt's column appeared in the newspaper the following day.

> *I suppose I spent more time covering news events involving Roy Gus-tafson than any reporter, including his prosecution of the Elizabeth Duncan case, which was undoubtedly the highlight of his career as district attorney and mine as a reporter of crime news.*
>
> *To the big-city press representatives who flocked to Ventura for that trial, Gustafson appeared, I guess, as the archetype of the tough prosecutor. They had never seen him, as I had, move legal mountains to clear the record of an unfairly accused person. And once in a while, you caught a glimpse of another Gustafson, gentle, humorous, an essentially private man, totally unconnected with the machinery of the law.*
>
> *I shall remember Roy Gustafson as a blunt speaker who reporters knew was good for a colorful quote. He never ducked an issue. But I shall remember him best, I suppose, as a teacher. He took the position that if a reporter like me had to hang around and report the court news, at least he ought to understand some of the rudiments of crim-inal law. I found his little dissertations crystal clear. It never made me a lawyer, but it has prevented me, over the years, from making some of the more egregious blunders of which I would otherwise be capable.*

After the trial, **S. Ward Sullivan** told colleagues that he'd hoped to get a hung jury or at least spare his client from the death penalty. He admitted that he had underestimated Roy Gustafson, the man he'd referred to as "a hick" the night before the trial began.

On February 1, 1968, Ward Sullivan was indicted on ten counts of child molestation by a Los Angeles County grand jury. The charges, dating back to January 1966, involved five young girls, ages nine through eleven. Investigators reported that the alleged offenses occurred in Sullivan's luxurious Wilshire Boulevard apartment. At the time of the indictment, Sullivan said through his attorney that the charges were "without foundation."

But three months later, he pleaded guilty to two of the counts, and on June 24, 1968, the sixty-seven-year-old attorney was placed on probation and ordered to undergo psychiatric treatment.

After his mother's trial and execution, **Frank Duncan** built a successful law practice in Los Angeles. In 1964, a short article appeared in the *LA Times* about one of Frank's cases. His client Arthur Moore had been "positively" identified in court by two sheriff's deputies as the suspect who attempted to sell marijuana to one of the deputies. When Frank pointed to Mr. Moore and asked the deputy if he was "sure" about the identification, the deputy responded that he would "stake his life" that Moore was the man who had sold him the drugs. A second deputy, who had observed the transaction through binoculars from a block away, concurred.

Unfortunately for the police officers, Moore had the perfect alibi. Frank submitted proof to the judge that his client had been in San Quentin prison, serving a three-year term for robbery, at the time of the supposed drug deal. The charges were dismissed.

He continued to represent clients well into his late eighties. After he appeared for a client in custodial arraignment court in 2017, at the age of eighty-eight, the judge described Frank as "sharp as a tack" and "gentlemanly and courtly in manner." The judge added that Frank seemed "very fit" for someone in his late eighties.

Frank married twice after Olga's 1958 murder. In 1960, he married fellow attorney Elinor Chandler. They had one child and divorced in

1966. He was married to his third wife, Margaret Rose, for more than forty years.

Frank Duncan has refused all interview requests since his mother's execution, saying, "I never speak of it. I never do interviews. That is all in the past."

The Investigators

Clarence Henderson, Roy Gustafson's chief investigator at the Ventura district attorney's office and the man who led the search for evidence in the Duncan murder case, retired from the DA's office in 1963, a year after the executions. Gustafson was quoted as saying that Henderson, who led the team of investigators that interviewed dozens of witnesses and developed hundreds of pages of evidence used at the trial, deserved much credit for the convictions of Olga Duncan's killers. Henderson died of a heart attack in 1971 at the age of fifty-four.

Forty-year-old Ventura County deputy sheriff **Ray Higgins** obtained the confession of Gus Baldonado that led to the discovery of Olga's body. He also developed a rapport with Luis Moya, who finally confessed to him on Christmas night after speaking with Reverend Gressett. Higgins left the sheriff's department shortly after the trials and went to work as a security guard at the Point Mugu missile test center. Gustafson gave Higgins full credit for obtaining the confessions and remarked that "it is too bad that under the county's civil service personnel system, a man of that ability was rated only as a Deputy I, lowest on the pay scale." Higgins died at the age of sixty-two in 1980.

In 2001, at the age of seventy-five, DA investigator **Thomas Osborne** told a reporter, "The Duncan case became my life for over six months." He said he was "most proud of the evidence I developed for the penalty phase of the trial that proved to the jury that you could not believe a word that woman said." When the trials were over, Osborne went to law school. He was admitted to the bar in June 1964 and joined Gustafson's Oxnard law firm to practice with his old boss.

Charles Thompson was a thirty-year-old Santa Barbara detective when he "cracked" the case surrounding the disappearance of Olga Duncan. After returning to work from an unpaid suspension for calling his lieutenant a "son of a bitch," he gained the trust of Emma Short, Mrs. Duncan's eighty-four-year-old constant companion. His interview with Mrs. Short proved to be the key to unraveling the conspiracy and solving the disappearance and murder. He continued to assist the Ventura DA's office throughout the trial.

After the conviction of Mrs. Duncan, Thompson was often in hot water with "the brass." He was a frequent critic of his bosses and an anonymous source for the press about unfair goings-on in the department. He wasn't afraid to stand up to his superiors when he believed it was the right thing to do. But maintaining close relations with the press did not make him popular with all of his colleagues. Some felt he was a grandstander. Nonetheless, Thompson was an excellent, street-smart detective who rose to the rank of captain.

Although Thompson had never been particularly religious, in 1979 he "found the Lord" and became a born-again Christian. Two weeks later, he was diagnosed with incurable bone marrow cancer. He retired from the department in 1980.

After leaving the police force, Charlie ran a profitable almond ranch near Bakersfield, owned a rental condo at Mammoth ski resort, built an affordable housing project in Santa Barbara, and started an advertising business, all while undergoing treatment for his cancer. Charlie Thompson died at the age of fifty-nine in November 1987.

The Judge and Jurors

Judge Charles Blackstock lived on a sixty-acre ranch near Oxnard. He was a TV boxing fan who loved horses and horse racing and never missed a Rose Bowl game. Long famed for quoting from Shakespeare and other literary classics while giving speeches to local civic organizations, he liked to reminisce about the Ventura he grew up in during the late 1880s during an era of mostly ranches and dirt roads. Judge Blackstock was usually described as a courteous and philosophical man, but when pushed, he pushed back, and he never suffered fools in his courtroom.

The death sentences of Mrs. Duncan, Moya, and Baldonado were the first handed down by the judge in his thirteen years on the superior court bench. Blackstock retired in 1959, soon after the Duncan trials ended, and died in September 1966 at the age of ninety. Charles Blackstock Junior High School in Oxnard is named after him.

The Jury

After reaching a guilty verdict at the trial, Elizabeth Duncan's jury made a pact to never speak about what took place during their four hours and fifty-one minutes of deliberations. None of the jurors ever granted an interview.

The Killers

Journalist Peter Wyden interviewed both **Luis Moya** and **Gus Baldonado** on death row at San Quentin for a chapter in his book, *The Hired Killers*. Moya told Wyden, "I thought I was such a hotshot. How come I let myself be persuaded? I could have done other things to get money. I pulled a lot of burglaries. I was handling thousands of dollars at the Blue Onion when I was the night manager. I could have walked off with it. I can't understand myself. It's one of the problems I haven't figured out yet."

What kept lingering in Moya's mind, Wyden wrote, was a deep resentment of Elizabeth Duncan for her part in his and Baldonado's apprehension. "I thought there was a good chance of getting away with it," the prisoner told Wyden. "We were living in an entirely different circle from Mrs. Duncan. There was no connection whatsoever. I was impressed by her. I trusted her. I thought her word was good."

Moya also blamed his death row incarceration on fate, what he called "bad luck." And he acknowledged that he had lost his lifelong struggle between "good Luis" and "bad Luis."

"I guess everybody has two faces. My bad one was quite extreme. I fell in with a bad crowd. I don't know about the good part, but I know about the bad part. It's very, very bad."

Moya never brought up God during the interview. Finally, Wyden asked Moya about his claim of a religious conversion during his visit with Reverend Gressett on the Christmas night before the grand jury hearing. The journalist told Moya that he'd read in a prison report that he'd signed up for a Bible study class when he'd first arrived at San Quentin but that his interest had lapsed.

Moya shrugged. "I just did it for a little while."

Wyden also talked to Gus Baldonado in the special visiting room for death row inmates. He described Baldonado as tall and lanky with a wide, smiling mouthful of perfect teeth. He said that he resembled a south-of-the-border, carefree version of comedian Jerry Lewis.

Baldonado talked to the reporter about Olga Duncan's murder in a conversational tone. "I just got caught up in it. It's just something that came up, I guess, that was meant to be. I guess nothing could have prevented it."

When Wyden brought up Gus's impending death in the gas chamber, Gus responded with a big unaffected smile. "If they're going to get me, they're going to get me regardless. Why be moping about it?"

When Wyden ended the interview and stood to leave, he wrote that Gus offered "a rubber-armed handshake" and quipped, "Take it easy! Don't run over nobody that'll get you manslaughter." Gus shook with laughter.

The Mastermind

After **Elizabeth Duncan** was found guilty of Olga's murder and denied a retrial, she told reporters that she would "be glad to leave the Ventura County jail and move on to the Corona women's prison." She was reported to be a model prisoner at Corona, popular with both fellow prisoners and the guards. She maintained her innocence until the very end, never wavering from her claim that she was being blackmailed by Moya and Baldonado—that she was the victim.

Ventura sheriff's deputy Mary Fogarty saw Mrs. Duncan every day for five weeks while transporting her to and from the trial and guarding her in the courtroom. As she reminisced twenty years later, "On the night we waited for the jury to come back with the penalty verdict, I asked her, 'Mrs. Duncan, if you could do all this over again, knowing the consequences, would you do it again?' She said, 'You bet I would. Nobody is going to have my son.'"

Elizabeth Duncan was the last woman ever executed in California.

The Sidekick

A few hours after Elizabeth Duncan was pronounced dead at San Quentin, **Mrs. Emma Short**, Mrs. Duncan's longtime companion and the chief witness against her at her trial, was buried at a Santa Barbara cemetery. Mrs. Short had suffered a fatal heart attack the previous week and died two days later. Her age was in question. When she testified at the 1959 trial, she was listed as eighty-four. But at the time Mrs. Short complained to reporters that this was wrong; she was only eighty. "My boyfriends don't want to go out with an eighty-four-year-old woman." Mrs. Short was listed in hospital records as age seventy-nine at the time of her death.

The Spiritual Advisor

Reverend Floyd Gressett was the pastor of the Avenue Community Church in Ventura and the man who encouraged Luis Moya to unburden his soul and confess to the police. He continued his prisoner outreach work after the executions. Country singer Johnny Cash, who lived in nearby Casitas Springs and sometimes attended Gressett's church, sought counseling and guidance from the reverend in the 1960s while battling drug and alcohol addiction.

Johnny and the reverend became close friends, and in 1968, Reverend Gressett encouraged Cash to play concerts at the maximum-security Folsom Prison, where Gressett made regular visits to minister to prisoners. The concerts at Folsom were recorded live and sparked a resurgence in Cash's career. Reverend Gressett continued to reach out to prisoners across the state to preach the word of God. He died in 1995 at the age of ninety-one.

The Victim

Olga Duncan, described at the trial as "a quiet young woman with a lovely disposition and very devoted to her work as a nurse," wrote a letter to her parents in Canada on July 20, 1958, one month after she married Frank Duncan. The letter was inadmissible at the trial because it was considered "hearsay," but Olga's words live on to tell her story in her own voice.

> *As you all have guessed by now, all is not well with Frank and me, or should I say, Frank and I and his mother. As I told you before, Frank's mother has lived with Frank for so long that she has an "uncanny" hold on him. She is a very possessive woman and has not allowed him out of her sight. Therefore, Frank has not really grown up. He's never been away from home.*

We had been planning to be married for some time, as you know. But Frank didn't tell his mother until shortly before. She phoned me at two in the morning and said that she didn't approve, that he was in love with another girl, that I was a foreigner. So the next day, Frank found out about the phone call and said that if I was still interested we'd be married that day. After weeping all night, you can imagine how I felt. Naturally there was not time for formalities, so we were married by a superior court judge at the "nationally famous" Santa Barbara courthouse.

Here are the events in brief.

1. *Mrs. Duncan came to the apartment and threatened to kill me and kill Frank, and she phoned me five or six times a day saying all kinds of horrible things.*
2. *She went all around the neighborhood saying I was buying expensive clothes at I. Magnin's.*
3. *She told people that I was already married and that I had two children!!!*
4. *And that I had a mother to support. What about you, Daddy? Ha! Ha!*
5. *She also put an ad in the paper saying that Frank was not responsible for my bills. Just imagine. The woman is nuts!!*
6. *She cut up Frank's birth certificate and all his baby pictures.*

All this was a shock at first, but I rather laugh now. I could go on and on, but all I can say is that she has not allowed Frank to live here. He has a great problem . . . so I have consulted many people. I have a lawyer who has told me to annul the marriage. Thank God I found out now instead of a year from now.

I know you all will want to help. You can do something. Write and tell me news about home and the children. That will cheer me up

more than anything. If I have anything else to say about the situation,
I will write to you.

The reason that I did not write about it before was the fact that
I thought time would work it out. But now I know it won't. So
please write about yourselves. I know about me so don't dwell on my
troubles. Life is short and I want to enjoy the rest of it.

Olga lived for another four months after writing this letter. A week after the discovery of her savagely beaten body, she was cremated at Ivy Lawn Cemetery in Ventura. Frank arranged for a small private service on December 30. Only Frank; Olga's father and brother, who had made the trip from Canada; and two of Olga's friends attended the service. Olga's mother was too bereft with grief to make the trip.

At first, Frank wanted to keep Olga's ashes with him in Los Angeles, but after the trial, he relented and sent her remains home to Canada to be with her family. In 1997, the great-granddaughter of Olga's brother told an interviewer that Olga has not been forgotten. The story of her short life and her death has been passed down to each generation of her family.

The Holt Family

In 1967, **Bob Holt's** prized Sears Powerboy lawnmower, the one he'd named the "Mrs. D." and sometimes called the "Orange Bitch" after his favorite notorious murderess, chopped off the ends of two of his fingers. He'd been trying to dislodge grass clippings from under the cover without turning off the mower. For the rest of his life, he had to wear a rubber tip on the end of his left index finger while typing news stories.

My father retired from the *Ventura County Star-Free Press* in 1983 after thirty-four years as a reporter but continued to write his twice-weekly columns for the paper. During his career he wrote over four thousand columns on every subject imaginable—from the mundane to the lofty. He wrote about anything that interested him—and everything interested him. He found most of the universe somehow important. At least one third of his columns were written about the trials and tribulations of our family and the goings-on in our Montalvo neighborhood.

When he retired, a piece appeared in the *Los Angeles Daily Journal*, a legal newspaper. "Bob Holt was as able as anyone I have ever encountered to render what goes on in a trial understandable. If the Big Press covered courts the way he did, the public's understanding of the legal process would be a hell of a lot less distorted."

The Duncan case continued to fascinate my father long after the executions. As the only reporter who'd covered every session of all three killers' trials, he was deemed *the* expert on the case. He considered the trial the highlight of his career as a crime reporter. In 1972, ten years after the executions, he wrote,

> *Twenty years from now, if I'm lucky enough to be hanging around some newsroom, I will doubtless be boring young reporters with accounts of that remarkable case.*

Unfortunately, he didn't live another twenty years. In November 1987, my parents phoned me as usual on Sunday night, after the national news and before *60 Minutes* started. My father mentioned that he was getting a little sore throat, but he sounded fine to me. I don't remember what we talked about. Probably my children, or maybe something amusing about one of my parents' cats. I pray that I wasn't impatient to get off the phone that night, because I never spoke to him again. Later in the week, his "little sore throat" turned into the flu. On Friday, he died from a fast-moving, aggressive form of pneumonia while watching the five o'clock news on TV. When my mother found him, he was still holding the notebook and pencil that he'd asked her to bring to him in case there was anything of interest on the news that he wanted to note for a column.

He was sixty-nine years old at the time of his death. Hundreds of people from all over Ventura County—fellow journalists, politicians, commissioners, neighborhood friends, judges, lawyers, even people who had never met him but felt they knew him because of his columns—turned out to pay tribute. A former county supervisor remembered him as compassionate but tough: "He kept a suspicious eye on me for twenty years." And one of his longtime colleagues at the paper remembered him as "the most un-phony man" he'd ever met.

Lois Holt retired from her career as a psychiatric social worker at Camarillo State Hospital in 1972. Soon after, my mother was appointed to the Tri County Board of Mental Health and Regional Center. She served two terms working to ensure that persons with mental illness and developmental disabilities in Ventura, Santa Barbara, and San Luis Obispo received high-quality services. Mother also enjoyed taking short trips up the coast of California with my father, going to lunch with her friends, visiting with her grandchildren, loving and caring for her many cats, growing roses and picking bouquets for the neighbors, and sipping tea in her kitchen. A memorial bench on the Ventura Pier is dedicated to my parents; it overlooks the beach she so enjoyed walking along with my father.

Mother lived fifteen years after Daddy passed away. She said that she missed his laughter most. She died in March 2002 at the age of ninety-two.

After college, my sister, **Betsey Holt**, made crafts and jewelry for many years and owned a jewelry store on Main Street in Ventura. Montalvo was annexed into the city of Ventura in 2012, and Betsey was elected to the Montalvo Community Council in 2014. She likes to keep her eye on the Ventura civic leaders in order to protect the character of our old neighborhood.

After both my parents passed away, Betsey moved back to our family home in Montalvo. She claimed that when she first returned to our old house, a ghostly presence occasionally roamed the hallway. She kept catching shadowy movement out of the corner of her eye, but when she turned to look, nothing was there. A roommate also said she felt an invisible presence in the house. Although the apparition seemed friendly, Betsey decided to consult a psychic, who told her that she was living with a benevolent male ghost who watched over the house. I asked Betsey if she ever heard any humming, but alas, she did not.

Debby Holt. During our junior year in high school, my friend Judi Smith and I officially became Episcopalians—baptized and confirmed. After graduating in 1966, we went off to college together at UC Davis and quickly lost interest in organized religion. It was the sixties.

Before I left for college, I'd told my father that I didn't know what I wanted to do with my life, except that I was sure that I didn't want to be a teacher. I had secret hopes of becoming a writer. But during my summer breaks from college, I worked as an intern at the school on the grounds of Camarillo State Hospital. My interest in helping children with mental illness like Cathy, the little girl at the hospital who wanted a doll, returned.

After college, I went on to earn a master's degree in the Education of Emotionally Disturbed Children at San Francisco State University. Just as I started teaching special needs students, Congress enacted the Education for All Handicapped Children Act, requiring public schools to provide equal access to children with physical and mental disabilities. I spent eighteen years teaching and administering special education classes before becoming an elementary school principal.

Olga Duncan's disappearance and murder ignited my lifelong fascination with the true crime genre, not because I like blood and violence but because of my own feelings of vulnerability. Now that I'm retired from education, I spend more time watching *Forensic Files* and *Dateline* and reading true crime and detective novels. True crime books are where I've learned about dark, terrifying, real-life messy stories. I want to understand what motivates someone to kill, to find insight into the psychology of a murderer so that I can avoid becoming a victim myself. Olga Duncan could have been me, my sister, any of my friends. DA Roy Gustafson said it well in his summation to the jury at Mrs. Duncan's trial.

> *One of the pities of this case is that the girl who was so brutally murdered on the night of November 17th might have been any girl . . . anybody's sister, anybody's daughter. Any girl could have been Elizabeth Duncan's victim if she happened to marry Frank Duncan.*

I still believe that we are responsible for our own safety, but Olga wasn't reckless. Like many female homicide victims, she was murdered by someone she knew. Her mother-in-law hired strangers to kill her. Mrs. Duncan shopped all over Santa Barbara looking for someone to help her "get rid" of her daughter-in-law, yet no one told Olga, or called the police. Olga didn't have a chance because nobody spoke up for her. My father's words from so long ago remind me again that, "We all have to look out for each other."

I sometimes still think of Olga and the "if onlys"—the decisions and choices that might have saved her life. I've spent nine years writing this book, contemplating the randomness of the world and my lifelong quest to escape evil.

I'm more accepting now, knowing that life is unpredictable and people imperfect. I no longer count on a higher being to keep me safe. If there is a God, I'm sure that She is way too busy with all the troubles in the world to intervene in my little life. But I'm still careful! *God helps those who help themselves.*

My father died so suddenly and unexpectedly that I never got to say goodbye, never told him that I loved him and how much he meant to me. He had always planned to write a book about Elizabeth Duncan, but he never seemed to find the time. This book is my goodbye to my father. I love you, Daddy.

-30-

Acknowledgements

Many people contributed to this book, and I am grateful to all.

First and foremost, I want to thank my lifelong friends, Judi Smith and Marilyn Waples, and my sister Betsey Holt, for their encouragement to write this book and for sharing their childhood memories. I couldn't ask for more enthusiastic supporters.

I also want to thank my Wednesday night 'read and critique' group at San Diego Writers, Ink. The book would never have been completed without the input, advice, prodding, support and all-around sounding board provided by this wonderful group of writers. Thank you to John Mullen, Laura Kelly, Ken Kaplen, Sandy Robertson, Diane Demeter, Indy Quillen, and many others who circled in and out of our group over many years. You all helped in ways both large and small. I especially want to thank our group's leader, Mark Clements, a constant source of inspiring critiques, witty observations, and laser-precise edits that all made my book so much better.

Thanks also go to Michael Mohr, who completed an early developmental edit on my manuscript, and to the reference desk staff at the Ventura County E.P Foster Library for helping me with old newspaper searches and for their endless patience teaching me how to load and operate the mircrofiche reader too many times to count.

To my wonderful sons, Nick and Jack Larkin, thank you for your good humor and understanding when our guest room gradually disappeared under a mound of newspaper clippings, trial transcripts, and manuscript drafts. But please never forget that the couch is always available! Also, a heartfelt thanks to Jack for insisting that I go with him to the Santa Barbara Writers' conference to find an agent. Brilliant!

And a million thanks to that dream-making agent, Charlotte Gusay, for loving and believing in my book and for tirelessly pitching it until she found the perfect publishing home at Pegasus. Charlotte, you are a miracle worker! And to Jessica Case, my editor at Pegasus, thank you for your willingness to take on a first-time author, for your edits and suggestions, and for coming up with my book's lovely title. I'm honored to be on Pegasus's list of authors.

The Elizabeth Duncan trial transcripts had disappeared from the Ventura DA's office sometime in the 1960s, and I could have never written this book without the serendipitous intervention of Los Angeles superior court commissioner Robert McSorley. Bob grew up in Ventura in the 1950s, and he became fascinated with the Duncan case as a boy while reading the articles in the newspapers he delivered on his daily paper route. In 2001, when Bob was a partner in a Ventura County law firm, he stumbled across the lost transcripts gathering dust on the top shelf of his firm's law library. DA Roy Gustafson, a founding member of that firm, had apparently brought the transcripts with him when he left the DA's office. Because of his boyhood fascination, Bob understood the significance of what he'd found. The Ventura County DA's office now has the transcripts preserved for history.

I also wish to thank Teri Lee, daughter of Santa Barbara police detective Charlie Thompson, whose interview with Mrs. Emma Short finally broke the case and linked Olga's disappearance to her mother-in-law. Teri told me her father's stories about Elizabeth Duncan, provided information about his personality, and gave me insights into his attitude about police work that brought his character to life in the book.

And last, but certainly not least, to my husband Tom, I am so grateful for your wisdom, your support, your belief, and your encouragement. Always my first reader, my cheerleader, my technical support, and my most valued editor. You put down whatever you were doing to listen to my endless worries and to read the many drafts of the manuscript. I truly could not have written this book without you.